Also by William Freedman

Land That I Love

Age of Certainty (Editor)

MIGHTY
MIGHTY

William Freedman

Rebel ePublishers

Detroit New York London Johannesburg

Rebel epublishers
Detroit, Michigan 48223

Mighty Mighty
© 2014 by William Freedman

For information regarding permission, email the publisher at rebele@rebelepublishers.com, subject line: Permission.

ISBN-13: 978-0615985060
ISBN-10: 0615985068

Cover design by J. A. Fludd
Book design by *Caryatid Design*

The greater danger for most of us is not that our aim is too high and we miss it, but that it is too low and we reach it.

Attributed to Michelangelo

PART ONE

MALL HEROES

BOOM! POW! A sharp left and a sharper right made quick work of the last two henchmen as Colonel America charged at the villainess. Maman Brigitte had dared to take hostage the Colonel's comrades, The Crusaders (THE CRUSADERS!!!), and he was the only one left to charge to the rescue.

Aside from the Colonel, his teammates, and Brigitte and her Institute minions, Park Avenue stood abandoned from 34th Street to Central Park South. Even the NYPD had been cleared out by National Guard troops who secured the famed, flower-basketed boulevard. Outside, the Manhattan air sat muggy and unseasonably warm in the pre-dawn. The Colonel was finding it hard to breathe, though he had the battle almost won.

The only thing that stood between Colonel America and his adversary was a glass counter, the entranceway into Tiffany's having been demolished in the early-morning donnybrook. The battleground that the previous day had been a shop of rare and unique objects of wonder was now a common shambles. Individually and in packs, the eldritch artifacts littered the store. Over here: cards that could conjure the strength of mighty athletes, long departed but still summonable to play their positions. Over there: cards that gave form to pocket-monsters or digital-monsters, so that their possessors could duel for supremacy. Behind the glass counter, Maman Brigitte intended to leave all these valuable talismans behind to escape with the rarest card of them all.

"The gig is up, Maman Brigitte!" Colonel America shouted. "Surrender ... or else!"

Maman was a ghostly figure, dressed in a diaphanous black shroud and matching headscarf. Her face, black as a moonless midnight, was as hollow and austere as her figure was tall and lithe. She confronted her adversary who was clad in primary-colored body armor and cowl, folded-over boots and famous bulletproof flag-cape.

"I think that's 'jig,'" she corrected in her thick Creole accent. "'The jig is up.'"

"Really? Are you sure?" the Colonel paused, perplexed. "I've been saying 'gig' all this time."

Suspended three feet off the floor in a cage composed of black magicks and white bones ripped from the security guards, the other four members of the Colonel's team shook their heads or rolled their eyes. The second-biggest one, made of soft, black, crumbly sediment spoke for them all. "Colonel!" the Carbon Avenger shouted. "Remember what we told you about banter!"

"Sorry, Avenger!" Colonel America said to his teammate while Maman Brigitte smashed open the glass counter and pulled out an ornate, two-by-four-inch tin with MALIFICIUM engraved across it in gothic letters, the u carved like a v.

The Colonel droned on, "Remember, even the best of us still has a couple areas he'd like to improve ..."

"Shut up and subdue her already!" the Carbon Avenger advised.

But just as the Colonel was vaulting over the counter

and ready to put a gloved hand across her throat, he was overcome with the fumes of a thousand Haitian fire peppers. His eyes burned as if dipped in ammonia. In a puff of putrid smoke, Maman Brigitte was gone. Her voice lingered on for a moment, "Now I need but one more ..." then degenerated into a fading cackle.

As the voodoo priestess's presence receded, the cage that held her captives disintegrated. All but insect-sized Midge, who had wings, fell to the floor. Pantagruel, the World's Largest Human, hit particularly hard, flat on his coccyx. Midge, his wife, tittered at this until Pantagruel shot her a killing look.

"She's got almost the entire deck," the Carbon Avenger exposited. "We've got to find that last Malificium card before she does or the world is doomed!"

"Wherever it is," Colonel America pondered, "Let's hope that it's protected by guardians worthy of their fateful role."

"For now, though, we should get back to the Pinnacle and see if we can figure out where this rarest of all Malificium cards is," the Carbon Avenger suggested. "As for who might currently be charged with its safekeeping, we just have to leave that to a higher power."

The Colonel, Midge, and Pantagruel all nodded in agreement. The fifth member of their cohort merely smiled his beneficent smile.

THE SUCK

I t was 10:37:09 a.m. It was also a Tuesday, but that is not important.

It being 10:37:09 a.m., Orville Ortley was walking past the Chesterfield Mall's Cinnabon and approaching the Auntie Anne's. Orville did this every morning at that tick. It was a point of professionalism. He was a proud member of an elite profession.

Orville was not an imposing-looking man by any means. Only five-foot-five, one hundred-forty pounds, he looked as if his arch-nemesis could be a snugly-torqued lug nut. From appearances, one would not expect that Orville Ortley was one of Earth's most powerful superbeings. He wasn't – one of the *most* powerful. But he was still a superbeing whom most mall shoppers would be ill advised to confront.

Despite his modest appearance, Orville did have a certain bearing about him. His TSA uniform was starched and pressed, the shirt the kind of white that only daily bleaching could produce. Although worn and frayed, it was plenty white. To go with it, the patent-leather uppers of his rubber-soled shoes shone to the point of being just a little creepy.

His features were obscured by the headgear which marked him as a mall hero, as opposed to a run-of-the-mill mall cop. Choice of headgear had been a highly personal choice among mall heroes. Some years before, they were pressed into the Civil Service and the choices of facial concealment became more limited, but that only affected the newbies. Orville, who had been taking the pace between Cinnabon and Auntie Anne's every work day at 10:37:09 for the preceding 1,981 workdays, was able to take advantage of a grandfather clause.

Orville went with the cowl, partly in homage to his idol, Colonel America, but also because he was a little self-conscious about his thinning hair. That is, it was thinning when he first took up the hero mantle; by this time, all he had left to him were a few stubborn follicles combed over a smooth scalp and a good memory.

How the cowl covered Orville's face, though, was unique in the hero field. His forehead, cheeks, and slate-gray eyes were clearly visible, as were his mouth and jaw. His cowl would have been little more than a bathing cap if not for the crystalline green band that stretched across his nose.

Orville had little life outside the job, so the purpose of this accoutrement had nothing to do with hiding a secret identity. It had everything to do with hiding his nose. His nose, incidentally, was not a source of embarrassment. It was pronounced, distinctive, without being outsized or gaudy. It was a regal nose, suggesting a man of lofty origins and a destiny of his own making. This was not a nose one would deliberately hide.

Rather, it was a nose from which others must be protected, for it was …

"Base to Unit One," crackled Orville's walkie-talkie. Yes, they still used walkie-talkies. "Disturbance in women's

5

wear in Macy's. Are you in the vicinity?"

"Unit One to Base," Orville replied. "Negative. My ETA for approaching the second floor of Macy's is 10:48:30. Suggest you contact Unit Two."

He maintained stride.

"Orville, get it in gear and head over there now!"

Orville hesitated. On the one hand, he saw his duty, the thrill of foiling a crime in progress, his dispatcher's urgent plea. On the other, his obsessive-compulsive disorder was quite severe, and he had resolutely quit taking his Paxil the month before.

"Now!" the walkie-talkie repeated.

"On my way!" he replied. The decision made for him, he obsessed about how to get there in the shortest time, using the most direct route, and metering out the fewest steps possible. The parents of the children frolicking in the play area were not amused. Nor was the salesman from the car dealer raffling off the Porsche.

BOOM!

At the other end of the mall was a hallway with no stores along it. It was for the offices. Closest in was the glass block, marble and mahogany enclave for the managing partners of the investment trust that owned the mall. Nobody ever entered it. Behind that were somewhat less plush offices hosting the group that managed the property. Behind that were the hardscrabble cubicles of the people who provided the computer and network services that kept the retail transactions running between the mall and the banks. Behind them was the janitors' closet.

Behind that was the security office. It didn't make any sense. That's just the way it was.

Sheldon Shapiro considered himself to be the demon responsible for that deepest circle of hell - as consigned to eternal damnation as any of the poor souls who found themselves punching his clock. Shel felt that the only difference between him and a true minion of Satan was that he actually felt bad for his charges.

So it was with some chagrin that, immediately after telling Orville, "Now!" he acknowledged the young man in front of him with the clipboard packed an inch thick with filled-out forms.

"I'm gonna have to monitor this situation, but we can get started with your application, Mister Kiley."

"Please, call me Kevin."

Twenty-something Kevin Kiley sat in a permanently unfolded folding chair to which the 40-something dispatcher gestured. Kevin handed over the clipboard, took back his pen. Somewhere in the background, fingers tapped at a keyboard, a laser jet printer engaged, and a resonant, bass voice muttered as low as it could.

"And I'm Shel," the older man with the bald scalp marked with scars – burn marks? – said. "Listen, as Lou Noble no doubt told you already, I have to hire you according to the Triple-A. I just want to get a sense of how long you expect to stay in this job." The dispatcher paged through some of the sheets on clipboard. "Grad school boys like you find better prospects after a while. Anyway, says here you go by 'Count Karma'?"

"On second reference," Kevin said earnestly.

"Say huh?"

"The full moniker is 'Count Karma, Comma, Master of Arts.'"

"What arts are you a master of?"

"Economics."

"Uh, right," Shel said skeptically. "I thought that was a science."

"It can be. It can be an art, too."

"No. I remember on the first day of class, the teacher called it 'the dismal *science*.'"

"You took economics?" Kevin asked somewhat too

7

archly.

"Yeah. So what?"

"Well, I took it for four years as an undergraduate, then two years as a grad student at the University of Missouri at Kansas City. I was graduated this past May with an M.A. in economics. So I'm a Master of Arts."

"But don't most guys ..." Shel started just as his base station crackled with Orville's voice. "Hold on ..."

{ POW! }

Meanwhile ...

... Mousy, mild-mannered Mindy Maguire was inwardly bemoaning her fate, outwardly counting sweaters on a table display elsewhere in that same mall. A graduate of one of the best fine arts programs on the East Coast, here she was working retail for sub-minimum wage. Mindy had interviewed for an assistant buyer position with Federated. They bucked her to the Macy's chain, which she was all in favor of. When she got the job, she could almost smell those pretzels and roasted peanuts sold by the pushcarts along 34th Street. Maybe they would let her decorate the windows for Christmas. Maybe ...

No.

They had over-hired that year. Still, Human Resources liked the earnest, creative Smith College magna cum laude and told her they would find her a temporary position somewhere on the Macy's management team. Would she accept relocation?

That was more than two years ago. Still "temporary," they never gave her a nametag of her own. For the past twenty-six months and two days, she had been walking around the floor of the Chesterfield Mall Macy's store in greater St. Louis wearing a pin that said HELLO MY NAME IS TRAINEE.

Being a trainee might not have been so bad under other circumstances. In the retail pecking order, a manager trainee still outranked an assistant manager. But Mindy was an *assistant* manager trainee. She still outranked the crew, but even that was a matter of perspective. If one of them failed to show up for a shift, someone would have to work it – usually the most junior member of the management team, i.e. Mindy. Everyone connected with that store made more per hour.

She had a talent for fading into the background, not that this was her superpower – far from it. Mindy could turn her career around with one little taste of her true ability, but she had her reasons for not using it on the job. And because she had no intention of using it on the job, she checked NO RESPONSE on the application's question enquiring about special abilities.

Federally mandated, so-called "Triple-A" set-asides were not for her.

So when the disturbance occurred at the Petite register, she was able to observe it from the obscurity of the Plus section. One middle-aged man at Petite could have been shopping for his wife ... or daughter ... or, uh, niece. Two men could have been enjoying shopping together during liberated times in which such self-expression was celebrated – though not so much in Missouri. But what were three men doing together in Petite? And dressed that badly, in *hoodie*s for Pete's sake.

At first, they seemed to be haranguing the cashier about something. Mindy went about folding the sleeveless frocks for those size 18 women who insisted on kidding themselves. She ignored the three men as if they were customers.

Two of them then drew guns – not the usual Colt pistols or cheap, improvised zip guns wielded by run-of-the-mill bad guys – but Ruger Super Redhawks, whose high-end appeal was beyond the grasp of most cash register robbers or, for that matter, most mall shoppers. Mindy viewed them with a derisive headshake.

Only people without superpowers used firearms. These were just regular villains, although what they were doing robbing the Petite counter - weeks after the end of the back-to-school rush - was open to speculation. Still, armed robbers were a concern of local law enforcement, not for Mindy's alter ego.

Unless ...

The third one didn't draw a pistol. Instead, he removed his sweater's hood to reveal ... a turban. Mindy recognized him instantly from a newscast a few months earlier. It was The Incomprehensible Singh.

An avid follower of superbeings - and one in particular - for years before granted her own powers, Mindy knew the book on Singh. No older than she, Singh was already a mainstay of the Institute. She knew not to look directly into the ruby that adorned his turban. It was an illusion-creating device.

Mindy crawled unnoticed out of range, then ran to the inconvenient and poorly marked ladies' room. It had been quite some time since she had used her abilities, but this was the moment. She never could admit to herself that she enjoyed it but, really, who wouldn't?

She burst into a toilet stall, cried out, "Sorry, ma'am," and burst into the next toilet stall. Then she began the brief ritual: dropping to her knees, supplicating Aphrodite, praising Lakshmi, adoring Ishtar, sticking her finger down her throat, and coughing up 16 ounces of Kona blend and that morning's blueberry bran muffin.

It only took an instant, but Mindy's experience of the transformation was slow and painful. Through gritted teeth that quivered as they grew whiter and more evenly spaced, she let her other self take over. It wasn't really an alter ego; this new persona had the same memories and thoughts as Mindy, but overflowed with the kind of courage and self-confidence she usually lacked. This superpowered version had experimented with many names, none of which was satisfactory. "Amazon" was Mindy's first thought, but she quickly dispensed with it; the name connoted an eagerness to battle, which just wasn't her. She couldn't take a goddess's name for risk of offending that goddess – or some other goddess, jealous types that they are. She tried "Bovary" and "Karenina", both of which were just too highbrow to take. "Rappaccini" was too obscure and, she was surprised to learn, already taken. But that at least pointed her in the direction of the name she wanted to be known as now: Georgiana. It has a ring, Mindy thought, you don't even have to get the literary reference.

Georgiana raised her head. She rose from her knees. She flushed.

She emerged from the ladies' room completely transfigured, her Charter Club ready-to-wear pantsuit mystically transformed by the goddesses into skintight blue-and-gold leotards. Her girl-next-door figure suddenly rendered corset-perfect. In place of short brown bangs, a blond Farrahesque mane sprouted.

And she was superstrong. And she could fly.

BAM!

The stable satellite, or statite, hovered directly above a certain point in the eastern Atlantic Ocean. Technically, this point was in the Gulf of Guinea, but the Gulf was huge and the point was hundreds of miles from any shore; by any human reckoning, it may as well have been in the middle of the ocean. Remote to be sure, but of all the satellites falling freely around the earth, only one could be deemed important enough to hold this prestigious address: 0'00" latitude by 0'00" longitude. The rest of the spacefaring community gladly ceded the distinction to this statite, the Pinnacle of Righteousness. For who would presume to have a more honored place in the sky than The Crusaders? (THE CRUSADERS!!!)

The spaceplane Steed One was tethered to the primary airlock and its solar sails glinted like pinwheels constructed out of a disco mirrorball. These were visible through the smooth, curved, triple-paned, floor-to-ceiling windows of the module The Crusaders called the Keep. Only two of the august group occupied that gravity-enhanced module at that moment: Midge, at full human size seated in an ergonomically perfect chair, waving her hands around a touchscreen computer, and Pantagruel, standing at her shoulder. He was also as close to his natural size as was comfortable, that being eight feet even. They were both clad in their dazzling spandex bodysuits.

"So what have we ruled out?" Pantagruel demanded.

Images slicked across the 42-inch screen in response to Midge's gestures.

"We can assume the Institute doesn't have the card, or they'd have used it by now," Midge said, as she looked into Pantagruel's familiar steely eyes. "What we do know is that the card's RFID code is unique, and mass marketers don't like unique. Big-box stores are out, as are dollar stores or middle-market chains. I think it's with a specialty retailer."

"That's supposing it's not with a private collector," Pantagruel noted, trying to maintain workplace detachment despite his rising lust. The two had been married for years but often had difficulty keeping their shared professional life and their shared home life separate.

"That's a safe bet, though," Midge replied, fighting the same fight. "The Institute's attacking retailers. No collectors have turned up dead. Maybe they know something we don't."

"So it's at a legitimate card dealer's," Pantagruel summed up. "In the States?"

"There were no export documents."

"Heartland or coastal?"

"We know it was loaded on a truck rather than a box-car, so I'm guessing heartland."

"I am so turned on right now, Midge."

"I know. Spandex doesn't lie."

"You're not wearing a bra under ..."

"Citizens!" Colonel America announced as he entered the module. "How goes the mission planning?"

"We're getting there, Colonel," Pantagruel replied.

"'We'?" Midge said, barely audible, but with a brass band's worth of sarcasm.

"Did you say something, Midgie?" the Protector of Patriots inquired.

"No. Yes. Uh, it's coming over now," she said, as the report from her database query popped up on her screen. "The card was in a shipment that left the Malificium factory in Jackson, Mississippi, two days ago, along with a ton of non-enchanted cards. It was part of a regular truckload, so it could be anywhere from Philly to Salt Lake City by now. We won't know which outlet of what card chain it's at until somebody tries to pay for it."

"Blast!" said Pantagruel. He often said random things like that when he was, for whatever reason, frustrated.

"So it could be at almost any card shop in three time zones," Colonel America said. "It could be at any Below Decks or Dalai Laminate or Plaquet Box."

BOOM!

There was a Plaquet Box in St. Louis's Chesterfield Mall, at a prime spot right next to the anchor store, Macy's. From outside the Plaquet Box, Orville Ortley stopped suddenly to observe the situation in the department store's women's wear section. Protocol demanded he go no further. According to standard operating procedures, TSA mall security personnel were not to enter the premises of an anchor store unless specifically requested by the store's management. They usually had their own security measures and injecting mall heroes into the situation could very well make matters worse. So Orville stopped and called it in to his dispatcher, Sheldon Shapiro. Mister Shapiro, he reasoned, would be along himself in a moment and could provide further direction if necessary.

Besides, it looked like the Macy's incident was already being handled. Orville recognized the villains: The Incomprehensible Singh, the mystical mage of the American Malevolence Institute, with two of his henchmen. He didn't recognize the hero flying to the rescue, but was fairly sure it was a female.

In the meantime, a disturbance in the Plaquet Box required the attention of a mall hero.

POW!

"Look!" screamed an acne-prone 12-year-old lad in a boys' choir soloist falsetto.

"It's Supermodel!" boomed a much deeper voice. It was the same 12-year-old, his acne already fading.

The complex, educated, life-examining professional woman flying toward her peril detested that name whether she was in her fighting leotards or her pantsuit, but she had been stuck with it since her powers first manifested themselves back when she lived in western Massachusetts. It's *Georgiana,* punk, she refrained from shouting. Instead, she let it go and flew past Singh, casually using her hair-toss power to whip him off his feet and into the 50%-off bin. Then she focused on the henchmen. She detested this part – the reason why she had gone years without summoning this persona.

"Nice guns, fellas," she cooed as she came to rest barest inches in front of them. She continued to hover a few inches off the floor to better maintain eye-breast contact.

"Uh, yeah, I am, thanks," stammered the first henchman, "miss."

"I don't like guns."

So they offered to hand their Rugers to her.

"Silly boys! I said I don't like guns. I don't want you to give them to me." She laughed engagingly. "But you want to know what makes me hawwwwt?"

Yes, they did. More than anything.

"Bulllllets," she said, knowing full well that either of these grunts would hand over his whole paycheck to watch her tongue pronounce the letter L. "Can you show me your bullllllets?"

They emptied their chambers into their hands.

"Why don't you just hand them over to li'l ol' me?"

The henchmen complied.

"Now you two be good boys and take your empty weapons downstairs to the TSA holding facility."

"Yes, Miss Model," said the second henchman. "Is that your secret place? Huh-huh. Huh-huh."

"Now it can be *our* secret place, sugar. I'll be down directly, but first I have to, sigh, prepare myself. You two run along now. I'll be down to visit you just as soon as I go make myself beautifulllll."

Then they were off, both running like Usain Bolt with an erection.

That was easy, she conceded to herself. Singh, though, shrugged off an assortment of petite leftovers, already recovering from the smack in the face by the world's most manageable hair. He would be a more daunting adversary.

BLAM!

Seth Hill, the owner and sole day-shift employee of the Plaquet Box, seemed to be a typical trading card geek: knowledgeable about the most arcane attributes of each of his cards, an authority on dueling tactics and rules of engagement, and single-mindedly dedicated to the craft of card gaming, regardless of publisher or canon.

This had made him a wealthy and respected young man. In a world in which superbeings were so common-place they worked mall security, gaming cards were one of the few paths to power available to what heroes and villains pejoratively called "mundanes."

The second the graying but spry Southeast Asian man entered his store, Seth knew he was trouble. As the man rummaged around a little to - unsuccessfully - avoid suspicion, Seth checked him out on his iPhone's villain database app. His visitor was Ta Mok. Affiliation: Ameri-can Malevolence Institute. Tactical genius. An ideology instead of a conscience. Cloven hooves for feet which, when he pounded the ground with them, sent shockwaves simulating a localized earthquake. And he had the power of persuasion - he was known for his ability to "reeducate" his foes into being his mindless minions.

Seth had bare seconds to prepare as Ta Mok soon am-bled over to the counter.

Focused on one another, neither noticed Orville at first.

"Hey, you gonna buy something?" Seth asked ingenu-ously. Orville was out of earshot when Ta Mok first started spouting his Marxist tirade against the use of currency. But Seth was close by, just across the display cabinet.

BOOM!

Don't look at the ruby in Singh's turban, the woman who preferred to be called Georgiana reminded herself. Get the upper hand first and don't let it go.

"Don't I know you?" she purred. "Haven't you been on TV?"

It worked.

"Uh, yes. Yes, I'm on TV all the time. I was all over the news last year when Pantagruel and Midge brought me in. Then I was on all the stations just this past week when I escaped from ..."

"How nice for you." Don't look at the ruby. Give him a

reason to take off his turban. "I really like your beard. How do you get it so thick and lllllluscious?"

"My mom's Italian," said the Incomprehensible Singh.

"I bet your hair is just as lllllluxurious," Georgiana continued. "I'd lllllove to see it."

Don't look at the ...

Too late.

PONT

"The proletariat must rise up and throw off the yoke of the elite capitalists and their bourgeois lapdogs," Seth repeated woodenly. The words made little sense to Orville, who stayed out of both Seth's and Ta Mok's line of sight until he could formulate a plan of attack.

"Excellent, my pupil," responded Ta Mok. "Now, do you have the card I seek? It is all the Party needs to bring about a workers' paradise in which the State shall wither away."

"Yes, Comrade," Seth said. "Let me set it down on the counter for you."

But the card he retrieved wasn't the one the Institute sought. This one was a simple Reversal card, the kind that could be found in any deck from the most current and complicated all the way back to Uno.

"You know, I just realized," Ta Mok said wistfully when the Reversal card was in play. "History will remember George W. Bush as a great president. He kept America safe for seven years, and he really had the right idea about tax cuts and deregulation. Of course, it was all Congress's fault he was forced to sign the Americans ... with ... Ab... "

The spell suddenly broke. Ta Mok had walked into the store with a Temporary card in defense mode tucked up his sleeve. He then attacked Seth with a Volume Up card.

"Now, young man, I know you can hear me," Ta Mok, the Butcher of Battambang, told the Plaquet Box's proprietor, who stood there in sudden terror. "Why you didn't simply use earplugs, I just can't fathom. Now I shall attack you again. You shall experience zero life and zero health."

Sheldon Shapiro and Kevin Kiley arrived in the concourse between Macy's and the Plaquet Box and immediately saw both battles underway.

"Let's split up!" Kevin announced before Shel had the opportunity. "I got Macy's!"

And with that, he raced off to see if he could rescue the beautiful damsel.

"Pretty." Georgiana managed before her mind went blank and her feet touched the floor. Without any volition, she shuffled slowly toward the mystic.

"Thank you," said Singh, regaining his composure now that the woman he thought of as Supermodel saw only what he wanted her to see. The same went for scent, taste, touch, and sound. "Thank you," as Singh willed, sounded to her like the voice Barry White might play to get in the mood.

The crowd, which had gathered when the hero had the upper hand, ran past Kevin, who attempted to get closer. Georgiana stood there blankly, staring off into a wonderland of hedonic, tropical vistas. She felt sand under her feet as warm breezes carried the aromas of cocoa butter and hibiscus. Singh presented her with an avatar he'd plucked from the depths of her unconscious fantasies. He was astonished that she preferred the wiry build to a more macho physique. And she had this fetish for a prominent nose.

"Respect me," the mage intoned in a New Jersey rasp that sounded like a smooth-rolling baritone to the enthralled Georgiana. "Have a high personal regard for me. Honor my opinion."

Georgiana's pupils dilated and her face contorted into an open-mouthed invitation to a wet kiss. Only she and Singh knew about a non-existent breeze blowing flecks of his skin onto her tongue. She fell in love with the very taste of his flesh, and could only guess at the thrill if he were to reach out and touch her.

POW!

Seth looked down at the counter. Ta Mok had merged his Volume Up with a Skip Turn card. Seth stood helplessly as Ta Mok held Swift Yet Agonizing Death at a menacing height ...

BAM!

It's unclear what Kevin did in Macy's at that point when he was supposed to be helping Georgiana. It looked like he simply leaned up against a rack of blazer-skirt combinations and took a power-nap.

Then a subsonic rumble preceded a rush of air and a whistle, which sharply rose then fell in pitch and volume.

BOOM!

... but in less time than it takes to tell, a gale-force wind knocked the Death card out of Ta Mok's hand. Before it flittered harmlessly facedown to the floor, the Butcher of Battambang was knocked sideways by moisture that exploded with the force of a hand grenade when it hit his shoulder.

Ta Mok turned to see Orville Ortley or, as he was known without his nose guard on, Mucus-Man.

One more sneeze from Mucus-Man, and Ta Mok was a shell-shocked lump on the floor of the Plaquet Box ...

POW!

Singh leaned over to claim his prize but, as he reached around Georgiana's waist, he was suddenly confused, blank. Simultaneously, Georgiana regained her composure. She fought against the effect of the ruby. Singh fought

19

against the effect of her glamour. After tense moments, the eternal battle between the man with the most precious of gems and the woman with the boundless beauty ended in stalemate, as it always must. Singh escaped.

BAM!

Kevin's eyes opened.

BOOM!

... Recoil from the second mucous blast knocked Orville flat on his back, sending him slamming into Shel - who was actually still out on the concourse. Shel sat there with Orville's head cradled in his lap.

"Kid, you all right?"

"Hnnngriiiihhhh," was Orville's immediate reply.

"Huh?"

"Hun-gry, Mis-ter Shapiro," Orville replied, regaining some of his strength. "Need food."

Kevin came ambling over, trying to chat up Georgiana who appeared still shaken by her brush with the Incomprehensible Singh.

"Where's the bad guy?" Shel demanded.

"Got away."

"Was that Singh I saw in there? How the hell did you let him escape?"

"I was on a spectral plane of consciousness that didn't permit ..."

"I sent his two lackeys over to your office to surrender themselves," Georgiana told Shel. "Maybe they can tell ..."

A flick of a card, a flash of light, a billow of smoke and dust, and Ta Mok also vanished.

"Oh, this day just keeps getting better and better," Shel said.

"Doesn't it, though?" Kevin replied, oblivious to the sarcasm. "Boss, meet Su ... Georgiana."

As concerned as Shel was about the two escaped villains, the apparently useless new hire he'd have to make work for, and particularly the depleted mall hero cradled in his lap, he still managed, "Pleasure to meet you."

"I get that a lot," Georgiana said offhandedly, her attention elsewhere. She focused on Orville. "Anyway, I hope you have someone back at the office to lock up the henchmen."

"We sure do," Shel said with a little braggadocio, leaning back on the hand adorned by a wedding ring. "One of the best. He used to be with The ..."

"Mister Shapiro, what time is it?" Orville interrupted, indicating the impact had stopped his watch. He had maintained eye contact with Georgiana for almost ten seconds – notable because Orville didn't do eye contact, and Georgiana wasn't accustomed to men looking at her eyes.

"It's nine minutes to twelve."

"My mucous blasts have a velocity of explosion of 1,250 meters per second at 15 degrees Celsius at sea level," Orville explained, as he picked himself up. "I must replenish my energy after each attack. I am going to the food court. Are you hungry as well, after your battle?"

Once done talking, Orville was able to direct his gaze back to Georgiana's eyes.

"I could eat," she said.

"Mister Shapiro," Orville said, helping his dispatcher back onto his feet. "I'm breaking for lunch. Eight minutes early."

And Mucus-Man and Georgiana rode the escalator down to the food court.

"Kiley," Shel said, watching them walk away.

"Yeah?"

"I don't buy all that 'spectral' or 'cosmic' stuff. If you can't prove to me that you got a real ability, you're gone before the end of your probation period. Got it?"

21

"Got it," Kevin replied. "So I'm in trouble with the boss already and I haven't even started yet?"

"That's right."

"And the only reason I'm being given a shot at all is because the government says you have to give me one?"

"That's the law."

"And the pay is minimum wage."

"That's going up year after next."

"And the most beautiful woman in the world won't give me the time of day but is going off to have lunch with Rain Man and his snot grenades?"

"I wouldn't believe it if I wasn't seeing the same thing."

"This sucks," Kevin concluded.

Shel draped an avuncular, and surprisingly heavy, arm across the young man's shoulder.

"Embrace the suck."

GODS AND LIEUTENANT COLONELS

Orville Ortley genuinely liked people, but in the same way he liked abstract art. He maintained an efficiency apartment adorned with prints of works by Pollack, Kandinsky and Mondrian. He appreciated them, but he never claimed to understand them.

So, although it registered with him that the most beautiful woman on earth was sitting across a glaring aluminum table, facing him, sitting on the same excruciating mesh of extruded plastic that Aristotelians would have difficulty mapping to the metaphysical concept of "chair," the experience had only the vaguest meaning to him. Lacking in social skills as he was, he was halfway through his three-course Chinese meal before Georgiana spotted where he was sitting.

All eyes in the food court followed the vision in a shimmering leotard, from the Chik-Fil-A to Orville's table – all eyes but Orville's. She sat down across from him, to the envy of at least half the other patrons. Her bright eyes virtually bathed him in blue. And he didn't even look up. He just sat there stuffing his too-often-indoor face, a napkin tucked into his collar to keep his TSA-issue shirt bright-white, his cowl pulled back to reveal his balding scalp (he was off-duty, after all), while his nose remained obscured by the crystalline green band. The groupthink from the others in the food court was almost audible: What was *she* doing with *him*?

And Orville was oblivious. Of course, he noticed that Georgiana had joined him at the table to which he had carried his lunch tray, but didn't understand the protocol for acknowledging that in any outward manner. The overhead speaker softly played the Counting Crows' "Rain King," but he didn't feel the need to display any awareness of that either.

So it fell to Georgiana to start the conversation.

"I can't believe I actually got to meet you!" she blurted out, to the visible incomprehension and jealousy of one man seated at the next table. "I mean, here I am, having lunch with Mucus-Man! The guy who singlehandedly stopped the Chauvinauts from taking over the earth!"

"Mmmhmmm," he grunted as he kept at his kung pao over fried rice.

"I was in middle school at the time," Georgiana continued, "You're my inspiration. Ever since that day, I dreamed of becoming a superhero."

"So why didn't you?"

She sat paralyzed for a moment. The hero who was the object of her schoolgirl crush had again spoken to her. It was enough to get her over Singh's lingering effects.

"Didn't I what?"

"Become a superhero. You never registered with TSA," Orville said, not with reproach, just factually. "You've only been involved in four actions, including this morning's. The first three were in the Springfield, Massachusetts, area and your presence in St. Louis was unknown until today."

"True. I'd hoped—" Georgiana began, but Orville had difficulty taking turns in conversation.

"Nobody even knew your name was Georgiana. The

24

press just referred to you as—"

"Supermodel. Yeah, I hate that."

She took a big bite of her chicken sandwich and was immediately transformed back into Mindy Maguire, her stretchy nylon morphing back into flannel, adorned with the pin reading HELLO MY NAME IS TRAINEE. Everyone who had turned their heads toward their table found other things to look at again.

"Why?" Orville asked.

"I was a women's studies major, for crying out loud. I had to change my whole curriculum over this. Of all the powers I could've developed, did it have to be—?"

"I meant, why Georgiana?"

"It's a reference to—" she began but stopped in response to a loud crash. A display outside the Suncoast near the entrance to the food court upended somehow, and a voice called out *"Oof!"* Before that voice could register, though, the chalkboard sign in front of Johnny Rockets tipped on its side followed by an *"Oww!"* About 20 yards of open floor separated Orville and Mindy from a caution-yellow sign that read AVISO PISO MOJADO. *"Nnnngh!"* called the voice as its source skidded flat on his back at tornado speed across freshly mopped tile straight at their table.

A sixtyish-looking, gray-bearded man with wild eyes leaned on Mindy's unwelcoming shoulder as he pulled himself up off the floor.

"'Scuse me," he said to Mindy as, with some difficulty, he regained his footing. Mindy wondered if he had some kind of buzz on. The man, whose hardtack, deep-fissured face sat atop the same uniform that Orville wore, but with a grimy shirttail untucked and the tie clipped on to only one collar wing. He wore the simplest of party-favor masks, and at that moment it was obscuring his forehead rather than his eyes. "Yo, Orville, your break's almost over. Clock back in so I can go to lunch, wouldja?"

"I'll be punched in within eight minutes," Orville said, the barest hint of irritation in his voice. It was apparent to Mindy that they'd had this conversation before.

"Fair enough, Orv," the man said, then gave a two-finger salute to Mindy and sped away at superhuman speed, bouncing off a mannequin in front of the Gap, then off to who-knows-where.

"Who was that?" Mindy asked.

"Guy I work with. His name's Bobby Botler," Orville explained. "The Blur."

"We could have used him against Singh. Why wasn't he called in?"

"He's road."

"Huh?"

"Road," Orville explained evenhandedly. "R-O-A-D. Retired on active duty. I have to get back to work."

{ POW! }

Here are a few things that don't go together well:

- Spent fuel from a nuclear reactor,
- A leak in the container that's designed to hold it for 9,997 more years,
- Shoddy maintenance on the controls that are supposed to alert the command center,
- A gentle, spring-fed creek trickling through the bucolic Wisconsin countryside nearby,
- The adorable woodland creatures who dwell along the creek, and
- The granola-crunching pinhead who thinks they want to be petted.

The result can only be bloody mayhem.

More on this later.

{ BAM! }

"Hey, I know that guy!" Kevin Kiley announced to Sheldon Shapiro. He was referring to the figure hunched over a

26

metal desk outside the cage that held The Incomprehensible Singh's henchmen.

"Thought you might," Shel said absently as he moved on to other administrative matters at his own family-picture-adorned desk in the outer office.

Kevin stepped back into the lockup for another look. Guarding the caged, moon-eyed villains still pining for Georgiana was a figure that, had he been standing up, would have been at least six and a half feet tall. Seated regally with broad shoulders squared and red-bearded chin thrust out, long, burgundy locks framed his high cheekbones and stormy, auburn eyes. Slung across his barrel of a torso was a broad strap of sturdy leather, which holstered this famous hero's fearsome weapon. For his own part, if this mountain of masculinity even noticed Kevin's presence, he gave no indication. He was aloof, mysterious – not just godlike. An actual god.

Aside from that, he was wearing a white short-sleeve shirt, black trousers, and a skinny clip-on tie.

Kevin returned to Shel's office.

"That's The Indomitable Lugh!" he exclaimed, as if this would be news to the boss.

"Yeah, he's been here a couple months now," Shel said. "Good guy. Keeps a clean desk."

Kevin struggled to keep his voice down, in part to tamp down his own excitement, but only in part. He didn't want Lugh to overhear him, a mere mortal, talking about The Sovereign of the Strong to another mere mortal.

"Why's he keeping any kind of desk? Do you know what kind of power Lugh brings?"

"Sure," Shel said, without breaking concentration on his paperwork. "He could kill all of us without taking a deep breath. But I can't put him on patrol."

"Well why not?" Kevin's voice went up an incredulous octave.

"Same reason he got released from The Crusaders. You got a lot to learn, kid."

BAM!

"You're late."

"Sorry, Ms. Penobscot Snodgrass," Mindy apologized meekly, standing with her head slightly bowed. The roar and diesel smell of heavy equipment on the Macy's loading dock seeped into the manager's office.

Eunice Penobscot Snodgrass was, as the I-love-me wall behind her desk testified, a Daughter of the American Revolution, a married maiden of the Social Register, a Mayflower descendant and a member of St. Louis's exclusive Wednesday Club. And, in her considered opinion, it was Mindy Maguire who was the insufferable snob. Smith girls! Ugh!

"In fact, I don't recall excusing you for lunch."

"I'm entitled to a lunch break."

"But not without checking with your manager. Me."

"Sorry, Ms. Penobscot Snodgrass," Mindy said again.

"I'm going to give you one last chance, young lady. But if you—"

"No need," Mindy said, correcting her slouch.

"How's that?"

"I quit."

"After all I've done for you?" Eunice said, rising out of her chair.

"Letting me be your scut puppy for two years?"

"In this economy, any job is a favor."

"Stop doing me favors. I can make more per hour as ... a ..." and then, out of her own mouth, she heard the plan her unconscious mind had concocted. "... security guard."

"Oh, that's brilliant! Next thing you'll be telling me you're some sort of ... hold it. You disappeared right before Supermodel appeared."

Oh well, Mindy thought. The transition back was wit-

28

nessed by the whole food court. There's bound to be video.

"I prefer 'Georgiana.'"

"Silly name."

"Yes, Ms. Penobscot Snodgrass."

BOOM!

It wasn't long before the events at Macy's and the Plaquet Box registered on Midge's computer screen.

"Well, well," she mused, "St. Louis. Chesterfield Mall."

"I bet Mucus-Man was involved," Pantagruel offered. "The lad's got guts. Always had."

Colonel America was about to enquire about Lugh and Shel Shapiro but, uncharacteristically, thought better of it.

"Are we certain the card is there?" the Carbon Avenger asked, shuffling along the floor, shale flaking off his massive form.

"Not a hundred percent," Midge conceded, "but it would be a heck of a coincidence for Ta Mok and Singh to go up against Mucus-Man, Supermodel, and whoever else—"

"Supermodel?" all the men, except the new guy, said in unison.

"We need to go down her right ... go down there right away!" the Avenger exclaimed.

"No, no need for all of us to go," the Colonel corrected. Colonel America - the current one and his predecessors - had long been the team's tactical leaders and not even the Carbon Avenger would second-guess the Protector of Patriots when it came to arraying personnel. "I'll go, taking Panty and Midge with me. Avenger, you and the new guy stay up here and keep watch. This could be a diversion. We'll signal you if we need backup, but this doesn't appear to be a hostile situation."

Without a further word, the Colonel, Midge, and Pantagruel boarded Steed One and strapped in. This required Pantagruel to shrink down to normal human height, at which he sighed his reluctance.

The reentry from the Pinnacle of Righteousness took their pilot more than an hour. By about halfway through, Midge and Pantagruel had enjoyed a giggly conversation full of inside jokes and *double entendres,* which made the Colonel fidgety, after which they entered a period of stone silence, which made him all the more fidgety. They repeated the cycle twice more before the Colonel stomped his foot in protest.

"If you two won't talk, how am I supposed to practice my repartee?"

"Well, you could talk to me," said a calm, matter-of-fact woman's voice in front of him.

"What?"

"Me, up here on the flight deck. This craft doesn't pilot itself."

"Ah, yes," the Colonel conceded. "Quite right, Major."

"That's 'Lieutenant Colonel' now, sir," she replied. "For the past two months."

That stopped Colonel America short. He stammered out a few generic comments to the effect of "thank you for your service," and "your work has been consistently outstanding," but didn't do anything to actually engage in conversation.

Rather, he regarded Lieutenant Colonel Nebraska much as Doctor Van Helsing would regard someone who had been bitten by a vampire three times. After the first time this is a victim who must be protected, after the second this is a soul that can still be saved, after the third, though, this is a ghoul that will feed on your flesh given half a chance.

He spent the rest of the flight muttering, "jig-is-up, jig-is-up ..."

{ POW! }

Evil had an address. And 24-hour doorman service.

That would be 1825 K Street NW, Washington, DC. And the regular second-shift doorman was named Edgar. He had been there eleven years. Evil tips well.

A black limousine pulled up and Edgar helped Ta Mok and The Incomprehensible Singh out of the conveyance. Singh, as was his custom, paid a gratuity in casually measured diamond dust. The next day, Edgar got $86 for it.

The two evildoers took the brass-and-mirrored private elevator up to the 19th-floor penthouse, headquarters for the American Malevolence Institute

In an office – not a corner office, but one with a beautiful view of Farragut Square and a squint of the White House – sat Maman Brigitte in regal repose.

"You're late," she stated after they had stood before her for an adequately humiliating period of time. "Do tell me you're not also empty-handed."

"A thousand pardons, Maman," Singh began. "There was an FAA ground-hold in St. Louis and—"

Ta Mok gave Singh a subtle hint that he was off-message. He kicked him in the shin.

"What my comrade is trying to express," Ta Mok took over, "is that we ran into unexpected resistance from the lapdogs of the capitalists. And Lambert Airport is just the worst."

"Yes, I know. Your failure was on YouTube," Maman Brigitte said. "You, Ta Mok, allowed yourself to be humbled by the likes of Mucus-Man. As for you, Singh, you lost your assigned henchmen to Supermodel! And before you complain about Lambert, consider yourself fortunate I didn't send you someplace where you'd have to connect through O'Hare."

"She wasn't alone," Singh replied. "There was a disturbance in the *Akashi*. I felt another presence on a transcendent plane, which distracted me and once more, I apologize. It shall never happen again. And have you been to LaGuardia lately? Last month I saw a raccoon in the United terminal. I swear, the place ought to be condemned."

"The question remains, gentlemen—"

"Yes, the only question that matters!" boomed a voice that sounded more tuba than human. As the deep bass rattled the three villains' dental work, a screen descended obscuring the park view. Maman Brigitte stood up and faced the screen, and she, Singh and Ta Mok greeted a mysterious, black-on-gray silhouette.

There was a moment of awkward silence. Maman Brigitte looked at her two subordinates. There was another moment of awkward silence.

"Uh, what was the question?" Singh asked.

Ta Mok kicked him again but deigned to explain, "The commissar would like to know if we were able to locate the card."

"No, *siddha*," Singh conceded, respectfully addressing the black outline.

"Do you," the thundering voice asked, "know whether the card is at the Chesterfield Mall?"

"Well," Singh replied. "That really wasn't my assignment, *siddha*. I was only there to create a diversion in case the TSA showed up. And I did ..."

"No, commissar," Ta Mok interrupted. "We have not ascertained the card's whereabouts yet. But I believe that it is very likely in that Plaquet Box."

"And why is that?"

"A couple reasons, commissar. First, by process of elimination we are running out of places it could be. Second, that we were so unexpectedly outnumbered by mall heroes suggests—"

"Suggests, *Gran Houngan*, that Harold and Kumar here couldn't handle the job," Maman Brigitte volunteered. "I beg you, let me try. I shall be successful. Have no fear."

"I agree, Maman Brigitte, that the number of second-rate heroes is immaterial, but Ta Mok has a point in that we have few places left to look. You may go, but take these two dolts with you and whatever henchmen you need. And Brigitte ..."

"Yes, *Gran Houngan*?"

"Never again tell me 'have no fear.' I fear nothing," the evil master rumbled. "Except for an abortive landing at Guarulhos in São Paolo. I just about soiled myself."

BLAM!

About that granola-crunching pinhead who thinks woodland creatures need to be petted ...

Bella Brock didn't know how long she lay asleep in the Wisconsin glade. She didn't even know she was Bella Brock.

Wakefulness is not consciousness. She was aware that it was dark, and instinct informed her that this was good and right. Wisps of memory intruded from another life: Waking up in the morning with the sun already over the hills. (Awake in the day! Hold on ... there are voles around. I can smell the rusty iron in their blood.) She remembered slipping on a sundress and wide-brimmed straw hat with a big, bright-yellow artificial daisy on the band. (Will this slow me down? I can tear it off if it gets between me and my prey.) She remembered packing a picnic lunch. (Where? Where? No matter: The den of voles is right below me.)

Without, literally, another thought, the still-mostly-human form that had until recently been Bella Brock dove straight into the rich black soil. She was not surprised that she had long, hook-shaped claws where her fingernails had been. The peace sign decals applied during her manicure the day before were stretched beyond recognition. In seconds, she had burrowed into a den of mouse-like rodents. She opened her mouth wide. And wider. The part of her that was still human marveled at just how far her jaw could drop.

Any species down the food chain might not agree, but humans are sweet, gentle creatures compared with many in the animal kingdom. So she hesitated, but only for an inconsequential moment. The family of voles - for that's what they were, a typical, Midwestern family with a mama, a papa, and a slew of kiddies - barely had time to register the intrusion.

None escaped.

Bella had developed, in addition to claws and another 30-degrees range of mandibular motion, a new array of teeth. The still-human part thought they were fangs, but that wasn't strictly correct. Her incisors had grown to extraordinary lengths. Her upper front teeth now descended to just above her chin as her lower ones now barely missed her nostrils.

With these tools, Bella dug into the belly of papa vole, tearing its soft flesh and, coordinated like ballet, her tongue lashed out, wrapped around its vitals, and dragged them into her mouth. The rodent's skeleton held stubbornly to its contents, which was fine with Bella. The whole animal went into her maw at once. The moment of satisfaction she took from the crunch would have allowed mama vole to escape had maternal instinct not anchored her to the spot. Still, the mother was helpless to do anything but protest as her offspring were taken up in twos and threes then chomped to bits. It wasn't until all her children had been devoured that it occurred to her to run away. And she was too slow.

Bella arose, shaky, upright on two legs, a position that felt a little awkward. Wearing a muddy sundress, a skewed straw hat, one Birkenstock and a face awash in the blood, gristle and fur of slaughtered rodents, she ambled downstream, toward human settlement. Bigger prey.

INTERLUDE: 1980

More and more, Olivia Ortley found herself stopping to reflect with amazement: Wow – this is really my life!

The excitement of being inducted into The Crusaders still hadn't worn off, and she'd been with the superteam for four years. Being Orville's mother was a thrill with which Olivia was still getting familiar.

Olivia had it all: A rare talent, a place in the pantheon at the top of her profession and the financial independence that came with those merits. Freedom to have a child without any permanent entanglements with a man came with that financial independence. Ten years earlier, or even five, society wouldn't have tolerated such an unconventional life choice from any woman, not even a superheroine. That was another thing about her life that Olivia celebrated: She was born into precisely the right moment of history.

And, most precious of all was little Orville. Olivia considered the past two months home alone with him as the best time of her life. But there was a world that needed protecting and, as the Carbon Avenger had been reminding her with increasing frequency, she had a sacred duty.

So, with keen regret, she prepared to leave her Upper East Side apartment. Before leaving Orville for the first time in the care of a nanny, Olivia had leaned over the crib that contained her infant son and brushed the wispy hair off his satiny forehead, rewarded with his first smile. She felt herself beginning to melt when he gurgled his contented proto-laugh. That, plus the four-tone tune from the geometric-shape mobile and the competing nursery smells of antiseptics and life, and she congealed into a spongy glob of pure motherhood.

On the other side of the crib, the nanny, a stern-faced Latina from the completely different world fifteen minutes away on the 6 Train, discreetly cleared her throat. Olivia took the signal to steel herself enough to sniffle a little, and walk backward out the door, savoring every second of watching her baby boy rock himself side to side, not quite rolling over.

Olivia managed not to cry because Orville didn't. He had her physical courage, as certainly as he had her patrician nose. He didn't have her eyes, where her power resided, but maybe some other power would manifest itself. The father – sperm donor, as far as she was concerned – also had a superhuman skill. Odds were that Orville inherited some ability, but would he take more after her or him?

She pondered this as she looked herself over, her face planted up against the full-length mirror on the armoire near the Manhattan Classic Six's front door.

Not bad for two months after childbirth, she concluded. The spots of acne and tangles of uncooperative hair, which had plagued her during pregnancy, vanished completely; instead, her strawberry-blond mane and alabaster skin were more luminous than ever. As for the rest of her, the new costume helped. Gone were the leotard and jog-bra (a look that, a generation later, the goddesses would bestow upon one Mindy Maguire). Instead, a well-tailored tunic and jodhpurs in earth-toned colors accentuated her athletic build without advertising any postpartum changes to her figure.

Her squinting eyes remained, as ever, hidden behind opaque green goggles. She permitted two teardrops to form. They instantly vaporized, fogging the goggles for a moment.

The grandfather clock in the living room chimed eight times, reminding her of the Town Car waiting for her on First Avenue. She found herself tripping over the umbrella stand on her way out the door, chalking it up to haste or nerves. She had, after all, been away from fighting evil for some time.

The car took Olivia to the heliport, which delivered her to the secret airfield in Connecticut where she boarded the private jet. The crew, sworn to secrecy, took her to the undisclosed location of Crusaders Castle, where she met up with the rest of the team.

Inside the Keep were the three mainstays of the group. The post-Vietnam era Colonel America was not somebody the free-spirited Olivia Ortley, whose *nom de guerre* was Looker, associated with. It was an age of experimentation and license, and it was as if youth, vigor and WASPish good looks were wasted on him. This Protector of Patriots was an anachronism – like the fairytale prince she gave up seeking by the time she was eighteen.

Next to him stood the Carbon Avenger. This was

many years before the accident which would turn him into a walking pile of slate; he was still a man, wrapped head-to-toe in a carbon-steel exoskeleton that was the source of his power. The Avenger had a slight build, some would say skinny and, standing next to his more bulked-up teammates, some would say scrawny. He didn't have the muscle tone of Colonel America, and nowhere near the beefy physique of that last mainstay, The Indomitable Lugh.

But she liked slender men.

These three highly regarded heroes greeted Olivia warmly, the Colonel smiling shyly, the Avenger asking to see pictures of little Orville, and Lugh greeted her with the sort of verbiage that was his trademark.

"And you remember Black Man," the Avenger said, indicating the hero they brought onboard weeks before Olivia's maternity leave. He was a burly man with a 48-inch chest and a 52-inch afro, dressed like one of the O'Jays.

"Of course I remember Black Man," Olivia said, and greeted him with the same lean-in hug and air-kiss with which she greeted the others.

After exchanging a few pleasantries, Olivia met the latest addition to the team.

"Looker," the Avenger said, walking her over to a man who looked as if he should be playing trumpet in a mariachi band comprised of masked wrestlers, "Meet El Hombre."

He pronounced the H.

There was a lot of milling about, catching up, and Olivia was soon bored beyond belief. No crisis had called them together that morning, just a team meeting. As much as she enjoyed the prestige of being a Crusader, and as much as she enjoyed the challenge of fighting bad guys on a level above the street thugs she'd tussled with in her solo career, she could've lived without all the mickey-mouse corporate crap.

Olivia couldn't wait for the meeting to begin, so that it would all-the-sooner end and she could go back to being with Orville. She never considered herself the maternal type until one day the year before, she just suddenly realized she wanted to be a mother. It still surprised her how much she loved bathing Orville, dressing him, singing to him, taking him around on errands, watching the effect a two-month-old baby has on people. Olivia looked forward to teaching him about the goodness that's generally in people's hearts, to exposing him to an optimistic view of life, to building up his self-esteem and to demonstrating how to consider others' feelings when ...

"Liv?" the Carbon Avenger whispered in her ear from behind. No, not the Carbon Avenger – the man *inside* the shell. "Can we talk a minute?"

"What do you want to talk about, Dirk?"

"In my study."

To the world, the Carbon Avenger was the private muscle behind Dirk Henderson III, CEO of Carbodyne Worldwide. To those in the know – The Crusaders and almost nobody else – the Avenger and Dirk Henderson were one and the same.

Although Colonel America was very much the battle chief of the group, it was the Avenger who handled day-to-day matters. The Colonel got unquestioned loyalty out in the field; the Avenger got the plush office adjacent to the Keep.

Olivia looked around at the art on the walls. She used to be impressed by the complex, detailed Rembrandts and Vermeers. But not so much that day. They seemed dreary to her, mazes of heavy-handed strokes.

It was quiet in there once Dirk shut the intricately engraved oaken doors. The air-conditioning ducts hummed as they cranked rose-scented air out of the vents; the in-wall exotic fish tank gurgled in a way that sounded almost like Orville.

Dirk's present awkward behavior wasn't his usual style. My God, Olivia wondered, is he coming on to me again?

"Listen, Liv, I'm not coming on to you again."

"I wasn't even thinking that."

He sunk down in his red leather chair and invited her to sit on the cushy wing chair across the desk.

"This is business. You've been away awhile and we need you to go in for a routine physical."

"Is it time for that already?"

"It was time for that a year ago."

"Been kinda busy the past year," she said. "And it's not like I didn't have about fifty doctor visits in that time."

"I know. That's why we let it slide. But I can't let you go out on any missions until you get checked out by Doc Rudy – someone who understands superpowers. Remember, we're all Carbodyne employees here. We got lawyers, insurance companies, risk management people ..."

"Whatever. Are we done?"

"Yeah. Yes, we're done."

They stepped out into the Keep, where a small, discreet staff had arranged six banquet chairs girding a round table with a bright white tablecloth, pads, pens, and tumblers full of ice water. The Crusaders took their seats.

"You're probably wondering why I called you all here today," the Carbon Avenger began. "Starting this

40

year, Federal regulatory compliance requires us to hold an annual diversity training session for all employees. I've asked Colonel America to give the briefing."

"Thank you, Avenger," the Colonel began.

Olivia's eyes rolled. Underneath the cowl, Colonel America was a 22-year-old naïf who still wasn't shaving every day. He was whiter than the napkins at Sardi's, grew up in a Rocky Mountain town where everybody else was white, and attended an all-male military academy. And he was giving the diversity training? For this, she took a car, helicopter, and plane? For this, she had to leave her baby?

She looked around. Black Man was visibly uncomfortable, as was El Hombre. She began to wonder how these two guys got into The Crusaders. Neither of them had much power beyond super-strength. Black Man was bulletproof and El Hombre was, she had heard, a skilled horseman who used mystically enhanced *charrería* gear – spurs, lariat, riding crop – to do battle. But surely there must be some psi-powered heroes out there, or shape-shifters, or elementals, or ... No.

It became clear to her in that moment. These guys got into The Crusaders just so Carbodyne could meet its affirmative action quota. These guys were ... were guys. She was the solitary female at the table. She was just as much a token as they were!

As Colonel America droned on about how to treat coworkers with divergent skin tones or genitalia, Olivia was about to stand up and leave, quitting The Crusaders in protest. She hesitated a moment – the job paid really well. But in the end ...

And then the claxon went off. There was evil to contain. The Crusaders scrambled for their customized Harrier jet.

Careerism and politics would have to wait. So would the diversity lecture. So would the doctor's visit.

Ninety-nine Percent Aspiration

"Henchman" is such a loaded term. It's a step up from minion, lackey, stooge, underling, scut-puppy, spear-carrier, gofer, bootlicker, suck-up, pissboy or bitch, but still. "Henchman" was on its way out as a job title even before anyone pointed out that it could be more gender-inclusive. What, after all, is a "hench"?

None of this was lost on the two victims of Georgiana's glamour. They slowly weaned themselves from puppy love as they sat in their cage under the neglectful proctoring of the Indomitable Lugh. It was as if they awakened from a dream of untold splendor to a world of unmitigated squalor. When the police arrived, the two men gave their names, their age (they were both 21) and, as an address, 1825 K Street NW, Washington, DC. When asked about their occupation, they recited, "research fellows at the American Malevolence Institute."

Many years earlier, henchmen were reclassified as interns. But nobody in Washington called themselves interns anymore. Not since Monica. Fellows.

The two were handcuffed and thrown into the back of a squad car, skin scraping off their foreheads from where the police "misjudged their height" guiding them through the vehicle's rear door frames.

Shel Shapiro tapped on the hood of the car a couple times to signal be-on-your-way to the cops. Both the police and the perpetrators felt the fillings rattle in their teeth.

The mall heroes' supervisor let out a melancholy sigh and stared at his feet as he shuffled back into the mall and his bare-bones office of shabby chairs, metal desks and industrial wallpaper peeling at the corners.

He slumped in his chair, splayed out in the good kind of exhaustion. It had been an eventful day. Two Institute incursions foiled – simultaneously. Although the villains got away, two flunkies were on their way to the lockup in Wildwood. Shel, and anyone else who watched the news, knew that villainous activity had spiked through the Central time zone over the past week. Maybe the county prosecutors could get them to explain why. Or maybe not. Errand boys like these don't get fed a lot of information.

Back in her civilian guise, Mindy Maguire had been unrecognizable to the two thunderstruck men in the cage. She had filled out her paperwork and would be starting the next day. Kevin Kiley would be starting the next day as well, although Shel was less enthused about that. If he was sure about anything, it was this: Count Karma, Comma, Master of Arts, was not going to work out. Kevin was just too smooth, Shel figured, there was too much of the con man to him.

And the way Kevin hung out in the security office until Mindy was done with her paperwork, then wrapped up whatever nonexistent business he had just in time to walk her to the parking lot? Come on. It was like Mindy was some hot chick's hatchet-faced sister whom he'd pretend to be nice to until he got under the skirt he had his sights set on.

Mindy and Kevin had left right before the cops got

44

there, Kevin chattering away like a man trying to hold up both ends of a conversation. Lugh was off taking his break. Orville Ortley and Bobby Botler were on patrol. Well, Orville was on patrol. Bobby was just on the clock. Window shopping? Girl watching? Napping? Nothing to be done about it. Drinking on the job? Probably, but Shel would have to catch him in the act. Catch the World's Swiftest Man in the act? Good luck.

In any event, Shel found himself with a moment of repose to reflect on just how eventful a day it had been.

But it was about to become even more eventful.

BOOM!

That afternoon was far less eventful for the senior staff of the American Malevolence Institute.

If they had simply called the charter flight operator at Gude Airfield, they could have been aloft ten minutes after a twenty-minute limo ride.

But, Ta Mok had thundered, that would be decadent.

So they flew coach on the last St. Louis-bound flight of the day out of Reagan National. And took the Blue Line train to get there.

Thanks to an all-too-common glitch in the FAA's software, they sat on the tarmac for over an hour. No cell phones. No electronics and, in the fading twilight, no view.

In the back row were two female fellows, their wide-ranging discussion bouncing at random off healthcare policy, Ethiopian food, defense policy, comparisons of happy hours at Capitol Hill bistros, monetary policy, and when the officers at Andrews Air Force Base get their next paychecks.

In front of them sat Maman Brigitte, engrossed in a hardcover edition of Louis-Philippe Dalembert's *Dieci poesie*, and Singh, puzzling his way through the airport news kiosk's current edition of *Penny's Finest Super Word*

Seeks. "Emu ... Emu ..." he chanted, over and over again, while his irritated seatmate turned twenty pages.

In front of them, Ta Mok had sat in utter silence for almost two hours. It was all one could do when seated next to a mere peon. But finally, curiosity and boredom caught up with the Butcher of Battambang.

"I could not help noticing," Ta Mok began, continuing to stare at the seatback in front of him. "You are male."

"Yes, sir," the man, toward the higher end of his twenties, replied with just enough respect.

There was more silence. Again, Ta Mok broke it.

"I thought we were going with female henchmen only this mission," Ta Mok noted. "Less susceptible to Supermodel's effects."

"Fellows. Georgiana. Don't worry about it."

"You must have a very high opinion of yourself if you believe yourself impervious to her power."

"Then again, sir, you're male and you're going."

"True, but I am a supervillain," Ta Mok explained. "Perhaps someday I will be an archvillain, but I won't get there unless I can demonstrate that I can defend myself against such influences. I believe I have proven such resolve in the past."

"If you say so, sir."

Ta Mok turned to observe the man sitting next to him. Standard Washington-issue blue blazer and gray slacks. The stocky build of a former Special Forces operative. The five-o'clock shadow, buzz cut and character lines in his face confirmed that. Although most fellows came straight out of college, there were enough ex-military types for the breed to be spotted with ease.

"What's your name, young man?"

"You gonna remember it?"

"No."

"Okay then."

Silence resumed.

Ta Mok, again. "This isn't the way, you know."

"Sir?"

"To become a villain," Ta Mok explained, suddenly taking an avuncular tone. "Most of us senior staff were never henchmen. Maman, Singh, me, none of us were ever where you are now."

"I know. You all started out as nemeses. You advanced when your opposite numbers were called up by The Crusaders."

"You've done your homework," Ta Mok noted. "Most people say 'nemesises'."

"What I can't figure out though," the fellow continued, as Ta Mok detected a distinct Piedmont drawl, "is how you get to be a nemesis. I'm just henching 'til I can crack that."

"Well," Ta Mok intoned, settling into a mentoring role, "the first step is to find a worthy adversary."

"That won't be hard."

Ta Mok chuckled. "No shortage of heroes. Remember Time Tempest?"

"The Mistress of Moments? Cool power: Jumped up to a day back in time whenever she needed to. She's been off the radar for ten years now. Whatever happened to her?"

"Works for UPS."

"Oh."

"And that's my point. Powers are a dime a dozen. There are more people with superhuman abilities than there are people with herpes. You must find one hero that has the brains, talent, tenacity, and self-motivation to take whatever skills they have to the highest level and stay there."

"And you have to make sure that your power and his - or hers - is evenly matched," the fellow volunteered. "You have to build the drama."

Ta Mok shook his head violently.

"No, no, no! You have to outclass the hero by a ton. Your opponent will not only have power, but also righteousness, cunning, the adoration of the innocent bystanders and an almost insurmountable pile of luck. All you have is power," Ta Mok paused. "You do have a power, don't you?"

"If I had a power, sir, maybe you'd be asking me for advice."

Ta Mok thought about that a moment.

"Well, like I said, they're a dime a dozen. You're still young. If you're lucky, you'll get a power."

"And if I'm not?"

"You'll get herpes. Meantime, you need to work on a persona."

"Isn't that premature? I mean, shouldn't that stem from whatever abilities I develop?"

"So young, so stupid," Ta Mok said as he let out a long breath. "What does being a tactical genius and master of persuasion have to do with being Cambodian? And you know Singh is a complete fabrication, right? He's no mystic from the Punjab. I've worked with him for five years. He went to public schools in Iselin, New Jersey. Maman Brigitte is the real deal, as far as I can tell, but that makes her the exception, not the rule."

"So how do you come up with a persona?"

"You have to read the American zeitgeist."

"Not sure I follow."

"Every year, America needs a new boogeyman, something that we at the Institute can use as a lever to turn half the population against the other half. Using a foreign connection helps establish you as a sinister 'they' to oppose the virtuous 'we.'"

The fellow nodded as Ta Mok continued.

"When I started in this business, America was still dealing with the aftermath of Vietnam. The Soviet Union was

48

in Afghanistan and Red China was still Communist red, not the Republican red it is now. People were wondering how we botched Asia so badly. Pol Pot was the best non-powered evil man going. As an off-the-boat Cambodian refugee, I had some serious street cred just coming from the same shithole of a country."

"Singh came along much later," the fellow said with a comprehending nod, "when America was growing anxious about losing jobs and its technological edge to India."

"Now you're catching on," Ta Mok said. "And Maman Brigitte? Black, female, foreign, non-Christian. She's a walking wedge issue."

"I heard that!" came the Creole-accented voice from the seat behind the fellow. "And I shall take that as a compliment."

"As it was intended," Ta Mok said.

"With all due respect," Ta Mok's new protégé interjected, "I think I have that topped."

"Really?" Ta Mok condescended. "Would you kindly tell us what you have that will make at least half of America hate you instantly?"

"While I was still in the service, you wouldn't have been allowed to ask me that."

"I'm asking now," Ta Mok replied, a little slow on the uptake.

"I'll put it this way," the fellow offered. "This trait that does so much to define me may be against the law depending on what state we're in."

Ta Mok paused a moment before venturing a guess.

"You're a gun collector?"

"Beside the point."

"OK. Then you smoke marijuana to control migraines."

"You moron!" Maman Brigitte called forward, a little too loud. "He's gay!"

Half the plane turned around, realized they were intruding on the conversation of masters of evil, and went back to thumbing through SkyMall.

"Are you sure you're gay?" Ta Mok asked.

"Yeah. Pretty damn sure," the fellow continued. "That's why I'm not intimidated by Georgiana."

"The reason I ask ..."

"... is I don't look gay to you," the fellow explained to the umpteenth ignorant person attempting open-mindedness. "I buy my clothes at Marshalls. I've never been to a Broadway musical. I'm a domestic beer-drinking, pork rind-eating, Chevy-driving, University of Michigan-rooting, all-American guy who happens to have a thing for Anderson Cooper."

"Singh! Have you been hearing this?" Ta Mok asked over his shoulder.

"Yeah," was the distracted response.

"What do you think?"

"Michigan, huh?" Singh pondered. "OK, I suppose I can believe he's gay. Now, if he'd have said Ohio State ..."

"Ladies and gentleman, from the flight deck: We're Number Three for departure," the overhead speaker crackled. "Flight attendants, please strap in."

{ PONY }

Some magazine once named Chadwick Point, Wisconsin, as one of the "Top 100 Places to Live." It wasn't *Harper's*, *Cosmo* or *The Atlantic*. But if one prefers the laid-back life amid bucolic splendor, Chadwick Point, population 25,327, was as perfect a place as any.

It certainly fit the bill for Reinette Ingersoll, a fifty-year-old divorced former high school math teacher from Appleton who regularly camped out at Chadwick Point's Lake DuBay Shores community. At the end of the last academic year, she realized that there was nothing holding her in Appleton anymore - no more husband, no more kids at home, and twenty-five years in with the school district was just enough, thank you very much. So she splurged and bought herself a cottage by Lake DuBay and became an official, year-round resident of Chadwick Point.

Her cottage wasn't remote – not during the summer at any rate. There were other cottages right over the lot line from hers, left, right, and back. Another row of cottages stretched across the gravelly path wide enough – barely – for two four-wheelers to pass.

But by autumn, these houses were empty. People went back to Appleton or Madison or Milwaukee or Sheboygan, dropping back in on the weekends with decreasing frequency.

This mid-October was her first encounter with an empty resort area. She was literally the only soul in a four-block radius, reminding her of a Wild West ghost town.

If one gives the animalistic husk of Bella Brock credit for still having a soul, then maybe there were two souls in that four-block radius.

To say Bella was a disgusting, filthy, repulsive sight would be misleading. She used the darkness to her advantage and no diurnal creature, like Reinette, would have seen enough of her to be revolted. She was quiet as a cloud and had rolled around in the silty soil enough to mask her scent. As far as any prey was concerned she was just another mound of prairie soil, no more or less acidic than the next pile of dirt. She had even rubbed her own vole-scented spoor on a tree down the road to throw off any of the more clever links down her food chain.

That turned out not to be necessary. Reinette was not that clever. After all, it was Tuesday night and she was watching NBC. To her credit, she considered the second hour of *The Biggest Loser* not to be must-see-TV. She decided, in the spirit of the show, that her time was better spent taking a walk along the lakefront. That was a fateful choice. Her next choice was not so fateful: She decided to TiVo *Loser*. The only distinction was that it was her last.

She experienced no foreshadowing, no sense of imminent danger. Reinette had simply thrown on a poncho and walked along the intermittently lit path along the lake. There were no other people around, but she expected none and reveled in the solitude. A slight breeze whistled through the drying, pre-peak autumn leaves, but gave no scent of danger, no sound of muted breath. Feral eyes actually were tracking Reinette's every move, hungrily, lustily, with a predator's ever-waning patience until she stepped into the kill zone. But there was no feeling she was being watched, whatever that is. Reinette simply walked along, her thoughts free to wander, until, with no warning, she was on the ground.

Stunned by the force with which her head hit a paving stone, she missed the first three seconds of the attack – not that there was much she could have done except endure another three seconds of agony.

Before she experienced any of it, though, she caught an horrific glimpse of her assailant. It looked like some perversion of the human form. In a filthy, tattered floral dress that exposed one shoulder and breast, it knelt over her rather than crouch on all fours, so there was definitely something of a person in there. But the face was elongated by a snout, the eyes rotated to the side with no whites showing, and teeth like diamonds dipped in whitewash. Fur and whiskers grew in clumps.

Then the jaw distended.

Reinette had just about registered the sharp but familiar pain of a knock on the skull when a whole new level of inhuman anguish was revealed to her. Two sabre-clawed, floral-draped forelimbs reached into her belly as easily as she could reach into a Jell-O mold. She ignored the pain from the breach of her skin as the more sublime torture of liver and kidneys being torn out entered her awareness. And even that pain was nothing compared to the shock. Shock, yes, in the physical sense of loss of blood as it squirted and sprayed around the path as her screams echoed futilely across the lake. But shock all the more paralyzing in the psychic sense: the shock of bodily violation, of helplessness, of realizing that she was no longer a viable, living person, but just a source of meat for something else, something perverse.

Objectively, it was eight seconds in a Wisconsin park. Subjectively, it was eternity in an archbishop's nightmare of hell. That's what it took for the one-time Bella Brock to devour Reinette's liver and kidneys, then draw a long tongueful of blood and lymph to slake its thirst. Reinette took it as a kindness that the creature went straight for the heart next, gulping it down in two bites. As a final kindness, the monster's nimble tongue sucked out her eyeballs so she need bear no further witness to her own dismemberment.

BAM!

"Sheldon Shapiro, we meet again."

"Well, well, Colonel America," Shel countered, leaning back in his squeaking chair, feet up on his desk, puffing on his illegal end-of-day Robusto. "I'm just about to head home. Let me get you an application to take with you. Bring it back tomorrow."

Colonel America strode through the doorway, threw his head back and laughed like a villain.

"That's what I always liked about you, Shel," the Colonel confessed. "You appreciate good repartee. It's lost on the kids."

From somewhere behind the Protector of Patriots was a tongue click of exasperation.

"Speaking of which, flagboy, who's that on your six?"

"Hmm? Oh. This is my, my, um ..."

53

"Pilot," the young woman in the flight suit said as she walked up to Shel to give him a firm handshake. "I'm an officer in the U.S. Air Force. My call sign is Nebraska."

"*Lieutenant Colonel* Nebraska," her superior officer emphasized.

"Oh, I see," Shel replied, then turned his attention to his new acquaintance. "Have a seat."

Nebraska waited until the Colonel sat first. Shel studied her. Small frame, but a toughness about her. The accent was pure blue-collar New York. Her smooth, straight hair pulled back in a bun, shimmering mocha skin tone and wide eyes the color of shadows on a bedroom wall suggested Latin origins. The next Colonel America is going to look like Anita from *West Side Story?* He liked the idea. Especially because the current Colonel America seemed to be having a problem with it.

"So how's my old boss, the Carbon Avenger?" Shel asked.

"He's as well as can be expected, given his condition," the Colonel replied. "He's disappointed you didn't stay in the clean coal industry."

"Some days, me too," Shel confided. "And Midge and Pantagruel? Are they divorced yet?"

"No," the Colonel said with a knowing smile. "They were supposed to be here with us right now but—"

"But they needed a moment," Nebraska continued. "They're out in the parking lot."

"How's The Indomitable Lugh fitting in down here?" This time it was Colonel America's turn to play catch-up.

"Real good, to tell you the truth. I haven't had a moment's problem with him."

"So he hasn't had any incidents while out on patrol?"

"Not a one," Shel said, not volunteering that he wasn't so dim as to actually put Lugh out on patrol. "What about his replacement? How's the new guy working out?"

"Ah, well, you know," the Colonel sputtered, trying not to be unkind. "We're still working through a few things."

"If you don't mind my saying, that's a pretty arbitrary staffing requirement you got," Shel sympathized. "Why Carbodyne insists that The Crusaders always have at least one deity on the payroll is beyond me."

The Colonel nodded. "Don't get me started."

"What name does this guy go by again?"

With a roll of his eyes, Colonel America spat out, "Christ the Son."

"He's supposed to be pretty powerful," Shel said. "What's the problem?"

"This doesn't leave this office," the Colonel insisted. Shel nodded. So did Nebraska, not that he noticed. "Ever work with one of those transcendent types that are supposed to have all kinds of abilities on some level that we mere mortals can't comprehend? He's one of those. Maybe they're affecting the outcome in some subtle way or maybe they're not but when the rubber meets the road, we're not philosophers and we're not priests. We're heroes! We need to count on each other in a bare-knuckles fight!"

Shel flirted with the idea of trading Kevin Kiley straight-up for this Christ the Son.

"All he does is just smile like an idiot and when we win, no thanks to him, he provides some kind of moral we were supposed learn from our adventure, then spends the rest of the day on the Xbox."

"Well, good luck with all that," Shel said to put a coda on that topic. "What brings you to St. Louis?"

"I can't tell you," a suddenly somber Colonel America intoned.

"You come all this way from halfway to the moon, you walk into my office uninvited while I'm packing up for the day, bring a guest and you're not going to tell me why?"

"I'm Colonel America," the Protector of Patriots announced as he rose to his feet and struck a parade-rest stance. "I don't do exposition. Only repartee."

Shel glanced at Nebraska.

"We have reason to believe that the last card of the Malificium deck is in the Plaquet Box here at the Chesterfield Mall," Nebraska began. "The American Malevolence Institute is also aware of that, as Orville's actions earlier today suggest."

Orville, Shel reflected. Not Ortley. Not Mucus-Man. He takes Supermodel out to lunch, then it turns out he's on a first-name basis with Colonel America's understudy. Shel wondered if Orville's supposed OCD and Asperger's syndrome were some kind of dodge.

"We wanted to alert you of the threat, and offer whatever assistance you require," Nebraska continued. "We all know what would happen if that last card were to fall into the Institute's hands."

"Yes, of course," Shel said. He hadn't a clue.

"We must remain vigilant," Nebraska summed up. "The Institute could strike at any time."

{BOOM!}

No, they couldn't.

Their flight cancelled due to mechanical difficulties, the senior staff and fellows of the American Malevolence Institute stayed the night in the Crystal City Howard Johnson's and would have to take the first flight out the next morning.

{POW!}

While Shel met with Colonel America and his eventual replacement, Lugh took a power walk around the Chesterfield Mall's parking lot.

Absentmindedly, like an archetypal beat cop twirling his nightstick, he swung around his enchanted adze, the weapon with which Lugh was so intimately identified.

But it wasn't a weapon, per se. It was a tool, similar to an axe but with the blade perpendicular to the shaft rather than parallel to it. An implement of a skilled artisan, the adze could be used to build or to destroy. And the Indomitable Lugh, Sovereign of the Strong, immortal scion of an ancient Celtic pantheon, was patron of all such artisans. No one was more skilled in the use of the adze, and no one could wield it with greater might.

If Lugh was aware how ridiculous he looked in a TSA uniform, his face did not betray that. It was with the dignified gait of the unbowed that he went about his unofficial rounds. (No patrols, Shel had directed.) This was Lugh's day to work the supervisor's shift from 6 p.m. to closing, and he had another ten minutes to kill before he needed to be back in the office to relieve Shel.

Very few things could shake Lugh's detached aspect. But, as he rounded the JC Penney entrance, he saw one of those things. There, taking up all eight handicapped spots, was a space-worthy, vertical-takeoff-and-landing craft with The Crusaders' logo on the side.

As chance would have it, the impenetrable craft opened its aperture just as Lugh approached. Loud arguing pierced the monotonous grind of engines that served as the usual parking lot background noise.

"... always about you, isn't it?" shrieked the soprano voice.

"If it wasn't for me, you wouldn't be a Crusader! You wouldn't even have a power!" boomed the bass.

"And if it wasn't for me you'd still be spending eighteen hours a day in the lab. Probably never gotten laid! Not that you ever showed any improvement at that!"

"Well, maybe if I knew how many guys you were comparing me to ..." Pantagruel paused. Both he and Midge emerged from the aperture, their disheveled costumes suggesting they had been thrown on hastily. "Lugh? Honey – it's Lugh!"

They ran down the gangplank, the aperture squeezing shut behind them as they ran to embrace their old comrade. A ten-foot-tall Pantagruel slapped him on the back. Half that size, Midge jumped up to throw her arms around the god's neck.

Lugh returned neither greeting. He just stood his ground, inscrutably, wordlessly.

"Oh, Lugh, don't be that way!" Midge said, flitting down to the ground. "I hope you don't hold us accountable for how things worked out."

No response.

"Yeah, buddy," Pantagruel continued. "We were always in your corner. Still friends, right? C'mon. What do you say?"

What does he say?

Lugh's lip quivered. His teeth ground together as if they were trying to hold the rest of his mouth shut. Lugh struggled to control himself and recapture his commitment to never speak an unguarded word again.

But it was a losing battle. He looked Pantagruel clear in the eye.

"Rot ... thy ... soul ..." Lugh choked back, but from those three pebbles, the landslide had begun. "Thou simpering, flaccid-skootched, misbegotten son of a whore and a baited bear! By all the fauns in Tralee, may thy gouch ne'er cease to itch 'neath thy cod more wide than long, ye ruptured bag o' bukkake from a whole village o' amented Varangian wankers!"

"Lugh," Midge said in soothing tones, after a short pause, "I don't think Pantagruel really deserved ..."

"And what knoweth thee, thou dry-blooded, pustule-misshapen twat? Art thou the one who must bear this discomfiture? Nay, thou art nothing but the hairy,

58

widespreading arse in a brothel's window, thou putrid trail of cunt sap!"

Pantagruel and Midge went back inside their craft. Lugh, head held high as ever, strode back toward his office.

Scores of people - dozens of children under twelve - gawped at this scene as they walked between their cars and the mall or vice versa.

All other conversation stopped as Lugh's tirade continued. His thunderous voice reached all the way to the outer ring, where Kevin Kiley was escorting Mindy Maguire to her Honda Fit.

"So that's the Indomitable Lugh," Mindy said, taking the driver's seat as Kevin held the door. "I can see why you're such a fan."

"Don't let the nasty mouth fool you," he cautioned. "He's by far the most powerful hero going. Granted, you can't be a Crusader with a piehole like that. They have to give post-battle interviews and you do *not* want that guy on the NewsHour. But there's no one else I'd rather have watching my back. I'm really looking forward to working with him."

He then hastily added, "But I'm looking forward to working with you more."

Mindy half smiled.

"He's a real god, huh?"

"Yeah. Certifiable deity."

"What is he god of?"

"Lugh was the Celtic god of carpenters, thatchers and stonemasons."

"Construction workers."

"Right."

BAM!

On a plane of existence that few mortals can conceive and no mortal can traverse, the goddesses watched.

Their fellow deity Lugh, who was not only on the same world as Mindy and Kevin but only thirty yards away, gave no sign that he was aware his new teammates were anywhere around. Still, the goddesses paid careful attention as Mindy drove away and Kevin stared wistfully at the license plate.

"We did not foresee this," Aphrodite said. "We cannot allow this to come to pass."

"But we have sworn an oath never again to interfere with the ways of the mortals," Lakshmi countered. "And even if we had not, who among us would willingly diminish herself to return to that horrid realm?"

"But the girl needs guidance, sisters," Ishtar urged. "Not only about the ways of men - that one in particular - but also in how to use her abilities. She has not called upon us since her powers were new. There is a new peril, or she would not have called upon us today."

"What she needs is a spirit guide," Aphrodite said. "Not one of us ..."

"... but one whom we might welcome into our circle," Lakshmi continued, "if she is successful."

"Perhaps we could find a soul with whom our ward - what does she call herself now? Georgiana? - can identify more closely," Ishtar offered. "We are all removed from her by thousands of schoenii and just as many years. We need a soul willing to risk eternal rest in exchange for a chance at goddesshood, but someone from a culture more similar to Georgiana's, perhaps someone born in the same century as she."

"Yes," Aphrodite affirmed. "But whom?"

NIGHT DIVIDES THE DAY

ey, you! It's Brigitte," the managing director of the American Malevolence Institute spoke into her Bluetooth as she plodded along on the elliptical trainer in the HoJo's fitness center. Instead of her usual black ceremonial garb, she wore shocking-pink stretch pants and an old, well-worn Washington Bullets T-shirt. These all the more revealed how emaciated she kept her body, like a heroin-addicted ballerina with cancer. "Yeah, I'm supposed to be there already, but we're stuck at a hotel near Reagan for the night. That damned AirTran! ... Next time, absolutely. But for now, I was wondering if I could call in a favor. ... Can you get away tomorrow? We may need someone with your firepower on this St. Louis job ..."

BOOM!

Wall Street didn't exist anymore.

There was a time when every major investment banker felt the need to have an address on that eight-block stretch between Trinity Church and Pier 11, but those days were long gone. To expand, banks relocated to TriBeCa, Midtown, New Jersey, Connecticut, London, Hong Kong. The New York Stock Exchange remained as Wall Street's anchor, but all the other exchanges – for stocks, bonds, commodities, derivatives – found less expensive digs out-of-town or evaporated entirely into the internet. On the one hand, Wall Street transformed from a hyperactive, white-knuckled street where dreams of fortune were fulfilled or dashed, into just another Manhattan side street of delis, jewelers, and souvenir shops. On another level, though, Wall Street came to intersect with every market lane and county highway. Every web site linked to it.

Still, the biggest players stayed close to the root of American mercantilism. One of them, a woman with a worldly, exotic air who still had Maman Brigitte's 202-prefixed cell number at the top of her desk phone's inbound log, was only five blocks south and 30 stories above physical Wall Street. Ending an exasperating call with the her employer's travel office, she didn't even notice the 12-passenger Sikorsky S-76C soar straight past her window, as a spotlight projected its shadow on the Statue of Liberty. Ordinarily, a chopper that close to the window would be noisy enough to distract, but the steady patter of rain masked all other sounds from outside.

The travel office was absolutely no help getting her a plane to St. Louis. There were no more flights there that night, not out of JFK, LaGuardia, or Newark. The squall that generated the rain which was splashing the window had canceled everything inbound, so the airlines were only taking standbys for the morning.

But this wasn't going to stop her – not the villainess known as Equity.

Though the hour was late, she was still at her desk. By industry convention, that meant her entry-level associate was there too.

Vijay bring UPS pkg 2 me plz, she IM'ed to the newly minted Cornell MBA outside her glass office.

"Right away, Equity," came the immediate, vocal response as Vijay got up from his cubicle and headed for the elevator bank.

Mindy Maguire trod into her one-bedroom apartment and went through the first few steps of her routine in darkness. She kicked off her shoes, set her purse and keys on the little Queen Anne table by the door, hung her coat on the rack, and transferred the mail from her teeth to her right hand to the table, then she flicked on the light to discover ...

She wasn't alone.

Seated regally, as if the recliner were the throne of the House of Bourbon, was a slight figure of a woman. Mindy envied of what she wore; if an impeccably tailored power suit could be woven from bright, tropical, floral prints, that's what draped her frame from padded shoulders to modest mid-calf. She wore the kind of shoes that would have Anna Wintour asking, "Hey, where did you get those?" At a startled first glance, Mindy could tell this was a woman not all that much older than she was. Still, this stranger exuded the weariness and knowing of a full lifetime.

The woman on the recliner - actually a finger's breadth *above* the recliner, as Mindy noticed as she approached - made eye contact, but no threatening motion. Mindy missed a breath - realizing at that point that the intruder didn't appear to waste effort on breathing - then settled down quickly and regarded her as an unwelcome trespasser, but no threat.

"Who are you?" Mindy demanded.

"In life I was called Maria Eva Duarte de Peron," was the reply, calm bordering on tedium.

Mindy, on the other hand, was surprised, starstruck even.

"You? You're Evita?" Mindy gushed as she stepped closer to shake the legendary figure's hand.

"Are you registered to vote in Argentina?"

"No."

"Then I'm 'Mrs. Peron,'" Eva said coolly as Mindy tried to shake her hand but discovered that she was an apparition, not a physical being. "The goddesses asked me to fill in for them. Tamora wasn't available. I'm your new spirit guide."

"Spirit guide?"

"Yes, apparently the goddesses feel some responsibility for you, but they don't like you very much. So you just do what I say, dearie, and you'll be a heroine, and I'll become a goddess."

"Did you know they made an opera about you?"

"No, but I won't feign surprise."

"I have the soundtrack around here somewhere," Mindy offered before getting back to business. She tried without success to keep a dismissive tone out of her voice. "Exactly what kinds of responsibility do they feel toward me?"

"First, do you know a young man named Kevin Kiley?"

Mindy blushed a little. "Well, we just met today."

"Good. Keep it that way: 'just met.' Whatever you do don't sleep with him."

"Why not?"

"Ah! So you were thinking about it. Don't."

"But why ...?"

"Just don't. The goddesses don't tell me every-thing. But the way I see it, if three immortal matrons of love and beauty tell you not to screw somebody, don't screw him."

"OK, so that's the first thing," Mindy said with a non-committal arching of an eyebrow. "Next thing?"

"They felt you could use some advice on using your powers."

"Oh, yeah. Really hard powers to use," Mindy said, pacing – no, stomping – through the room. "Show up in tights, shake my boobs and guys do my bidding. It's degrading."

"That's where I come in," Eva said evenly. "Using womanly charms need not be so, shall we say, overt. You have a far broader palette of abilities than you know. And if you weren't so ungrateful, perhaps the goddesses themselves would have given you some pointers rather than leave you to your own devices."

"They granted me the powers, so maybe they could've spent some time teaching me to use them," Mindy agreed, still pacing angrily. "But what's this got to do with you? What do you know about any of this?"

Eva's upper lip curled a little, for a precise ten-count, before a cleansing breath brought her back into self-possession.

"I secured the right to vote for eight million wom-en," Eva said, wagging a slender, white-gloved finger. "in one of the most macho nations on earth. You couldn't have done that on your best day, dearie."

At that, Mindy sat down, shut up, and started lis-tening.

BAM!

"Here you go, Equity," Vijay said casually, as if there was nothing unusual about carrying a writhing, body-

65

sized canvas bag from the elevator to his boss's office.

He deposited the package on an ergonomically designed guest chair that was comfortable only in theory. Vijay then took the sack off the captive's head, revealing a woman with sharp features, steely gray eyes and close-cropped red hair. Her brown collar was also visible, marking her as a uniformed UPS courier.

Equity rose from her desk chair, affording her captive a good look. The villainess wore a pinstriped, cinch-waisted suit with a choker-length strand of lustrous, subtly rose-tinted pearls. Obviously a product of the American melting pot, there was something WASPish in her erect bearing, but that was the only noticeable European trait. Equity had more diverse roots –some Asian in her background and some African as well. Asking questions about her kidnapper's origins was the last thing on the courier's mind, though.

"That will be all for the evening, Vijay. You may go," Equity said and Vijay took her up on that without comment or hesitation. Equity walked around her bound captive three times before offering the requisite villainous introduction. "So, Time Tempest, we meet at last ..."

BOOM!

Up in the Pinnacle of Righteousness, the Carbon Avenger and Christ the Son kept vigil. That is to say, the Avenger did his best to manipulate Midge's data tracking console with his oversized, crumbling, coal-black fingers while Christ stood by the window, looking down on the Earth and smiling beatifically.

Somehow, The Avenger happened to be looking in the right place at the right time. There was a call from

Maman Brigitte's cell to a 212 number. He had a good idea whose it was, and a moment's search confirmed it: Equity.

The Crusaders' rogues gallery database brought up all he needed to know about this particular villainess. Firmly aligned with the American Malevolence Institute, she preferred to stay in the private sector. With her ability to siphon off half the power of any super-powered being she touched, she presented a threat potentially more deadly than all the Institute's senior staffers combined. For that matter, she could conceivably battle The Crusaders themselves to a stand-still. The more powers you brought to bear fighting Equity, the more powers she could throw right back at you.

The Avenger had a quick decision to make.

"Christ," he directed, "Let's get to Steed Two. We're going to St. Louis."

Christ floated over to the docking station, even though the artificial gravity was on.

POW!

One brush of Equity's hand against Time Tempest's cheek, and it was suddenly many hours earlier in Equity's office. Vijay was bringing her midmorning coffee — no, it was her first cup of coffee, Time Tempest had a little more giddy-up than Equity knew — as green and red digits and ticker symbols swirled around the light boards and other officers of the bank and their assistants went about their business.

Equity took the elevator down to street level. She turned to walk two blocks downtown to the heliport when she realized she had an errand to run. Fortunately for her, she stood in one of the few neighborhoods on earth where she could pick up what she needed at the card shop in her building's lobby, so she could catch the next shuttle to JFK as the first rain clouds peered over the horizon.

An uneventful flight later, and she checked into the Renaissance Hotel across I-70 from Lambert-St. Louis International Airport. In the morning, she would reunite with her friends, they would set about taking the last Malificium card and, with the deck complete, they could finally destroy the world.

THE SECOND-BEST DEFENSE

Plaquet Box franchisee Seth Hill entered the Chesterfield Mall through the doors between the Sears and the Gaylen Ross, as he did most mornings around 8:30, and took the stairs up to his little shop on the second floor next to Macy's. He casually greeted some of the old-timers who strolled the mall for exercise before the shops opened.

He also nodded to his latest neighbors; the mall never seemed to be able to find a permanent tenant for the space on the far side of the Plaquet Box from Macy's. Its latest incarnation was as a holiday store - the kind that sold Christmas ornaments or Easter baskets or Fourth of July bunting, depending on the season. That month, they were selling Halloween costumes. Seth wondered if they'd still be around to mark the birthdays of Washington, Lincoln, and King.

Most storefronts in the mall had grille-style gates that allowed people to window-shop even if the stores were closed. Not the Plaquet Box. Too much valuable merchandise would be in full view. Seth favored rolling fire doors - the kind that, in a downtown area, would be a magnet for graffiti, but not so in a suburban shopping center. Seth found this barrier eminently practical. Titanium-alloy steel, a quarter-inch thick, designed to withstand up to 80 pounds per square foot of force – there was little any normal human being could do to argue with it.

Within the hour, it would be shredded like confetti.

BAM!

Shel Shapiro was draping his jacket over his desk chair when Mindy Maguire showed up for her first day at work. She seemed tired, as if she had been up most the night, but was still there precisely on time – that is, just a pace behind Orville Ortley. Mindy was surprised that Bobby Botler, the haggard, dissipated Blur, had beaten them all in. Shel and Orville understood that he must have slept in the mall again. Kevin Kiley ambled in a few minutes later, a five-dollar vanilla chai soy latte in his hand, and nothing for anyone else. It took Shel all of one second to determine who to pair with whom for training day.

"Mindy, you're with Bobby. Kevin, Orville."

BOOM!

Midge and Pantagruel stayed at the Drury Inn across the parking lot from the Chesterfield Mall. After a few complaints from guests in adjacent rooms and a brief appearance by the local police, management requested them to never stay there again.

Before the first cycle of loud mutual recrimination, followed by louder mutual reconciliation, was completed, Lieutenant Colonel Nebraska moved out of her Drury Inn room and slept, peacefully if uncomfortably, in Steed One.

POW!

Colonel America didn't sleep at all.

As the gate to the Plaquet Box clattered open, the Protector of Patriots was standing in his usual parade-rest stance.

"Fear not, citizen! I am here to protect you and your merchandise," he informed Seth.

"I was wondering when The Crusaders were going to show up," Seth said nonchalantly as he took off his jacket and began stocking the display cases. "How did you get in?"

"The Clam let me in," Colonel America replied. "But aren't you supposed to be expressing how glad you are to see me and how relieved you are that the greatest team of ..."

"Huzzah. Great job you guys did in New York last week. Our TSA mall heroes did a better job of protecting my Malificium card than all you jokers put together," Seth said without paying the Crusader any further attention as he continued his pre-open shopkeeping rituals. Then he looked up suddenly. "'Clam'?"

"Yes, The Clam. Sh... uh ... the TSA supervisor for this location."

"You mean Shel Shapiro?"

"So he's revealed his secret identity?"

"I didn't even know he had a power. Clam?"

The Colonel shook his head violently.

"I've said too much already."

"OK, I'll ask him myself later. By the way, where's the rest of your team?"

"Close at hand. They'll be here before your first customers arrive."

And that's when three twenty-somethings walked in: two impeccably if economically dressed young women and a solidly-built man in a blue blazer, their clothes rumpled a little, as if they had just gotten off a plane.

"Are you open yet?" the man asked Seth, as he gave Colonel America a too long, and too unwelcome, look.

"Yes," Seth said as he surreptitiously pressed a button under the counter. "Yes, we are."

BAM!

Mindy regarded the cavernous, incense-perfumed hideaway in a forgotten stretch of the Chesterfield Mall.

It must've taken some dedication, Mindy realized in a flash.

"Bobby," she half-whispered, "did you do this yourself?"

The expanse, almost ten times the size of her apartment, was a mixture of dangling, unshaded, 100-watt incandescent bulbs with corners black-lit to highlight the kind of velvet posters once sold by Spencer's. There was a full-sized refrigerator, a dorm-sized freezer and a microwave. A patchwork of carpet remnants covered the cold concrete slab of a floor. More lined the walls and ceilings in the obvious attempt to dampen sounds. Loud noise emanated from the piecemeal stereo system, which at the moment was tracking a Green Day CD. At any time, solos could erupt from the amps attached to the electric guitar and bass, the stripped-down Zildjian drum kit or the Xbox hooked via a series of technology-bridging connectors into a big-screened but archaic console TV with similarly big but archaic speakers. These speakers looked like they could blast a monstrous wall of sound if called upon, but they put out a mellower level at the moment, not even drowning out the whirring of machinery coming from behind the far wall.

"Yeah. This used to be the main loading dock," Bobby recounted as he unclipped his tie and stuffed his mask into a pants pocket. "Then – and this was before my time here – the state said the mall needed more handicapped spaces so management expanded the other three docks and added the spaces right in front of this one. Nobody's come down here since. They never did get around to installing surveillance cameras. Beer?"

"No thanks."

"First day on the job. I get it," Bobby nodded as he went into the fridge to pull out an Old Milwaukee then went into the freezer to pull out a frosted glass mug. "Pull up a beanbag."

She did.

"Is Mr. Shapiro aware of this place?"

"Yeah, I guess, in a Sergeant-Schultzian sense," Bobby said, blowing the foam off his lager. "Orville does, but he never comes in here. I like the guy, but he's too much of a straight-arrow to hang out."

"What about the regular mall security guards? I mean, at some point they must've stumbled ..."

"Jim! Deke! Say hi to Mindy! She's a new mall hero."

"Hi. Mindy," came two strained voices from a dark and distant corner, obscured by a support beam, as they tried not to exhale as they spoke. The greeting was preceded and followed by the sound of water gurgling, and the billowing of a cloud past a busted smoke detector.

"Hi."

As always happened when Mindy was about to get comfortable, she suddenly found a new reason to be uncomfortable. The weight-bearing pillars that stood at 16-foot intervals - some connected by base paths painted in white primer on the carpet - had been virtually wallpapered with voluptuous, female nudes printed out on an inkjet. Mindy glanced away. She tried to make eye contact with Bobby, but where he had been a moment ago there was just an empty beer mug resting on a milk crate. She noticed a breeze and a bass rumble that didn't seem to have anything to do with Green Day. Mindy looked around the dock again and the cheesy pictures were gone. Bobby was pouring himself a fresh mug.

"Sorry about that," he said, puffing a little from exertion. He downed the beer in one chug and poured another.

"Thanks, I appreciate the effort," Mindy said. "Should you really be slamming those drinks? I mean, having a beer at work is one thing - I spent my junior year in Europe and it was considered perfectly acceptable there. But three before the stores even open?"

Bobby's boyishness turned off like a movie projector in a

blackout. All of a sudden, he fully inhabited his grizzled, hard-worn visage.

"You don't know anything about me," he said, staring Mindy straight in the eye in a way that made her push back in her seat. He drank the beer in his hand then popped open and drank another.

"They call me 'The World's Swiftest Man'. Do you know what that means? On a practical level?"

Mindy shook her head. She noticed a Texas twang working its way into Bobby's voice as he became more emotional.

"It means I have the world's fastest metabolism. The alcohol from the first two beers is already out of my bloodstream," he said. "Another thing: How old do you think I am?"

"I don't know."

"Guess."

"Maybe fifty-four or fifty-five?" she said. For an honest estimate, she'd have had to add ten years.

"I'm thirty-five. A year older than Orville," he said, to Mindy's amazement. "Whenever I use my power, the world slows down for me. To you I'm a, well, a Blur. To me, you're a statue. The world's a museum full of statues. I'm all alone, aging."

"So you drink to handle the loneliness," Mindy said, trying to comprehend, "and to slow down your metabolism."

"Yeah, you might say that," Bobby granted. "But to be honest, my powers didn't manifest until I was twenty-two. I was in tenth grade when my friends started calling me the Blur."

"All units!" Shel Shapiro barked via the tinny walkie-talkies on both Mindy's and Bobby's belts. "Plaquet Box! Now!"

Mindy was already up off the beanbag and at the fire

door before the order was finished.

Bobby opened another beer.

"You go ahead. I'll catch up," he told Mindy. "It's what I do."

"Acknowledged," she replied into the walkie-talkie then, with the regular mall guards trailing, burst into the fluorescent glare of a mall concourse. They trotted toward the up escalator.

"You guys keep moving," she said as they passed a ladies' room.

Meanwhile ...

"It's 9:41 a.m., straight up," Orville said in patient tones. "By now I like to be in front of Aeropostale. So we're four storefronts behind schedule already."

"Sorry for throwing you off," Kevin said, making only a half-hearted attempt to match his lackadaisical gait to Orville's purposeful stride.

"It's fine. Training is a valuable part of my role."

"Shel must think a lot of you to trust you with the responsibility," Kevin said in a transparent bid to get on Orville's good side. But Kevin realized that Orville was not all there in terms of social skills: was it ADD? OCD? Both? Both, plus Asperger's, or something out of the autistic range? What constituted Orville's good side? And how could someone tell if he were on it?

"Yes, he does," Orville said evenly. "It takes eight paces to pass a standard storefront at approximately one second per pace."

"OK."

"You should be writing this down," Orville advised. It wasn't an order and didn't sound like one. "You were issued a notepad."

"Uh, yeah," Kevin said. "I didn't bring a pen, though."

"Here," Orville offered as he reached for his breast pocket without breaking stride. "I have three spares. Take two."

"Eight paces per store, one second per pace," Kevin recited as he scribbled down what an absolute tool. "Why is this important?"

The question momentarily confused Orville. It's not that he didn't have an answer. He just thought it was obvious.

"Your ten-minute break starts at 10:50. Before it starts, you must make three full circuits of the mall concourses. There are 184 storefronts. If you stick to the route and schedule I'm showing you, you'll be right in front of the security office at exactly 10:49:30," Orville explained. "Otherwise, you might have to waste your own time racing to the punch clock."

"Ah, now that you've explained it, let's make up for lost time," Kevin agreed and up-shifted into a racing walk. He actually got half a dozen stores in front of Orville before he realized that Mucus-Man couldn't be baited into a contest like that.

He slowed again to allow Orville to catch up, then matched his speed.

"So, Orville," Kevin said, trying another topic, "What's up with you and Mindy?"

"Up?"

"I mean, of all the guys in the mall she could've had lunch with, it was you. It was me who saved her from Singh, after all," Kevin said. "Do you know her from somewhere? Are you wearing a particular antiperspirant I should start using? Are you hung like a barnyard animal of some kind?"

"She was familiar with my work prior to joining TSA."

"Well, you must've made one hell of an impression. In real life, she's a cutie-pie. When she's got her powers on, she is made of gorgeous."

"She's the most beautiful woman in the world," Orville said in a matter-of-fact monotone then added, in exactly the same cadence as if it were a fact of equal weight, "She likes Chik-Fil-A."

"All units!" Shel Shapiro barked via the tinny walkie-talkies on both Kevin's and Orville's belts. "Plaquet Box! Now!"

Then it became a race.

First across the threshold were Jim and Deke.

"These three must be Institute henchman," Seth told them. "I can spot 'em a mile away. Escort them out!"

The security guards took a look at the large man and the two rather petite women and decided to take on the two women. There wasn't much of a struggle.

"Are there any heroes on the way?" Seth asked. "Lapdogs like these are never far away from their supervillain bosses."

"TSA is on the case!" came a seductive, airborne voice. As Georgiana flew into view, Seth, Colonel America and the two guards all swung their necks. They were only mildly disappointed by the wardrobe choice. The diamond-shaped face was the same. The golden mane remained wild and long, like the martial banner of some ancient, sun-worshipping empire. But the body was covered by more than a sheath of nylon. A sheer blouse exposed an immodest amount of décolletage, though nothing scandalous. A gauzy jacket served the double purpose of accentuating Georgiana's waspish waist and obscuring her nipples. A pleated skirt fell halfway down her thighs, and thigh-high leather boots covered most of the rest of her long, shapely legs. The ensemble didn't exactly shout "corner office" but at least it didn't remind anyone of a 1980s workout video.

And there were dangly earrings, a tennis bracelet, and a handcrafted brooch. For the first time since being granted her powers of limitless womanly charm, the hero still most widely known as Supermodel had accessorized.

The two women from the Institute took the opportunity

to escape from mall security and run for the exits. The guards gave chase.

"Colonel America?"

"Yes, I am me," the Protector of Patriots said. He may have sounded vain and vacuous but, to his credit, he was the only male in her presence who could speak at all.

"The Blur is on his way. Mucus-Man and Count Karma too. Where are the rest of The Crusaders?"

"Pantagruel and Midge should be here by now," Colonel America said, increasingly composed. "The Carbon Avenger and Christ the Son called a few minutes ago. They'll be landing at any moment. But even without them, we're more than a match for Ta Mok and Singh. If they brought Maman Brigitte along, we could still make a stand."

"Might they be bringing more reinforcements than just her?" Georgiana asked.

"It's possible," the Colonel said. "Let's find out what this underling knows about that."

The Colonel pointed a thumb at the remaining Institute fellow.

The fellow was, of course, immune to Georgiana's allure. But he could look at Colonel America all day. Sure, the flag-waving costume was over-the-top, but that's not a bad thing. If he didn't love red, white, and blue, he'd have never joined the Service after all. And the Protector of Patriots, standing in that body armor and folded-over boots was a stunning specimen of masculinity. There, up close, the fellow noticed something about Colonel America that never came through in news photos: his crystal-clear blue eyes. Under that cowl, the fellow imagined, this man might have a tousled crop of sandy hair to go with it.

Anderson Cooper wearing nothing but a flag ...

Colonel America locked his crystal-clear blue eyes on the fellow, whom he intended to pummel for information. Suddenly the eyes staring back glowed, shooting sparks at him. That pummeling idea quickly left Colonel America's brain. The fellow seemed like such a wonderful individual. Too bad he dressed so shabbily – the Institute must by paying him peanuts. Colonel America wanted no more than to take the young man out shopping, buy him a proper wardrobe, buy him a hearty meal, walk it off along some riverside promenade, hand-in-hand ...

After a long, very confusing moment for everyone present, Colonel America stammered out, "That's, uh, quite a power you have there, young man."

"Power?" the fellow gasped, then realized what just happened. "I have a power!"

"You turn straight people gay!" Colonel America announced. "I'm so confounded I'm doing exposition."

"I knew the boy had potential," Ta Mok said. He was at the threshold of the store, flanked by Maman Brigitte and the Incomprehensible Singh.

"Take him to safety, Ta Mok," Maman Brigitte ordered. "Get him back to the Institute. We don't want to lose him before we find out more about his abilities."

"Can we take Colonel America too?" the no-longer-fellow asked. "As my prisoner."

"Yes," the Colonel responded. "I could be your prisoner."

"No," Ta Mok said with a hearty, villainous laugh. "You'd like that too much. I want you to suffer."

The Colonel said, "I'll keep fighting you, Ta Mok, no matter what my sexual orientation. I'd keep fighting against my nation's foes even if you chopped off my hands and feet. I'd keep fighting for my country even if I were dying of cancer. I'd keep fighting for America even if I were a Democrat."

"Ridiculous!" Ta Mok retorted, his words carrying the weight of all his powers of propaganda. "You're useless now. You can't be Colonel America anymore. Colonel

America can't be gay. You can't be gay and serve your country with distinction - you should be glad they finally decided to let you serve at all. That's like saying you could be gay and in a lifelong commitment. That's like saying you could be gay and a good parent. That's like saying you could be gay and enjoy going to church."

The fallen hero simply curled up in a fetal position on the floor and wept.

Ta Mok slammed his foot on the floor and the shock-waves scattered people, card, and glass everywhere. Sections of the Plaquet Box's titanium-alloy gate rattled and crashed to the ground. He and his charge rode the shock-waves out of the store. The concourse buckled and shoppers fell to the ground or scattered as they passed. Emerging from the Macy's exit, they encountered something they didn't expect:

The sharp end of the adze of The Indomitable Lugh.

Ta Mok dropped down on the ground in an instant, writhing in pain - some of it phantom pain, as he would soon discover.

"Whither goest thou, thou hatful o' cock cheese?" Lugh shouted at Ta Mok as he hovered six feet above the villains in the loading zone. He tossed a haughty glance at the other villain. "And what manner of meadow didst thou traverse to get this pile o' loose *merde* stuck 'neath thy boot heel?"

Ta Mok wasn't paying much attention as he stared at the source of his power - his severed left foot and calf - rolling down the sidewalk, the blood spraying from his popliteal artery blinding both him and his new associate and showering the pavement, the exterior walls and doors and a dozen panicky bystanders in sticky, staining crimson.

"Do it to him!" Ta Mok shouted at his companion, who was applying his belt as a tourniquet above the wound. "Make him love us!"

"I can't."

80

"What do you mean?"

"Well, first of all, even if I could turn him, that doesn't mean he'd be attracted to either you or me," the man in the blue blazer explained. "But I can't make him gay. I've been trying. I don't know why I can't."

"Ach, ye stool-brained, mortal bottom-bandits," Lugh laughed as he raised his weapon triumphantly over his head. "I come from a time 'fore there was shame in buggery. E'en so, mine adze didst e'er swing but one direction."

"Send maintenance to the Macy's entrance – oh, and EMS too," Shel Shapiro said with a big smile, speaking into his walkie-talkie. Then Lugh glided to the ground and offered a hand in friendship, which Shel eagerly grasped. There was a sense of equality and mutual respect between the two, despite Lugh's godly stature and Shel's pasty, pudgy appearance. "Thanks for coming in on short notice, bud."

"Nay, to come to the aid of an honored comrade ... 'tis a pleasure akin to having one's scrotum nibbled by all fifty o' Poseidon's Nereid nymphs."

"I'll have to try that sometime. In the meantime, you stay here with ..." Shel began, but was distracted by Ta Mok's protégé's intense scrutiny. "What are you staring at, dirtbag?"

"Nothing, I guess," was the ineffectual reply.

"There's a lot of nothing on the ground. Lie on your stomach and stare at that," Shel said. As the young man complied, Shel continued. "Lugh, stay here with these two until an ambulance comes for Ta Mok. The city cops didn't get anything out of the last crop of henchmen, so get buttboy here down to the cage and we'll sweat it out of him ourselves. Meantime, I'm going to check to see how we're doing inside."

"Speed thee on thy way, O Clam!"

Shel ran as fast as his atrophying physique would permit

81

through Macy's and back to the Plaquet Box.

Colonel America writhed in tears on the ground. The rest of The Crusaders still hadn't arrived. Georgiana had succumbed to Singh's ruby again. And Orville and Kevin were still running down the concourse, which was badly buckled and in danger of falling to the floor below. Fortunately, most the stores had not yet opened and the crowd was virtually non-existent before 10 a.m.

"Every chromosome in every cell in your body yearns for my DNA," Singh informed a very receptive Georgiana.

"My uterus cries out for you, master," was the trancelike response as she shuffled slowly but certainly toward Singh.

There was a crash outside. Shel checked. A portion of the buckled second-floor concourse that Orville and Kevin were climbing over gave way. A landslide caught and dragged Kevin twelve feet down to the first floor. Orville was able to scramble for a rail and swing his way back up.

"I'm okay!" Kevin shouted at Orville. "Keep going! Keep going!"

It was painfully slow going, but Orville worked his way onto more solid ground and approached the Plaquet Box.

As all this was going on around her, Georgiana - and no one else - heard a still, small voice.

"Think, dearie, think," the disembodied echo of Eva Peron whispered. "What has this man ever done for you? What is he ever going to do for you?"

"But he's so ... perfect ..."

"Thank you," Singh said. Then, after a moment, he added, "Who are you talking to?"

"I know, dearie, but you have the power here," Eva counseled. "You have more of what he wants than he has of what you want. You're never going to get that ruby. You're never even going to get the man. You're going to get two minutes and three milliliters."

"Then he's going to turn me into an amusement park.

82

Charge admission. Put free naked pictures of me up on the Internet."

"That's right, dearie. What's an internet?"

Suddenly, Georgiana was clear-eyed. No longer shuffling up to Singh, she punched him in the face hard enough to knock teeth loose, dislocate the jaw, and bloody a lip, but not break any of her perfect, manicured, nails.

"You go, girl!" shouted Colonel America, who started sobbing again.

Then Shel and Orville stood side-by-side with Georgiana as they moved in on Maman Brigitte.

"The jig is up," Shel said.

"See?" the villainess shouted over at Colonel America, who just went on an even more pathetic crying jag.

"It's over. Lugh has Ta Mok and whoever that C-lister is on the ground outside," Shel broke it down. "Singh isn't waking up anytime soon. The rest of your gang has fled on foot. Surrender now, 'cuz you don't want to know what Count Karma is going to do to you once he—"

Sparks flew as an adze came down on Shel's arm. It wasn't Lugh's adze, though; it was only half the size. And it was wielded by an exotic-featured woman in a banker's suit.

"Darn it to heck, beeyatch!" Equity shouted at Maman Brigitte. "What did happen to thy gang of dried lumps of excrement?"

"Who's that?" Georgiana asked.

"Equity," Shel replied, through teeth gritted in determination, not pain, despite the damage his arm just took. It hung by a tendon that appeared to be made out of the same kind of cable that held the Gateway Arch together.

"If she touches you, she leaves you with half your powers while she hosts the other half," Orville explained. "And she keeps them until she touches someone else with abilities."

"And I have of most late touched Lugh," Equity said as

she threw her half-sized adze at Shel's other arm. "Right on his tushy."

Shel was able to deflect the haft so that the adze sailed harmlessly into the titanium-alloy gate. Another section of that gate came crashing down, though. Orville had to duck to avoid the debris and momentarily lost his balance. Equity pounced on him, brushed her hand across his face, being rewarded with nostrils full of explosive snot as she took half his power.

She thought hard about ragweed, long-haired cats, her ex-boyfriend's Aqua Velva, dusting the mantel at her cabin by the Finger Lakes. She sneezed.

And she kept thinking about dusting. She couldn't help it. Equity looked around the store, which was already a disaster area, but zeroed in on the powder shaken loose as ceiling tiles and drywall crumbled. It took a mighty act of will to tamp down the compulsion to clean. This too she had absorbed from Orville.

Shel dove behind the counter with Seth. Georgiana flew out of the store and up, to avoid the conflagration. Kevin, having just found his way into the store, was knocked back down to the first floor. Orville nimbly – and with a rare gleeful expression as if he was enjoying the thrill of battle – ducked under the flying mucous, not even looking over his shoulder when the explosions blew out the windows of the store across the way and blew thousands of dollars of Macy's inventory to tatters.

Orville rose to his feet and sneezed right in Equity's face, blowing her up against a wall, but not through it.

"Your snot is all over me," Equity said, in much less expressive tones than usual, as she picked herself off the floor. "Where can I wash up?"

"It shall be over soon," said a preternaturally soothing voice. It was not Orville speaking. "For you are like a whited sepulchre, which indeed appears beautiful outward, but is inside full of dead men's bones, and of all unclean-ness."

"Christ the Son," Equity said with some hollow preten-sion of awe for the saintly figure gliding past the store's crumbling threshold. "I am unworthy to be in your pres-ence."

"Don't believe anything she says, Christ!" Orville called out in full throat. "She's not capable of expressing these feelings right now!"

"Please, Lord, just being in your presence has changed me. I am putting aside childish things. Take me into your embrace."

"Don't do it, Christ!" Orville said forcefully.

"We must do all that is required. For Midge and Pantagruel are indisposed, discussing how they as husband and wife can render one another due benevolence. The Carbon Avenger will be with us as soon as he pays for the damages made to the inn. Orville," Christ said, and the mention of his name by God Incarnate was a thrill on a level that Mucus-Man had never felt before. With half the static of his autism washed out of his neural pathways, Orville felt doubly blessed as Christ continued. "Be not forgetful to entertain strangers, for thereby some have entertained angels unawares."

And so he allowed Equity to kneel down and kiss his hand.

She arose with an inner light, as if she had absorbed half of all the beneficence of the God of Abraham.

"The good that I would, I do not," she said with a sly smile, then blasted Christ the Son with all the power of a host of seraphim. "But the evil which I would not, that I do!"

That pretty much destroyed the entire eastern half of the Plaquet Box and the entire second floor of Macy's.

"Oh, no you didn't," Colonel America cried out and Orville reflected how, a moment earlier, he might have laughed out loud at how Colonel America was conflating his newly acquired homosexuality with Ta Mok's stereotyped propaganda of what homosexuals are like. But the static was back. It was no longer enjoyable to Orville any more than the rest of the battle - although he had a fleeting sense that he actually enjoyed that for a moment too.

"These powers are to serve our heavenly Father," Christ cautioned the newly omnipotent villain.

"Ye cannot serve God and Mammon," Equity laughed and let loose another blast more powerful than the first.

Christ answered with a blast of his own which destroyed the Halloween shop and the next three stores on the other side. Sword-wielding cherubim, summoned by both combatants, spread the mayhem throughout the mall. Baby-faced angels with broadswords lashed out at each other from one end of the mall to the other, slicing through displays and merchandise racks, cash registers and fountains, walls and ceilings and floors. There was little left of the Plaquet Box's ceiling. The store stood exposed to the midmorning light and October chill.

"Stop it!" Georgiana called out to the combatants. "This can only end in stalemate. Neither of you can win. When you split omnipotence right down the middle, both of you will still have unlimited power."

"I'll stop," Equity said, overturning a table full of cards as if she espied moneychangers seated behind it, "When I have what I came for."

"We can't let her have it," Shel said. "If she completes the Malificium deck, the Institute would have the power to destroy the entire world."

"Look around, Shel," Georgiana said. "They got that now."

"There's only one way to stop me," Equity gloated.

"We know," Shel said. "If you touch another hero—"

"Are you kidding?" Equity chortled as she launched another broadside at Christ. "Why would I ever touch another hero?"

Then, suddenly, Christ stopped fighting.

"The last enemy that shall be destroyed is death," he intoned and, in his right hand, a sachet of frankincense and myrrh appeared. He tossed it gently into Orville's face.

The sneeze that erupted ripped through Christ the Son's painfully thin torso and tore inexplicable holes in his wrists.

Silence echoed through the mall as seraphim and cherubim dissipated into the heavens. Equity slumped, weakened, to the floor.

Maman Brigitte was making gestures to invoke a voodoo curse with origins far older than Christian scripture when she was undone at the last moment by a supersonic punch from Bobby Botler, the Blur.

"We're back to the jig being up," Shel told Equity. "You're the last one left and you have no powers."

"Don't bargain with her!" Seth begged the heroes. "Even without her powers, she's dangerous."

"He's right," Equity said, regaining her feet. "You all right, Brigitte?"

"It'll take more than one punch to take me out of a fight," Maman Brigitte replied.

Seth took matters into his own hand. Going on a hunch that anyone intending to rob a card store might have some of her own cards along to use on the errand, he threw a Magic: The Gathering deck onto what was left of the main counter, and drew a Discard card, which compelled Equity to show whatever she may be holding.

"Too fancy, shopkeeper," Equity gloated as she followed the compulsion to show the card she brought from New York. It was a Yu-Gi-Oh! that, as she played it, took half her opponent's cards away.

Maman Brigitte disappeared from view and reappeared

through the crack in the ceiling. Standing on the roof, she boarded a waiting helicopter. A parting gesture from Maman Brigitte and her accomplice Equity shimmered out of the store and onto the roof, her Yu-Gi-Oh! in hand. As the 'copter sped away, a random half of the Plaquet Box's still-functioning cards leapt up from their drawers, counters and tabletops and soared up through the hole. They trailed behind the villainesses' escape vehicle like comet gas.

"Crusaders to Steed One, come in," said the man slumped against the remnant of the Plaquet Box's front counter, speaking into a transceiver in his glove. The cowl was off. He did have sandy hair. The tone of voice shocked all those who had heard it before. Gone was the pompous ring of command. It wasn't defeated, but it was plaintive, humbled, relieved.

"Colonel America? Are you all right?" the woman known by the call sign Nebraska responded via transceiver.

"I should ask you that," he said, "Colonel."

{BOOM!}

Something in her vestigial human memory told her the stuff was called "cheese." It smelled appetizing to the wild animal. There was a whole cache of it in a big cave on wheels, so the creature who was once Bella Brock climbed in.

The door shut behind her. The cave rolled away amid loud noises and nasty jolts, starts and stops.

It was cold in there. Very cold. But a nocturnal creature from the north woods can tolerate almost any frigid temperature for a while. Sooner or later, the door would open again, and woe to whomever had trapped her.

INTERLUDE: 1980

How much he looked like a bird!

The nanny didn't know it at the time, but she would come to love Orville Ortley as much as she loved her own four-year-old daughter. The nanny, her name was Esperanza, kept staring at him as he lay sleeping in his basinet, the last metallic strain of Brahms clinking as the mobile of black, white and red shapes wound down. Orville breathed fitfully and without rhythm in the way babies do sometimes, causing any adult nearby to keep listening to ensure there would be another inhalation.

Esperanza had tucked him in with a blanket bought from the same catalog as the mobile: There was a large red circle in the middle, surrounded by a white triangle, all against a black background. Curled up as he was, with little sticking out of the blanket other than the already nobly hooked nose, Orville looked like a nested, black-winged bird.

And, like a bird, he slept fitfully. There was something restless about the way he kicked at the blanket, making sounds as if he were about to cry but didn't have the strength.

As if he knew that, at that moment, his mother would soon be fighting for her life.

{POW!}

It wasn't some grand, evil mastermind. It never is. Masterminds only fight when they have to. Then it's almost always to a stalemate, just to get Good off their backs so they can go back to scheming and plotting and acquiring the wealth and power they need to someday rule the world. Masterminds, in short, are a bunch of pussies.

The most dangerous villain is the one with something to prove. He's a long way from the easy life of a mastermind. Not yet a qualified nemesis, he won't be satisfied with revenge against a particular adversary. No, it's always the new villain – with the unknown power, the unfamiliar vector of attack, the youthful disregard for his own safety – who gets in the lucky shot.

Neither Looker nor any of her Crusader colleagues had ever heard of Ta Mok before.

So they didn't know what to expect when their Harrier-style transport dropped them at the Port of Miami's Maersk terminal and pried open the ranch house-sized shipping container which Carbodyne's government contacts had alerted them to.

One of the many such containers that had come in that spring from Mariel, Cuba.

At least fifty Cuban refugees in that container stood perfectly silent, listening to one man. That single, reedy voice spoke haltingly, as if Spanish were not his first or even second language – as if he were struggling for words. But all the Marielitos hung on every syllable.

"Ach! Ye half-stepbrother to a Jew's bastard!" Lugh called out to the speaker as the Carbon Avenger tore a hole through one of the long walls and a contingent of The Crusaders (THE CRUSADERS!!!) charged through the opening. "Shut thy tit-sucking hole ere mine adze joins it to thine unwiped shitcrack!"

The speaker, whom the heroes could now tell had Asian features, smiled broadly and said a few words in Spanish. This caused the entire host of refugees to turn to face the superpowered team.

"What do you make of it, Colonel?" the Avenger asked as the first of the Cubans stepped into his gloved fist and Ta Mok continued to exhort in broken Spanish.

"He's a persuader," Colonel America assessed, throwing a couple punches himself. "No wonder so many of these people from the boatlift have been turning against us."

"How do we beat him?" *BANG. POW.*

"First, don't use deadly force on the Cubans," Colonel America said, but directed that more toward Lugh, who was holding his adze over his right shoulder like a 3-wood.

"Bacchus cum in thine eye!" Lugh seethed, then consoled himself by flying a lap around the container, clubbing the taller Cubans with the adze's shaft, knocking them to the ground.

"Any chance he can put us in thrall as well?" the Avenger asked as a head-butt bounced harmlessly off his diamond-hard carbon-fiber suit.

"If he speaks English, maybe," the Colonel replied in the middle of a complex maneuver in which he simultaneously put a compression lock on one opponent's thigh, a cattle-catch on another's neck, and kicked teeth out the mouth of a third.

"Or if he has some other power besides persuasion," the Avenger added as he made his way toward the Asian man who stood against the far wall, continuing his string of commands.

"I wouldn't rule that out," the Colonel replied as he advanced shoulder-to-shoulder with the Avenger and as Lugh flanked him on the other side.

The trio of Crusaders had all but forgotten that Black

Man and El Hombre stood directly behind them. And next to Looker.

THE AMERICAN WAY
PART 1

With finger-like phalanges extruded from graphite fiber, the Carbon Avenger controlled Steed Two's flight back to the Pinnacle of Righteousness. Midge flew Steed One. Evidently, the makeup sex was unequal to the fight the previous night, and Pantagruel begged the night manager for permission to stay on alone at the Drury Inn for another night. Maybe longer.

Two black helicopters out of a paranoid militiaman's wildest delusions of fascist government stopped at the Chesterfield Mall. One was for prisoner transport. Singh slumped unconscious through it all. Ta Mok stayed cruelly conscious as a corpsman stanched the bleeding out of what was left of his right leg. Lugh's slice had been clean, or matters could have been much worse for Ta Mok, not that this was of any great consolation as he screamed in anguish as they lingered over Missouri and Tennessee.

Eventually the painkillers caught up to the pain. The corpsman turned in for a nap. Two guards - obviously professional, elite soldiers - kept their sights trained on Ta

Mok's forehead.

"You okay?" asked the Institute fellow whom Ta Mok had taken under his wing.

"Been better, young man," Ta Mok conceded. "But let's talk about you. What is this unique trait you've developed?"

"Evidently, it's not herpes."

"Touché," Ta Mok chuckled. "But you deliver white-bread America's ultimate fear – an unwelcome, unanticipated breach from normative sexual orientation. Can you imagine the shock of such a sudden realization?"

"Yes, in fact. Me, and around four percent of the population."

"Including these two gentlemen in front of us?"

"Wouldn't help us. Their sense of mission is too deeply ingrained to be altered along with their sexuality," the fellow said. "Besides, the guy on the right is already gay."

"You can tell? Does your power also give you the ability to detect homosexuality in others?"

"No, but a month in a two-man tent in Kandahar answers a lot of questions," the fellow replied, then addressed that captor. "Hi, Terry. Long time gone."

"'Zup, Ray," the guard responded. "Looks like you got yourself in some shit."

"Been through worse, as you know."

"I hear that."

"I hate to break up the reunion," Ta Mok interjected, "but are you saying you can't get us out of this? We are villains. We escape. It's what we do."

"You said 'we'?"

"Your power manifested. I'm giving you a field promotion. Can you get us free?"

"Terry, you want to free us?"

"Wish I could. Orders is orders."

"What about you, Mick?" the fellow asked the straight guard.

"We been through two wars, brother," was the response. "Don't make me scrub your brains out of my 'copter."

"Well, Ta Mok, it's up to you. You're the master of propaganda. Talk them into landing this bird and giving us an hour's head start."

"No can do. That ability was tied up with my earthshaking power. When I lost one, I lost them both."

"Nothing we can do, then," the fellow said. "And we still have about an hour to kill before we get where we're going."

Ta Mok was stunned.

"You know where we're going?"

"Yeah, we're heading for a top-secret facility outside Huntsville, Alabama. It's where the mil does its superpower research – my last station before I left the service."

"An hour, you say?"

"About that, yeah."

"Plenty of time to invent a supervillain name for you."

"Hadn't thought about that."

So he did. And so did Ta Mok. They sat there in silence for long minutes until Ta Mok's eyes brightened.

"That guard," Ta Mok said, indicating the gay one. "He called you 'Ray.'"

"Maybe because that's my name," Ray said. Then paused. "No. Oh no."

Ta Mok laughed. The guard named Terry laughed. The one named Mick laughed. Ray did not laugh.

The prospect of Gay Ray being his professional name brought him closer to tears.

BAM!

The other black helicopter contained the once and future Colonels America.

Ta Mok's brainwashing had worn off already and the man who wore the star-spangled costume realized that his new orientation wouldn't affect his ability to perform as a superhero. But he didn't care. Having carried the mantle of

95

Colonel America for a quarter century, he took it as a sign. He was ready to hang it up.

Lieutenant Colonel Nebraska was expecting the silent treatment from the retiring superhero, or some juvenile hazing, or his customary bluster. But there was none of that. Instead, he treated her to equal measures of entertaining and instructive battle stories, avuncular advice, and turns to tell him her own story.

After the 'copter landed on a pad to the lee side of Alabama's Weeden Mountain, the outgoing Colonel ("You can call me Elias") continued to engage Lieutenant Colonel Nebraska in conversation. They sat and chatted in the otherwise empty commissary of a building on the Redstone Arsenal army post, the existence of which was known to only a hundred people. That included not only the Protector of Patriots and his successor, but also Ta Mok, Singh and Gay Ray, who arrived moments earlier and now lolled in a reinforced stockade in the building's sub-basement.

"After the transformation," Elias told the soon-to-be-promoted lieutenant colonel, "you'll feel invincible. You will be. Every muscle, every sense, every synapse will be heightened to superhuman levels. The whole gamut of martial arts skills and small-unit tactics will be, literally, in your blood."

"It's an awesome privilege, Elias," Nebraska said. "You have every reason to be proud of your service."

"You start out proud," Elias replied wistfully. "All that power coursing through your veins! But then you put away a couple bad guys, get on a few magazine covers, start believing all the hype on TV. Proud becomes prideful. You become a swaggering, buffoonish caricature of yourself. Guard against that. Guard against that."

He held Nebraska's gaze over empty coffee cups for long moments before she finally said, "Let's call it a night."

"Yeah. Time to hit the rack. See you at oh-dawn-thirty."

Looker and Black Man rushed into the container, having hung back in reserve per Colonel America's orders. El Hombre had as well but, like Orpheus's backward glance, he couldn't resist poking his head through the hole that Lugh's adze had made in the container wall. And now something had gone wrong.

The Carbon Avenger, Colonel America and Lugh had knocked out all the Marielitos and were closing in on the man they would soon come to know as Ta Mok, who still spouted, in broken Spanish, what sounded more like propaganda than orders. In response, El Hombre moved as if in a trance, twirling his lariat as he stealthily approached the core members of the team from behind. In one giant loop, his rope encircled all three, paralyzing them with its touch.

The remaining two Crusaders burst into the container. Black Man leg-tackled El Hombre as Looker grabbed the lariat from his hand and freed her captive teammates. They turned their attention to Ta Mok, leaving Black Man to subdue El Hombre, whose unblinking gaze and flailing limbs suggested he still had plenty of fight left in him. Black Man was much stronger, and his skin was almost as impervious to harm as the Avenger's carbon-fiber suit, but El Hombre still had his spurs and riding crop.

Cognizant that this new villain might have another trick up his sleeve – they always do – the other Crusaders moved in on him with caution. But move in they did. Victory was assured.

Ta Mok knew this. Having nothing left to lose, he charged straight at the one he perceived he could beat one-on-one: Looker, Olivia Ortley. His full-throated war cry echoed loud and shrill, but his heavy-lidded expression begged the woman he knew only as Looker to end his misery quickly. She nodded obligingly before removing her shades and letting loose with an optic blast ...

... that went all over the place. The beam out of her right eye went so far astray that it ended up winging Colonel America. The left beam was so diffuse as to hit everything but hurt nothing and nobody, least of all Ta Mok.

Olivia realized suddenly that Dirk was right. She should have made the time for a checkup with Doc Rudy, who specialized in people with exceptional abilities. All the gynecologists, obstetricians and internists she had seen over the past year marveled at how well she'd carried the baby, given birth to the baby, nursed the baby and returned to her original, athletic self. But none of them thought to give her an eye test. After all these months of pregnancy, delivery, and maternity, the only real damage baby Orville did was to her retinas. She didn't drive or watch much TV, so she didn't catch herself squinting. She had been walking into doors every now and then, though, and tripping over things – still, a condition that almost anyone in the world would tolerate for years before seeking medical attention.

Almost anyone, that is, except Looker. Her eye beams had the force of 88-millimeter artillery shells. If they worked. With uncontrolled astigmatism, they didn't.

The villain revealed his secret, a secondary power that the Colonel had guessed at. One pace in front of Olivia, Ta Mok stomped his foot causing a shockwave that threw her straight up into the air. On her way down, she encountered that same foot as it kicked her in the head - no, *through* the head. She died impaled on Ta Mok's shin.

It would be nice to say that her last clear thoughts were of her beloved baby son, Orville, but death came too quickly.

The shock of seeing Looker fall shook Black Man and El Hombre out of their duel. The gauntleted fists of the other Crusaders, the ones who knew her best, pounded Ta Mok past the point of submission. The Carbon Avenger then cradled Olivia's body as Lugh and the Colonel strode over, knelt down and put massive arms around him in grim silence.

Police appeared, statements made. First the paramedics, then soon after the medical examiner arrived. Reporters showed up, some with trucks full of video equipment, others with slim-line notepads and a flash photographer in tow. Desultory interviews ensued, but none of The Crusaders felt much like talking.

BOOM!

Olivia Ortley had been perfectly clear on this point: Her schedule was unpredictable. She might have to leave suddenly, stay away for an extended period, and not be able to send word as to when she would be home. Esperanza Rivera was amenable. She was like-

99

wise raising her child on her own, but had extended family who could watch four-year-old María de la Soledad while Esperanza was caring for baby Orville.

Neither mother could have expected this trust to be tested so soon and with such finality.

It got quite late in Olivia's East Side apartment, and Esperanza's pager buzzed annoyingly. The nanny glanced at the green screen to find her sister's number. A quick phone call confirmed that little Marisol was tired and cranky as only a four-year-old can get and needed to be picked up. So Esperanza made a fateful decision: She grabbed a diaper bag, the mobile, and some formula. She swaddled Orville and took him out of the apartment, down the private elevator, out the door as it was opened by an accommodating man in a black, woolen uniform, two blocks up Lexington Avenue, and down onto the subway platform to catch the 4 train.

She didn't bother to leave a note, being unlettered in English. If the lady should return home before morning, she had Esperanza's pager number. A quick, Spanglish phone conversation would alleviate most of the anxiety.

It was a long wait on the platform at that hour for the short ride uptown. Esperanza sat on the chipped, graffiti-tagged bench and talked to the baby, who paid rapt, unblinking attention.

"Your mommy will be home soon, precious," she said in Salvadoran-accented Spanish. "Until then, you can stay with my little girl and me. How does that sound?"

By reply – not that a baby that young could possibly reply – Orville stared pensively off to the side for a moment, then met the nanny's gaze with a big, gummy smile.

"Well, I'm glad you're happy about that," Esperanza continued, as Orville kept staring up at her with the expression of a retriever puppy giving its owner the impression it understands every word. "You'll like Marisol. She likes to play with trucks and airplanes, just like boys do. She's always running and climbing, and getting bruises and rug burns, God help me! Of course, you're still too little to care about what's for boys and what's for girls."

The train clattering down the track was becoming audible. Esperanza watched how its headlights glinted off the rails a minute before the engine itself emerged into view.

"Maybe you'll be good for her, little one. She won't play with her dolls, but she never had a doll as beautiful as you. Maybe you can make a young lady out of this tomboy!"

But Orville was no longer paying attention. The thunder of an approaching train – which could scare anyone regardless of age the first time they heard it – only intrigued the infant. Through vision that was still not completely focused, he observed the metallic cars follow one another as they barreled into the station, accompanied by the shriek of marginally maintained brakes – another sound that failed to frighten. Esperanza carried the boy on. By the time they reached the next stop, no more than two minutes later, the motion had put Orville to a peaceful sleep.

Esperanza picked up a petulant Marisol from her equally petulant Tía Luz, who advised Esperanza to come for the demon-child right after dinner from now on, "Or there won't be a from-now-on."

The walk from Luz's tenement to Esperanza's was only a block but not without danger, particularly for a woman and two small children late at night. They passed without incident, but not without menace.

Marisol at first viewed this new presence wrapped in thick blankets with deep suspicion. But as he blissfully slept through the boom boxes, domestic disturbances and occasional gunplay that marked that time and place – while her mother fretted and muttered prayers – Marisol decided he was all right.

Olivia Ortley never called that night, of course. Esperanza couldn't sleep a wink, though, for fear of slumbering too soundly to respond to the beeper. At one point, she did nod off, only to be woken by the sirens that regularly blared down the avenue.

Marisol fussed on and off through the night, as she sometimes still did, but Orville managed to sleep through on a pile of hand towels after one late-night bottle of formula, soothed as he was by the clinking lullaby and simple, familiar patterns of his mobile, which Esperanza had clamped to the arm of a chair. He woke up hungry and needing a change early in the morning, but was otherwise none the worse.

Bleary-eyed, Esperanza watched Channel 11's first newscast of the morning on the small, rabbit-eared black-and-white set on her kitchen counter as she fixed herself a large mug of Eight O'Clock coffee. Orville sat in Marisol's old highchair and casually glanced at the news too, as if this weren't his first time watching TV.

Esperanza didn't need to understand the voiceover to comprehend the image behind the flashing red lights: The building that contained Olivia Ortley's apartment was a pile of smoldering ruins dripping water, foam, and debris onto the yellow-taped sidewalk below. She remembered the sirens racing down the avenue in the night.

After a minute and a half, though, there was another story of mayhem in the outer boroughs, then something about the hostages in Iran, and something else about the Mariel boatlift. Only after all that did the newsreader mention "The Crusaders." Esperanza's jaw dropped when she saw a picture of Olivia over the anchorman's shoulder, the kind of softly lit picture that could only mean one thing. The caption read, "Looker." She was horrified but, as a war veteran as well as a war widow, she was able to steel herself. A palm rose to cover her gaping mouth. After a moment, her muscle memory made the sign of the Cross.

Her mind, however, remained engaged in analyzing the situation. As far as the news media were concerned, then, there was no known connection between the blaze - Esperanza parsed the words "under investigation" - and the death of a Crusader.

Esperanza knew better, and knew better than to say anything to anyone about it. It occurred to her that someone or something had demolished the entire building, having just killed the mother, to destroy the son as well. She didn't know why, and she didn't know who would be so callous with regard to the lives of dozens of others who lived in that building. She prayed that their souls, and Olivia Ortley's, would rest in peace. On the premise that this would require vengeance, she prayed for a righter of wrongs to arise. But that was not her role. She was a nurturer, which often means being a protector, but she was the farthest thing from a warrior.

Orville had lost his mother, then his home. He needed a new one.

Esperanza understood her friends and family would wonder about this alabaster-skinned boy who was now under her roof. She also knew that casual acquaintances and any acquaintances she would make going forward would jump to wrong conclusions about his

103

parentage. She resolved to stoically weather all the gossip and humiliation, as well as the added financial burden of another mouth to feed, but she was going to keep this baby safe, with her, where nobody who had just tried to kill him would think to look. Then, maybe someday, this pale, scrawny infant with the bright eyes and hooked nose would grow up to mete out justice and lay his mother's soul to rest.

And five years went by.

THE AMERICAN WAY
PART 2

Strapped to one of two operating tables, hooked up to what looked like an industrial-sized apheresis machine, Lieutenant Colonel Nebraska was ready for the transformation. Old, mustachioed Rudy Goldman M.D. and his staff monitored the machine and the patient. The doctor himself struggled to keep his clinical detachment in the presence of such a toned, tawny-skinned beauty wearing nothing but the flimsiest of hospital gowns. He reminded himself that she could kick his ass at that moment, and he was about to transfer the power of Colonel America into those long, luscious limbs, and his libido was suitably curbed.

"So where's Elias?" the doctor asked no one in particular. "Not like him to be late."

As if on cue, the hydraulic doors swung open and the man himself stepped in. Instead of the cape and cowl, the neatly parted sandy hair and crystal blue eyes were perched above the dress blue uniform of a U.S. Army officer. The castles pinned on each lapel of the four-button coat designated him as part of the Army Corps of Engineers, the eagles on each shoulder identified him as a full colonel. Ribbons marked him as the recipient of the Distinguished Service Cross, Silver Star, Legion of Merit, Purple Heart, Joint Service Commendation and a dozen other honors. The nameplate read O'NEILL.

Just as he stepped in, alarms started going off. A team of MPs in riot gear ran down the hall alongside the operating theater. The overhead PA system announced a breakout from the stockade. Lieutenant Colonel Nebraska reflexively struggled against her restraints.

"Sounds like you two might be needed," the doctor suggested. "Maybe we should postpone."

"No," Colonel Elias O'Neill decided quickly, before his successor could suggest otherwise. "The transformation always takes place during a crisis. You should remember that, Doc. Let's get this done."

He took off his uniform, carefully folding it on a stool in the corner. Before he did that, though, he unpinned one of his eagles, walked over to Nebraska, and without any outward display of emotion fastened it to her gown. She received it with the same military bearing.

Elias then lay down on the other table and heaved a sigh of relief.

The transformation was at once something clinical and something spiritual. Elias's Type AB-blood coursed out of the venipuncture needle in his right arm, through tubing that led to the centrifuge where the unique organelles - he was only the fifth human being to host them - separated out, and returned through other tubing and another needle into his left arm. The organelles transferred to artificial cells suspended in saline and pumped into Nebraska's arm.

The donor's face was a mask of peace, but it quickly became clear why the recipient was restrained. Her breath became short, shallow pants as her body shook violently. Drool foamed around her mouth as she lost the impulse to swallow. Four hefty assistants - two of them the Special Forces

106

soldiers who had guarded the villains the night before – lay crosswise on top of her or else she'd have burst her restraints.

The critical period was over in less than a minute.

The organelles were just receivers. They had no power of their own. The clinical task completed, the spiritual task could begin. The true power of Colonel America flooded the newly promoted officer: The transcendent might of the Homeland. She became the embodiment of all that was good and decent about America, all its strength, all its confidence and can-do spirit, its quintessential virtue, its destiny to lead, its perfection that can never be improved, its exemplary status among the depraved nations of the world which have nothing left to teach the New World – not about culture nor art nor courtesy nor conflict resolution nor mass transit nor economic efficiency nor dietary health, and certainly nothing about those silly foreign languages.

Her eyes, clenched shut during the transformation, sprang open. Her fists unclenched. As Elias got up and put his Class-A uniform back on, the new hero received her costume: Elias's bulletproof, star-spangled cape draped behind a new version of the body armor, tailored for the first time to fit a woman's curves.

As the search for the fugitive went on up and down the hall, the two faced each other, exchanging a salute and a handshake.

"Congratulations, Colonel America," Elias said.

"Godspeed, Colonel O'Neill."

As the new Colonel America turned to leave and join the search, the former called out, "Colonel?"

"Yes?"

"You probably told me once but it, uh, didn't register," Elias said. "I've only known you as 'Nebraska' and that's not your call sign anymore. What's your name?"

"Rivera," Colonel America replied. "María de la Soledad. Call me Marisol."

At one end of the mall was a hallway with no stores along it. It was for the offices. At the end was the security office.

In front of that was the janitor's closet.

In front of that were the hardscrabble cubicles of the people who provided the computer and network services that kept the retail transactions running between the mall and the banks.

In front of that were somewhat plusher offices hosting the group that managed the property.

Closest in was the glass block, marble and mahogany enclave for the managing partners of the investment trust that owned the mall.

Nobody was ever in it. Except that next morning.

Most obviously, there were the mall heroes lined up: Shel Shapiro, Lugh, Orville Ortley, Bobby Botler, Mindy Maguire, and Kevin Kiley. In front of them was a big chair behind a bigger desk, all to serve a small man. His name was Johnson or Jackson or maybe it was Johnston, and he was a scrawny, jaundiced, graying man with the nervous twitches, short wheezes and yellowed fingers of a chain smoker whose habit wasn't allowed in the office anymore. None of the heroes had ever seen him before and none expected to ever see him again. He was the executive vice president of the shell corporation that owned the Chesterfield Mall, a general manager of the real estate investment trust that owned the shell corporation and a mid-level manager of the diversified corporation that owned the trust: Carbodyne.

"You're all fired, of course," the man in the suit said. "The damages to the infrastructure, destruction of merchandise, personal injuries ..."

"You can't fire us," Shel protested. "We're TSA. We're federal employees."

"If I were you, Mister Shapiro, I'd check my conditions of employment," the man replied, waving a crooked, yellow finger at Shel. "I can terminate your positions here at the mall.

You'd go back into TSA's labor pool, which is already saturated with supervisors and, as a supervisor, you don't have any union protection. The feds will fire you themselves within the month. Lugh too."

Shel turned to his friend to see the god standing there stoically. He turned back to the executive.

"OK, fire us if you have to, but the rest of the—"

"Maguire and Kiley are probationary. All it takes is one phone call from me. I already made it. Botler!"

"Uh, yeah?" Bobby mumbled after a distracted moment.

"You're the World's Swiftest Man, right?"

"That's what they say."

"How swiftly can you fill up a 100-milliliter sample cup?"

"Or I could just quit," Bobby conceded.

"Or that. And as for you, Mister Ortley—"

"Hold on!" Mindy shouted, as all eyes and ears attended to her defense of her new friend. "Orville's the reason this mall is still standing. He didn't just save the day, he saved two days in a row. What did Orville ever do wrong?"

Johnson or Jackson or Johnston gave her a puzzled look. His face froze for a second in reaction to the obtuseness of the question and the obviousness of the answer.

"He killed Christ."

"Yeah, but besides that?" Kevin asked, and no one was sure if he was serious, kidding, or taking Mindy's side out of sheer tactical machination.

"If you have any personal effects, you've got an hour to pick them up and get them out of what's left of my mall. That's all. Goodbye."

"Fine, we're leaving. But before we go, there's one thing that needs to be said," Shel stated with dire intensity. "Lugh?"

Lugh inhaled deeply before speaking at some length.

BAM!

With time to kill and no personal effects to clean out, Kevin convinced Mindy - and this took some doing - to join him for a cup of Dunkin Donuts coffee at the food court. She grabbed a table while he ordered two French Vanilla lattes.

"Here you go," he offered as he sat down.

"Thanks, Kevin. What do I owe you?"

"It's on me."

"No, I insist," she said, tearing the receipt out of his hand. It informed her that the drinks were $4.06 each including tax.

"Honestly, four bucks doesn't obligate anyone to anything."

"Four dollars and six cents is a small price to pay for principle," she countered as she fished the exact change out of her purse and handed it to Kevin.

He handed back the one-cent piece.

"Not even Dunkin Donuts cares about the penny," he informed her, then changed the topic. "So what's next for you? Going back to Macy's?"

"Not even if it was a choice between that or prison. I'm just going to go home, put on some Sarah McLachlan, and figure things out."

"Any thoughts of doing the hero thing full-time?"

"Yeah," Mindy said. "And you saw how that worked out."

"No, in private practice."

She stopped drinking her coffee in mid-sip.

"That's illegal," she whispered. "The Triple-A ..."

"It's what we economists call 'the informal sector,'" Kevin explained. "If you were to hang it all up, that would be a loss to the entire world, Mindy. Or do you prefer 'Georgiana'?"

"Why do you think I'd prefer to be called by my alter ego's name?"

"Because you really put a lot of attention into what to name her," Kevin said. "I really like it, by the way. The literary reference. Nathaniel Hawthorne's ethereal beauty from 'The Birthmark.'"

"Well, Mister Kiley, I must say I'm impressed," Mindy said brightly. Kevin hadn't seen her anything but dour up to that point. "How did you know?"

"I'm ... Master of Arts," he intoned.

"Yeah, and just how does that qualify you as a superhero? I haven't seen you actually *do* anything."

"I operate on a heightened level of existence. What I do on the astral plane directs outcomes that manifest themselves on earth."

"Sure."

"No, really. I can't lose."

"Uh, didn't you just lose ... your job?"

"A job that I didn't need, and held onto long enough to meet you and talk you into having a cup of coffee with me."

Mindy thought about that for a second before Kevin continued.

"I want to see you tonight."

"Kevin, that's very sweet," she said. "But the timing is all wrong. I just met someone I've long admired and ..."

"Orville?"

"Yes," Mindy said with a downward glance and a little blush.

"But he's a ... great guy. Really. I'd like you both to come out tonight."

"Huh?"

"Yeah, and Shel, Lugh and Bobby, too. This is business. I want to pitch the non-TSA hero thing to everyone. We could be like The Crusaders."

"I don't know."

"You got any other plans tonight?" Kevin asked. "You got any better ideas for tomorrow?"

She didn't. Together, they went back to the security office and talked to the others. None of them had any other plans or better ideas either.

{BOOM!}

Mindy was back in her apartment barely an hour, as eventful as it was, after she had left that morning. Eva Peron was sitting there on the couch to greet her.

"I didn't fuck Migaldi," Eva declared over "Waltz for Eva and Che." Mindy had the Madonna-Antonio Banderas movie playing on the DVR to keep her guardian spirit company while she was at the mall.

"Really?"

"Well," Eva said indignantly, "not in Act One, Scene One. I was fifteen and sharing a room with my mother. How exactly was that supposed to work?"

"I'll take your word for it."

"And I never even met Che Guevara, if that's who that character is supposed to be. Although I wouldn't mind meeting this Banderas fellow."

"Me either," said Mindy who, anticipating this reaction, already had *Philadelphia* and *Spy Kids* queued up on the DVR. "Listen, Mrs. Peron, we need to have a chat."

"Can it wait? I think my death scene is coming up."

Mindy introduced the incorporeal spirit to the pause button.

"As you probably guessed, I lost my job today. I'm not a hero anymore. I can't legally turn into Georgiana again. So I might not be needing your services anymore. You should let the goddesses know."

The ghost rose from the couch. And kept rising.

"What!" she screamed from the ceiling. "No! That's unacceptable! This is your destiny!" Eva calmed down a bit after that. "My deal with the goddesses is that I become one of them if I can get you started on the path. If you think going back to eternal rest is an option for me, then maybe you need to watch this movie again. If you take godhood away from me, I will haunt you for the rest of your mortal life, then torment you through all eternity. Now, are we done with our chat?"

Eva fluttered back down to the couch.

"There's another option," Mindy said meekly. "I was going

to ask your advice about it, but I guess I have that already."

"Go on."

"Some of the guys from work are getting together tonight to talk about keeping the team together and going underground. If it's a choice between that or finding another retail job, I guess you're in favor."

"Are you meeting at an office?"

"No, at a bar."

"Is this Kevin Kiley fellow going to be there?"

"Yes, it was his idea."

Eva found herself floating again. It was turning into a nervous habit.

"A date? You're going on a date with Kevin Kiley after what I told you!"

"There will be four other people there," Mindy said adding, just to calm Eva down, "including a man I'm much more interested in."

This did soothe Eva's sensibilities – to some degree at least.

"All the same," Eva responded, "I'm coming with you."

PONT

Johnson or Jackson or Johnston wasted no time replacing Shel Shapiro.

Pantagruel was noticeably uncomfortable in the TSA uniform because he had to shrink down to wear it. The largest uniform they had was Lugh's and, while Lugh was considered beefy by the standards of men or gods, size wasn't his superpower.

So Pantagruel concentrated on the job. And the most immediate was to survey and make detailed notes of the damage from the previous day's battle. He forced out all thoughts of how he could have prevented some of that damage if he had joined the fray instead of fighting with his wife, bothering everyone else staying at the Drury Inn and taking the Carbon Avenger, who had to physically restrain him, out of the fight at the mall.

113

His first stop was the hardest-hit store. The Plaquet Box. Seth Hill was taking inventory of what cards were left, and what cards were left undamaged.

"So how many do you think they got away with?" Pantagruel asked, ready to record the answer on a clipboard.

"Hard to say until I clean up a little."

"Can you give me an estimate – just a rough figure? It would be exactly half your inventory if it was Equity who robbed you."

"Half by count or half by value?"

"I don't know," Pantagruel conceded.

"And that would be after who-knows-how-many cards were destroyed in the battle."

"I see," the man in Lugh's uniform said with a shrug. "But I have to fill in this report. Can you give me some idea how many cards are missing?"

"A lot."

"How many's a lot?"

"How many girls named Melissa have slept with Gregg Allman?"

"That's a lot."

Maman Brigitte and Equity stood in the former's K Street office as the screen came down between them and the view of Washington's Farragut Square.

The silhouette of the mysterious leader of the American Malevolence Institute appeared.

"Your mission was successful, I assume," he stated without any hint of a question.

"Yes, *gran houngan*," Maman Brigitte announced, without going into detail that two senior staffers and a fellow were captured, and that the other two fellows ran away and hadn't been heard from since. "We have half the cards that were in the store, and I have temps sorting them out now."

"And this must be Equity," he said, his shoulders squaring

toward the villainess in the pinstriped suit. "A pleasure to meet you at last."

She knew the custom of addressing the leader with the most respectful term from one's frame of reference. Thus, the voodoo priestess called him *gran houngan*.

The Wall Street financier replied, "The pleasure is all mine, Warden."

"I thought you'd go with 'Mister Chairman,' but 'Warden' plays," the leader replied cheerily. "What assurance do I have that the last Malificium card is in our possession?"

"I can only offer you a one-in-two chance. That's all my powers can produce."

"Well, it's more than anyone else has been able to do so far," he said, knowing that Maman Brigitte would bristle at the backhanded comment. "How many cards do we have to go through?"

"I don't know precisely, Warden."

"Rough guess. Order-of-magnitude. Budget-and-planning number."

"Uh ..." Equity stuttered until Maman Brigitte came to her rescue.

"How many hundred-dollar bills can an Afghani diplomat stuff into his attaché case?"

"So it's going to take a while to go through."

"That's all I'm saying."

BOOM!

Colonel Elias O'Neill, formerly Colonel America, requisitioned a Ford Crown Victoria suitable for his rank and drove through the Redstone Arsenal auxiliary parking lot to the side gate. There was a wait while the guards searched all vehicles leaving the premises for signs of an escapee.

When the Crown Vic got to the gate, the guard recognized the driver and asked him politely to pop the trunk. "Just a precaution. Maybe the fugitive is hiding back there."

No, nothing in the trunk. Elias was waved through.

A half mile down the deserted road back to Route 72 he turned his head around and said to the hollowed-out leather shell of a back seat, "You can come out now, Ray."

{ POW! }

Singh's criminal history was not particularly remarkable. Despite his powers, most of the charges against him were for the kind of felonies inspired by greed or lust, not pure evil. Stripped of his turban, he was remanded to the custody of the Alabama State Police who would sort out which other state would get first crack at prosecuting him.

Ta Mok was another story. His injury tended to, it was time for him to start answering questions. He would be treated as an enemy combatant. Eventually, he would see either a military tribunal or a federal court and respond to charges of sedition and conspiracy, as well as a host of felony assault, robbery and murder charges.

He decided on the course of least resistance and willingly answered all questions posed by the Judge Adjutant General attorney who visited his cell. Yes, he did this. Yes, he did that. Here are the names of his co-conspirators. Here's where you can find them. Yes, I killed Olivia Ortley, a.k.a. Looker.

No, I didn't have anything to do with destroying her building, killing seven of her neighbors and endangering the life of her child.

PART TWO
THE STUFF IN THE MIDDLE

WITNESSING THE BADGER

There used to be a dot on the map called, as hackneyed as this sounds, Plainville, Illinois. A place where 250 people lived, mainly construction workers who paired off with medical techs to raise their families in a remote and inexpensive milieu. If anyone felt like a little nightlife, he or she drove over to St. Peters, Missouri, the nearest city of 50,000. That trip ate up an hour, so maybe they'd only drive as far as Quincy, Illinois, or Hannibal, Missouri.

Nothing ever actually happened in Plainville, and that's just how its residents liked it. Until one day when something happened that none of them liked at all, according to the survivors.

The only restaurant in the ZIP code, Bayard's, did business a mile north of the main drag, 200th Avenue, along 1700th Street, the inflated road designations a quirk of Illinois's Adams County.

The owner of Bayard's ordered from a cousin in Bancroft, Wisconsin, who ran a small cheese factory. Every month, this cousin would fill up a small, refrigerated truck with something called squeaky cheese, a delicacy little known outside dairy country. It looked like cheddar, tasted like cheddar, but chewed like bubblegum. Kids loved it. So did grownups. Trouble was that these curds needed eating within hours of being processed. So, once a month and only once a month, the patrons of Bayard's restaurant enjoyed an evening of fresh squeaky cheese, deep-fried squeaky cheese, and French fries topped with squeaky cheese and brown gravy.

So it was with some excitement that the familiar rumble of a particular delivery truck with Wisconsin plates broke the cool of an early evening in October. The owner of Bayard's - like the plurality of restaurateurs, he was named Nick - met the truck as it pulled into the parking lot.

His cousin Lee Ann jumped out of the driver's seat as the diesel engine sat idling. They shared a short hug and peck on the cheek.

"You made really good time today," Nick said, as they walked around the back of the truck, adjusting his pale blue apron. "I bet it'll be fresh as daisies."

"Have I ever delivered less?" Lee Ann countered, fumbling with her keys. "The family around?"

"Rhonda's working second shift, but I just left the kids to finish their homework. They'll be your first customers, as usual."

Lee Ann found the key to the padlock which secured the back of the rig. As she turned it and felt the tumblers fall, she could swear she heard something or someone moving in there. Before Lee Ann had a chance to register that as a cause for caution, though, she had already started rolling up the rear door.

She and her cousin Nick gasped; she'd hauled more than squeaky cheese.

BAM!

As daylight dimmed, the government-issue Crown Vic had crossed into Mississippi. Soon after, Colonel Elias O'Neill and his new plus-one pulled into a budget motel just past Meridian on the road to Jackson.

Elias and Ray had changed into the kind of cheap, hard-wearing work clothes available for purchase at gas stations throughout rural America. While Elias folded his Army uniform neatly and placed it in a plastic bag in the trunk, Ray had chucked his tattered blazer-and-slacks ensemble into Holt Lake outside Tuscaloosa.

Now the former Colonel America took the lead as they walked up to the desk. He wore a black T-shirt and six-pocket pants. The desk clerk, old enough to work full time but young enough to sport terrible acne, stared at the officer through squinted eyes. Elias hoped that civilian clothes rendered him inconspicuous. He wasn't about to get caught aiding and abetting an escaped federal prisoner. Elias O'Neill may have given up Colonel America's powers, but he was still a formidable man and braced for battle. His hand rested on the loaded sidearm stuffed into a cargo pocket.

"I recognize you," the young man behind the desk drawled slowly, deliberately. "You're Anderson Cooper."

"Yes. Yes, I am."

BOOM! POW!

On an astral plane beyond the imaginings of most mortals, Count Karma thrilled at the victory that was within his grasp.

The ghostly figure had Kevin Kiley's face but its ornate ceremonial garb hinted at a more impressive man.

On Earth, Kevin wore the body of a man who had been on the track team in high school and most of college and still, just a couple years later, spent forty minutes a day on the treadmill and worked out lightly with free weights. While in fine shape, he didn't possess what one would call a heroic physique. His disembodied spirit, though, rocked the ethereal world.

With the otherworldly analog of a right hook, he pasted Acedia, the personification of Neglect, to the spectral equivalent of the canvas. A left jab would have knocked Tristitia, Despair's anthropomorphic aspect, unconscious, had the entire dimension not been constructed out of pure consciousness.

These twins, servants of the sloth-demon, Belphegor, were vanquished but not truly defeated. That could never be as long as human nature endured. But as their essences faded away to a plane so inhospitable to the human soul that even Count Karma dared not follow, the Master of Arts could take comfort that their sway over the physical world would not be increased. Not on that day, anyway. Not on Count Karma's watch.

The hero of the astral plane stood like a statue of triumph, thick hair tousled by the winds of war, noble chin high, broad shoulders squared, rippling chest bedecked with arcane talismans and tapering down to a slender waist knotted with musculature.

Then he woke up.

It wasn't a dream, Kevin knew. It did happen. That paragon of might and right was indeed him. The battle he won did influence events in the real world. He did tip the scales ever so slightly toward Good. In some subtle manner, he had successfully defended the Earth from evil powers.

Yay.

There he lay, chest heaving to the point of stabbing pain and a pungent layer of sweat adhering his whole body to the sheets in the world he had saved: on a thin mattress on a squeaky bedspring, no frame, in an efficiency apartment with a shower stall instead of a bathtub, and no proper closet.

Aside from the dresser, the only furnishing was a second-hand treadmill which, at the moment, did double duty as a hanger rod. On it hung his Brooks Brothers suit, the ski jacket he'd owned since high school and would soon need for at least one more winter, and one garment bag, which contained the costume he had never dared wear in public.

The treadmill and all that hung from it accounted for ninety percent of his net worth.

Kevin wept.

POW!

"What's your name, hon?" The question floated into the back of the truck, tender as a lullaby. The face that formed the question was an unblinking, open-mouthed mask of concern.

A black- and purple-blotched visage, wheat-colored hair matted against a grimy forehead, paused in thought as if she'd misplaced it, but soon gathered enough of her faculties together to reply, "Bella ... Brock."

Lee Ann, kneeling over the young woman crumpled in the fetal position in the back of her truck, wrapped her in the blankets she used as cargo padding and half-carried her over the rear bumper. Bella leaned on her heavily as they staggered into the restaurant and into Nick's office. Fortunately, it was still a little early for supper, and there were no patrons in the dining room.

A couple of old men, permanent fixtures at the bar, were the only others who saw their host and his cousin from Wisconsin escort the wretched-looking young woman into the back. The summer dress, shredded asymmetrically, exposing a breast, failed to elicit crude comment. Prairie clay, blood, and who knows what else caked its owner. Smelling like offal and urine – some of the grotesque bouquet could have been human, other notes clearly weren't – she was bruised and scraped and lacerated like an animal that had just been in a fight – the kind of fight where the winner was decided by who was still alive.

Laying Bella down on the originally white, 1970s vintage modular couch, Lee Ann noticed her shivering as if with fever.

"I think she's in shock," Lee Ann told her cousin as she took off her spring jacket and threw it over Bella's torso.

"That ain't gonna do anything," Nick pointed out. "You already got her wrapped up in the stuff from the truck."

"Get more, then!" she ordered, and Nick complied. He had a shelf full of cotton-blend tablecloths.

Nick didn't need telling how to respond after that. He went and grabbed the first aid kit out from behind the bar, ignoring the two regulars who demanded he top off their beers while he was there. He brought a case of bottled water into the office, which Lee Ann used to wash the wounds before cracking open the kit for antiseptic and bandages.

Bella was incredibly thirsty – thirsty enough to fight through whatever haze she was under to form the word "drink." As soon as she could sit up, she downed three half-liter water bottles in as many breaths. Nick's last favor to the young woman from the back of the truck was to fetch a spare waitress's uniform, place it on a chair, and leave unobtrusively.

Lee Ann gave Bella a gentle hug and noticed that she wasn't shaking anymore, and actually felt warm.

"Anything broken, hon?" Lee Ann asked.

In response, Bella slowly kicked off her covers and tried, with ultimate success, to stand.

"I don't ... think so."

"Bella, is it?" Lee Ann asked as she handed her the uniform. "We'll get you a proper change of clothes as soon as we can. You'll probably want to shower off before we do that. In the meantime, you can wear this-here."

Bella took the garment but looked confused as to what

she was supposed to say. After a long pause, she ventured, "Than...k...s."

"By the way, I'm Lee Ann Bayard. You also met my cousin Nick. He owns this place," the middle-aged woman said by way of introduction. "I just drive in from Wisconsin once a month to make some deliveries. You may not believe this, but it's a good thing you climbed in the back of my refrigerated truck. When I make supermarket runs, I use a freezer truck, and you don't want to be in the back of that for seven—"

"Wis ... con ... sin." As she climbed into the waitress frock, Bella chanted this word, which evidently held some obscure meaning for her. Then her eyes brightened. "I'm from Wisconsin. I go to school ..."

Her legs buckling, she collapsed back on the couch as Lee Ann guided her down.

After a moment's near-catatonia, Bella's eyes opened wide.

"Lee ... Ann?"

"Yes, Bella?"

"Not in ... Wisconsin ... now?"

"No," Lee Ann said with a headshake. "We're in Plainville, Illinois."

Lee Ann could tell that confused Bella but, then again, everything seemed to.

"Don't worry about it, hon. Nobody's heard of it 'cept those of us who were born here," Lee Ann volunteered. "It's downstate, way west of Springfield, almost to the River."

"Miss ... is ... sippi," Bella replied, almost immediately, as if to demonstrate that she was a Midwesterner as well, and knew what *the* River meant.

"Yes, indeed," Lee Ann said, with a smile that was as much gums as teeth. "Listen, you got banged up pretty good and you should probably get an X-ray or something.

But I think for now you should just rest yourself some and stay warm, maybe take a couple Bayers 'cause I bet you're in some pain. Truth is, it's over a half-hour's drive to the nearest people-hospital from here and that's all they're gonna do for you anyways."

Bella replied with an "OK," that convinced Lee Ann that she understood one word out of every three.

"If you want to use the toilet, it's the door right opposite this one," Lee Ann said as she grabbed the knob to leave the office. "You got plenty of water bottles left on the desk if you get thirsty."

"Thanks."

"And let me know what you'd like to eat. Nick is really a great chef. Spent ten months up in Chicago at—"

"Not ... hungry," Bella said, pressing on her solar plexus as if smothering a fire.

BAM!

This would go a lot faster with henchmen, Maman Brigitte thought.

The windowless, clockless boiler room was crammed with six-foot folding tables on which were stacked what had been half the inventory of the Chesterfield Mall's Plaquet Box. Around those tables were folding chairs occupied by a motley assortment of has-beens, head cases and losers – exactly the type of people the Americans with Abilities Act was passed to protect. They plodded along, carefully inspecting and cataloging each card.

Equity had suggested henchmen, and Maman Brigitte was sorely tempted. They were plentiful and they worked for free.

But they could be ambitious, Maman Brigitte had explained to Equity as they set up the boiler room. With superpowers increasingly plentiful, it was tempting for a mundane human being to acquire cards such as those Seth Hill traded in as an edge. It was only natural.

126

It was also a waste of time.

Managing by walking around, peering over the shoulders of the washed-up heroes and villains in the folding chairs, Maman Brigitte recalled the exact words she used to explain why people with special abilities were more trustworthy than non-powered people for this kind of exercise.

"Think back to when you were in school." She recollected the lecture she'd given Singh when he had first signed on. "The student council president you thought would be living in the White House someday, is living in a ranch house and managing a Bennigan's. The homecoming queen you figured was going to make it in Hollywood. She married her dentist. Even the chess team captain who was going to cure cancer, or have a billion-dollar idea for a high-tech startup – well, he either got a Ph.D. and went to work as a mid-level bench chemist at a drug company, or else he had that billion-dollar idea, but never got around to writing up the business plan because he didn't want to miss any of the *Babylon Five* marathon.

"Most people are their own worst enemies." Maman Brigitte remembered Singh nodding in agreement at this point, as she continued. "It doesn't matter what gifts Fate gives them, they'll find a way to squander it. People tend to be comfortable in the middle, except for those who are even more comfortable at the bottom. But there are exceptions. If you get a roomful of henchmen in here, odds are at least one of them is the kind of go-getter who'd grab the Malificium card for himself. Or he might even try to use some lesser card against us. But if we fill the room with villains who never got offers from the Institute and with heroes who couldn't hack it with The Crusaders, they've proved their mediocrity. And the mediocre can always be trusted."

And to Maman Brigitte, that formulation was worth the

short-staffing delays, not to mention the $40 an hour.

Coincidentally, it was at that point when Equity returned to the boiler room, tucked between the elevator shaft and the restrooms of the nineteenth floor of 1825 K Street N.W. The unmistakable smell of Pizzeria Uno's Chicago-style pies preceded her. Maman Brigitte's eyes rolled.

Equity flashed a big smile though, recognizing the through-the-looking-glass irony of the moment: a villainess making a pizza run for her subordinates.

Everyone else served, Equity relished a slice of her own. Maman Brigitte declined the offer.

"Chicago style!" Equity gushed. "You can't get this in New York."

"Yes," Maman Brigitte replied. "And with good reason."

{BOOM!}

Bella Brock found the restroom just in time. She was exploding from both ends.

She went for the bowel movement first. Brown fluid splashed out in five spasms. The first four found the bowl, but that fourth one coincided with Bella's mouth inflating with vomit and she had to invert to empty the puke.

Bella crawled over the excrement-splattered tile floor trying to identify what she must have eaten. It had fur, and tiny teeth, in addition to a tooth that was big enough to be human.

It even had a filling.

That thought didn't so much trigger another heave as accelerate it. Another and another came right behind.

The last one featured something shiny. She fought another round of physical disgust and reached into the fetid bowl for it.

It was a bracelet.

Bella brushed the murky fluids off with her thumbnail - the peace-sign laminates now looked like mosaics with half the tiles missing – revealing a MedicAlert bracelet belonging to a diabetic. She cleaned an inscription on the back, also with her thumb. Bella searched her memory for any trace of someone named Reinette Ingersoll.

She began hitching her panties back up but, after one glance and one sniff, she decided to throw them away. Bella flushed, let the tank fill up and flushed again; in between, she washed herself off in the sink as best she could and made some effort to wipe up the tile and porcelain, but she was too weak and the job too extensive. Then she returned to Nick's office.

Bella started shivering again, but now from terror, and no amount of covering was going to stop it.

I was there, and then I wasn't there, or else I wasn't me, Bella pieced together. It didn't make any sense. All she knew, and this was on a visceral rather than a verbal level, was that she had undergone some kind of transformation, had then changed back, and might once again become whatever it was she had been. What she didn't know, and what she desperately needed to know, was what would trigger the change.

{ POW! }

Nick had been tending bar, but now the wait staff prepped the dining room as the kitchen crew geared up, and the first dinner guests arrived. He was doing his favorite part of his job: playing host. He gleefully welcomed a family that had been friends with his own family since their great-grandparents' time, poured them some ice water, set them up with menus and apologized that the squeaky cheese was unavailable.

The bad news taken in stride, Nick went back behind the bar. At this time of day, the bar was a thing of incredible beauty. The ornate stained glass along the edges of the bar mirror glinted like the scattered remains of a rainbow. And smack in the middle of the mirror, which ran the whole twenty-foot length of the bar, was the reflection of the sun hanging low and red over the freshly harvested plain.

His cousin Lee Ann had pulled her truck around back and was tossing her inventory into thick, Hefty yard-waste bags. She couldn't sell those curds. They'd been bled on, peed on, and she stopped her imagination right there and set it to work thinking up a story for the folks at the insurance company. They'd probably call what happened a preventable act of vandalism and deny reimbursement. Lee Ann wallowed in uncharitable thoughts for a moment.

But then she gazed across the plains at the setting sun. It was so beautiful, she felt inspired to go back inside for Bella.

The despondent young woman objected but was too weak from her ordeals to resist Lee Ann's persistent good cheer. Together, they watched the orange-red orb drop into the Mississippi.

Lee Ann, in her flag-motif T-shirt and Wranglers, smiled as if she were watching a miracle unfold. Bella, with fresh vomit stains on her baby-blue uniform with bright-white lace, shuddered as if dreading an omen of doom.

SUPERPOWERS AND ALCOHOL

Kevin intended to be the first to arrive at Hawk's, but the vagaries of the Clarkson Road bus schedule conspired against him. Shel Shapiro and The Indomitable Lugh already had a couple tables pushed together in the back, under the black mask and two-holstered gun belt mounted on the wall. Four empty Budweiser longnecks cluttered the scene.

Shel and Lugh were arm-wrestling.

"I knew it!" Kevin announced. "Shel, I knew you had a power. You have super-strength. Why the big secret?"

Lugh took advantage of the distraction to pin his opponent's knuckles to the laminated teakwood table then, with his other hand, signal the waitress for two more Buds and that Shel would be paying for them. Lugh laughed heartily.

"Sorry," Kevin muttered in Shel's direction.

"It's okay, kid," Shel replied with a resigned shrug. "Not the worst thing that's happened to me today."

"Expecting a crowd, better switch to pitchers," Kevin advised the waitress as he pulled up a chair, then turned back to Shel. "I figured you had some really lame power - ruler of the traffic lights or world's greatest speller or something like that. But you just arm-wrestled The Indomitable Lugh to a standstill."

"Not quite, but I did beat him one time out of three."

"Still, Lugh here is strong enough to toss SUVs around like they're bricks."

"Yeah, well, I can't."

"The Fates have rendered our compatriot thoroughly fucked," Lugh explained. "He be sorely and roughly penetrated from his anus even unto his windpipe. Destiny's own foreskin doth tickle his tonsils from behind."

Kevin didn't know how to reply to that.

"Spake metaphorically, I."

"You get used to that. What Lugh here is trying to say," Shel explained, "is that I have super-strength in my arms only. My legs are normal and so's my spine. I can curl Escalades, but I couldn't pick one up from a standing position, no less throw it like a brick. So this is my power – I'm the greatest mortal arm-wrestler. 'Lame' enough for you, Kiley?"

Fortunately for Kevin, the awkward moment was cut short by the arrival of the first pitcher. It was empty before the waitress set it on the table. Suddenly Bobby Botler was sitting across from Kevin.

"I got the next one," Bobby said with a belch. "Hi, guys."

Then Orville came in Hawk's front door and strode to the back with his metonymic gait, seating himself with perfect posture. He was still in his TSA uniform. It didn't occur to him to say hello to any individual until they each in turn greeted him. A moment later, another full pitcher arrived and Bobby poured everyone a glass faster than pony-sized bottles could be filled at the brewery; he did this by blowing into the top of the pitcher, producing a Category 5 blast that displaced the beer more rapidly than Earth's gravity was able.

As the rest of the former teammates drank, Orville studied patterns in the foam.

When Mindy walked in, Kevin was the first to greet her, warmly and graciously, complimenting her outfit – this being the first time he'd ever seen her in casualwear: a pretty peasant blouse and ankle-length, camel-colored skirt. He pulled up a seat for her. The others left it at, "Hi, Mindy." Orville waited his turn to greet her, but then Lugh inexplicably added, "Well met, Maid Maguire, and who be thy friend?"

BAM!

The motel off Interstate 20 in Mississippi had a tiny restaurant. Or not so much a restaurant, as a half dozen tables in a nook off the lobby that served continental breakfast in the morning, and chicken-fried steak with cans of Coors for a couple hours each evening.

It was there that Elias and Ray settled down for a meal in the glow of their intimate consummation.

"That's a common misconception," Elias explained, staring into Ray's eyes, staring back. "But you, having been in the Airborne, are a more elite soldier than I'd ever be."

"How do you get more elite than Colonel–" Ray stopped abruptly, looked around at the other guests and staff members whose attention they were attracting, "than Anderson Cooper?"

Elias also glanced around the lobby. One by one, people went back to minding their own business, except for two young men wearing green Mississippi Valley State Delta Devils varsity jackets. "Get a load of them queers," Elias heard one stage whisper to the other. The tension broke when one collegian's phone buzzed and he had to reply to a text.

"I got a civilian job with the Army Corps of Engineers straight out of school – me and about a hundred other guys

133

from Drexel," Elias recounted. "Just a skinny, pigeon-toed mathlete. Despite having 'army' in the name, the Corps is mostly a civilian agency."

"I know," Ray said.

"After a couple years, I was encouraged – strongly encouraged – to apply for a commission, which was granted before the ink was dry on my paperwork. Turns out the former ... Anderson Cooper ... was retiring and they needed someone with AB-negative blood to take over."

"And that's all it takes?" Ray asked. "A commission and the right blood type?"

"That's all that's needed," Elias replied. "The transformation gave me all the physical prowess you'd expect, and the muscle memory of every previous ... anchorman ... was literally in my blood. I had to keep up the training, of course, but it was all a matter of being in the right place at the right time with the right hundred-to-one blood type."

"Even so, there were probably over a thousand other officers who—" Ray stopped. The two Delta Devils, done texting, were snapping cellphone photos and chuckling. Ray stared them down. "You got a problem?"

"Yeah," one of them said as they strode over to the table. "We got a problem."

Ray stood up. "Then take it somewhere else."

Elias also stood up, giving the youths something to think about: a glimpse of the steel grip of his sidearm sticking out of his waistband.

With a long, tense hesitation but without another word, the two Mississippi Valley athletes turned toward the motel's front door. As they were walking out, though, they stopped and looked at each other.

Elias noticed that Ray continued to gaze intently at the pair. Elias knew that gaze. He had felt it on the back of his own neck, only a day and a half before.

The varsity men shared a smile and turned right around.

Their footsteps quickened as they crossed the lobby for the elevator. When the elevator was too slow to arrive - that is, after two seconds - they bounded into the stairwell. Elias and Ray could hear their footsteps echo as they took the steps three at a time.

"I'm still not clear," Elias confessed as they sat back down to finish their meal. He could still savor the saltiness on his tongue from before. "Under what conditions can you do that? When can't you?"

"Still figuring this out for myself," Ray said, contemplating how best to carve steak with what was a repurposed butter knife.

"You are going to change them back, aren't you?"

"You want me to change you back?"

"No, of course not."

"Then why do you care?"

BOOM!

Lugh was the only one at Hawk's besides Mindy who could see Eva Peron, and he liked what he saw. It was hard for Kevin to make his pitch with Lugh making eyes at a point on the wall. Judging from Lugh's giddy waving and kiss blowing, the point on the wall welcomed the attention.

"Let's get down to business," Kevin announced. "First of all, I want to thank you all for coming, and don't forget to tip the waitress. If any of you need the restroom before we—"

"Shut up and talk," Bobby said, a demand which could only make sense in that context.

"Right. Well, here's the situation. Since the Americans with Abilities Act was, uh, enacted, our career choices have been greatly curtailed. Millions of people just like us are prevented from taking heroic services jobs in the private sector, and there's room for only a handful of us in the only independent super-team that can legally function

135

in the U.S., The Crusaders. Our only option has been to join the special branch of TSA or to take jobs that ought to go to Mundanes."

"I beg your pardon," Mindy said, staring a gentle dagger.

"Excuse me, Mundane-Americans. The point is," Kevin recovered, "we've all tried straight jobs, and it never worked out. We've all tried to get in with The Crusaders. And with the exception of Lugh here ..."

Kevin gestured to the Sovereign of the Strong who was, at that moment, proving that he could touch both the tip of his nose and the tip of his chin with his tongue, a puckish twinkle in his eye.

"Anyway, here's my point. There's nothing The Crusaders can do that we can't. It was them, not us, who trashed the mall. It was us, not them, who fought off the Institute two days ago when they first tried to capture the Malificium card. And we can probably count ourselves two-for-two by now. It's been a day and a half since their second attempt. If they had it in their mitts, it would be Game Over for the whole world by now."

"You're right," Bobby said.

"I am?"

"Surprised to hear me say that?" Bobby asked in a tone of voice that signaled to Shel that they shared the same dim opinion of Kevin Kiley. "But don't get me started on how little you actually had to do with any of it. You don't want to have that conversation with me in public."

Orville stared dispassionately, as if what they said was no more than random monkey chatter, devoid of all meaning or subtext.

"What I'm saying is," Kevin ploughed on, "We could stick together as a team. We work well together. We belong together."

He stared at Mindy as he said that.

"We need to decide a few things," Kevin continued. "Are we going to go rogue – operate here in the American heartland without legal cover? I'm sure there're a lot of people who'd pay in cash for our talents. Or do we want to relocate to Canada where we can operate without reference to the Triple-A? Also, who's going to be our leader? And what shall we call ourselves?"

"Call ourselves?" Shel asked.

"We need a name."

"Why do we need a name?"

"Am I the only one here who went to summer camp? 'Everywhere we go-oh ... people want to know-oh ... who we are ... so we tell them ... We are the Somethings, the mighty, mighty Somethings ...'"

"Stay here. Cash business. Shel stays on as leader. No dumb-ass name," Bobby said.

"Seconded," Mindy added.

"I also think we should make our stand here," Kevin concurred. "And Shel's the man. But we do need a name."

"As leader, I say the hell we do," came Shel's first executive decision.

"Come on, Shel," Kevin cajoled. "What if we were to call ourselves 'Shapiro's Heroes'?"

Shel didn't miss a beat.

"I'd change my name to Shasshole."

"I suppose we can table that discussion for now," Kevin said, not ceding the metaphorical gavel. "What do you think, Orville?"

"No."

"Orville, please," Mindy intoned. "This is a chance to do some real good. Shouldn't we at least–?"

"No, what?" Kevin demanded, cutting Mindy off.

"The whole idea. We're heroes. We uphold the law. We don't break it. I'll be going now," he said, taking out his wallet and change purse and leaving exactly one-sixth of the tab plus twenty percent tip on the table.

"Good, because I've had too much beer and need a lift," Shel said. "Orville, are you going my way?"

"Dropping you off would take me six-point-five miles out of my way. I get an average of nineteen miles per gallon in city driving. My last fill-up was at $3.19 and nine-tenths cents per gallon. Do you have $1.09 in gas money?"

"Got you covered. Good night, team."

As Orville and Shel left, Kevin returned to holding court. "If we're going to stay local, then, we'll need some kind of base of operations, a place only we know about that we can use as a secret lair."

"I got just the place," Bobby said. "Mindy can show you where it is. Meet you guys there in the morning. Not too early."

"Why don't you stick around?" Mindy asked.

Bobby assessed the scene. It was obvious that Kevin was into Mindy and entirely possible that Mindy was into Kevin. Lugh was definitely into whatever spirit-wraith he was leg-humping as they tangoed around the open floor to "La Vida Loca." Whatever he thought of Kevin Kiley, and it wasn't much, he wasn't going out of his way to cock-block.

"This place is boring," Bobby said, the last syllable barely audible as he was already out the door.

"Will *you* stick around for a drink?" Kevin asked Mindy.

"You'll let me pay?"

"The rules are the rules," Kevin said with a forced smile. "Dutch treat."

"No. I mean, I'll pay for the round."

{ POW! }

Kevin was right about the Malificium card. The Institute didn't have it. Maman Brigitte and Equity came to that conclusion hours earlier; they still had hundreds of cards to go through, but the odds at that point were vanishingly small.

As the night wore on and the pizza slices evaporated, Maman Brigitte began sending the temps home. And now, well past eleven at night, it was just herself, Equity and one gnarled old man with a cumulus of white hair that contrasted with dark, leathery skin. His concert shirt from the recent S.O.S. Band reunion brightened the dim room. He overturned the last card on his pile, leaned over his clipboard, and put a hash mark next to the line that read "Kingdom Hearts 2."

"Nothing," he said to Maman Brigitte.

"I'm not surprised," the Institute's managing director replied. "Thanks for hanging in this long, Myron. We'll pay you through the full hour. Just send us an invoice."

"Will do, ma'am," Myron said as he got up to leave. Another gracious nod and "ma'am" to Equity and he was on the service elevator down.

"Nice old guy," Equity said once he was gone.

"Yeah," said Maman Brigitte. "Myron Masters. Hard to believe he used to be a Crusader."

BAM!

Midge - Millicent May Peale - had changed out of her battle togs as soon as she arrived at the Pinnacle of Justice. She favored the blue jumpsuit of the support staff she used to belong to. It constrained her wings a little, but she didn't need wings in microgravity, did she?

The Carbon Avenger had no need for clothes for either comfort or modesty. He was no longer what one could call a man, or even male. Since the accident, he looked like nothing so much as a mobile pile of roofing material with eyeballs, albeit one with the strength of carbon-steel sinews and the intellect of the keenest industrial engineering mind on the planet - the one that once belonged to the brilliant inventor and entrepreneur Dirk Henderson III.

"We have to move past this, Dirk," Midge explained firmly as she harnessed herself into her console seat. "The new Colonel America won't be here for another couple days. Even then, we'll still be far from full strength. We've got a lot of work to do."

"You're right," Dirk said. He understood what attracted Porter Peale, Pantagruel, to her, but never understood the giant's simultaneous repulsion from her. But now he was beginning to. This wasn't the first time they'd been alone together, but this was the first time alone together while Dirk was in a foul mood.

"Look, I know how you feel. Christ is dead. Porter isn't coming back. Elias—"

"What about Elias?" Dirk demanded. They had been colleagues and friends for twenty-five years.

"Whereabouts unknown," Midge admitted. "I've been monitoring the secure military channels. Elias got a car from the Redstone Arsenal motor pool and just drove off without a word to anyone."

"I can't believe he'd do anything like that, no matter what kind of changes he's been through."

"The base was actually in lockdown, but nobody questions Colonel America. He bluffed his way past the gate. You know why the base was in lockdown?"

"Don't tell me Ta Mok or Singh escaped."

"No," Midge explained. "Their henchman, Raymond Novinsky. The one who—"

"Right. Not a coincidence."

"We have to assume Elias has, well, switched sides in *every* sense."

"He doesn't have the organelles anymore, does he?"

"No. Nebraska - María de la Soledad Rivera - has the power. But after a quarter century in the cape and cowl, Elias knows all our strengths and weaknesses, and has learned a few things about fighting at the Crusader level. He's still a dangerous man."

Dirk suppressed his annoyance at being told what he already knew - and knew better than Midge.

"Changing the subject - how fast do you think we can get replacements for Porter and Christ?"

"It's never easy," Midge said with a shrug. "It'll proba- bly take a couple weeks to identify somebody who can step up to Porter's role. Lots of super-powers out there - but damn few *heroes*. And as for Christ ..."

"Damn fewer *gods*," Dirk concluded.

"So what we should focus on now," Midge continued - Dirk would have said *lectured*, "is the same thing we've been focusing on, finding that last Malificium card before the Institute does. It's clear they don't yet have it. We need to find out more from Seth Hill."

"Right, the card dealer. He didn't strike me as the type to leave anything to chance. Hill probably anticipated this attack and squirreled the card away somewhere offsite."

"But where?"

BOOM!

"Hill, Seth J." Maman Brigitte read off her ViewSonic 23- inch, 1080p monitor as Equity stood at her elbow. "Age thirty-five, graduated from the John Burroughs School in St. Louis, BS in Mathematics from Duke, Finance MBA from Berkeley. Stayed in the Bay Area after graduation. He's been a derivatives trader, a currency and exchange rate speculator, and was involved as a consultant on 'special projects' at Carbodyne, whatever that means. He was a high flier. Then out of nowhere, this past year, he chucks it all, moves back to St. Louis and buys a card shop."

"There's a lot of money in those cards," Equity pointed out.

"There's a lot of money in everything he's ever done.

Just like you," Maman Brigitte replied. "And I don't see you moving to St. Louis."

"Nothing I'm considering," Equity conceded. "But that's simply what we found out about this guy from his LinkedIn page. This is what he *wants* us to know. I wonder what he's hiding, besides the card."

POW!

"So we're finally having a drink," Kevin marveled. "What brought you around?"

"Well, when I first met you, I thought you were just this glib, feckless smart aleck," Mindy said. "But I'm beginning to believe there might actually be some substance to you."

"I'll consider that a compliment."

"Consider it whatever you want. But you took what was a terrible situation for all of us and found a way to make something positive out of it," she said.

Her eyes were deep pools of caramel brown, bookending a button nose. Her lips, not as full as the ideal set by Georgiana, made a straight, horizontal line that matched her matter-of-fact style of speaking. Even so, the very shape of her face - a perfect diamond, the top obscured by wayward bangs - cast its own allure. Kevin assessed that, if an absolute pulchritude scale existed, Mindy's would be well inside the bell curve. Still, there was something about her, that something within him found compelling. He wanted her more than he'd ever wanted any other woman. Even more than he wanted her alter ego.

"And you've made no secret you find me attractive. Even so, you've been respectful to me, and patient," Mindy continued. That last word was out before she caught it. Patient? She'd known him a day and a half. And yet Mindy couldn't escape the feeling that she was reuniting with this man after a long, lonesome time apart. "I've been going on and on, haven't I?"

"And?"

"And you've been listening."

They paused for a sip of their mojitos, never taking their wide irises off each other. On the jukebox, Billy Corgan seemed to speak for Kevin as he sang, "Tonight, Tonight." It was a long time before Mindy spoke again.

"I don't know how to put this any other way, Kevin, but every moment I spend with you, it feels more and more like I've known you all my life, then somehow lost you and half-forgot you, and now I have you back."

"That's not what you were saying this morning."

"Orville? He's sweet but ... that was just a crush. Hero worship, if you can believe that. I really admire him as a professional, and I'm going to miss him as part of the team. But I've come to realize that, on a deeper level, there's nothing there."

"And with you and me there is?"

"I think there could be. I want to find out."

"I do too."

"One problem, though."

"What's that?" Kevin asked, with an expression as if someone had sprayed seltzer in his ear.

"I have a roommate, and she doesn't like you."

Kevin glanced over at Lugh, who appeared to be groping thin air as he spun in a slow circle to the Smashing Pumpkins' power ballad.

"I don't think that's going to be an issue."

BAM!

"Are you feeling any better?" Nick asked Bella.

After the restaurant closed for the night, he'd invited her into his home. Bayard's wasn't in Plainville proper, but that was the nearest post office. The residence of Nick and Rhonda Bayard and family, though, was right on Main Street and just a half block from Church Street. Bella looked cozy on the soft, cushy mattress in the guest bedroom. The Early American furniture, although solidly built, looked spindly under ornate, colorful patchworks of quilting and the occasional accents of linen or cretonne.

It seemed to soothe Bella. Unknown to Nick, what Bella had most taken comfort in was the fact that sundown had come and gone, and dusk, and nightfall, and she had not transformed into ... whatever it was. That was far more soothing than the sight of any bench chest or straight-backed chair.

Still, it was nice. Bella had relaxed a little and regained more of her faculties. She was able to dress herself in a spare set of Rhonda's terry-cloth lounging wear.

"Bella?" Nick asked again. "Any better?"

"Oh, yes, much."

Nick, seated in the chair in the corner, kept the door open in deference to his ingrained, Midwestern sense of propriety. His fifteen-year-old boy was drumming in time with a group called Bullets for My Valentine, whose music ran out of his computer and through an amplifier. That was down in the basement, two flights away, and it was still a little on the loud side. The ten-year-old twins - their door was also open - managed to sleep through it.

"So how much do you remember?"

"Things are hazy but here's what I've pieced together," Bella said, marveling at her rediscovered ability for organizing her thoughts. "I'm originally from Milwaukee. I'm a graduate student at the University of Wisconsin and now live in Madison."

"What are you studying?"

"Environmental Science," Bella said, after a short pause. "Sorry. It's like I have to translate my thoughts into English, but I don't remember learning any other language. I don't know how else to describe it. Anyhow, I was doing some fieldwork up in the boonies along the Little Eau Pleine River. Water and soil testing. I remember there being lots of fauna around. Just the cutest little critters ..."

The phone rang and Nick was quick to answer it before it woke the twins; it was instinctual – the kids had been sleeping through Bullets for My Valentine. His wife was calling in.

He explained to her that they had company and under what circumstances and that he'd appreciate it if, when Rhonda went back to work the next afternoon, she could take Bella in with her.

Rhonda said she'd be happy to, and agreed that a nice, comfortable bed in a cheery room in a private home was probably the best place for someone so traumatized.

Nick mentioned that Lee Ann had decided to drive back up to Wisconsin and re-stock, planning to drive back the following day. Then he asked Rhonda what kind of day she was having. Rhonda told him it was "one of those."

"That was my wife, Rhonda," Nick explained to Bella, as the drummer decided to call it a night and go to sleep. "She works at a hospital in Quincy – she's a technician in the medical imaging department. They just got dinged in a health-and-safety audit. Damn state bureaucrats. As you were saying, though?"

"That's about it. I remember the animals just romping around me, I just wanted to reach out and pet them. And that's it. That's all I remember until Lee Ann helped me out of the back of that truck. I have no idea how I got in there."

But that wasn't entirely true. Even as her mind readjusted to human form, her memory of what happened in the meantime was encroaching. Only her sense of denial (it all had to be a bad dream!) kept the consequences of her savagery from the front of her mind.

There were any number of reasons that a tooth and a MedicAlert bracelet were in her digestive tract. Or maybe they were there in the bathroom before she ever went in, and she just didn't notice them at first.

There's nothing wrong with me, she kept telling herself. I just lost a couple days. It happens to everyone. (I hadn't had a drink all week.) I'll just get some rest and get myself checked out in the hospital tomorrow.

"Bella? Are you okay?" Nick asked in a near whisper, as he got up from the chair. Bella was, in fact, holding her knees to her chest, rocking back and forth in the bed.

"Yes," she said. "I'll be fine." (I am not placing you or your family in any danger.)

A small clock with serif numbers and a pendulum in a square, pinewood frame sat on the nightstand. Bella hadn't noticed it until that moment – the moment it struck midnight.

Not Talking of a Hurried Night

It wasn't the first time the Hinds County supervisor representing District 4 checked into that motel along I-20. It wasn't his first time paying cash for a room.

As always, he swung his Lexus across two parking spaces and left the engine idle. As always, the buxom woman in the shotgun seat stayed there for a few minutes so that they would not be seen entering together. Her cell phone rang.

Usually, this was the part when the supervisor would tell her to wait another five minutes, then come up to room such-and-such. But this time, it was the supervisor calling to tell her not to bother, it was all a mistake, she should drive the Lexus back to town, he'd get a lift back and pick up the car in the morning. Goodbye.

Around the corner of the building, another luxury car with another woman - not as busty but with legs that crossed at the knees and then again at the ankles - received a simultaneous phone call.

Another twenty minutes later, Elias O'Neill came out of the closet. Literally. And he had a camera.

He took a succession of still photos, then a 30-second video with sound, all of the same thing: the county supervisor with a mouthful of a senior vice president of Cellular South.

Ray, who had also been hiding in the closet, sealed the deal like a past master – it was their third mark of the night – acknowledging but not really listening to whatever these two local community leaders had to say. "You don't have to explain to *us* ... but how embarrassing if these images should impact ... your careers ... your families ..."

Wallets were tossed on a nightstand. PIN numbers hastily scratched onto the scrap paper motels place next to the phone. A diamond-studded tie clip came off the tie. The county executive also threw in his class ring. Liberty University.

After a quick ride to the ATM at a Conoco station, Elias and Ray retired to their own room counting the money. Elias sprawled out on the queen-sized bed and clicked on the TV. He flipped through the channels before settling on a toggle between *Project Runway* and *SportsCenter.*

"So that's a total of fourteen-thousand one-hundred and twenty-two dollars and I figure we'll pawn about another five grand in jewelry," Ray beamed after a couple commercial breaks, as he spun around in the desk chair. "We can afford a LodgeNet movie."

"I don't want to watch a movie," Elias replied. "I want to talk."

"Right, our plan," Ray said, as he stood up and started pacing in time with his cadence. "First thing tomorrow, we check out of here and move into the Marriott in Jackson, or some other place that's big and classy. Run the same scam. Then we take I-55 North to Memphis—"

"Why?"

"Because I-55 South takes us into New Orleans, and blackmail just doesn't work there," Ray explained, words rushing out of his mouth, shoeless feet scraping along the carpet. "So up to Memphis, same deal. Then Little Rock, then the Big D. Then we loop around and see how much these guys are willing to pay to be straight again. Then—"

"I mean, why blackmail?" Elias queried. "Can't we use our powers for good?"

"By *our* powers, you mean *my* power?"

Elias's downward glance was answer enough.

"Because I'm evil?" Ray reminded him, with an upward inflection that indicated the obviousness of the response. "So I figure after we clean out the whole Bible Belt, we hijack a plane for someplace warm, dry and sexually repressed. I'm thinking Saudi, but open to—"

"This isn't really what I wanted to talk about," Elias said, shutting off the TV.

"OK, what do you want to talk about?"

"Us," Elias said, with a vocal tremor.

That stopped Ray in his tracks.

"You don't have to be evil, Ray," Elias continued, earnestly. "Let me help you find a way of using your skills for the protection and betterment of humanity."

Ray stood with his back to Elias, and spoke to the door. "I spent three tours in Iraq and another two in Afghanistan plus some time in Pakistan I can't talk about," Ray said, staring at the emergency exit map. "All that was for protection and betterment, and to find WMDs and to be hailed as liberators and yadda-yadda-yadda. I'm no better off, neither's anybody else, and some good friends died. If there is any good in the world, I've done my bit in service to it."

"And I'm impressed with that," Elias replied, although he fought the urge to go into detail about what he himself had been doing for almost a quarter century. He got up off the bed and gave Ray a gentle rub on the back. "But I want us to—"

"Us?" Ray said, turning around to reveal a raised eyebrow and dropped jaw. "You keep using that word. Look, thanks for busting me out, man, but I've been waiting for years for the opportunity to step up to full-fledged villainy. You're a great lay so you can come along for the ride, but there's no 'us.'"

Elias removed his hand from Ray's shoulder and stood as tall as he could. His face was a thin veil of comportment over a storm of conflicting emotions.

"That comes as a surprise."

"Look, you knew I was evil when you met me."

"I know, but ... this is difficult ... I don't just want to have gay sex with you," Elias sputtered, then steeled himself and gazed piercingly into Ray's eyes. "I want to gay-marry you. I want us to have a gay future together, greeting each other gaily every morning and having gay dinner together every evening. I want us to adopt gay children and live together in a big gay house in a quiet, gay neighborhood as a big gay family."

Ray laughed aloud. "I guess you didn't get much tail when you were straight, either. That's not how things work. You think you can change me?"

The sheepish expression on Elias's face suggested, yes, he did think he could change Ray.

"This is something I've thought about for a long time," Ray went on, dropping the haughty tone in favor of patient explanation. "It's part of my core - who I am. I believe that the strong should subjugate the weak, that the cunning should treat the simple as if they were prey. It's the natural order of things. Without these principles, all would be chaos. Fairness and honesty and all that other Boy Scout junk only confuse me."

There was little more to be said, aside from the four words that signify the end of any relationship, gay or straight, long-term or short.

"Whatever."

"Whatever."

"Fine."

"Fine."

Elias left, taking the car. Ray could always steal another, he figured. And he took a few hundred dollars in cash, promising himself he'd pay it back to the victims as soon as he could.

The next day, Ray left without formally checking out. The bill went to CNN. Anderson Cooper had some explaining to do.

BOOM!

"Sure you won't come in, Orville?" Shel asked as he got out of the car.

"Yes," Orville replied as he continued to stare straight through the windshield. "I'm awkward in social situations."

"Well, okay, but you seemed to be all right back at Hawk's."

Orville paused a moment before offering the rationalization, "That was business."

"If you say so," Shel said as he walked backward up the path to his split-level tract home in the St. Louis suburb of Bellefontaine Neighbors. He fished out his cell phone. "But Lisa is sure to have a pot of coffee ready, and it's still early enough that the kids are still up. They'd all love to see you again. Let me just make sure everyone's decent."

"I have a schedule to keep."

"You're unemployed."

Orville turned off the engine, applied the parking brake, pushed the controls for the windows to confirm that they were all rolled up and jotted down the mileage on the trip odometer and the reading on the gas gauge. Then he got out, straightened his floor mat, shut his door firmly but without slamming, walked around the car to test all the door handles to be certain all the locks properly engaged, checked for body damage or rust that he didn't already know about, and ensured that his license tags were clearly visible and properly bolted on. Then he accompanied Shel,

151

who had by then finished his phone conversation with his wife, into the Shapiro home.

As Shel kissed his wife of thirteen years, swung his eight-year-old daughter around in circles until he almost lost his balance and played a head-butting game with his six-year-old son, Orville watched impassively.

Lisa Shapiro soon scooted the children upstairs and Shel excused himself for a couple minutes as he went to tuck them in. As they sipped their half-caf, Orville and Lisa sat in silence – but not an uncomfortable one. They had met dozens of times before and Lisa learned early on that Orville seemed comforted by having people around, although he was easily flustered if he had to talk to them. So she just sat and smiled at him, and was gratified when he risked eye contact and smiled back.

Shel soon came down to the cup Lisa had expertly poured for him, with just the barest splash of 1% and half an Equal, in the World's Greatest Dad mug. Shel knew Orville's quirks better than anybody and took it from there.

"Hey, Orv, did you see that article in the Post-Dispatch on the Keith Milow show at the Art Museum?"

Orville spoke at length about contemporary abstract art.

He was unaware of the passage of time but, in reality, the Shapiros were the epitome of gracious hosts for about twenty more minutes before they started signaling it was time for him to leave. They weren't rude, but they did get more and more focused on each other – stealing glances into each other's eyes then glancing up the stairs – and less and less attentive to their guest. Orville, true to his nature, failed to pick up the hint.

"Orville, Lisa and I would like to go to bed now. You should go," Shel eventually volunteered, his voice betraying no sentiment except patience.

"'Bye," Orville said, and left. As he stood on the front stoop, he turned around and added cryptically, "And I'm not."

"Not what?" Shel asked.

"Unemployed. Mister Noble arranged for me to be put on administrative duty until replacements can be found."

"Lou Noble got you your job back?"

"Yes," Orville said, then quoted a line he had heard innumerable times in movies and on TV. "If you'd like me to put in a good word for you ..."

And, just like in the scripts, he declined to finish the sentence.

"Hey, if Lou wanted me, he'd have gone to bat for me too. Good luck, Orville," Shel said. "It's okay. Really, I was getting sick of all the bureaucratic mickey-mouse anyhow. It's better if I stay in with those other knuckleheads."

As he walked to his car, and around it, twice, and got in, Orville could hear Shel begin to explain the minutes of the meeting to Lisa, to be met with an impatient "Tell me all about it tomorrow." Then peals of laughter and delight emanated from an upstairs window where a light had just gone out.

Orville started up the car, studied every light on the dashboard, checked that the rear- and side-view mirrors remained perfectly adjusted, drove a block, pulled over, and pounded his fists over and over on the empty passenger seat, screaming and crying in inchoate rage.

POW!

Sunset had come and gone. Midnight had come and gone. Bella Brock was still herself.

She even allowed herself to believe her nightmare was over. Maybe she could work up the nerve to turn off the bedside lamp. This nice Nick Bayard was kind enough to give her a meal and a bed for the night. His wife worked at the hospital at the other end of the county and would take Bella in with her the next day. After a thorough checking out, she'd be able to call the departmental office in Madison, have someone wire her down some money and a bus ticket, then ...

The front door opened with a jingle of cowbells and the shuffling of a draft stopper along the foyer's hardwood floor. Bella could hear it all faintly through her shut bedroom door. That must be the Rhonda whom Nick had mentioned.

It was. There were pictures of Rhonda around the house, mostly from their wedding day and the carefree year or two after. The woman who trudged up the creaky steps after a hard, second-shift workday was a much plumper and slightly grayer version of that twentyish girl, but she had managed not to develop spots or care lines in her still captivating face.

That face would be the last thing Bella Brock would remember seeing for some time.

Nick, who had retired to his own room to watch a few minutes of Jimmy Kimmel, greeted his wife at the top of the stairs with a smooch loud enough to be audible through Bella's door. Seeing the light on in the guest bedroom, Nick rapped on the door and opened it a crack.

"Bella? Are you still up? I'd like you to meet Rhonda," Nick said tentatively.

"Sure, come on in," Bella replied, sitting up and modestly holding the bedspread up to her collarbone.

"We can all sit and chat in the kitchen after the kids go off to school," Nick advised. "Apparently both you ladies have had awful days."

"I really don't remember what happened," Bella corrected.

"Maybe you're the lucky one," said Rhonda, as she crossed over to the bed and offered Bella a hand to shake. Rhonda wouldn't have been able to explain why, but a sense of dread crested over her. "Cardiograph went on the fritz again today - right when the weenies from the state were there on an inspection. Couldn't have happened on a worse day."

"Sounds awful," Bella agreed, shaking Rhonda's hand.

"It was just a matter of time, I suppose," Rhonda said as she kept pumping an increasingly agitated Bella's hand. "The thing never worked right. Would you believe someone actually misplaced a thallium rod? To the patients, it's a one-time event and so it's nothing to worry about but for those of us who work there every day, we could all get cancer from it someday."

Someday would never come. Those seeking palliative care for cancer might consider Rhonda lucky to die so quickly, even if it were in such a gruesome fashion.

"Bella?" she asked, as her new acquaintance's grip grew suddenly coarse, and constricting, and hairy. "You okay, honey?"

But Bella wasn't there anymore. Rhonda was looking into the soulless eyes of a predator that might be considered superhuman if it were not so less-than-human. Rhonda's right arm came off at the shoulder with a snap that didn't seem loud enough. What had been Bella took a giant bite out of the upper arm, slurped the blood, and spat out the ample fatty tissue. An unaccounted-for rod of thallium-201 spilled out of Rhonda's coat pocket.

"*Nick!*"

But Nick had disappeared into their bedroom – to get his shotgun, he told himself, to justify leaving his mate and mother to his children. She kept screaming, sometimes his name, sometimes God's, sometimes just a pre-verbal shriek. Then it ended. Nick saw Rhonda's blood splatter on the far wall of the hallway outside the guest bedroom. He searched frantically in his closet for the 12-gauge, until he remembered taking it out to the garage for a cleaning he never got around to. From the top shelf, boxes of shells scattered uselessly on the floor.

It was then his turn to shriek.

The body, wakeful or not, is keenly aware of its end in pain and terror. The Bayard children were no better off than their parents just because they died in their sleep.

Soon the house was still. The bodies lay lifeless and half-chewed. The predator had shattered the glass backdoor and escaped.

The stillness was broken after only a minute by the ring of Nick's cell phone. That stopped and, ten seconds later, the landline began ringing incessantly.

BAM!

Mindy knew that Orville lived in the same complex she did, Willowbend. Half the people who worked at the mall did. Still, it was an unprecedented event when she and her childhood hero pulled into adjacent parking spots.

She didn't notice him until after she got out of her car, laughing easily with Kevin who was emerging from the passenger side. That's when she tripped over the curb, lost her balance, and stumbled into Orville's arms. She looked up at him and knew from the redness of his eyes he had been crying.

Neither spoke. Neither knew what to say.

"Hey, Orville, no hard feelings, huh?" Kevin said, oblivious to the moment.

Orville and Mindy shot him identical looks of disfavor.

"I mean, about forming the team," Kevin added. "We all have to make our own decisions. I respect yours. Hope we can still be buds."

Mindy fished out her keys, tossed them to Kevin, gave him the apartment number, and told him to let himself in. He reread the situation and left without a word.

"Orville, I want you to know that I really do like you," Mindy said, giving the speech she hadn't had to use since high school. "And I know that there's someone out there for you. But Kevin and I just kind of clicked, you know? You understand."

He didn't or, if he did, his face didn't register comprehension. It was completely dispassionate. His tears from earlier were dry.

"You're making a mistake," Orville said tonelessly, then went through his post-drive ritual before heading up to his own efficiency.

BOOM!

Eva and Lugh had already arrived at Mindy's Willowbend apartment. Eva could have just walked through the wall, of course, but it was much more thrilling to be carried by a god as he smashed his way through the patio door.

The neighbors would complain in the morning about the howling sounds from Lugh but, in his own experience, Eva was equally enthusiastic and expressive.

Decorum requires that the scene end here.

POW!

Kevin had, contrary to instructions, waited outside for Mindy, then escorted her through the front door. The spirit guide and the god were so involved in their own coupling that they didn't notice. Mindy had to look away from what she saw. Kevin, who couldn't see Eva, took a long, bemused look at what looked like an audition piece from *Oh! Calcutta!* acted out by bulky, crimson-maned, impressively manly figure.

After a quick, nervous snicker, though, Kevin's attention was entirely on Mindy. The world was reduced to her angular face. He gave in to the temptation to obsess over each spiral in her ear, over each wayward lock of chestnut hair splayed across her forehead.

She forced any thought of Orville from her mind and returned Kevin's inviting kiss. It was gentle – a closed-mouthed invitation to intimacy that barely brushed her own lips. As the kiss lingered, intensity mounted. Mindy soon realized that was entirely her doing; Kevin allowed her to set the pace, but eagerly matched her passion as she gave in to it.

Without breaking that kiss, Kevin scooped her up in his arms and carried her into the bedroom, kicking the door shut behind him, which slightly muffled the operatic noises from the couch. His nostrils flared at the blend of vanilla, almond, and cocoa butter which scented Mindy's room. They reminded him of some place, long ago, where he was carefree and loved without condition. He hoped it wasn't a memory. He hoped it was *déjà vu*.

Tenderly, Kevin sat her on the edge of the bed, ending the kiss with a cool, puckered exhalation that ran left-to-right across her lips. Mindy expected him to tear off her peasant blouse and obsess with her breasts but instead he removed her strappy shoes expertly, staring straight into her eyes all the while. The pumps had been constricting her feet for hours and she reveled in the relief. He caressed her arches, rubbed her heels, lapped at her toes for what seemed to be the perfect amount of time, before his hands and tongue were redirected slowly, slowly up past her ankles, calves, knees, and thighs. Her panties came off, saffron-colored to match her skirt, which stayed on. The ankle-length skirt obscured Kevin from Mindy's view. She could not anticipate what he might do next, only hoping that he would understand she was not physically ready yet.

She need not have been concerned. He was her captive. Kevin had no impulse at that moment to take his pleasure. Seeking nothing but to see her fulfilled, he caressed, kissed, tickled, nibbled all around her well-toned thighs and abdomen.

Relaxing into the first ecstatic stirrings, she leaned back on her elbows, welcoming whatever came next.

He loosened her waistband and tugged off her skirt with a flamboyant, *torero* motion. Naked from the waist down, she loosened a giggle that elided into a sigh.

Kevin glanced approvingly at Mindy's womanhood. He was impressed by his intimate partner's natural growth of hair, unmarred by shaving, piercing, or ink.

Growing hard, Kevin arrested his throbbing by rising to his feet. He stared sonnets into Mindy's widened pupils and she welcomed his admiring gaze as both pairs of eyes moistened.

He unbuttoned his pinstriped, button-down shirt and draped it on the back of Mindy's desk chair. As he turned completely around, Mindy ached for him with a yearning somewhere beyond admiration and just shy of worship. His knotted abs, powerful shoulders, summoned her primal lust. Her breath grew short and her teeth chattered as she felt the first, warm dampness between her flexing thighs.

Kevin sat on the edge of the bed. She quivered, anticipating how he might reach for her. Every inch of her flesh awaited his touch. But he just smiled and swung his legs toward her. Mindy rolled over, smiled back, a tease of cleavage spilling from her blouse, and untied his tan, calf-leather dress shoes. She playfully threw them over the other side of the bed. As she rolled his socks off, Kevin masterfully removed Mindy's blouse with his feet. But for the delicate task of taking off her blue, nylon-mesh bra, he preferred to press his own chest against hers, reach behind her back and deftly work his fingers.

Mindy's breasts, though not as massive as her alter ego's, had their own charms: perfectly proportioned to their owner's body type, upturned in that precisely ideal angle that isn't meant to last, and large, dark, deeply ridged nipples that stood out in stark relief against smooth, alabaster skin.

The two lovers leaned in to kiss. This time, it wasn't a tender summons. It was an urgent demand. Open lips and twining tongues were still not enough to contain their passion.

Tearing off her man's denim trousers, Mindy was surprised by Kevin's taste in underwear: none at all. That was only the beginning of her surprise. Erect, as it was and as it remained for a very long time, Kevin's ample manhood glistened as if it were fresh from Heaven's forge.

Awkwardly, Kevin reached down to the jeans lying on the floor - neither bending at the waist nor squatting from the knees quite worked by itself - and pulled a bright gold cube of wrapping foil from the front pocket.

"Do you want me to use a ..."

"Not yet," Mindy replied, tossing a pillow down on the floor where it instantly became a kneeling pad.

She was ready now. Kevin could smell it, so he resumed licking and caressing her upper thighs. She responded to something delicate about his hands as he guided her to spread. Mindy gasped immediately as his tongue entered her and found the spot as if in response to her own will. After that, she had no more will of her own, only pleasure building as flicks of Kevin's tongue became long laps from all directions.

Mindy came easily over and over at Kevin's ministrations, his hands reaching up to tug firmly on her nipples.

Consumed by more than pleasure, this man enraptured Mindy more than she ever bargained for. What started as bare tolerance had, over the course of only a couple days, turned into amused flirtation, physical attraction, sexual chemistry, obsessive lust and now, who knows? She was willing to admit it: she was falling in love with him. Falling in love!

In her own mind - not from anything *he* said or did - she had elevated him to be her lord and master. It was fantasy play, but effective. She imagined Kevin to be a figure of untold might and authority before whom she should kneel in obeisance. And here he was, deigning to gratify her so kindly, so thoroughly, so expertly. He was a nobleman of the peerage, a knight of the round table, a hero ...

Kevin's motive might not always be entirely pure, Mindy rationalized between rapturous waves, but he was a good man with an instinct to do the right thing. And if he was an unblemished hero, what use would that be? If he weren't a little bit of a rogue, a little bit of a mystery, would she have been attracted to him? Oh, so what if he turns out to be a scoundrel? He ... he ...

That was the point where the pleasure finally overtook her and her mind shut off completely. She had no way of knowing how long she lay there, spasmodically thrusting her hips and arching her back, screaming and spitting her own hair out of her mouth, ignoring the torture her dangly earrings and pearl choker offered every time she swung her head around. The pleasures from all the places where Kevin touched her swirled and merged and radiated through every nerve in her body.

Kevin sensed her breath becoming dangerously irregular and slowed gradually to a stop. He gave her a moment to catch her breath as they both noted the silence.

Mindy was enraptured as Kevin climbed into the bed and held her close by his side. Neither moved for long minutes until he finally asked, "Now would you like me to use ...?"

"I want you," she said between heavy breaths. "Nothing else."

He caressed her downy patch with one hand and with the other fumbled to turn on the bedside lamp. He wanted, needed the light on as he entered her. Her eyes bewitched him by the soft light of the bulb. Taking all the time they could, they took each other through roiling flames and shearing winds, like shooting stars colliding and combining in the firmament of night until spent, when he gathered her to him in blissful embrace. She collapsed in his arms for the little that remained of the cool, October night.

Bobby Botler had retired to the apartment he rented above a video store across the street from the mall. He slept for an hour before the need to urinate woke him. He watched a movie on fast-forward and forced himself back to sleep.

He woke again after another hour and tapped into a dozen chat rooms at once. That killed some time. Then he tossed and turned for another hour, after which he decided to get a jump on the day. He took from the back of his closet a garment bag containing something he never thought he'd put on again: the costume he wore before the TSA usurped the hero business. Rubberized red and black, with gold and silver piping. Over-the-top, sure, but it looked great in motion. And, as soon as the perma-tread boots were clamped in place, he dashed off to the mall, too fast for cameras to confirm. He sped unnoticed through a loading dock as the Au Bon Pain assistant manager greeted the first delivery of the day, then he zigzagged through the mall to the cavernous room he'd taken to calling the Blur Cave.

And there he sat, drank beers and toked off his bong for another four hours before anyone else got there.

BOOM!

Fifteen miles away, Seth Hill, owner of what was left of the Plaquet Box card store, snored peacefully in his king-sized bed in fashionable Kirkwood. He slept through the night without waking, as if he hadn't a care in the world.

162

INTERLUDE: 1985

S e llama la senora de Rivera?" the youthful white man in the all-weather coat asked. "Me llamo_Roger Chadwick y..."

"I am Esperanza Rivera," the woman behind the apartment door in the upper Manhattan housing project said. "I am learning English and I think it is now better than your Spanish. What is this about?"

Roger heard peals of laughter that could only come from a room full of grade school-aged children having fun together.

"I was a friend of Olivia Ortley."

Esperanza drew a quick breath at the name she hadn't heard in five years.

"This is not a good time, Mister Chadwick. Come back in an hour."

With that, she unceremoniously slammed the door in the face of the man who, until very recently, was renowned as Colonel America.

With an hour to kill, Roger wandered aimlessly, chasing his steaming breath around nearby Central Park. Crime had peaked and was now on the downtrend, but this far uptown it could still be dangerous for a lone pedestrian. Roger, even after having ceded his powers, was hardly going to be a mugging victim - but he had no protection against the random violence that plagued the neighborhood.

Alone with his thoughts in the snow-covered park, he remembered the brave if reckless woman whose tragic end changed so much for so many. Maybe that was the definition of a hero: not just someone who makes things better, but someone whose absence changes things for the worse. That was Looker.

Dirk Henderson took it hard, losing her. He apparently had feelings for Olivia that he didn't share with anyone else on the team. Dirk became withdrawn, inconsolable, reclusive, and eventually hostile. He kept bankrolling The Crusaders, even ponied up funds for some platform in orbital space that would someday serve as their headquarters. He even sold Carbodyne's promising but not-yet-profitable video game subsidiary to do that.

But Dirk suited up as the Carbon Avenger with decreasing frequency until he went into complete seclusion. Nobody had seen him either in the flesh or in costume for more than a year. He was too busy burying himself in his latest obsession: some alchemy he called "clean-coal technology."

The rest of the Crusader faces changed as well. Looker's successor was half woman, half puma. She was succeeded by a half woman, half bird. And on like that.

El Hombre never recovered from his injuries in the battle against Ta Mok and the Marielitos. He was replaced by a Japanese martial arts master. Black Man worked out a little better, but he left after only a couple years, replaced by a rapid succession of heroes of increasingly exotic ethnicities and national origins. The Japanese guy didn't work out either, and ceded his place to a Chinese man, and Indian woman, and eventually a Syrian man. At one point, the team had both the Arab and an Israeli. They didn't work together well and neither lasted. The only thing they could agree on was that they both hated the name, The Crusaders.

Lugh remained. Roger was sure Lugh would always remain.

The last major change was the man inside the Colonel America suit. Roger wasn't the first Colonel and he knew he wouldn't be the last. In fact, he barely lasted six years in the body armor; when the history of Project America was written, the chapter on Roger Chadwick would be the shortest in the book.

There was the World War II Colonel, the Korea Colonel, the Cold War Colonel. Roger considered himself the weak link: the post-Vietnam Colonel.

The country he symbolized was defeated, humiliated, financially ruined, and morally adrift. Roger's on-camera presence at the end of a battle was more likely to draw derision than awe. But with Dirk out of commission, the undependable string of rookies unqualified and Lugh, well, being Lugh, it fell to him to be spokesman. Roger was never comfortable in that role. His experience as an airborne officer rendered him a competent tactician and a courageous fighter, and that's all he ever wanted to be.

The costume needed more.

It needed someone with a little more brass, and that kid from the Corps of Engineers fit the bill. Sure, at first glance, he was just another pallid gearhead, but once he warmed up to you, he'd talk your ear off: his exploits, real or imagined, his opinions, his occasional zingers. This was a guy who loved to talk. There was a flamboyance about him, a zest for living out loud that four years of engineering school had repressed. He met all the other criteria: As far as Roger was concerned, 22-year-old Elias O'Neill was welcome to the job.

So Roger set up the transformation, had the organelles

removed from his bloodstream and inserted in Elias's, then faded into the obscurity he desired.

Obscurity, not penury. It wasn't long before the phone rang in the house he had bought for himself in Ottumwa, Iowa. An executive with MarCom, the video game company Dirk had spun off, called and said his company was working on "multi-POV shooter," whatever that was, and asked if Roger would be interested in working as a consultant. He mentioned a number. Roger liked the number a lot. He had consulted on two more video games since then, and was now as rich as he cared to be; any more money he made in this lifetime would strictly be an exercise in record keeping.

There were only two things that Roger wanted to do. One was to find the right woman, settle down and raise a family. Of greater urgency – considering he had barely aged in six years and still had plenty of time for family life – was to prepare the next generation of heroes.

A man of his means had any number of research sources at his disposal and was able to compile a list of children who had the potential to manifest powers. He wanted to focus his attention on a small number of kids who might be so gifted, and decided that the best option would be to attract siblings. There was one family, less than a three-hour car ride away, that looked promising. Those children were still very, very young, so there wasn't much training that could be done for several years. Meanwhile, there was another family in New York that not only had school-aged children, it was the sentimental favorite.

That was the family in which the adopted son was really Olivia Ortley's boy.

After an hour, Roger wandered back to the Riveras' apartment.

Esperanza let him in. There were specks of plaster and unwanted licorice-flavored candy underneath where a piñata recently hung. A sign on the wall read, *Feliz 8° cumpleanos*

Marisol.

The birthday girl, already recognizable as an athlete, was teasing her light-skinned, five-year-old brother. He'd throw a punch; she'd duck out of the way, maneuver behind him and kick him in the fanny.

He'd throw another punch. She'd evade and counterattack again.

The boy never tired of the game. He just laughed.

"Let's sit in the kitchen, Mister Chadwick," Esperanza said. "Take off your coat. They will go like that all afternoon."

Esperanza offered a cup of coffee, which Roger gratefully accepted.

"It's a pleasure meeting you Señora Rivera," he began. "I am, of course, honored to speak with the widow of Major Marcos Rivera. Freedom-lovers everywhere are grateful for his work with MILPAS during ..."

"My husband was a great man," Esperanza interrupted staring daggers at Roger. "The man was not a great husband. When he was killed, he left his wife and daughter with nothing, and lucky to find a way out of the slaughter in Nicaragua. I am no longer *la señora de Rivera*. I'm just Esperanza. So, what can I do for you?"

Roger made his pitch: he had enough money to take care of her and her family for the rest of their lives. He knew the origins of the boy she introduced as Marcos Segundo and he wanted him to have his identity back – privately, not publicly, for his own protection – in tribute to the great woman who was his mother. He intended no disrespect to Esperanza, whom he hoped would agree to continue raising him. Orville was special because he was genetically predisposed to manifesting a power, but María de la Soledad was also special in her own way. She had her Contra father's fighting spirit – and his rare blood type.

"What if I say no?"

167

"There are other candidates," Roger informed her, "but I hope you'll say yes."

She did.

They moved out of Spanish Harlem that day. After a night in the O'Hare Hilton, they settled into Roger's new Iowa home - quite a trade-up from the ranch house - and the two children began training for their destinies.

It took a year and a half, but Roger and Esperanza discovered that they had much in common. They were both dedicated to the cause of freedom. They had each paid too high a price for it. They both loved Marisol and Orville dearly. They were married.

And they lived happily ever after.

{POW!}

Not everyone did, though. One family's gain was another's loss. Elsewhere on the Great Plains, a woman was left alone to raise two children - "Irish twins" was the term for siblings born less than a year apart. Their father, an amphetamine-addicted alcoholic with a nasty temper, died in the seven-car pile-up he caused a month before the birth of his baby girl. No great loss, the mother conceded, considering he had never so much as changed the 11-month-old boy's diaper.

She had no way of knowing how close she had come to having a millionaire/former superhero sweep her off her feet and take in her two children.

Instead, she married the first guy who would have her. And he came with a condition: no kids. He wanted her to put her children up for adoption. She said no. The negotiations began, and she had to make a modified Sophie's Choice: she could keep one but she had to put the other in an orphanage. Otherwise, this new husband had convinced her, her life would degenerate into poverty, crime, and who-knows-what. He would save one child from that. God would have to protect the other one.

MAGNIFICENCE

Good morning," Kevin said as soon as Mindy opened her eyes.

"Good morning," she beamed back. "How long have you been awake?"

He glanced at the clock.

"I've been lying here watching you sleep for twenty-two minutes."

"You're sweet."

They kissed tenderly.

"Any regrets?" Kevin asked.

"What? No! What makes you ask that, silly?"

"No reason," he said and let a moment go by. "Well, of course there's a reason. I feel like I can be honest with you ..."

Mindy noted the hesitation in his voice. "Kevin, honey, you can tell me anything," she said. "Even after so short a time, I feel like I've known you forever."

"Well, I'm cursed by the gods," Kevin said after some searching for the most straightforward words. "Jehovah, Allah, and Zeus were having an argument about who was the most powerful. They picked a mortal at random - lucky me - and asked me to decide."

"What did you answer?"

"I told them I didn't believe in any of them," Kevin explained. "I thought they were friends of my college roommate and I was being punked."

"Guess that didn't go well."

"As bad as could possibly be. It amused them to give me an ability so subtle it can't be detected in this world, even though I'm the ultimate hero on the astral plane."

"That doesn't sound so bad."

"That's not the curse," Kevin explained. "The curse is that's where all my power would be and that absolutely nothing I do on Earth would ever amount to anything good. So I asked ..."

"I know what you asked," Mindy said, rolling over so she lay directly on top of him. She stared straight into his eyes and spoke with the earnest tone of complete sincerity. "And I'm telling you, you did nothing but good last night."

Torn between the prudence of keeping her own counsel and the naïve impulse to share everything with her lover, naïveté won out. "That was the best thing that ever happened to me," she continued. "You fulfilled me in ways I hadn't even known about. I'm still dazzled by you."

Kevin cast his eyes down in humility, then looked back at her with his devilish smile. "I don't know how, Mindy, but you broke a curse."

"If anything broke the curse, it wasn't me," Mindy said, gathering her courage. "It was love."

The word hung there for a moment.

"I love you, Mindy."

"I love you, Kevin."

170

They kissed. They embraced. They joined together in a morning encore.

When they were once again spent, Mindy spoke a little of her own origins.

"Funny you should say the gods forced you to choose between them. The goddesses did the same to me."

"What did you do?"

"Punted, same as you. When Aphrodite, Lakshmi, Ishtar, and Tamora ask you to judge a beauty contest, there's no graceful way out."

"So you end up with the one superpower that no women's studies major from Smith would ever be caught dead with."

"Exactly," Mindy said. "But to their credit, they did send Mrs. Peron to show me how to use this power for good – in at least some proto-feminist way."

"That's important to you?"

"Yes, it is."

"Then it's important to me, my love."

They embraced again.

"Isn't it funny how much we have in common?" Mindy asked.

"Yeah," Kevin agreed. "Except I'm trying to figure out where you're from. That's not a Midwestern accent."

"I grew up in Pennsylvania, where my stepdad got a job when I was around five years old. And then, as you know, I went to school in Massachusetts."

"Well, Mister Maguire's little girl sure grew up right."

"No thanks to stepdaddy, that's for sure – or to my biodad, who I never met," Mindy said. "Both were a couple of losers. ' Maguire' was actually my mom's name. I took that when I turned eighteen. Anyway,

171

where are you from, lover?"

"Me? I'm from around here. Upriver a little. My parents were dirtbags too, I suppose. The Reids gave me up when I was a year old. I grew up in an orphanage in East St. Lou until I was ten, when the Kileys adopted me."

"The Reids? That's funny, my stepdad's last name was Charles, but biodad was also a Reid. What are ... the ... odds ...?"

"John B. Reid?"

"From Palmyra?"

"Ewww!"

"Ewww!"

They dove out of opposite sides of the bed - Kevin wisely picked the side closer to the door - and they had a brief tug of war with the linens. Kevin ended up with the sheet and Mindy with the quilt. They covered themselves as best they could.

"We can't ever do this again!" Kevin screamed. "Ewww!"

"We can't ever even talk about it!" Mindy screamed. "Ewww!"

"But this is personal - we still have to function as professionals! Ewww!"

"I'll do my best! Now go! Ewww!"

Kevin slipped on his shoes, left his socks, and held his shirt and pants in front of him like a fig leaf. "One question," he posited.

"What?" she replied with mounting impatience.

"I'm not technically related to Georgiana ..."

"Get the fuck out of my place! Ewww!"

Fighting the revulsion of touching him again, Mindy ran around the bed and physically shoved Kevin out the bedroom door.

He stumbled into the living room with a naked Lugh

lying there, nestled in bliss with thin air.

"... Do thy will then; then subject and degree / And fruit of love, Love, I submit to thee. / Spare me till then; I'll bear it, though she be / One that love me," he whispered into a throw pillow before acknowledging Kevin's presence. "Needst thou a lift, young Kiley?"

And soon the two were half-dressed and airborne, on their way to the Blur Cave, with a brief stop at Kevin's.

Mindy sheepishly shuffled out of the bedroom, still shuddering in the quilt.

All Eva had to say was, "Told you."

Mindy took a bath. And then she took a shower. And then she abraded every inch of herself with pumice and took another bath.

After getting dressed, she stepped out of her apartment and hurried to her car. Along the way, she ran into Orville picking his copy of the Post-Dispatch off his front stoop. It registered with her that he wore his bleached and pressed TSA uniform.

Mindy didn't know what, if anything, Orville knew about her background, Kevin's, or what happened that night. She was just grateful that he didn't repeat Eva's comment.

INTERLUDE: 1985

There are a few things that nice Jewish boys from nice Jewish neighborhoods don't do.

One is shave their heads. It's not unheard of and there's no doctrine against it, but it's evocative of something that fascists do, so it's not a style sported around the JCC's squash courts.

Two is get tattoos. The rabbis actually do frown on that. They believe that there's something holy inherent in circumcision, so any other marring of the flesh cheapens that covenant with God. This teaching led to the persistent myth that anyone with a tattoo can't be buried in a Jewish cemetery, so the children of Abraham tend not to get ink.

Three is join the U.S. Marines.

So it was with some drama that Sheldon Shapiro, recently graduated from college and still under his parent's roof in St. Louis's University Park section, came staggering home late one night with gin – and no lemon – on his breath, bald as an eagle, a globe-and-anchor expertly applied to his right deltoid.

MEANWHILE, BACK IN THE BLUR CAVE

They eyed each other in their full, pre-TSA regalia.

Count Karma sported a loose-fitting, midnight-blue tunic with a broad lavender sash, a hood sculpting shadows across his face, every inch the man of mystery.

The Blur carried himself with unaccustomed dash and bearing in his yellow-and-red nylon tracksuit, the two inches of tread on his matching high-tops providing him with the illusion of height.

Even so, he fell well below the height of the Indomitable Lugh whose shoulders, bare and no longer understated by the white TSA shirt, were revealed to be as broad as a bookcase. They also began at the altitude where the Blur's head ended. Lugh's long, wine-colored mane protruded from under a conical helmet, providing still more elevation. He no longer carried his adze. Instead, a spear slung across his back and a triangular shield rested on his massive left forearm.

The spear was speaking, muttering really, in some long-abandoned Gaelic dialect. The voice didn't come from a mouth, but rather from the way it vibrated in its holster, which emitted a pleasant fragrance, like a black tea accented with sweet nuts. Except for Lugh, no one understood what the spear's deep and raspy voice was saying, but it sounded impatient, and it sounded angry.

Lugh himself was the farthest thing from angry. As the Blur zipped around, simultaneously playing a Colonel America-themed shooter game on the Xbox, surfing the Web and drinking a six-pack, and as Count Karma fidgeted nervously at the arrival of awkward company, Lugh was a tower of serene composure.

And when the ladies walked in, the three men were all smiles. Eva was in a perfectly tailored, velvety, red jacket-and-skirt number – a tropical floral pattern, of course – and a fresh orchid in her blond-streaked hair, tied back in a tight bun. Whatever her role in any battle to come, she was going to take it on in suggestively-seamed black stockings and strappy four-inch heels. Knowing that nobody but Lugh could see her, she unbuttoned her jacket, leaned forward enough to spill out of her dainty camisole, gave a little shimmy, and covered back up, ending the show with a contorted pucker of her rose-red lips.

If mortals could have seen her, Eva would have dramatically upstaged Mindy Maguire, still in her non-super persona. At Hawk's Tavern the night before, Mindy had demonstrated that she did indeed have a casual wardrobe, but this morning she was back to her frumpy self in a Macy's ready-to-wear salmon pantsuit. It wasn't that horrible an outfit. Others could have pulled it off; on a better day, Mindy could have. A smile, a little blush, chin up, shoulders back, and the wearer would be dressed to impress. But her expression and posture didn't suggest that she had just entered the secret hideout of a newly formed underground superhero team of which she was an integral member. Rather, her shuffling gait, slack jaw, knitted brow and unfocused gaze suggested she had just entered the day room of a long-term psychiatric ward.

As the rest of the team mingled, Mindy kept very much to herself – studiously averting her vacant stare from Count Karma's direction. Count Karma did his best not to draw attention to himself, tapping away on a cell phone, pretending to be texting when all he was doing was refreshing ESPN over and over. Lugh gallantly tried to include Mindy in the conversation he was attempting to have with Eva, but the disembodied essence of the Spiritual Leader of the Argentine Nation shooed him away. They needed some girl-talk time, she said, and promised-without-words that it would be worth his while later if he gave them some space right now. So Lugh threw back some beers with the Blur, making a game attempt at keeping up.

"Attend!" he ordered Count Karma, handing him a can of brew with a distinctive blue ribbon on the label. "The best thing for what pains thee."

"Pabst?" Count Karma said, processing slowly. "You drink this stuff?"

"I was not e'er a god," Lugh said, as if that explained his fondness for hoppy, unrefined, mass-market lager from a can. "Drink, lad."

And he did, and he was having his second when there came a retching sound from a far corner of the hideaway. All heads turned. Even before their eyes caught sight of her, the men in the room reacted to the charisma of – the knowledge of the presence of – Supermodel.

Or, as she preferred, Georgiana. She was dressed in an outdoorsy outfit this time: soft, brown-leather jacket over a spaghetti-string shirt, hip-hugging britches and riding boots. Her golden mane gone, a no-muss bob of dark, chestnut hair stayed well away from her eyes, which were a deep, chocolate brown. The bone structure was the same, though: the perfect diamond. A creamy mocha complexion now stretched across her face.

And there was something else that was distinct from her earlier incarnations. Georgiana was a healthy, well-proportioned, transcendently beautiful girl next door. A proud representative of Size Tens everywhere.

"Hello, Lugh," she said with casual cool, to the god whose eyes were darting between her and Eva. Then she swung her eyes toward Count Karma.

"Kevin," she said with an offhand nod, as if she'd buried whatever happened the night before in the past, as deeply as an Egyptian sarcophagus. Just for good measure, she missed not a beat and turned to the Blur.

"Bobby."

The men were standing around gripping their beers a little too tightly when the final member of the team arrived.

Shel Shapiro's colorfully costumed teammates were stunned by what he wore: tan windbreaker. Polo shirt. Dockers.

"What?" he asked, in reaction to the scrutiny.

After a moment, the Blur spoke.

"To tell you the God's-honest truth, Shel, I always thought this get-up was ridiculous. I wore it 'cuz all the other heroes wore, well ..." and he gestured around the room. "When the TSA came in and did away with all that, I was relieved. But now that we're not with guvmint no more, I figured ... and I guess everyone else did ..."

"I was too late to the party," Count Karma said. "I spent every dime I had on this outfit, figuring I'd make The Crusaders and get a chance to put it on every day. I've never worn this in public before."

Shel walked up to Count Karma and threw a heavy arm over him. Kevin Kiley's alter ego had to summon all his will not to let his knees buckle.

"It's okay, kid," Shel said. "We're still not in public."

"But what about you?" Count Karma asked. "Why aren't you in costume? What did they call you? 'The Clam'?"

Lugh, who knew the story, laughed heartily.

"Don't have a costume," Shel said. "Can't wear the TSA white-shirt-and-clip-on any more. Before that, anytime I fought evil I was wearing the uniform of the United States Marine Corps. That was superhero costume enough, and it doesn't fit any more."

"So you're going to fight in ... Dockers?" Count Karma asked.

"No," Shel explained. "*You're* going to fight. I'm going to *lead*. In Dockers."

"Well, there's not a lot of leading to do at the moment," Count Karma said, falling into a beanbag chair and picking up a PlayStation controller. "I don't think anyone knows we exist yet. Until we get the word out that there's a team of heroes for hire, we'll never—"

"Money!" The Blur announced. He moved so fast between the computer on one milk crate and the printer on another, he appeared to be in both places at once. "We got our first customer."

"Leave it to the World's Swiftest Man," Shel said, in rebuttal to Count Karma.

"Leave it to Craig's List," the Blur corrected, as he picked up a sheet of paper from the printer tray. "Anyone ever been to a place called Plainville, Illinois? That's what it says here. I'm not making it up."

BAM!

The notice had been posted to St. Louis Craig's List just in time. Lee Ann Bayard wondered what kind of heroes would be up at four in the morning.

Somewhere past Springfield she had a premonition that things weren't right back in Plainville, took out her Nokia smartphone and, despite it being nearly one in the morn-

179

ing, called Nick's cell. When he didn't pick up, she called their house phone, which rang until it went to voicemail. It didn't mean anything, Lee Ann told herself. It's late. The kids are asleep. Maybe they're *busy*. So she waited another five minutes and called again. Voicemail.

She U-turned right in the middle of I-55, driving south and honking wildly in the northbound lanes until she found a point where she could cross the median. Then, she lead-footed it all the way back to Plainville. On the way, she called 9-1-1, something she'd wanted to do the moment she first saw that Bella person, but which somehow seemed rude. The Adams County sheriff's office said they'd send a patrol car, but she should relax. Maybe the nice couple just needed another five minutes.

Lee Ann kept calling, but that accomplished nothing except to increase her anxiety level and drain her phone's battery. When she was down to one bar of power, she gave up.

Lee Ann left the diesel engine running as she pulled in front of her extended family's home. She bounded up the front path to the stoop and, when she reached the edge of the front light's illumination, she saw the blood trail running along the Victorian's wraparound porch. Lee Ann was close enough kin and a frequent enough visitor that she never bothered to knock on the door – she'd just walk around back and let herself in from the sliding glass doors to the deck.

But that night, there was no door to slide – just shards of clear glass scattered on the porch. She crossed the threshold into the family room which, in the dim, indirect light, she could tell wasn't similarly littered with glass slivers. Whoever left that blood trail started on the inside of the house and headed out.

So, despite the overturned chairs and end tables, that made the Bayard house the safest place in town, Lee Ann reckoned. What remained was to find the safest room in the safest place, but that would have to keep. She had to check on Nick and Rhonda and the children.

Inching upstairs, careful not to step on those risers known to creak, she immediately saw Rhonda's dismembered remains scattered through the hall.

Tougher in the situation than she thought she'd be, Lee Ann not only kept from screaming or puking but even from drawing a sharp breath. By the ten-watt glow of a night-light, she studied her sister-in-law's remains. Something with great strength had torn Rhonda apart. Something with a mess of needle-sharp teeth had eaten what it killed. From the blood spatter up and down the hall, up and down the walls, even on the ceiling, anyone could tell this was a feeding frenzy. Lee Ann hunted a little. Everyone she knew did. So she knew from the lack of necrotic odor and swarming insects that this was a fresh kill.

Where was Nick?

There would only be one reason to leave his wife to such a fate: he must have been in one of the kids' rooms, protecting their young.

But as she skulked silently from room to room, Lee Ann saw that fifteen-year-old Nicky had met a similar fate and, of all the footprints left in the pooled blood in his room, none were human. They might be those of some kind of rodent if they weren't so big.

The twins, Veronica and Annalee, were apparently too small and fatty for the predator's tastes. It did seem to have drained as much fluid as it could out of those corpses. Again, no sign of a human footstep.

Pushing on to the master bedroom, she solved the mystery of what happened to Nick. Like his wife of two decades and his namesake son, he had also been killed for the meat of his muscles and organs, his blood shed on all surfaces. Nick's body core came to rest atop the ceiling fan, still turning, slowly, groaning with strain as Nick hung up there facedown, almost like a primitive trophy, his viscera wrapped randomly around the fan blades.

Still, Lee Ann fought back hysterics, suppressed the urge to vomit, and turned slowly to head back through the hall, down the stairs, to the most secure place she could think of to wait out this episode. But she slipped on a shotgun shell, tried to regain her balance, lost traction in a blood slick, and fell down. If she had simply dropped with a dull thud onto her fleshy hindquarters, that would have been bad enough. But she tried to catch herself, twisted around, and ended up going down hard on her kneecap. The sound of bone shattering on the floor echoed in the prairie night. So did the scream of pain she couldn't rein in.

When that echo cleared, she realized that the town was not as still as she first assumed. Focused as she was on finding her relatives, she must have tuned out everything else and just gone with the given that a small town in the wee hours of a weekday morning was going to be as calm as a pothole puddle. But now her senses were heightened and, past the rumbling of her truck engine, there were tires screeching, boots clicking on asphalt, shrieks, and contradictory orders shouted, "Get inside!" "Get out!"

Lee Ann's internal voice was also giving her mutually exclusive direction, "Get up!" "Stay down!" She went with the former. Less concerned with noise now, she hopped on her good leg down the hall, slipping once in a pool of blood, banging the crushed knee, and whiting out from the ratcheted-up pain. After a full minute, the agony subsided enough for her to continue on her way. She took no joy in sliding down the banister for the first time in thirty years - it was simply the only way she was going to make it down the stairs.

From there she hopped on one foot to the closet where she knew they kept the folding chairs, and she commandeered one as a makeshift crutch. Lee Ann hobbled over to the basement door – the very, very heavy basement door, technically the storm cellar door. This was where the family went to ride out tornadoes. This was where she was going to ride this out.

But she hesitated. Sure, she could go underground now, but then what? In her state, she wasn't sure she could keep her balance on the steps while she bolted the door behind her. And whether or not that was the case, she felt a moral obligation to see if there was anyone else she could help. Arguing against that, though, was that she'd be putting herself in far greater peril if she got close enough to any door or window for the purpose of attracting attention.

The dilemma solved itself.

In much the same way she and Nick and their siblings and their neighboring friends would do, a column of people suddenly diverted through the back yard as if it were a shortcut to somewhere.

"Hey! In here! We're going to the cellar!"

There was a cop in front – the county patrolman who drew the unlucky assignment after she called 9-1-1. He waved everyone into the Bayard house with one hand and with the other ... Lee Ann suddenly realized he didn't have the other. Something had sheared it off.

A dozen people of all ages and states of dress piled in. The policeman never made it. A hollowed out husk of his severed arm, though, skidded across the floor, tossed by an as-yet unseen limb.

Then it appeared. It moved too fast for Lee Ann to get a good look, but it was some kind of fur-bearing animal, a patchwork of neutral colors, whose teeth and claws glinted in the light from the bathroom window of the house over the fence. Its pointed face immediately began to burrow into the officer's abdomen.

While whatever-it-was feasted on its prey, a teenage girl

and a fifty-ish man insistently forced Lee Ann to drop her makeshift crutch, then carried her down the basement stairs. An old woman slammed the tempered steel door shut just as the predator pounced, the race decided by the barest moment. The people in the basement could all hear the creature carom off the outside of the door, howling in an alarming voice none had ever heard before, conveying both pain and boundless disappointment.

They settled in. Like any well-stocked storm cellar, there was ample food and beverages, a first-aid kit, lights and a radio that could run off either grid power or a backup generator, and a supply of books and board games. No firearms, though.

Nobody had any life-threatening injuries; Lee Ann was the most banged up. There was no doctor among them, nor nurse, nor EMT, nor lifeguard - not even a Boy Scout who might have a first aid merit badge. But most people can puzzle out how and why to make a splint, and four extra-strength Tylenols took the edge off her suffering.

While waiting for them to take effect, she looked around the room. Having grown up in Plainville for a portion of her childhood, she knew half the people there. Others were either strangers or long-forgotten acquaintances. For the next few hours, though, they'd all be closer than septuplets.

"Does anyone know what that thing is?" Lee Ann asked, trying to make conversation to take her mind off her knee.

"Looks like some kind of mutant rat," someone offered.

"Or more like a weasel or ferret."

"Kinda looks like a skunk."

"Yeah, but it don't stink."

"Are there any other police around?" Lee Ann asked.

"They're on their way, baby," the grandmotherly woman said. Over the next few hours, Lee Ann would come to realize she called everybody "baby."

"Doug – the cop – was able to radio the situation in."

"The police can't really do anything, though. They're not equipped to deal with this."

"It's got to be a super. Which means all they can do is cordon off the town and call in the feds."

"Then the National Guard secures a perimeter inside the perimeter, TSA supers secure a perimeter inside that. Then they call in The Crusaders."

"How long's that going to take? When should we be able to leave?" Lee Ann asked. Nobody had an immediate answer.

"Let's turn on the radio, baby."

They found it already tuned to the emergency broadcasting frequency at the top of the AM dial. A looped message advised Plainville residents to stay in their basements until the unspecified emergency ended.

They turned off the radio after about ten minutes, or around 2 a.m., which allowed them to hear some snarling and hissing at the top of the stairs. Whatever-it-was was still there. Those who could, slept. Overstressed and loaded with acetaminophen, Lee Ann fell into that camp.

She woke up to, not silence, but an absence of snarling and hissing. Some of her fellow survivors were snoring or talking quietly among themselves or stirring spoons in cups. Straining her ears, she could hear the low rumble of her truck, which had to have been running on fumes by that point. And if she really filtered out everything else, she could make out the hopeful cheer of birdsong.

"We're safe," Lee Ann announced in a sudden moment of perfect clarity, bounding with an intuitive grasp of the situation.

"Bullshit," said a more reasoned voice, that of the fifty-ish man. "We open that door, that thing's gonna eat us."

"No, it's not going to get us now."

185

"Baby, I believe you, but not a hundred percent. Even if there's a one percent chance you're wrong, then that's too high a risk to take with all our lives. How can you be so certain it's gone?"

"It's not gone," Lee Ann said. "It's asleep."

"Henh?" asked the teenage girl as only a teenage girl can ask.

"What did we all say it looked like?" Lee Ann asked. "A rat? Or a weasel or a skunk? What do they have in common?"

Greeted with pop-quiz silence, she answered her own question. "They sleep during the day."

It took a moment, but there were nods of agreement.

"We need a volunteer to go topside, and two more to secure the door. The rest of us build a fort out of the appliances and shelving and hide in there."

Nobody jumped to play hero.

"I'd go up myself if I didn't have a broken leg."

Still no takers.

"Fine," she relented and popped four more Tylenols. "Wusses."

As she hopped up the stairs, Lee Ann was able to recruit only the grandmother to get the door. She secretly hoped the others would die, even if that meant the thing would have to go through her first.

After a deep breath, she squeezed through the door, which the grandmother wasn't going to open a millimeter wider than she had to. It clunked heavily behind her.

Using the folding chair as a crutch again, she shambled around the family room, dining room, and kitchen, checking in every closet and cabinet, peering under and over every piece of furniture. No predator.

She dreaded going back upstairs. The adrenaline had worn off, and she didn't know how she'd react to seeing all those bodies of people with whom she'd shared so much of her life, people she loved. She did know that the smell was wafting down, and the flies were buzzing.

Lee Ann dispensed with the folding chair as soon as she got to the steps, which she ascended in a sitting position, her splinted leg stiff, the other pushing. Once she got to the landing, she continued in a modified crabwalk down the hall, pieces of Rhonda adhering to her clothes and skin. Going no farther than Nicky's room, she regained her one good leg and hopped over to the boy's computer.

Lee Ann was of a certain political persuasion common in the rural Midwest: a strong libertarian sensibility with the accompanying distrust of government authority. She simply didn't trust Washington to handle this.

And, whether or not her views were applicable more broadly, she was unequivocally right in this case.

She needed private-sector heroics. Unfortunately, it had been a decade since such services were widely available. Where could she find one? Private heroes wouldn't be in the phone book and, now she thought about it, Lee Ann couldn't remember the last time she'd consulted a phone book. So she booted up Nicky's computer (she got his password on the first guess: b00bies) and did a Google search. No luck. Same with eBay. With a shrug, she tried Craig's List. And there was the listing, not three hours old, under Services:

HEROES AVAILABLE: If you need rescuing in the St. Louis area, call us first. Team of former Crusader/former TSA heroes with diversity of abilities. Reasonable rates, no official bureaucracy, no questions asked.

Reply to serv-f4rsbj-2129815189@craigslist.org and we'll be their.

BOOM!

"You know, 'diverse abilities' reads better than 'diversity of abilities,' and 'their' should be spelled T-H-E-R-E in this case," said the Master of Arts.

"Who cares? We got a customer," Shel replied, scan-

187

ning the paper the Blur had just handed him. "Some kind of giant carnivore, possibly nocturnal. Killed at least a couple dozen people in a town of just a couple hundred. Everyone else has either run away or they're hiding in storm cellars. Cops and the Guard have sealed off the town but are waiting for a TSA team and The Crusaders to step in."

"They're screwed then," the Blur pointed out. "Crusaders still haven't replaced Christ or Pantagruel, and I know those TSA pukes based at Lambert – they're the '64 Phillies of superheroes."

"'64 Phillies?" Count Karma asked.

"Come on! Even I get that reference," Georgiana said. "They're sometimes mentioned in the same breath as the '67 Arabs."

"Oh," Count Karma said. "Hey, you're talking to me again?"

"And just talking."

"I don't want to know the details—" Shel began.

"That's right!" Georgiana and Count Karma said in unison.

"—but we have a town to save."

"Lugh and Georgiana can fly, and I can take one with me in my car," the Blur said. "We'll have to take a second—"

"We travel as a team," Shel said. "Let me show you why I was late."

Shel left unobtrusively through the still-functional loading dock gate, pulled an old, black GMC conversion van with a jagged, red racing stripe out of an adjacent handicapped space, and backed it up. The team piled in.

POW!

It didn't take Maman Brigitte long to locate Ray in the concierge lounge of the Memphis, Tennessee, Marriott.

"Do you still work for us?" she asked from her K Street

office.

"As a henchman? No," he replied into the lounge's house phone, as he watched the closed captioning crawl along the bottom of the rerun of the previous night's *ESPN SportsCenter.*

"As a villain."

"Yes."

"Good. There's something going on in some pisswater called Plainville, Illinois. ... No, I'm not making that up. They just called out the Guard in response to some kind of monster that's on a massive killing spree. Eats its victims. We need to know if it's truly evil, in which case we want to sign it up, or if it's just chaotic, in which case we want it dead as much as the good guys do. You up for making that contact, then making that call?"

"Hundred percent," Ray replied. "Would I be going up against any heroes? I might need backup."

"Equity and I will show up as soon as we can, but you'll be there hours ahead of us. As for heroes, I can't imagine who. Crusaders are down to just the Carbon Avenger and Midge, and they're all the way up in their satellite. The new Colonel America is still getting outfitted. And the TSA out there is underpowered – and also probably understaffed. Those mall heroes we tangled with over the past couple days were all fired."

"How do you know all this stuff?"

"Buh-bye."

BAM!

General Giacoia, head of the secret operation in the nondescript building at Redstone Arsenal, was the only one who could give Colonel America orders. And she had one.

"Rivera, you check out medically and we're ready to put you in the field," the general said as the new Colonel stood at attention in front of her desk. "Would you like a shakeout before we send you on to The Crusaders?"

"Yes, ma'am!"

"There's been an anomaly in Plainville, Illinois, and no, I'm not making that up."

"You want me to take care of it, ma'am?" Marisol asked, brimming with confidence born of something besides experience or exceptional intelligence.

"Negative," the general replied. "Someone else is going to take care of it. I want you to take care of the guy who's going to take care of it."

THINGS GO BAD

lmost one-third of the Chesterfield Mall had been damaged as a result of the battle that started in the Plaquet Box the day before. That gave Porter Peale, formerly the Crusader known as Pantagruel, that much less area to patrol - which was a good thing considering how shorthanded he was.

Actually, he was no-handed. Hired at the supervisor level, he had nobody to supervise except for one guy, who was only permitted to work at a desk. So the supposed security guard was back at the office and the supposed supervisor was on patrol.

Macy's checked out largely intact, but entry from the mall was prohibited. The rest of that concourse, upstairs and down, was little more than rubble: jagged metal born of security gates and clothing racks, apparel and housewares torn and dented beyond any hope of salvage, and reams of paper scattered like the confetti thrown at a parade celebrating the final victory over consumerism. It saddened Porter to look at the wreckage; his mind kept going to what he could've done to minimize it if he and Midge hadn't picked that moment to have the last and worst of their marriage-in-its-death-throes fights.

And he didn't want to think about that at all.

Instead, he focused on the one small, green shoot of growth amid the ruins. At the far end of the first level, next to the Gaylen Ross anchor store, Porter watched as a team of moving men helped a new merchant set up shop. Three burly men struggled with a mash-up of a school cafeteria freezer and a law office filing cabinet.

"Excuse me," the merchant, a middle-aged woman in a well-tailored black suit, called out to Porter, her placid face calming to the point of chilling. "Would you lend us a hand?"

There was no reference to Porter's size – he was still at Lugh's height and feeling claustrophobic about it – but he understood that the woman could only be talking to him and only for that reason.

"Sorry," Porter replied. "Union rules."

"These guys are union too," she said, indicating the men who had put down the filing freezer to take a break, making a conscious effort to be exhausted and sweaty.

"There's a principle at stake," Porter said. Then thought about it. She was kind of cute. He was kind of single. It would only take a minute. The men really did need the help. "But I'm hazy on what that is. Which is the heavy end?"

The movers backed away from the end with the compressor and, in no time, the icing cabinet was in place at the very back of the store.

Well, not exactly a store. Scattered around, setting on gurneys, awaiting shelving and inventory, were face shields, latex gloves, cake makeup, metal syringes with finger holes, all kinds of fluids in all kinds of bottles and wooden crates big enough to fit just about any human being in – including his current six-and-a-half-foot frame. It had never occurred to Porter before: a coffin – the last box you'll ever need – comes itself in a box.

He watched another group of workmen raising an understated sign – two names with an ampersand between them in

192

elegant script - over the storefront.

"So, are you Savini or Nicotero?" Porter asked the woman.

"I'm Forrest," she replied. "I just work here."

"Never heard of a funeral home in a mall before."

"No, that goes in the office!" she said to one of the moving men who was about to put a filing cabinet for actual paper down in the front room, then turned back to Porter. "Does everything here have to be about sneakers, jeans, and cell phones?"

"Um, no."

"Just put all the folding chairs in the viewing room for now! You got banks here, right? And an optometrist and a dentist?"

"I suppose."

"None of that sounds like retail therapy. District manager wanted to try this and got HQ to go along as a pilot program, so we'll see. Meantime we'll pay our rent on time - at a premium because of the electrical upgrade we needed - and I promise you we'll be very quiet neighbors. Stop by sometime when you're ... Are you going senile? That's an urn - zip your fly back up!"

Porter's cell phone rang, and he faced a moment of inner conflict. He was single again, and here was a woman to whom he was attracted and who - though clearly distracted with her own very busy day - wasn't giving him any sign of the cold shoulder. On the other hand, he had always been one of those people who couldn't let a phone ring. So he looked down at the caller ID. If the picture of somebody important came up, he'd answer. If not, he'd go back to chatting up the girl.

The ID showed a portrait in black-and-white of a man with dark, slicked-back hair and a cigarette perched on his lower lip. The sullen, smooth-shaven face framed dark eyes that had seen too much and sat above a broad tie with a skinny knot. It was his new boss: Just like this Forrest lady, he too had a district manager to report to. It was an important call. A quick glance at the lady's left hand - no ring. See you later, *Miss* Forrest.

"Pant ... Peale," he said to his boss.

"Pantpeel to you to, you big lug," said a raw voice etched onto a carrier wave of cheap whiskey and unfiltered Camels.

"What can I do for you, Lou?"

"Stop glomming dames and get your keester back to work," Lou the district manager said. The R in keester was an unvoiced H. The R in work was more like a Y. Porter was left to wonder how he knew about the dame in question. "And while you're at it, you mug, send that boy of yours out here to Lambert."

"I beg your pardon?"

"Why? Did you stink up the joint?"

"First, I'm supposed to fire the guy. Then I hear from you to keep him on in a probationary capacity, now you're telling me to reassign him? I don't think—"

"You're a civil servant now, highpockets. Stop the blamed thinking. Get Ortley into his jalopy and send him over here. And tell him to step on it!"

Time of call: forty-eight seconds.

Porter put his phone away and passed the word along via walkie-talkie to Orville.

He pouted as he continued his rounds. Orville wouldn't be called away from desk duty unless there was a situation somewhere in the region and Lou needed some additional firepower. Then Porter realized that he should have had the call. Pantagruel – a longtime Crusader, passed over for a career mall hero who didn't last a year at the Pinnacle of Righteousness.

But what could he do? The chain of command was the chain of command, and he was just a mall hero himself now, taking orders from Lou.

Lou Noble: the scrappy, quick-witted but underpowered knight errant of another day, preserved in stasis from 1958 until just a few years ago. And all that time, gathering seniority in his sleep.

BOOM!

Orville pulled out of the Chesterfield Mall parking lot behind a black conversion van. He got on I-64 eastbound toward the outer belt freeway, which would take him to the airport. The black van went westbound, toward Hannibal and the crossing into Adams County, Illinois.

POW!

"You know what I don't understand?" Count Karma asked the Blur.

"How to read a boxscore? Driving a stick-shift? Righty-tighty, lefty-loosey?"

Kevin realized in that moment, seated next to each other in the back of the van, that the only time Bobby made eye contact with him was when he was being hostile. And Bobby was staring straight through him now.

"Why are you riding in the back of the van with the rest of us?" Kevin asked, ignoring Bobby's tone and the fact that he'd picked three things that Kevin truly didn't understand. "If you ran, you could be there by now."

"It's over a hundred miles," Bobby replied with a heavy sigh intended to mask his antipathy with ennui. "I run fast. Doesn't mean I run far."

"How fast can you run?"

"How fast can you shut up?"

"What's your beef, Blur?" Kevin asked after a short pause.

"You, you useless, lying goldbrick," Bobby replied, his face contorted by anger that would no longer be contained. He kept his voice under control so that the rest of the teammates, involved in their own conversations, didn't pick up on his seething fury. "And that's coming from me. I spent years seeing how little I could get away with doing, but when there's an immediate need for a hero, I find some motivation some-

195

where and get the job done. You just pass out. And the worst of it is, when you wake up you right away go into story mode about how you saved the day."

Kevin sat there passively.

"We both know what happened at Macy's when Singh showed up," Bobby said. "That was me, at super-speed, taking him out – not some spirit-world manifestation of you, you suck-ass." Bobby waved his fingers in the air mockingly at the mention of the spirit world.

Kevin stared back impassively. "I never said it was me," he said. "I don't even claim to have been there. I projected my essence into the astral plane where I did battle with the minions of the archdemon Belphegor, the Moabite deity of sloth. As I defeat those evil forces on the spectral plane, my victories are duplicated in this world through other's efforts – yours in that instance. As the pace of technology has quickened, Belphegor's power has ..."

Then he realized that Bobby's eyes were closed and his ears were sealed with iPod earbuds.

Shel drove, Georgiana rode shotgun. Lugh and Eva canoodled, oblivious to all else. So nobody really noticed when Count Karma seemingly passed out with his head on the Blur's unwilling shoulder.

BAM!

Private jet this time. No delays this time. Airfone coverage this time.

"... so I figured, you're in Chicago, our guy in the area is still new, he could probably use your help, Prof, and we have the budget to cover your fee. I know it's short notice, but what do you say?"

"Anything for you, Maman," came a heavily-accented, middle-European voice. "You said it's about 300 miles away. I can jet and be there within an hour of hanging up. Plainville?"

"Yeah."

"Never heard of it. Are you making that up?"

Seth Hill had slept very well indeed – late into the morning, contrary to his custom. But he had no responsibilities – his shop was demolished and insurance would cover his losses. And he had no worries. As the Institute had certainly figured out by now, the last Malificium card was safe and sound.

So it was almost noon by the time Seth showed up at the Chesterfield Mall. He had to meet an insurance adjuster at the Plaquet Box, the only real work he had to do that day, or for the foreseeable future. He was looking forward to keeping the meeting short, then taking advantage of what might be the last summer-like day of the autumn season. Fishing, it occurred to him, would be the perfect ...

Oh no.

As he strolled through the end of the mall that was still open to business, he saw an impeccably dressed woman directing a team of burly moving men opening ... not a store.

A mortuary. In the same domain as the Malificium card. This could be very bad.

Seth stopped in mid-stride to gaze at the sign: SAVINI & NICOTERO funeral home.

He allowed himself some smug satisfaction in how he'd played the odds so far. He wasn't so precise in his calculations as to expect Equity, but Equity was in a class of villains, well known to Seth, who could take the card from anyone's possession. It was important, then, that he have neither physical custody nor titular ownership of the card.

So in addition to moving it out of the Plaquet Box, he had quote-unquote sold it to someone else for a penny. He trusted that someone implicitly. But that someone could be in grave danger at any moment. If anything should happen to Seth's partner in guile, the card would have a 50-50 chance of falling into Equity's hands, which would give the Institute possession of the entire deck, which could doom the world to a reign of evil. Or worse.

Seth kept up his veneer of nonchalance. He would head to the insurance meeting for which he was already late, maintain his poker face. Best not to draw attention to the potential weakness in his – and the world's – defenses.

It was, after all, just a potential weakness. And he'd be able to tend to matters in no more than an hour.

What were the odds that an unemployed mall hero would be in grave danger within the hour?

{ POW! }

The Ford Crown Victoria.

Infiniti, Mercedes, Cadillac – Ray had all these choices open to him. But he decided to stick with the same make and model ride in which he had sailed into Jackson. Nothing, in his experience, compared with the size, the comfort, the stability, the roadworthiness, the suspension made of cumulus clouds.

A quick stop at the nearest Best Buy for a Tom Tom GPS system, and he was on the road to Plainville, Illinois, at an average speed of 90 mph, which felt like thirty in the Crown Vic.

Maman Brigitte had called on his cell phone. She sought him out and summoned him. By name! Not, "You in the striped tie!" Not by some approximation of his surname.

She said "please".

This was Ray's big chance to prove his villainy, and he wasn't going to disappoint. After all, he'd already taken one hero out of the fight. Maybe he could make it two in two days. Or more.

Ray realized that this was the first time he'd reflected on Elias O'Neill since he got in the car three hours earlier, and it was a dismissive thought at that. He chuckled.

"Fine," he said to nobody but the road.

{ BAM! }

Elias had nowhere to go, little money to get there, and oh by

198

the way, was on the FBI's Ten Most Wanted List. He couldn't go back to the Redstone Arsenal. He certainly couldn't go back to The Crusaders.

There was only one destination he could parse out: the Chesterfield Mall. Maybe Clam Shapiro would help him. He was not as well acquainted with the Blur, but Bobby Botler seemed like the kind of fellow who would bend the rules to help somebody out. Mucus-Man? No. Orville Ortley was hard-wired to follow convention. Better make sure he ran into Clam or the Blur first.

And, come to think of it, wasn't the mall the last place he saw his old pal Pantagruel? No way would The Crusaders take him back after not even showing up for the last fight, even though he was only a parking lot away. Maybe Panty was stuck in the St. Louis area. Elias knew he could count on Porter Peale.

So with that in mind, he had boarded the St. Louis-bound Greyhound bus from Jackson so many hours ago. Cramped, uncomfortable, stopping at every wide spot in the road, a fetid smell flowing at annoying intervals from the back, Elias O'Neill had been spending the night inching his way back to St. Louis.

{BOOM!}

"So, Count Karma, we meet at last," the archdemon Belphegor announced, his voice echoing throughout the astral plane. "Now you shall know the humiliating sting of defeat."

"Prepare for your end, Belphegor," Kevin said in return to the challenge.

They floated in ether, an otherworldly landscape out of a Dali painting dancing around them but nothingness above and below. Count Karma was a 3D-animated etching devoid of color in the outlines of his ceremonial garb.

Belphegor hovered naked, a flabby torso with atrophied limbs and oversized hands and feet. Fingernails and toenails, uncut for millennia, formed intricate swirls, punctuated by

199

occasional sharp angles. Disdain for all mortal striving was expressed through a contorted perversion of a face, from the smirk hidden in the impossibly deep jowls to the upward thrust of the misshapen broccoli floret of a nose. Framing this unholy visage, pointy horns rose in parallel alignment with pointy ears, and a beard grew to his toes from a narrow patch of chin. And behind it all, a jackal's tail swatted randomly at non-existent flies.

Dispensing with any further banter, Count Karma bent his fingers in directions that flesh would not permit and recited an incantation that vocal cords could never utter. Great, glowing lights formed in his palms, swelled around his hands and expanded to spheroid fireballs a cubit in radius. Contrasting with their wielder, who was completely blanched of color, these two flares were as vividly hued, as green as green can be and as orange as orange can be and still register in the visual range.

As such, they were not true flame. They were strange fires, what Count Karma thought of as metafire, transcendent representations of ideals which bring humankind closer to Infinite. The green was pure Splendor, the orange pure Judgment.

As the balls of metafire gained in size and intensity, the sounds hanging in the ethereal gas around them grew louder. Crackling turned to roaring, roaring to thundering. Heat like Hell's boiler room built up until Kevin could take it no more. Incorporeal, he could neither sweat nor burn; but he felt the pain as intensely as if he had fallen into an ocean of torment. He took as much agony as he could, the fireballs - their blinding light, their searing heat, their deafening blare - growing with each shallow, reflexive, useless breath. Then, furrowing his brow around his squinting eyes, Count Karma launched the maximum manifestations of Splendor and Judgment at Belphegor. At where he was.

Belphegor was there no more. In his stead reigned stillness, silence, dimness and blessed chill.

Kevin allowed himself a moment of hope. After all these years vanquishing Belphegor's chthonic minions, had he finally dispatched the embodiment of idleness and disputation?

No.

A cackling laugh rang loud from behind. Count Karma spun round. The tip of the nose of the ugliest countenance he had ever seen was a dime's breadth away from him. Belphegor made no move, just hung there in the ether, as if to double-dumdum-dare Kevin to make the next move. The cackle's cadence suggested the juvenile taunt, "Does-this-bother-you?-I'm-not-touching-you!"

The pain from the fireballs had only just begun to abate, but Count Karma willed his fingers to bend and his voice to scratch out the incantation. But before he could speak two syllables, the demon lord was gone. Then he appeared off to the right, halfway to the vanishing point. Kevin wouldn't have known he was there if not for the "Yoo-hoo!" Belphegor called out.

Then Belphegor blinked out of existence again and reappeared over Count Karma's left shoulder. Then he ceased to be yet again and returned to the astral plane directly overhead. Randomly, he popped up near, far, left, right, up, down. Sometimes he was nowhere to be found for long, disquieting moments. Sometimes he was briefly in two places at once. While this was going on, he mocked Kevin.

"You vain, useless child-man! ... You are ineffectual even by mortal standards ... I let you strike me once with your attack of abstractions, and I won't lie to you. It hurt me ... a little. Like a baby teething on my finger. You think you are so far above other mortals because you have such facile victories over foes in this astral plane! Well, let me tell you something ... this is the highest plane of existence you can comprehend but ... it's as ordinary to me as your sidewalk is to you ... I can be anywhere ... everywhere ... in worlds upon worlds you cannot even imagine ... this image you see dancing around you ... is not me. It's the portion of me that fits on this plane. You have defeated all of my minions here, but there is only one way you can best me."

"And how's that?"

"Am I supposed to tell you? I leave such self-defeating gloating to ... earthly villains. You remember the prophecy?"

"Yes," Kevin recalled, and recited what the gods had told him. "I would be invincible here but of no consequence on earth 'until time turns back before me.'"

"And you know what that means?" Belphegor asked, bounding to a spot not an inch in front of Kevin, who paused before confessing, "No."

"Neither do I ... but it hardly matters. You see, I have no intention of challenging you on the astral plane. Because of the prophecy, it would be a useless exercise on my part. All those lesser sprites you've beaten here? ... you've accomplished nothing, not on the astral plane, not in what you consider the real world. All you have done is entertain me. I have no more challengers to offer you here, which is just as well because ... I tire of you. I shall now remove myself to my plane of origin. I deny you victory. ... I deny your world the assurance of good besting evil. You and your tiny band of miscasts will succeed or fail on earthly terms now. ... Goodbye, Kevin ..."

"Kiley!" a voice screamed in his ear. A too-harsh slap struck his cheek.

He was back on earth, in the van, Kevin realized as his eyes adjusted to the light. His head drooped on the shoulder of Bobby Botler, who slapped him again for good measure, and he sat up straight in reaction.

"Don't ever do that again, creepy-boy," Bobby said.

The Blur's approbation aside, Kevin realized, for the first time, his team's likelihood of winning out over whatever peril was about to face them was very much in doubt.

INTERLUDE: 1990

Rudy Goldman was a busy man. The black, baggy patches under his eyes that would be his most prominent feature as he got older were already in evidence.

As the U.S. government's leading suprologist, his caseload was unsustainably heavy. If all his patients were local to the Huntsville area, it wouldn't have been a burden. But people with abilities were scattered randomly, so Rudy was among the last MDs in America to make house calls.

About every six months, he dropped by the Chadwick home in Ottumwa, Iowa, which he once joked was the Sioux phrase for, "no direct flights here."

"So how are we today, Marcos?" he asked the ten-year-old boy.

"Speaking only for myself, I am in vigorous health," he said. He stared out the window of his foster father's home office, fascinated by a blackbird perched on a maple branch hanging low with big, heavy, September leaves.

As Roger and Esperanza stood in the doorway beaming pride at how bright their boy was, Rudy saw the familiar pattern: vocabulary far above grade level, flat speech, no eye contact, a deep focus on a narrow range of interests. Marcos displayed telltale signs of being autistic – though without a doubt high-functioning – and might also exhibit symptoms of obsessive-compulsive disorder. A psych consult was in order.

In the meantime, a brief checkup revealed Marcos's heart, lungs, and reflexes to be in vigorous good health. As Marcos stared intently at the bird's pitch-black wings, he didn't even notice the flu shot. When it was over, though, and Rudy went to tousle Marcos's hair, the boy ran screaming from the office, screeching without words, violated.

"He does that sometimes," Esperanza said, a factual statement delivered with all stoicism.

"Why don't we all sit down?" Rudy suggested. The office was large and comfortable enough that three people could sit without anyone grabbing the authoritative high-backed leather chair behind the desk. "So, how's Marisol?"

"She's wonderful," Esperanza beamed.

"So Kemper is agreeing with her?"

"She's really taken to military school," Roger agreed. "And I can't tell you how proud I am. At first, I was disappointed that you weren't able to find any special abilities in her, but ..."

"... but Type AB-neg blood is special enough, especially considering her upbringing," the doctor finished, sharing a smile with the retired Colonel America. "She'll make it, Roger. Call it a hunch." He winked. The fix was in.

"And how are your students?" Rudy continued. "I expected to see three other kids while I was here but I don't see anyone around."

"Caltech offered Porter early admission, so he's off to college already. Sixteen years old and in such a rush to grow up! He started over the summer."

"Good for him, although I think he had more to learn from you two. And what about Tara?" Rudy asked.

"Oh, she's around," Esperanza said, eyes rolling. "She saw you driving up and jumped into the past. She can travel about four-and-a-half hours back now."

"That explains it. I parked the car down the hill and walked up the path three hours ago – no Tara," the doctor said, then sighed. "I suppose we can expect her ability to intensify now that she's past puberty. And Bobby?"

There was an awkward silence.

"He's no longer with us," Esperanza said, measuring the syllables.

"Doc, I'm not sure how accurate your genetic tests are," Roger continued. "The only ability he's demonstrated is getting into the liquor cabinet."

"After a month of this," Esperanza added, "we had to send him back to his family in Texas."

"Marcos must have taken that hard," Rudy replied. "The Botler boy was the only other pre-teen in the house."

The Chadwickes just shrugged.

"It's as if ..." Esperanza began, then choked up.

"It's okay, hon," Roger said, draping a comforting arm over his wife, then addressed Rudy. "It's as if Marcos hasn't noticed. If he doesn't have anyone to talk to, he just doesn't talk. He reads up on birds, or he paints."

"Paints?"

"On canvas, abstract art." Roger replied.

"Basic shapes, bright colors," Esperanza added. "He loves arranging them in patterns. They get more complex all the time. We don't know much about art, but we save them all. Maybe I'm just a proud ... mother ... but I think they're very good."

"I'm sure it keeps him out of the liquor cabinet," the doctor quipped.

"Spice rack," Esperanza said, and Rudy was left to wonder what that had to do with anything, until Roger explained.

"He's fascinated with scents, as best as we can figure. We don't know why he feels the need to—"

BOOM!

Something in the kitchen exploded. Not a light bulb - too loud. Maybe someone put metal in the microwave.

The three of them ran into the kitchen and, indeed, found that appliance crumpled like a soup can, its door hanging off one hinge. But why would the microwave have imploded rather than exploded?

Sitting on the floor looking up at it was Marcos, a shaker of cayenne pepper in his hand.

His power had manifested. Marcos - Orville - was his birth mother's son.

He was also very much his birth father's son, but nobody knew who that was at the time. Doc Rudy might have been able to figure it out, but just then a loud beeping came from his leather satchel back in Roger's office.

The biggest device in Rudy's black bag was something the size and weight of a brick with a telescoping antenna.

From Doc Rudy's end of the conversation - which involved a lot of *say-agains* and *repeat-thats* - it could be surmised that there was an emergency. Sure enough, the doctor quickly rushed out the front door. The blackbird flew away a moment before the branches began flapping in the breeze. A helicopter landed on the front lawn.

206

Rudy climbed aboard, abandoning the Ford Taurus he had driven up in.

POW!

The blackbird that provided the ten-year-old Marcos Chadwick/Orville Ortley with so many hours of fascination looked much like another blackbird being contemplated by another ten-year-old two thousand miles away.

That other blackbird was strapped down to an intricately carved teakwood table on an even more intricately tiled veranda in the back garden of one of the most fashionable homes along Port-au-Prince's Rue Champs de Mars.

It squawked desperately and noisily as the cutest, most precious little girl recited Ghanaian incantations, twirling the handle of a four-inch blade between her palms.

She wore the green-plaid uniform of a girls' boarding school in North Carolina – just trying it on, she wasn't flying out until the following day. Long pigtails framed a face that was smooth as syrup and richly hued as a chocolate milkshake with just a dollop of strawberry jam stirred in. As high-caloried as that sounds, she was actually a little underweight, not gawky, but she apparently had little appetite for syrup or milkshakes or jam.

Her appetite was for blood.

Not to eat it, but to look at it, stare at it, immerse herself and her oh-so-darling uniform in it. She felt the warm stickiness all over her hands and face, admiring how it spotted the bright white of her blouse. She licked it off her lips.

The four-inch blade sliced protest from the blackbird's throat, then cut a line – jagged from the bird's deathly twitching – from breast to pinion. With bare hands, she untied the carcass, picked it up, turned it over, and pulled out its entrails. The viscera formed an abstract pattern of red and blue and black all over the table, random to the casual observer but imbued with meaning to the little girl.

She stared at the entrails as if they foretold her own destiny, and smiled with gap-toothed delight, her teeth the same luminous white as her pearl stud earrings, which could have been mistaken for her two missing incisors.

"Mademoiselle," a husky alto called in flatly deadpan Creole from the enclosed porch nearby. "Mademoiselle Brigitte, your father wants to see you in his study right away."

The complete lack of intonation in the domestic's voice would have seemed eerie to most people, but it was part of Brigitte's upbringing so it was unremarkable to her. In response, she dutifully stood up and primly brushed away a thin veil of dust and creases that had worked its way into her blouse – nothing to be done about the blood. Just as she was about to turn toward the main house, though, she caught movement from the corner of her eye.

A wing twitched on the bird. This captured her attention. Its eyes, frozen open at the moment of the bird's death, blinked shut then opened again. And despite its digestive tract being scattered around the table, the bird opened its beak like a nestling looking for a worm.

The servant again uttered, "Mademoiselle."

BAM!

Myron Masters's skin, eyes and teeth were once as clear as Brigitte's, back when he was an up-and-coming hero, destined for The Crusaders (THE CRUSADERS!!!). But that was a decade ago.

Now he was just another middle-aged man with a beer belly whose forearms were atrophying from never holding anything heavier than a twelve-ounce pop-top.

208

At the moment, he was clutching a one-ounce blue Sharpie, signing pictures of himself in a breakout room at the Dallas Sheraton.

Some early-teen white kid, probably from Copper Canyon or Highland Village, had just spent the past two minutes telling Myron his life story. Myron, though, didn't register a word of it. All he knew was that he netted five of the ten dollars charged for a personalized signature, a moment of time, maybe a photo. The convention also paid his transportation from his place off Georgia Avenue in Washington to the Sheraton: airline ticket, ground transfers and the cost of the room for two nights. Myron was doing okay – there was a line in the hall an hour long to meet him.

The year before, it had been two hours.

"Here you go kid," Myron said, handing over the signed photo of him in his prime, scowling war face atop an Adonis sculpted in ebony and satin. "Stay in school. Don't do drugs."

The kid skulked away muttering something about having aced the goddamn PSATs.

In the wake of Jim Crow, Myron had been the first black in America identified as having a genetic predisposition to superpowers, and the first to have that strength and stamina and invulnerability manifest. He picked the name Black Man for the straightforward way it conveyed his pride at having been so selected by Fate. But it turned out to be an unfortunate choice.

Between the time he settled on the name and the time he was inducted into The Crusaders, the world had changed and "Black Man" had become a laughable anachronism. The papers were no longer filled with announcements of "the first black chief of medicine" or "the first black CEO" or "the first black mayor." Certainly, Myron knew of at least half a dozen other black people with abilities that might someday qualify them for Crusader status.

Some of them – hell, all of them! – had powers that put his to shame. He was well aware that he was where he was due to tokenism. Myron hung onto his seat at the table in Crusaders Castle for a couple years, but it wasn't long before he decided to bow out gracefully and let some better suited individual represent the increasingly diverse array of younger heroes.

He was already drinking habitually before he left, and then just switched to drinking cheaper stuff, starting earlier in the day.

"Next!" a handler from the superhero fan convention called out.

A boy who looked to be in sixth grade shuffled forward, moving with no deliberate speed. One look and Myron could tell: slacker. Useless. Never amount to shit. Oh well, his mommy must have worked three jobs to save up the ten bucks. Be nice, Myron reminded himself.

"What's your name, young man?"

"Uh, Bobby Botler," he muttered as he handed over the picture to be signed, so shy he was staring at his own shoes.

"Well, Bobby Botler, is there anything you want me to write on here?"

At this, Bobby glanced up and made eye contact with the former Crusader.

"Um, if it's not too much trouble," he began, "I'd like you to say something about what it's like to have a power. The doctor says I, uh ..."

"Doctor. Rudy Goldman?"

"Yeah."

"What can you do, kid?"

"Nothing. Nothing yet, anyway. Doc Rudy says that

once I'm old enough to shave and beat off and like that, something will develop. But we don't know what yet."

"Or when. Sometimes these genetic powers don't show up 'til later," Myron said, stopping short of saying or sometimes they don't show up at all. "I was twenty. Hey, I bet you're looking forward to it."

"Uh, just the shaving and beating off," Bobby confessed. "Tell you the truth, sir, I don't want any part of being, like, special. I'm not scared of fighting the bad guys. It just sounds like more trouble than it's worth."

Myron considered this with his head tilted to one side.

"So what can I do for you, Bobby-boy?"

"Well, I suppose I could use some advice from a guy who's been there."

"How do you spell your last name?"

Bobby told him, and this is what Myron wrote:

Dear Bobby Botler,

You may have heard that with power comes responsibility. That's a bunch of horseshit. You can save the world, destroy it or sit back and watch others fight over it. You still have the same power.

The only thing power comes with is limitations. Get to know yours early. Respect them. And get out of the game before you run into any of them.

Stay in school and don't do drugs,

Myron Masters
"Black Man"

Myron signed more than two hundred eight-by-ten glossies that day. He remembered Bobby Botler for years. Everyone else was just a blur.

BOOM!

When he was in his final year of medical school, the news that a Crusader had been killed in the line of duty shook Rudy Goldman. He would admit to having a little crush on the slim, strong woman in the leotard and jog-bra, her mysterious face obscured by the goggles that kept her optical beams contained. The waste of such a remarkable woman was made all the more tragic by the senselessness of it all: Surely The Crusaders could have handled one rookie villain, even at less than full strength? The news reports were sketchy, but the tightly controlled media were able to state that her beams were diffused and off-center after several months of inactivity.

Rudy correctly surmised that the misfiring beams were probably caused by a detached retina. And if she had a detached retina after maintaining a low profile for all those months, he again correctly surmised, she was a new mother. Which made it all the more tragic. All those trips she must have taken to OB-GYNs over the course of a nine-month pregnancy and three-month maternity leave, and nobody realized what a common, minor complication like hers could mean to a Crusader.

That's when he decided to go into suprology, the treatment of people with special abilities.

Rudy had seen a lot of weird things in the meantime: a kid who could step in and out of the timestream; the human DNA of a Celtic god whom the pantheon had elevated from mortal origins; the dizzying equations drawn by a tenth-grade boy, that proved a sufficiently agile mind could control the size and density of the cells in its body. And, of course, he now had the keys to the lab that had created four iterations of Colonel America.

None of this prepared him for what he was about to see as the chopper dropped him off at Crusader Castle.

All the message on the cellular telephone told him was that there had been an accident involving Dirk Henderson, the Carbon Avenger.

Rudy regretted that he hadn't met Dirk when he was at his best. The other Crusaders told Rudy about a supremely impressive man on every conceivable level: a brilliant engineer, a successful business titan, an intrepid hero, a respected leader of heroes, and the ladies loved him.

But that changed for Dirk after Looker was killed. The change wasn't sudden, but the solemn expression he wore as one of Olivia Ortley's pallbearers never faded. The Carbon Avenger continued in his role with The Crusaders for more than a year, but then faded into the background. He went from the group's headquarters leader to its ATM. After designing the Pinnacle of Right-eousness and approving funding for it, he was rarely seen anymore.

One of the Castle's support staff led the doctor at a full run from the helipad through the vaulted foyer and into a suite of rooms where nobody - not even the other Crusaders - had access. Within that suite was a suprology room which made the one at Redstone Arse-nal look like a medieval barbershop.

A sickening smell imbued the room, far worse than anything Rudy had ever experienced. Not in his oncolo-gy rotation, not in his recent tour with a combat support hospital, had he ever endured anything so awful. Flesh had been burned, deep, he could tell, as he instinctively tucked his nose into the elbow crook of his jacket. But it wasn't just flesh. The air hung heavy with hydrocarbons. Rudy had smelled oilfield fires, and this was worse. A haze hung in the room, making it difficult to see.

Through watering eyes, Doc Rudy looked around for his patient. This was the first time that Rudy would have a chance to meet the reclusive hero, and hoped that there was still enough of him left, considering the evidence his nose provided. Rudy didn't know what he was looking for. He squinted for a glimpse of the sleek Carbon Avenger costume, or a business suit, or a lab coat.

Doc Rudy wasn't really surprised to find Dirk naked. The shock was that he was no longer human. Lying there, strapped to a table underneath a menacing-looking piece of equipment, Rudy could neither name nor guess the function of, was a four-limbed pile of shale with iron slag running through it, a face composed of soft coal.

THE BATTLEFIELD

olonel America and Doctor Rudy Goldman arrived on the scene before anyone else, the Colonel piloting their Black Hawk helicopter up from Alabama, wringing 180 knots out of it the whole way up. Rudy couldn't help feeling a little queasy on the ride, but his stomach settled as soon as they touched solid ground in Plainville.

That's when Colonel America threw up.

"You all right, Marisol?" Rudy asked, crouching down beside the doubled-over Colonel.

"I will be," she replied, confidence surging. "You never have to smell this in the Air Force."

Rudy was sadly better acquainted with the intricate bouquet of fluids and bacteria that accompanied scattered, unburied bodies. The unusually high humidity of that October mid-morning kept the stench from blowing away; fortunately, the temperature was seasonably cool. As the doctor rose back to a standing position, it was the visual that nearly sickened him: bodies on the ground, scattered randomly, victims of the most savage, grievous wounds. They were shredded, which disturbed Rudy most. In a moment of self-loathing, he realized that if the cuts had been more precise, more surgical, the scene would hardly have affected him at all.

As the rotors wound down and the dust settled, the two could see that the quadrangle of dirt they landed in was the infield of the ubiquitous town baseball diamond. Up on the scoreboard they saw the mangled, broken, torn remains of what had been a man who wore overalls and carried a key card to work – a silo filler maybe. The head was folded back so the bald spot nestled between the shoulder blades.

"What could do something like that?" Marisol asked.

"Something that could climb – that could chase him up there."

"Or drag him up there."

Rudy considered that and countered, "Or maybe something that can fly."

"I don't think so, Doc," Colonel America replied, a reflexive but uncalled-for hubris tainting her voice. Rudy knew that this was a side effect of her transformation, and remembered that Elias O'Neill's reaction was much more pronounced. He wondered if Marisol was struggling to keep that arrogance in check.

He raced to keep up with her as she strode swiftly, purposefully, toward the body, then picked up a limp hand.

"Fresh kill," Colonel America said. "Extremities are still warm. Guts haven't been ripped out yet. Not a lot of blood. When we landed, we must've interrupted something. Take a look around."

Rudy counted eleven other bodies within easy eyeshot. They were all on the ground or draped over a car hood or first-floor windowsill, gore spilling liberally, blood pooling.

"The chopper must have frightened it," Rudy surmised. "It instinctually dragged its prey up to where scavengers couldn't get to it, then disappeared."

"That suggests a couple things," Marisol explained. "First, it's running on instinct, so it's not evil in a villainous

216

way - just an animal trying to survive. Second—"

"Second, it's probably hiding somewhere close, watching us right now."

POW!

"Puh-leeeeze?" Georgiana supplicated, batting her eyelashes so forcibly that the youthful Illinois National Guard corporal felt the breeze on his goosebumped neck.

"There's nothing I'd rather do than help you, Georgie," he said. She'd just told him it was okay for him to call her that, then she motioned past the sawhorse cordon to the stretch of State Highway 96 that led into Plainville. "But it's not safe in there. I don't know what I'd do if any harm came to you."

"But my friends will be right there with me."

"Are you trying to make him jealous? He's already jealous," Eva Peron advised, unseen and unheard by the sergeant or the rest of his detail. "You probably just flubbed our last chance of getting past this poor, dumb beast."

"I see," the corporal said through gritted teeth. "But I could do a better job at protecting you than they possibly could."

"Of course you could, Sergeant," she said, knowing damn well his rank and that he'd take the compliment without correcting her. "But our country needs you here to protect all the rest of the citizenry."

"Stand down," Eva Peron advised, unseen and unheard by the sergeant or the rest of his detail. "You triggered the protective response. There's no getting past that. He'll die for you, he'll kill for you, but he'll never let you risk yourself."

Eva had become almost as good at reading her protégée as she had long been at reading men. She knew that Georgiana was about to let loose with a very unladylike piece of her mind.

"Don't say it, dearie," Eva advised. "He can't help being

217

male. Just get back to the van."

She did, Eva hovering alongside her all the way.

"No go, Shel," she said, climbing back into the front passenger seat. "Sorry."

"We'll find another way in, Mindy," Shel replied. "Don't sweat it."

"What I don't get ..." Kevin began, leaning forward from the bench seat in back.

"Is this about tying shoelaces, Kiley?" Shel asked. "Just wear loafers."

"Ha. Ha. But why don't we call on Lugh to kick some Pansy Patrol ass and just drive on in?"

Georgiana and Lugh exchanged exasperated glances until Shel summed it up: "Because we're the good guys."

"We're only as good as what we do," Kevin replied, not backing down.

"No, meat. We're only as good as how we do it."

"OK. We're only as profitable as what we do."

"Well, you got a point there," Shel conceded. "Let's think of another way in, one that respects authority but still gets us to the rescue."

It was then that the black Ford Expedition with flashing lights dragged up the dust-blown county road at sixty miles per hour and screeched to a donut-inducing halt next to the team's van.

"Just great," Kevin dripped sarcasm. "We need this like we need a skin rash."

"How long have we known each other, Kiley?" Shel inquired.

"Three days."

"Apparently you're right once every three days."

"Huh?" Bobby called out from the back. He had nodded off and was just waking up. "Who's flashing those strobes at us?"

"TSA," Shel announced. "The real TSA."

Out of the shotgun seat bolted an eager young man in the standard TSA uniform, but draped in a cape with red, yellow and green spots. Behind him emerged a sixty-ish woman who was also in the TSA white-and-black, but with her eyes hiding behind what Georgiana initially thought were retro, Looker-style goggles but on second glance were revealed to be exceedingly thick eyeglasses with a light tint.

Stepping authoritatively out from behind the steering wheel was a flickering, grayscale-skinned image of a man with a cynical set to his jawline, an unfiltered Camel dangling from his nearly black lower lip. His trench coat, a halftone lighter gray than his skin, flapped in the breeze as his intricately patterned foulard necktie stayed clipped to his shirt. Lou Noble.

Behind him came Orville.

Mucus-Man observed Shel and Kevin without engaging them, or even intimating that he recognized them. Nor did he respond to Kevin's gasp of surprise and betrayal. Rather, he stayed with the vehicle alongside the other three while their boss stepped over to the van. Shel got out to greet him.

Neither team leader extended a hand to shake.

"Lou."

"Shel," Lou replied. "Whaddya know, whaddya say?"

Shel just nodded, having no clue how to respond to a greeting that many decades out of date.

"When did you find out about the trouble here?" Shel asked after an uncomfortable pause.

"About the same time as you," Lou replied. "Your boy Orville here tells me he blew the joint right after you mugs."

Shel considered this.

"Then he drove miles out of his way to meet up with you at the airport, then you all arrived together five minutes after we did," Shel observed. "You made great time."

"We got Semaphore to thank for that," Lou said, indicating the man in the red-yellow-green cape.

"My first interview was with Lou – I've met these jokers," Kevin stage-whispered. "Semaphore controls signaling devices, like traffic lights. In the coke-bottles is Glyph, the spelling savant."

Shel thought back to the moment at Hawk's when Kevin learned about his arm strength.

"You thought I was making that up?" Kevin asked rhetorically. "I could handle these geeks myself."

"I knew your puss looked familiar," Lou said to Kevin. "Captain Knish, right?"

"Count Karma, Comma, Master of Arts."

"For my money, you're just another chump out on the street." Lou said. "Sorry you weren't up to snuff to work with me. I was kind of hoping Shel could find some use for you. Guess that didn't work out either, kiddy-o."

"Remains to be seen," Kevin said, standing toe-to-toe with Lou.

"So, Lou, seems you know young Kevin here," Shel said, draping an arm – gingerly – around his former manager's shoulders. We got Lugh and Bobby in the back there. But I don't think you met Georgiana. Georgiana, I'd like you to meet my old boss."

The woman known broadly as Supermodel got the hint, pushed open her door ever so gently, dropped a shapely leg to the ground and waited for Lou to come around and lend a hand to help her out.

"Charmed," Georgiana breathed.

"Likewise. I'm Lou Noble," the man in monochrome responded. "America's Greatest Dick."

"I beg your pardon?"

"That's what they used to call me. For eighteen years, I was the one you went to if you needed a dick and only the best would do. There were hundreds of others, but none was ever half the dick you see before you now."

"Um, okay Mister Noble, it is very important that my colleagues and I are permitted to enter the town," she said, bright eyes darkened by wide, receptive irises. "Would you be so kind as to tell the Guardsmen that we're here on TSA business?"

"We both know that ain't even a second cousin twice removed from the truth, dollface."

"You're so clever, Mister Noble, but we are desperate for your help," she said, willing forth tears.

"Dry up, sweetheart. I just don't know if there's anything I can do for you."

"But you're the only one who could possibly help," she pleaded. "You see, we're heroes. We have to play by the rules. But not you, Mister Noble. You're no hero. You're an anti-hero. You get to cut corners, use guile, do what's necessary to make sure that evil doesn't win out."

Lou considered this.

"Fine, glamourpuss, but we anti-heroes have to follow certain rules as well. Like the one that says we don't invite trouble in. There's got to be something in it for me, see?"

Georgiana paused for a moment before erupting, "I will not!"

"You will not *what*, gorgeous?"

"Never mind. I was talking to somebody else."

"You got bats in that pretty little belfry of yours, sugar-gams," Lou said and backed away toward his own patiently waiting team while keeping a leering eye on Georgiana. "You should know by now that I'm no sucker for a pretty dame."

"I'm from the 'fifties too. I remember him from back then," Eva confided to Georgiana. "He's *always* been a sucker for a pretty dame. Virginia-Mayo-hair-toss with a Veronica-Lake-tug-at-the-sweater! Quick! Before he turns around!"

Lou changed course so fast he almost tripped over his

own black wingtips. Standing behind him, Semaphore wiped a trace of drool from the corner of his lip as Glyph simply rolled her eyes behind her horn-rimmed spectacles.

"Perfect!" Eva shouted with pride. "Just as I showed you!"

Georgiana flashed Lou a come-hither look. He responded by going thither and was rewarded with a sly whisper in his ear.

Five minutes later, a black Expedition and a ratty old conversion van were driving in tandem toward the center of Plainville.

"These mugs are with me, see?" Lou Noble, America's Greatest Dick, told the Guard corporal as they drove past the cordon.

BAM!

The haggard man, who looked far older than his mid-fifties, took his roll-aboard suitcase out of the overhead bin as if it were empty.

In fact, it was nearly empty. It was a prop to keep this man – dark-skinned and holding a one-way ticket – from being hassled going through security at Reagan National. It contained a toothbrush with half its bristles missing, a comb with strands of his thinning hair stuck in it, and a change of underwear. But according to Homeland Security standards, having a suitcase made him a solid citizen and not having one made him a terror suspect. The non-superpowered TSA employees who scanned the roll-aboard knew that it was sham, but they were just following the rules.

Even if the suitcase were packed with masonry material, though, Myron Masters could have lifted it with his left pinky. Still, the only thing he had of value on his person was a card, thin as a paper cut, which was sealed in a hard-plastic case and tucked into his front jeans pocket.

In fact, handling that card had given Myron his first paper cut since he was a teenager. His powers, he realized, were beginning to fade with age and chemical dependency. His strength, though still considerable, was on the decline. Once as strong as Lugh, now Pantagruel could kick his ass. Maybe even Clam Shapiro. On a bad day, he supposed, Supermodel could. But what gave Myron pause was that his invincibility factor was nothing but a memory. He could be felled by a bullet. He could even be killed by a tic carrying Lyme disease.

Myron wasn't a hero anymore. Just an errand boy. Just a mole. Such wannabes as Glyph and Semaphore were now considered more valuable than he. But recently, in retirement, with endless hours to ponder over endless 40-ouncers, he regretted ever hanging up his costume and mask. He knew he had wasted the better part of a lifetime, had nothing to show for it, and could never fix the problem or make up for it.

The "Black Man" persona was an anachronism, and maybe it was a bad idea from the start. But Myron came to realize he could have re-branded himself in some way and kept up the fight.

Too late now, though. Myron was beginning to think he was nothing more than a useless vestige to the side of good – an appendix that can never help but could even be a danger if it ever actually tried to do anything.

So when he got the call asking if he could help by being eyes and ears inside the American Malevolence Institute, he volunteered without hesitation.

Now, as he hustled as fast as calcifying knees and hips could carry him through the concourse and out to the Lambert-St. Louis International Airport taxi stand, his job was nearly done.

"Chesterfield Mall," he told the cabbie.

And he was off to the appointment he made with the man who plucked him out of obscurity to help save the world one last time: Seth Hill.

The creature Bella Brock had become was indeed watching Marisol and Rudy. It could have been from any of a thousand tree limbs, telephone poles, rooftops, awnings, or second-story windows. Or it could have been from under some front porch or within an open garage or any other ground-level place with deep shadows.

"I don't even know where to look," Rudy confessed.

Marisol responded, "I don't even know what to look *for.*"

"Let's get back to the Black Hawk and figure out our next move," the doctor posited.

"Negatory," Colonel America replied, and began lecturing the learned oldster without whom she wouldn't even exist. "We didn't come all this way to sit in the chopper. We're going to draw this thing out, and we're going to capture it. Here's what we'll do ..."

Rudy followed her suggestion that they move - slowly, so as not to trigger a pursuit reflex - toward the baseball diamond's center field. That way, whatever it was that had brought slaughter to Plainville would have to cross open terrain to attack. Marisol draped them both in her bulletproof cape and hoped that would be enough protection - and wouldn't provoke the same response in this predator as it would in a Pamplona bull.

But the invading carnivore wasn't the only one watching the pair as they inched past their helicopter and into the field.

And it wasn't the heroes in from St. Louis. Having approached from the opposite direction, they hadn't yet laid eyes on the Black Hawk.

Ray had arrived, and the National Guard sentry from the County Road 53 checkpoint had a newly liberated look on life.

INTERLUDE: 1992

S o what do you do?" Lisa Lorenzo asked, sitting on a high-backed wooden bench in the Crusaders Castle dining hall, then drew a long straw sip from a Diet Coke can.

"Nothing," the shaven-headed guy in the olive-drab flight suit said between bites of his cheeseburger. "I'm just an airplane driver."

Lisa, who was wearing a midnight-blue leotard without any sort of logo which might give a clue what her own power might be, was skeptical but took him at his word. The question however prompted the young man, who had introduced himself as "Clam," to ask her the same.

"How's your burger?" was her random-sounding reply.

"Okay, I guess," Clam replied, his head tilted on his 18-inch neck. Lisa's words carried the text of an innocuous question, but Clam detected a subtext. He just didn't know what it was.

"Just okay? I mean, this is Crusaders Castle, the home of the mightiest heroes the world has ever seen, and bankrolled by the limitless wealth of Carbodyne World-wide and the Henderson fortune," Lisa recounted with a high degree of snark. "Most of us are here at The Crusaders' personal invitation to present ourselves as candidates for future membership in their august company. You telling me they can't get you a good cheeseburger?"

"When you put it like that ..."

"What's wrong with it?"

"Nothing, it's just a little bland."

"That's what fixin's are for, Clam. You didn't put anything on your burger. Why didn't you stop by the condiment counter?"

"Well, we were talking in line," Clam said, and Lisa was flattered to notice that his macho swagger was cracking. "And, um, I was just enjoying our conversation. You walked over to the table here, and I guess I just kinda followed you."

The Marine lieutenant was actually blushing.

"That's sweet," Lisa said. She wasn't blushing. Did Larry Bird blush after the Dream Team's 116-48 victory over Angola? "What can I get you? Ketchup? Mustard? They got the spicy-brown kind."

"Thanks, but I can get it my–" he started to rise from his seat before Lisa interrupted.

"Don't get up."

With a *boiiing*, her arm stretched across the twenty-yard expanse between their table and the condiment bar, picked up two packets each of Heinz and Gulden's and a packet of sweet relish just in case. As Lisa's arm *boiiinged* back to its normal length, spicy contents in her hand, she never broke eye contact with her astonished companion.

"So why do they call you Clam?" she asked, as she set the packets nonchalantly in front of him.

For his part, he also tried to be as nonchalant as he could, considering how very impressed he was with this woman's ability, how very impressed he was with her wit and poise before he even knew for a fact that she had an

226

ability, and how very likely it was that he had just fallen in love.

"My name's Sheldon, Shel for short," he began, fumbling with the ketchup. She used her steadier hands and well-manicured nails to help, then went ahead and squeezed the contents onto the patty. "Um, thanks. Anyway, when you become an aviator, they give you a call sign. Sometimes it's something that suits you, like Maverick or Iceman in *Top Gun*. But a lot of the time it's just a bad play on words."

"I thought you had a power and the name had something to do with that," Lisa said. "Maybe you got a hard shell – bulletproof, like Black Man was. Or maybe you're impervious to interrogation – you 'clam up.'"

"No, it's just that 'clam' was the first word that popped into some Pensacola redneck's head when he first learned that there were people named 'shell'. But it stuck."

"Would you mind if I called you Shel?"

"I wish you would."

(POW!)

At the next table, another couple destined for the altar made their first acquaintance as well.

"Seventeen?" Millicent May asked.

"Yes," Porter Peale replied, though he'd still be sixteen for three more weeks. "And you?"

"Twenty-one." She was twenty-three.

That was old enough to have defined her taste in men and she was, as the song went, holding out for a hero.

In Millicent's typology, though, there were two kinds. One was the standard-issue, bold, courageous, shining-armor variety. She considered them entertaining fantasy, but not terribly interesting in real life. And, since they were always oh-so-noble, they were hard to seduce for one-night stands. She wasn't entirely unsuccessful: she'd been through Lugh, Black Man and El Hombre, but they

227

were the exceptions rather than the rule. She was oh-for-two with the Colonels America she had met, and the Carbon Avenger reacted to her advances with a mélange of anger, repulsion, and shame, she found devastatingly insulting.

Which was too bad, she thought, because Dirk Henderson - she did at least get past the mask - was more the kind of hero she could go for. Hero-geek. He achieved his status by dint of his brilliant, agile, focused mind designed for solving problems - the more complex, the better. Dirk had taken his passion for organic chemistry and engineered materials - these were actually things he was passionate about! - and turned them into a super powered fighting suit that made him one of the most powerful heroes in the world.

Not content with that, he had led the project team that designed what would become, over the next five years, The Crusaders' new home: a statite 22,000 miles above the earth's surface. Over the past few months, though, Dirk had been spending more time by himself. He had become obsessed, it was whispered, with developing a process for burning coal without releasing carbon dioxide into the atmosphere. Millicent couldn't remember the last time anyone had even seen him.

But this Porter Peale fellow sitting across from her, unselfconsciously eating French fries eight at a time, was supposed to be the next Dirk Henderson; still in his first year at Caltech, he already had upperclassman standing. Porter carried with him the results of his efforts in the maze of labs on the Pasadena campus. He was in a constrictive spandex body suit that revealed an unfortunate little pudge of baby fat. Connected to that body suit via an inch-thick cable was something best described as a gizmo - all dials and levers and meters - about the size of an industrial carpet salesman's sample kit, which Porter

228

wheeled along behind him.

"So what is that thing?" Millicent asked, her curiosity getting the better of her.

"It's a dark matter converter," Porter said, his mouth full of starch, grease and salt. Then his voice went up an octave as he enthused over the subject of his baby. "It was the last piece of the puzzle to fall into place. I figured it out just in time to get invited to today's conference.

"You see, matter and energy and space itself must be held constant," he went on, denying Millicent a chance to say the opposite of 'Go on.' "So if you're going to expand an object – eye-ee a person – to a larger size, then you have to be able to expand not only the molecules but the space between them. Otherwise, the person wouldn't just become bigger, he would lose cohesion. He'd pass through everything, wouldn't be able to touch anything and so he'd be useless in a fight. Now, where do you find matter just lying around, not part of something else? And where would you begin looking for space? The answer is simple."

"Dark matter," Millicent replied. She had no idea what it was, but if the gizmo was called a dark matter converter, that was a safe guess.

"Exactly! Wow, you're smart, uh ..."

"Millicent," she said, introducing herself for the third time.

"Millicent. As you know, then, there's five times as much dark matter as atomic matter in the universe. So, with this converter," he gave it a love tap, "I can grow to five times my usual size, along with any organic fabric attached to my body. Gotta be organic, a co-polymer like spandex is ideal. Found that out the hard way when I wrecked my first costume, which had aluminum and nickel in its composite."

Millicent dutifully chuckled at the laugh line.

"It also helps with expanding the size of air molecules as they enter my mouth, because otherwise the oxygen molecules would be only one-fifth large enough for me. So what's your power?" he asked finally, as soon as he was done talking about himself.

"Oh, I don't have one. I work here," Millicent explained. "I'm a computer nerd. Dir ... Mister Henderson has me working on minimizing the size and maximizing the power of the processors required to operate the new Pinnacle of Righteousness."

"Must be quite a challenge," Porter said, leaning in with genuine interest.

"It is," she replied. "But fortunately, I don't have to do all the development work myself. I have a whole staff."

"I didn't know there were more than a few dozen people who knew the exact location of this place," Porter said. "Where's your team?"

"Scattered around the whole country," Millicent said. "We communicate via the Internet."

"You're on the Internet!" Porter gushed. "I'm on the Internet too! Wow! Two of us meeting just by chance and we're both on the Internet! What are the odds?"

"Hey, we're cutting-edge. You know," Millicent said, as her eyes followed the umbilical from Porter's spandex togs to the dark matter converter, "a lot of what my team is focused on is nanotech. We could probably help you compress the insides of that carry-on bag onto a printed-circuit card you could slot into one of your gloves."

Porter got up and started to pace around, wheeling the converter behind. Millicent looked at him, wondering what kind of freak she might be getting involved with. He repeated the word "shrink" a dozen times.

Then he stopped and looked at her, at the converter, then back at her.

"How much do you weigh?" he asked her. "In milligrams."

BAM!

Millicent, Porter, Shel, Lisa and a couple dozen others were ushered into a lecture hall after lunch. The lights went down, except for a blazing pin spot on the red-white-and-blue cowl of Colonel America.

Millicent didn't know what to make of this Elias O'Neill character. He seemed to be getting more arrogant every day.

Like many computer geniuses of her generation, Millicent dropped out of college to pursue opportunities that wouldn't wait. In her case, it was developing systems to support the world's most powerful assemblage of super-heroes. Back then, it was Roger Chadwick in the Colonel America uniform – humble, idealistic, Roger. But after an all-too-short tenure, he passed the torch to Elias who, in Millicent's opinion at the time, seemed like the type who, as a boy, was more interested in Lego blocks than in armies of green plastic figurines. A builder, not a fighter.

But America changed and Elias, her symbol, changed with her. He used to walk into a room. Now he swaggered. He used to ask questions. Now he gave orders.

"Be seated," he told the young adults in the audience. They already were. "Welcome to the annual Crusaders Young Heroes Conference. Those of you with super-abilities have been invited to spend some time with my colleagues Lugh, Saban, Sheikh Teshkeel and of course myself. The Carbon Avenger sends his regrets. We will inform you what you can expect from a career in the heroic services industry and we will see what you are capable of bringing to the fight. Are there any questions."

That itself wasn't a question.

"Not all of you have been blessed with the skills for front-line work in the industry. Your abilities are almost as important, though. You candidates for support staff positions will be meeting with Millicent May. Millie, stand up."

Millicent, who had gone her whole life without finding a nickname she liked - *Millie* particularly grated - was already standing up. She was just very short.

"Millie will be briefing you in breakout room Hombre. The rest of you will follow me to the Looker conference hall. In case you don't know why you're here, Lieutenant Rhode Island will read the list of support staff candidates."

Lisa was stunned when just-an-airplane-driver-called-Clam walked up to the podium and read off a dot-matrix printout.

"Applebaum, Richard. Delacort, Suzanne. Evans ..."

THE BATTLE OF PLAINVILLE

Well, that was humiliating," Georgiana said to no one in particular, though Shel was closest. Eva was busy giving Lugh a reason to smite the evildoer and return unscathed.

"Hey, it got us through," Shel countered.

In the middle of town, the team climbed out of the van, just as their TSA counterparts stepped down from their Expedition a block behind.

"Even so, it's demeaning," she said. "Have you ever been in a place in your life where you know you could be, should be, making more of a mark?"

"Yeah, I know that place," Shel said, placing an avuncular hand on Georgiana's shoulder. He was being gentle but even so, she winced. If not for her goddess-enhanced strength, her scapula would be in a dozen pieces. "I live in that place. I'm mayor of that place."

He was still staring wistfully down the dust-blown street when his tone of voice changed from empathetic to commanding. "Let's get moving! Start with basic recon. We got to locate, identify and end the threat before those TSA pee-pants do or there's no payday. Georgiana, Lugh, take to the air. Bobby, take ground level. Kiley, just try not to—"

"Done," said Bobby, before Count Karma could say anything to match the scowl he had for Shel. Bobby was sitting on the hood of the van, panting for air, an empty Mountain Dew bottle on the curb by his feet. "I didn't, heh, find whatever it is we're looking for but, heh, there's another problem, Shel."

"No one said this would be easy. What's the situation?"

"Colonel America - the new one - is in town."

"Where?" Shel inquired.

"Three blocks east and a block south. There's a ball field. You can see the scoreboard from here. I don't know if they attracted any other attention, but the new guy from the Institute has his eye on them," Bobby said, emphasizing *new guy* with a politically incorrect limp-wrist affectation.

"Who's 'them'?"

"She's got Doc Rudy with her," Bobby said, and that got the whole team's attention. "And as for the gay guy ..."

{BOOM!}

Yes, as for Ray, he was lying flat on the bleachers behind the right-field fence, an evil eye on both Colonel America and Dr. Rudy Goldman, unseen by either.

He'd had a long drive up from Mississippi, and plenty of time to muse about the nature of his power. He could change people, sure, but not everybody and not all the time. Elias O'Neill was easy - he became both gay and evil, although only gay stuck. Ray's power had no effect at all on Lugh. He altered the sexual orientation of each of those rubes in Jackson easy enough, but Ray spent hours pondering how long they'd remain so. Hours? Years? The rest of their lives? Maybe they were all straight again already. He didn't care so much, but he was intensely curious.

What he was more focused on at the moment was tactical. Could he turn this new Colonel America evil? What if he tried and failed, as with the last one? This power of his was still experimental; he wasn't sure what he could or couldn't do, and barely had a handle on the mechanics of focusing his will on his targets.

And as for her companion: could that be Rudy Goldman? The leading suprologist's identity was top secret, but the American Malevolence Institute had ways of peering behind such screens. With all he knew about correcting, refining and enhancing abilities, the doctor would make an excellent addition to the Institute's senior staff.

Ray had selected his target. His brow furrowed in concentration.

Then a hand reached from behind him. Ray felt it clasp over his mouth as a syringe jabbed his throat and a fast-acting neuromuscular blocker coursed straight up his jugular, paralyzing him.

As he stared up at the sky at an odd angle, Ray was the only one to notice a fur-bearing creature the size of a human being bound off the scoreboard and into the treetops. No doubt that was the new entity Maman Brigitte sent him to investigate. Was it spooked, he wondered. Or had it found easier prey?

{ POW! }

Orville listened to Lou Noble much as he did everything, intensely.

"Stay close to me, you mugs," the monochromatic TSA manager said as they moved northward. "But not too close. Stay in line, see? Stay low, and I want a full body length between you and the sap in front of you."

With that, he led his quartet up the street in a jagged path, from tree trunk to SUV to lamppost to brick wall.

Orville followed along last in line, keeping the less experienced Semaphore and the visibly jittery Glyph between himself and Lou. He didn't see the point to Lou's tactic; after all, they weren't dodging sniper fire. Whatever killed Plainville could dodge and hide better than any four low-level, government employees.

But then the column came to a halt.

Lou had led them to a garage that was, unlike most of the other garages up the street, detached from the property's main house. And its door was rolled up open. Once they were inside, protected on five sides by brick walls, slate roof and concrete floor, Orville realized that they had only traveled two blocks, and Lou must have sighted this redoubt as soon as they were out of the Ford. Orville himself spotted it while they were all still buckled up. That's what he knew he was good at: spotting things – things, and people. Interpreting them – useful, useless, friend, foe, mate – was beyond him. Lou had interpreted a garage door two blocks away as an ideal hunting blind and worked out a strategy for luring the beast toward it.

"Enough of this monkey business," Lou intoned. "If I was a ferocious predator, and I'm not saying I'm not, all that zigging and zagging would've caught my beady little eye."

Lou was met by cricket chirps.

Orville could identify his own emotions despite his difficulty of reading anyone else's, and he envied Lou for having the kind of tactical insight that can turn a battle. He welcomed the way envy ceded to self-loathing because it would turn to rage and rage was what he needed. Rage would give him strength. Fury flooded his nasal membranes, imbuing them with the explosive power that he would need to subdue the adversary. He reached into his pocket and put his fingertips on his pepper shaker, removing his nose guard with the other hand.

"Hey, lame brain!" Lou shouted at the daylight. "Come on, chucklehead, show yourself! What are you, yellow?"

What Bella Brock had become wasn't yellow. Her tawny coat was tinted a little ochre, but that wasn't the first thing the TSA team noticed when she appeared in the doorway, silhouetted by the daylight.

What they noticed were the immense incisors and the conic snout above them caked in blood. The sunlight's glint off the saber-sharp claws didn't escape their observation either. Something suggestive of a woman underneath the fur also registered with Orville.

It lunged for Lou, who was already ducking. His trench coat had four gashes across the back, spaced perfectly to fit his thoracic vertebrae. As the wild creature skidded along the concrete floor, nobody had time to express relief. Soon this thing would regain its footing and, now that she was in there with them, which party became caught in the trap was an ambiguous concept.

Without a wasted motion, Semaphore bolted out the door. What was Bella Brock ran after him. She pinned him down and, just as Orville noticed Glyph turning away from the expected gore, Bella wiggled her snout, licked Semaphore's face and purred. Before Orville had a chance to charge to the rescue, Lou rose to his feet and shut the garage door, ending that scene.

Barely a second later, Semaphore screamed, loudly, in pain and in something else. It didn't sound like fear to Orville. It much more closely resembled triumph. In any case, the shriek ended abruptly, like someone pressed the "off" button on an MP3 player while a death-metal track was playing.

"I don't want either of you mugs to think for a blink that Semaphore ran away," Lou said as he jammed the garage door chains with fishing poles that had been hanging on wall pegs. "He gave himself up. You think I kept this joe around just to get past red lights? He was master of all kinds of signals, see? That includes the smells that animals go by. I've seen Semaphore do this in gin joints. He made himself irresistible to whatever that was."

That prompted Orville to ask the obvious: "Whatever

was that?"

"Some kind of hybrid," Glyph replied, with crisp, quiet, calm precision.

"Hybrid?" Lou asked.

"H-Y-B-R-I-D," the world's greatest speller – and orthologist and mistress of all library sciences – continued. "Obviously, the creature is female. Judging by the triangular head and badge patterns on the facial fur, she could be a synthesis of *homo sapiens* and *taxidea taxus.*"

"I caught the first ninety percent of that," Lou said.

"T-A-X-I-D-E-A-space-T-A-X-U-S, commonly called the American Badger, a nocturnal predator of the Great Plains."

"So how do we kill it?" Lou asked.

"I don't know," Glyph replied in her soft-spoken, schoolmarmish way. "But whatever we have to do, I'm sure I can spell it."

"Which is the only reason you're not working at the DMV," Lou was resigned to saying. "Listen, chickie, I'm sorry I got you into this. We're in way over your head. Just stay close to Orville and me and don't try to help. We're going to lie low here for an eternity or two. Then, as soon as Minnie Mouse's nightmare moves on to other prey, we get you back to the hooptie, hightail it out of this burg and dial up The Crusaders. You follow?"

"You are in charge, Mister Noble," Glyph said with some hesitation, "but do you think that's wise, considering that badgers are fossorial?"

"Fossorial?" Lou asked, looking at Orville, who managed a shrug.

"F-O-S-S-O-R-I-A-L. It means that it hunts by burrowing into its prey's den. To a human-badger hybrid, this garage might look like a gopher hole," Glyph explained. "And she knows we're here."

"We should get to higher ground," Orville said, trying to demonstrate an ability to synthesize information.

238

"That wouldn't help," Glyph countered. "She's half human."

Orville looked at her quizzically, unable to form the follow-up question.

"We're related to apes and shrews. At the instinctual level, we're arborial. A-R-B-..."

"We know how to spell that," Lou said. "But I get your drift – no place is safe. Maybe we should—"

Whatever Lou was thinking mattered no longer. There was a scraping noise on the bricks outside the garage followed by a skittering across the roof. It took only one slash of her powerful claws for Bella to shred through the worn-out shingles and rotted wood. She dropped to the concrete floor.

Orville, acting swiftly, brought the pepper shaker up to his nose. One sneeze, packing the force of a 105-millimeter howitzer, knocked a hole in the wall behind Bella, but not directly behind Bella, since she had dodged the blast.

Glyph couldn't move that quickly. In Bella's crushing jaws, though, she did die quickly. Orville watched as the predator tore her throat before she had time to scream. As Bella quenched her thirst on the dark blood fountaining out of Glyph's jugular vein, he realized that he had never witnessed anything that gory before. He began to search for an emotion to connect to that experience, but decided he didn't have time.

"Leave now, Mister Noble," Orville said, deadpan as ever despite the desperate circumstance. "Warn the others. Get help."

"Nix to that, bunkie!" Lou replied as the smell of hot, shredded entrails mingled with the petroleum fumes native to the garage. He found himself shouting to Orville over Bella's primal growl. "You scram! You don't have enough firepower left to—"

Orville didn't argue. He simply proved Lou wrong by

sneezing again. The force was lighter, but that just meant that the hole he knocked in the far wall of the garage was smaller, that bricks were strewn over a shorter radius, and that Bella Brock and what was left of Glyph were thrown barely clear of the garage.

Orville could see the hybrid was knocked out by the percussion. He also noticed that he himself was trembling, which he knew to be a manifestation of fear. But if he were afraid, for some reason that didn't register. He looked over at Lou Noble, and saw that the TSA manager was shaking too.

Then he realized the whole garage was shaking.

"This whole joint's going to blow!" Lou summed up the thought that was too slowly congealing in Orville's mind. Mucus-Man ran over to his team leader, picked him up off his feet and tossed him through the first hole he'd blasted, the one farther from the predator.

Lou Noble was lying flat on the neighbor's lawn when the garage came down on Orville Ortley. Lou tarried a moment as he thought about digging him out. But the hybrid was stirring, and someone had to live to get help.

And to tell the tale.

BAM!

Meanwhile, back at the Chesterfield Mall, Pantagruel was making his rounds. It was lonely business, being the only hero in the St. Louis Metropolitan Statistical Area not deployed to a hot zone. Lonely, and pathetic.

And boring. He was still new in town, but he'd already walked dozens of laps around the first floor. He knew every stand in the food court and the names of every store surrounding them: The Gap, Suncoast, Hallowed Grounds, Gaylen Ross. But he kept making the same loop. Porter Peale wanted to keep walking by Savini & Nicotero, hoping to catch a glance of Forrest, the latest object of his affection – and he was honest enough to admit that to himself.

It was the only thing that kept his mind off Millicent, how deeply he had loved her, and how badly that ended, and how much of that was his own damn fault. He loved her, was faithful to her, but he found out the hard way that those are just table stakes in a marriage. It took much more, and he didn't ...

Porter's neck craned when he saw the man's face in a crowd. At first glance he thought, this guy looks familiar. At second glance, no, it couldn't be. At third, yes, it's him! Fourth, I'm ninety-nine percent sure it's him, but what if it's not - I'd be so embarrassed if I've got the wrong guy and, considering he's black, there's the whole race-fail thing. Fifth, he just caught me looking - I'd better look at something else. Sixth, he just caught me looking again - I'd better say something.

"Myron?"

"Porter," Myron Masters said, extending his arm to offer a simple, uncomplicated handshake that required no training. "Good to see you. It's been years."

"I almost didn't recognize you," Porter confessed. "You really let yourself go."

He regretted that comment as soon as he said it, but it was plausible and sounded just slightly less heinous than, I have trouble telling black people apart if I don't see them every day.

"Thanks for pointing that out," Myron deadpanned. "I thought I might find you here - heard you weren't with The Crusaders anymore," saying, in effect, I know exactly why you didn't recognize me at first, you latent racist, and here's my revenge.

"That's right. I decided to step aside, let in some new blood."

"And how's Millicent?" Myron asked, knowing that was a sore subject too.

"She's good."

241

"She's always been," Myron said with a wink that could have been interpreted as a tic. Or not. Then he piled on. "But she's still up in the Pinnacle with Dirk, right?"

"So what brings you my way, Myron? What can I do for you?"

"Actually, I'm not here to see *you*, Porter," was Myron's last dig. "Do you know where I can find a guy named Seth Hill?"

BOOM!

"Did you hear that?" Colonel America asked the doctor.

"Sounded like a house coming down," Rudy Goldman replied but, before he finished, the new Protector of Patriots had already sprinted a block ahead.

"Hey!" he called out, and that was enough. She realized that locating the threat was Doc Rudy's mission; hers was to keep him safe. Just as quickly as she left, she was back at his side.

"Sorry," she said, and felt the organelles in her blood recoil at apology.

"No problem. Stick to a jog and I'll keep pace."

So it was at a jog that the two left the field in pursuit of their objective.

Ray heard all this but couldn't respond. The neuromuscular blocker froze him.

"Do you know who I am?" asked a voice heavily flavored by central Europe. As Ray lay on one of the footboards high on the bleachers, the face that belonged to the voice hovered over him. It bore a slight resemblance to that of Rudy Goldman. He was an older man with a white mane, stouter and paunchier than Goldman, eyebrows not so bushy. And instead of the American doctor's thick moustache, this man had a meticulously cropped line of beard. Ray presumed that he didn't grow a full beard because he wanted to draw attention to, rather than cover up, the pronounced scar on his left cheek. A nose that had

242

been broken more than once hosted a pair of pince-nez spectacles.

Ray tried to reply and managed only a gurgle – and that only because the effects were beginning to wear off.

"Blink once for yes, twice for no," the accent said. "I ask again, do you know who I am?"

Ray blinked twice.

"Then allow me to introduce myself. You may address me as Herr Doktor Professor Franz-Joachim Maria von Schadenfreude."

"R ... ruh ..."

"I well know who you are, Mister Raymond Novinsky. Ex-Special Forces, eh?" the professor said with obvious relish. "It must gall you no end that an old man like me could sneak up on you so easily and render you utterly helpless."

Put like that, yes, Ray thought, staring tracer fire at the man standing over him. It occurred to him to focus his power on his captor.

"Maman Brigitte asked me to keep an eye on you," Schadenfreude continued. "And it looks like I found you just in time. Did you actually have a plan, or were you simply going to apply your power and hope for the best?"

"Tr ... try ..." he began getting his voice back but abandoning his plan to alter the professor's orientations. If he was this formidable an opponent as a fellow evildoer, turning him good would just aggravate the situation.

"Yes, of course. Every first-time villain with delusions of grandeur wants to try to prove himself. Always going for the glory rather than just doing the job you're told to do. We will kill Colonel America. We will capture Doctor Rudolph Goldman. And did you know that the piddling mall heroes who have of late kept the Institute from our prize are here in Plainville? I thought not. We will dispense with them as well, but we will do it all in an orderly, efficient manner.

Listen to me."

POW!

From three different directions and in staggered time, they met in the town square. Lou Noble lumbered down the street, his monochromatic trench coat in tatters, his face a grayscale mask of misery. He recognized his former employees charging toward him alerted, he assumed by the crash of cascading bricks. Clam Shapiro was in front. A couple steps behind were Lugh and Georgiana; in between them was enough space for another person to stride in step with them. The appendage who called himself Count Karma tagged along. The Blur, out of breath for some reason, straggled in the rear.

"Lou!" Shel called out. "Where's your team?"

"You're looking at us," Lou said, doing his best to mask the pain. He knew that it wasn't the loss that tormented him. It was the guilt. Both were part of being an anti-hero.

"Oh my god!" Georgiana called out. "Orville?"

She had given guilt a name. Semaphore had the guts to make the most of his abilities, Lou reflected, but he was impetuous and was bound to meet an end like this sooner or later. Glyph was also gutsy, but she had no real power that was going to matter in an all-out fight, and should have been content to stay behind at the airport. Mucus-Man, on the other hand, was a true hero, whatever his oddball tendencies. Orville saved his life and, for all Lou knew, he was still alive buried under the pile. But when faced with his own fight-or-flight choice, Lou ran. He rationalized it, he justified it, but he wasn't about to risk his own life for the man who rescued him.

"Sorry, doll," Lou said. "I've been in this racket since nineteen-forty. I never met a braver man."

Lou tried to read Georgiana's face, and figured that a little more information might comfort her.

"He was a hero, lady," Lou continued. "He gave his life

244

saving mine."

As he pondered whether they should go back and re-claim Orville's body, Georgiana walked over to Lou. For a moment, it looked like she was going to throw herself into his arms and sob. Instead, she slapped his face with just enough restraint that his jaw stayed connected to his skull.

She stormed off to be by herself for a moment. Well, by herself and Eva.

"They call me America's Greatest Dick," Lou muttered. "But I guess there's one thing no dick will ever figure out – women."

"You may be right about that," said a voice with a trace of the Midwest, a taste of New York and a smattering of Nicaragua.

"Nebraska?" Shel inquired of the face under the cowl.

"Not anymore. Your friend Elias retired. Of course you know Doctor Goldman."

"I think I know everyone here," Rudy said, then glanced at Kevin, "except him."

"Count Karma," he said, omitting *Master of Arts*.

"Well met, good medicorum," Lugh said. "But we are all of us in peril. Shall we not seek a redoubt? We know not what we battle."

"I know plenty well," Lou said. "A human-badger hybrid. And it doesn't matter if we're indoors or out, on the ground or up a tree. It'll try to pick us off one by one. The smart play, see, is to stay out here in the open. She'll see we outnumber her. We should also make it clear what kind of power we're packing. That'll make her think twice about crossing us. And if she's more badger than dame, then she's probably thinking of getting some shut-eye now and not flashing her peepers again until dark. We could nab her while she's in dreamland."

"Forsooth, a wise and worthy plan," Lugh said.

"You're welcome, Red," Lou replied. "And did you just

245

say a dozen straight words to me, all of which I can repeat?"

"Aye, and more," Lugh said wistfully. "Love doth change
a man, or a god."

"Glad you met the right pantheon, big fella," Lou said as
Eva, unseen, came as close as a ghost can come to blushing.
"Look, Orville's buried under a brickyard that used to be a
garage. I don't hold out much hope, but he might be alive if
we get to him now. And if he is, he'll need a doc."

All eyes were on Rudy.

"You folks dig him out if you can, but I'm here on an
assignment from the government. The local EMS—"

"Orville? Orville Ortley?" gasped Colonel America as
she grabbed Rudy by the scruff of his lab coat and sprinted
up the street to the garage. Marisol Rivera was not going to
leave her foster brother to die.

The rest bolted along with her.

"We can't all rush to the rescue," Shel said as he panted
along. "We have a hostile around here. Somebody has to
stand guard against this, uh, badger. Volunteers for guard
duty? Anyone? No? okay, Georgiana."

"Why me? I have super-strength and—"

"So does Lugh. So do I. Now just take to the air and give
us high cover."

Reluctantly, she agreed. Eva gave Lugh a spectral kiss
and floated up to accompany her protégée. And Count
Karma planted himself firmly in the middle of the street.

"I volunteer for guard duty too," he said, then heard
Shel's response trail off under the sound of boots on the
run: "I don't really care what you do as long as you stay out
of ..."

BAM!

The wondrous thing about downstate Illinois is that a small
plane can land almost anywhere. If no one happens to be
looking in that direction, if there's enough noise and ex-

citement going on, and if it has its transponder turned off, any Gulfstream or Piper can function as if it's loaded with stealth technology.

BOOM!

It took Ray a good ten minutes to get to the point where he could gain his feet.

He staggered in the direction Colonel America and Doc Rudy had rushed, stumbling and rising, over and over. The professor, far from helping, stood idly by and greeted each attempt at walking with a hearty, contemptuous laugh.

Ray tried to form the words, but most of what he said next was an unintelligible mumble.

"W-w-wizzuh, izzumah ...," he began, then found enough diction to issue one coherent word, complete with upward inflection, "p-power?"

Ray was also getting steadier on his feet. The professor walked slowly along with him, not offering any help.

"Ah, my power," the professor said as he pushed his pince-nez back up the bridge of his nose. "I have an innate ability to orchestrate events so that the mighty will meet their undoing in the most deliciously ironic manner. I radiate this event field that causes my enemies' undoing in ways that make them look inept and ridiculous."

"S-saw for myself," Ray said. "And already knew. Part of Institute fellow training. Was asking, 'What's *my* power?'"

"You haven't figured that out yet, young man?"

"N-not completely," Ray admitted. "I stare, c-concentrate, and the object of my focus changes on some basic level. I've used it mostly for turning straight people gay. But I think I can also turn good people evil."

"*Kuhscheisse*!" the professor called out, leaving Ray to pick up the meaning through context. "It doesn't work very reliably, does it?"

"The straight-to-gay runs about ninety-ten, but I have no idea how long the effect lasts. Good-to-evil only happened

247

once, and less than two days later the guy was back on the side of the angels."

"Still gay, though."

"Last I checked."

"Dear lad, you don't have the power to turn anybody anything. All you do is erode the barriers that people set up in their own minds. And you do this by affecting their neurons, which is why I reveled in getting your attention by affecting yours."

"So the people I turned gay ..."

"... had those tendencies all along. Most of us do to a greater or lesser extent. Those you 'turned' would likely have been happily, exclusively heterosexual for their entire lives, but you unleashed their curiosity, and freed them from the self-enforced strictures that their society imprinted on them. I heard about what happened in Mississippi. When these men have exhausted their new fascination and see their lives in ruins, though, I doubt they'll thank you."

"I don't plan to be anywhere around there when that happens. Now you say you had a plan."

"Yes, it involves waiting for reinforcements," the professor said. "We've been keeping to the shadows so far but, before we get to the town square, we should secure—"

"Brilliant, except for one thing."

"What's that?"

"We've been spotted."

A block away, twenty feet up in the air and closing fast, Georgiana was swooping in, leading with her fashionably gloved fist.

That fist landed on Ray's jaw. For the second time that hour, he got planted on the ground.

In a blink, Count Karma was on top of him, landing half a dozen punches to Ray's face. His elbows were at odd angles and skin came off his knuckles. There was more rage than technique involved with the pummeling.

"Ah!" said Professor Schadenfreude with amusement, "You must be that Count Karma we've all heard so little about. How many hours did you put in before you were fired from your last job?"

"Don't play head games with me, Schadenfreude," Count Karma commanded, his words punctuated by another swooping punch from Georgiana, who laid out the professor.

She landed, grabbed him by the lapels of his tweedy Norfolk jacket and pinned him against a tree.

"Go ahead, take your best shot, either of you," Kevin Kiley screamed as he kept up his feckless pummeling of Ray. "It doesn't matter. Turn me gay? So what! Straight hasn't exactly been working for me lately. Turn me evil? Like that's going to make a difference!"

He switched from punching every third word or so to punching after each word.

"I'm. Completely. Useless!"

Then Kevin got up and walked over to Schadenfreude, still in Georgiana's clutch.

"And what've you got?" Kevin asked mockingly. "Do you really think you can do or say anything to humiliate me more than I've already been over the past three days? I'd love to see it."

"My dear boy, I quite agree with you. Nevertheless, you really don't matter. Even as you spoke so eloquently of your own irrelevance and shame, I've already seen to this lovely young lady's ruination."

"Min ... Georgiana?" Kevin inquired. "You okay?"

"Hmm?" she replied. She was obviously distracted, but Kevin had no idea by what. Her grip on Schadenfreude loosened, but tightened up again quickly as soon as he tried to squirm away. "Yes, Count. I'm fine."

And with that, she laser focused on her captive.

"Oh, one more thing," Schadenfreude mentioned, "Ray

has escaped."

Kevin turned. There was nothing but empty concrete where Ray had lain.

{ POW! }

"Mister Hill?"

"You must be Myron Masters," Seth said. "I'm a big fan of your work."

He stuck out his hand, grabbing the base of Myron's thumb then, moving seamlessly as if by long habit, into a finger curl, a shared finger snap and a series of three fist bumps. Pantagruel stood there between them, outside the storefront that had been the Plaquet Box, rolling his eyes.

"I got one of the cards you asked for," Myron said. "I came just as quick as I could. As we discussed ..."

"Let's keep discussing, but not here," Seth advised, as the lunchtime mall-walking crowd presented far too many ears. "Remember Bobby Botler? He has a little *pied-a-terre* on the ground floor. I got a key."

Two minutes later the three men were entering the Blur Cave. As usual, two security guards were smoking from a bong and playing a simulated baseball game with trading cards they had purchased from Seth. Actually, the game was in a delay; four-inch representations of Ty Cobb and Orlando Cepeda had caused another bench-clearing brawl.

"Jim, Deke, do you guys mind giving us a minute?" Seth asked.

After they left, Myron fished the case containing the card out of his jeans and handed it to Seth. Opening the case, Seth studied the card intently – front, back and along all edges – with a jeweler's glass.

"This is of some interest to me," he said without emotion. "The triskelion pattern on the back holds and focuses the mystic energy better than anything they're engraving nowadays. It's a fairly standard trap card, but I do like my trap cards."

"We agreed on a price," Myron prompted.

Seth took out his smartphone, tapped the touchscreen a few times, and announced, "It's in your account now. More than I wanted to pay for it, considering it was stolen from me."

"Is that the card the Institute's been looking for?" Pantagruel asked.

"No," Seth said, taking two steps over to a beat-up end table next to the couch in the Xbox pit. There was a corkboard coaster on the table and an empty beer mug on the coaster. Seth set the mug aside, picked up the coaster, and revealed that taped to the bottom, was the last Malificium card.

"I thought they might send someone who could redistribute my possessions – someone like Equity – after it, so I transferred ownership out of my name," Seth explained. "Weeks ago, I sold it to Bobby for a penny with the proviso that I can buy it back for a penny at any time. And, if anything happens to him, it reverts back to my ownership."

The two former Crusaders exchanged uncomprehending glances.

"This is just a Domesticus card," Seth continued as if either was listening. "It's powerful in its own way – it seals off a domain so that nothing can exit – but it's not a world-changer like a complete Malificium deck."

"I'll stick to superpowers," Pantagruel said.

BAM!

Ray, on the run, ran straight into Maman Brigitte and Equity.

"You're a bloody mess!" Maman Brigitte exclaimed.

"She usually means that as a compliment," Equity explained.

"Not this time. Who did this to you?"

When Ray explained it was Count Karma, they couldn't suppress their laughter.

"But he wasn't alone. Supermodel was with him!"

"And Professor Schadenfreude was with you," Maman Brigitte continued. "So can we safely assume he's captured?"

Ray nodded.

The voodoo priestess called on Simbi, the Marasa and the loa of twenty-one nations to aid her in a spell. At the end of it, amid a column of black smoke and a roar like thunder as gravity stepped aside, clouds parted and a cylinder of sky turned black and starlit.

That cylinder sucked Ray off his feet as if he were jet-propelled. He landed minutes later in a motel parking lot outside Jackson, Mississippi.

One man witnessed it and ran inside to announce, "Hey, it's that guy!"

A small lynch mob of men recovering their lost heterosexuality knocked Ray out cold before he could focus his eyes. Rough justice, irreversible and beyond appeal, prevailed.

BOOM!

Lugh was oddly comfortable in his assignment. He was, after all, the god of construction workers, and knew how to salvage a site such as the garage that had collapsed on Orville.

He had instructed Shel, Lou, Bobby, Marisol and Rudy - in no uncertain terms - not to rush. As instinctual as it was to pull Orville out as fast as possible to get him into the air and light, rushing could lead to further collapse and, if he weren't dead already, that was more likely to kill him.

"We got it, Lugh," Shel said. "Why don't you go check on the other guys? Sounds like there's been a fracas."

Lugh reluctantly left, pulling his talking spear out of its sling.

"Slake me! Slake me!" grumbled Areadbhar, for that was the spear's name. "Let me swig a draught of blood from thine enemies!"

Lugh saw no reason to respond to it. Seeing that Georgiana had matters well in hand, and it was only that poser, Schadenfreude, Lugh sheathed Areadbhar again, over the spear's persistent objection. The poppy scent of its sheath soon mellowed it out again.

"Accolades of the highest, lass!" Lugh said to Georgiana, then turned his attention to the man she was tying with strips of her jacket. Just as well, because Georgiana wasn't much in the mood for conversation. Kevin, who was a half block down the road at an intersection trying to keep an eye on threats coming from all directions, was too busy to add an, "I helped." "Ach, Professor, hast thou not enow? How oft must I hand thee over to the magistrates?"

"Ach, Lugh," the professor said with his customary laugh. "How well-spoken you have become of late. That could only mean one thing."

Lugh was getting a lot of that assumption lately and frankly found it a little embarrassing. It didn't help that the woman who had put him on his best behavior was right there, unseen by all who made such comments.

"It means," the professor continued with an ironic lilt, "you've found a way to forget Bui. Congratulations."

Lugh stood there stunned, as if he'd been punched in the solar plexus without warning.

"Lugh," Eva inquired, "Who's Bui?"

"Bui was my wife."

"Of course she ... wait, you're not talking to me!" Schadenfreude pieced together. "Your new love is here with us now. A ghost!"

"You've been married before?" Eva asked incredulously. He'd never brought it up.

"And thee."

"Yes, but we're not talking about me now. How long were you going to—"

"The funny thing about ghosts is, you're not immortal. Not really. You might haunt this world for years or even centuries, but sooner or later you fade away," Schadenfreude continued. "But not gods. Gods are eternal. And they will carry the scars of daring to love a mortal until the crack of doom. Such loneliness, such emptiness, forever and ever. It's really quite sad."

But still he laughed.

Lugh just walked away. He would not let anyone, certainly not Eva, see his tears. So of course, she followed after him.

With Schadenfreude tied to a lamppost, Georgiana asked Count Karma to keep watch over the prisoner while she lent a hand with the rescue efforts.

Kevin agreed but, before he got two paces closer, the Badger had sensed her opportunity, sprang down from a low-hanging branch, tore the guts out of Schadenfreude as though they were sausage tubes, and leapt back into the early autumn foliage. The body twitched for several minutes as Lugh fought back tears, Georgiana returned to try to rescue Orville, and Kevin just stared at the life ebbing out of his adversary. He had never seen anyone die before. He wouldn't have to wait long to see another such spectacle.

The sound of a sudden battle blared from the direction of the wrecked garage.

Georgiana, Lugh, and Eva rushed back. Kevin Kiley, though, was nowhere to be found.

INTERLUDE: 2000

Austin, the capital and major university town, is the one place in Texas where young men in their late teens and early twenties referred to each other as "dude." As in:

"Dude, you smoked down that joint in, like, a second."

The aforementioned "dude," who also answered to Bobby Botler, was apologetic to the lad, who still displayed the erupted skin and indifferent haircut of the nerdy high school boy he had been just ten months before. He was one of three other collegians, all younger than he, with whom Bobby shared a dorm suite.

"Sorry, man," Bobby replied, a cloud of fragrant white smoke billowing from the depths of a very comfortable, well-broken-in sofa. "I didn't think you guys wanted any more. Y'all just toothpasted your tongues, so I figured you were heading out."

"Want to come with?" another of the roommates asked.

"No thanks," said the perpetually broke Bobby. "I'll just hang here."

"Suit yourself, Blur," said the last roommate on his way out the door with the others. "Happy birthday, anyways."

Bobby tended to lose track of time; he had the record of missed classes and deadlines to prove it. He thought it was March. The calendar on the fridge door said it was. He remembered flipping it up from February just a week before. Or was it two weeks? And how far into March was it before he got around to changing the calendar page?

Damn, he realized, it was April. Apparently it was the 4th, his twenty-third birthday. And the day before the 20-page Comparative Lit paper he hadn't yet started was due.

He looked at the clock on the cable box: 9:21 p.m. Too late to even get started. It didn't matter if it was a day late or a month late. It was going to be late. A quirk of this professor, which had become undergraduate lore at UT Austin, was that a late paper was destined to be graded a C- providing it ever got turned in.

So he had two more reasons to be pissed at himself, part of the slacker cycle of ever-declining self-esteem. Too broke to celebrate his own birthday. Oh well. He remembered, not for the first time, a piece of stoner philosophy that dated back to the 1960s: "Pot gets you through times with no money better than money gets you through times with no pot."

So he went back into his bedroom, got a fresh eighth of Maui hybrid from his sock drawer, returned to the outer room, sat down on the couch, rolled another joint on the coffee table, got up and wandered around until he found where he had set down his lighter, then sat back down and leisurely smoked the joint to a spitball.

As he got up to turn on the TV - God knows where the remote was - he glanced again at the cable box.

9:21.

Got to cut down on the weed, Bobby thought. It's playing with my sense of time. I'd better come down a little.

Forgetting about the TV, he decided to walk down The Drag – the street signs called it Guadalupe Street – to the 7-Eleven for a Coca-Cola Slurpee, the most satisfying blast of head-clearing sugar and caffeine he could afford. The six-block walk would do him some good, too.

But the automatic door wouldn't swoosh open for him, so he turned around and headed back to campus. It was at this point he noticed how slowly people were walking. As stoned as he was, it was as if everyone else was even more so.

Opening the door to his suite, he saw the cable box against the opposite wall: 9:21.

Bobby knew the day he dreaded had finally arrived: his power had manifested. And it was worse than he feared in that he had no way of controlling it. He noticed his T-shirt had been torn away – nothing left but a webbed collar around his neck. His jeans, which had long been a little threadbare at the knees, were shredded into horizontal strips like a heavy metal bass player's. The plastic soles of his gym shoes were sticking to the carpet like glue on Velcro. Bobby took note of these things without analysis. He was stoned, he was on the verge of panic, and he was also unpleasantly aware of how stale the air smelled if he stood in one place.

Holding a bandana over his nose and mouth, Bobby picked up the phone and called the number he was compelled to memorize during his brief stay at the Chadwick home: the 205-area extension for an office at Redstone Arsenal, outside Huntsville, Alabama. That's where he could reach Doctor Rudy Goldman, the only man who could help him.

It took forever for the dial tone to kick in, and Bobby didn't immediately recognize the 600Hz tone – it sounded to him like the low rumble of a power line knocked down by a storm. A slow, pulsing rumble from the handset informed Bobby that Southwestern Bell couldn't process the phone number that he'd entered. So he tried again.

He pressed a button, took a walk around the dormitory suite, pressed another button, took another lap, and repeated until all eleven digits were entered. After what seemed hours, he was rewarded with nothing but a slow-motion, bass-shifted spoof of the three-tone wrong-number prompt. This wasn't working.

Bobby tried willing the world around him to speed up, to no avail. He would just have to ride it out. Not ruling out the possibility that the world slowing to a crawl, had in some way been triggered by the THC in his blood-stream, he laid down and got some sleep, the top sheet pulled over his nostrils. When he got up, at 9:24, Bobby took a minute to read his Comp Lit assignment and write the term paper.

That's when the refrigerator turned on. Well, not really, but that was Bobby's experience of it. He couldn't hear the low hum of the compressor before, but suddenly he could. The cable box now read 9:25 and, a reasonable span later, read 9:26. Bobby dialed the 205 again. A recorded message told him the area code had changed to 256. Armed with that information, he was connected to Rudy's office and, moments later, to his cellular phone.

"Doc? Hi. Sorry to call so late. I don't know if you remember me ..." Bobby began and went into a brief introduction.

The doctor replied that yes, of course, he remembered, and how could he help.

"I seem to have this ability to stop time – or at least slow it down. A lot."

He went on to explain about the automatic doors, the frustrations with the phone, the stale air.

"And your clothes, son. Do they look worn, like you left them out in a storm in the middle of the desert?"

"Uh, yeah. How did you know?"

"The world didn't slow down. You sped up. Better get down here as fast as you - on second thought, take a plane."

POW!

There were more superhero teams back then.

The Crusaders (THE CRUSADERS!!!) were always the class act but, in the days before the Americans with Abilities Act and the TSA takeover of the heroic services industry, there were many others. Prairie Fire, Street Justice and The Warrior Guild were among the myriad teams who protected particular cities or regions. With Carbodyne's financial backing and contacts in the federal government, though, it was The Crusaders who attracted the best and the brightest. If you wanted to do heroics full-time, you had to sign up with The Crusaders, and that was by invitation only.

A young man who until recently had been called Marcos Chadwick was about to get his big break.

BAM!

Brigitte La Vallette thrived in America. Certainly, she had a head start in that she was heiress to a family fortune. But a fortune in Haiti doesn't go as far in the Northeast Corridor. And considering her father had made the money himself - stolen it, actually - and never completed the eighth grade, he was hardly in a position to secure her admission to Harvard. She had done that on her own. She even secured a scholarship; Brigitte didn't really need the money, but she took it anyway. La Vallette *père* was proud.

She was going into either politics or banking. Brigitte left that decision up to her inseparable roommate of the past three years and eight months. Whichever field her constant companion chose for herself, Brigitte would choose the other just so each would have a virtual sister in a position to exchange favors.

As for her roommate's name, what does it matter? She never answered to it. Every branch of her family – Huguenot, Indonesian, Yoruba, and Arabic – insisted on having at least a couple syllables, so it just took too long. In sympathy with the oppressed of the world – and as a thumb in the eye to all those family members who were in the oppression business – she chose a *nom d'ecole,* and that was all she would respond to.

"So have you made up our mind yet, Equality?" Brigitte asked as she came in one afternoon with a reusable shopping bag filled with the makings of a salad-for-two. They often ate light dinners together in their room in the former Radcliffe dorms.

Equality was sitting on her yoga mat – which she also insisted on using as a bed – wearing a Guatemalan hemp hoodie and a pair of loose-fitting Capri pants she'd sewn together from homespun and tie-dyed herself.

"Haven't really thought about it," Equality replied, then belched out a cloud of white smoke. "Where's Phish playing this weekend?"

Brigitte consulted the concert schedule stapled – they couldn't find magnets or scotch tape – to the refrigerator door.

"New York. The Garden."

"Oh. I'll drop by the drycleaner tomorrow, schedule a couple interviews in Manhattan and leave a day early," Equality said as she began going through her warm-up stretches. "I guess I'll just go and be an investment banker on Wall Street."

260

"Don't you love going to Harvard?"

BOOM!

Bobby never went back to Austin.

He spent the next six months under Dr. Rudy Goldman's care at Redstone Arsenal. The trick was to find a
way to control Bobby's bursts of speed. If he could
manage to turn on the jets when the situation called for it
then slow down afterwards to the pace of normal life, he
could be an indispensable addition to The Crusaders (THE
CRUSADERS!!!). If not, he would go through his time on
earth solitary and useless.

All that became abundantly clear after his first week
which, to him, seemed more like a year, alone among a
colony of snails. By the end of his second night there, he
had gone from clean-shaven to sprouting a bad beard. His
facial hair was sparse enough that, pre-manifestation, he
could skip a day or even two of shaving and nobody
would notice, but one morning Rudy had come into his
quarters to find the young man with a growth that was
sparse and patchy yet four inches long at the chin. This
contrasted with the hair of his scalp, which grew in thick,
loosely curled and streaked ever so occasionally with
gray. And Bobby smelled like an abandoned fish tank.

They tried everything: biofeedback, meditation, decaf.
These all worked to some extent, but only in combination
with ethyl alcohol and THC – and in prodigious quanti-
ties, considering how fast Bobby's body passed its toxins.
The doctor fretted, briefly, about how dependent his
patient was becoming on the chemicals, but considered
this the lesser evil.

Then came the day. Buzzcutting off his hair, shaving
close enough to abrade his cheeks to a dull orange-red,
filling a backpack full of soap and deodorant and another
full of George Dickel and a Doc Rudy-prescribed kilo-
gram of the Master Kush strain of medical cannabis, then

261

packing fresh Depends in opaque trash bags that would soon serve as containers for soiled Depends, Bobby Botler was ready to take a long trip.

"Be seated," Colonel America told the young adults in the audience. They already were. "Welcome to the annual Crusaders Young Heroes Conference. Those of you with super-abilities have been invited to spend some time with my colleagues Lugh, Time Tempest, Anniella, Pantagruel and Midge, and of course myself. As this is our first gathering in our new Pinnacle of Righteousness, the Carbon Avenger is on the premises and promises to make an appearance. We will inform you what you can expect from a career in heroic services and we will see what you are capable of bringing to the fight. Are there any questions."

Of course there weren't. Midge, despite being a full member of the team, was still expected to brief the support staff. Their names were read aloud for the eleventh year in a row, by Major Rhode Island, Shel Shapiro.

But that's not the crowd Bobby was attached to. Centrifugal force simulated normal gravity - normal for the moon - and it was in this environment that Bobby bounded toward the Saban room. Behind him was a short, skinny guy with thinning hair and a nose hidden by a crystalline green band. The man, who appeared to also be in his early to mid-twenties but much less weathered, didn't speak. He didn't even make eye contact, but there was something familiar about him. And the man obviously felt some kinship toward Bobby, standing behind him on the lunch line, eating at the table with him and a few other Crusader wannabes, sitting next to him through Colonel America's opening remarks.

Maybe if Bobby's synapses weren't addled on pot and whisky, and maybe if he weren't preoccupied with the constant mental exertion required not to accelerate, he would have recognized him right off the bat. But eventually the memory of the summer before he started middle school, the time he spent in Iowa, waiting in dread for a power to metastasize, deliberately getting into trouble in the hope of getting thrown out, as if that might stop it from happening: the weird kid who didn't look like either Roger or Esperanza but whom they claimed was their son.

It took an hour of real time. It felt like days to Bobby until he turned around to face his ever-present shadow with the green nose guard.

"Marcos?" Bobby asked. "Marcos Chadwick?"

The other paused as he walked down the hall, decorated with photos of Crusaders posing for news cameras after an assortment of their victories over the decades. In one glossy, disco-era photo, a stunning woman whose goggles weighed more than the rest of her costume turned to give a full-faced grin as her boot heel rested on the neck of Sensei Zaibatsu. Switch the goggles for the nose guard and it was the same face.

"My name is Orville Ortley," the young hero said flatly, as he said everything. "I was known as 'Marcos Chadwick' as a boy."

Amid a thundering crash, a huge pile of shale tumbled out of the door to the room they were about to enter. Bobby might not have noticed that the pile of mudrock had eyes if those eyes had not been wide open with amazement. He still wasn't sure the sediment could talk; if it could, it was at a loss for something to say.

Orville paid it no mind, as if landslides occur all the time on space stations.

"My code name is Mucus-man. Hello, Bobby."

BANG!

Meanwhile, in New York's financial district, a recent

Harvard graduate was hard at work.

The quantitative stuff came hard for her. She had, after all, studied anthropology rather than finance, her capstone paper focusing on the similarities and distinctions of containers that the women of various primitive river cultures made by interlacing their indigenous reeds. Yes, she actually majored in basket weaving.

But that had ended months earlier. Gone were the hemp and tie-dye garments, replaced by smart skirt suits, linen blouses, and pearls, her once long and layered hair cut short enough so that she would never miss the 7 a.m. daily squawk. She looked important.

She wasn't. She was an associate - a new hire, a trainee. Technically an officer of the bank, associates were still the lowliest of the low in terms of those who wore jackets to work on Wall Street. That's why they were collectively known by their betters as "whale shit."

Everyone in the training program aspired to a career in mergers and acquisitions, but they had to go through the entire loop before they could network into any particular department. So the young woman who was no longer being addressed as Equality toiled on the trading desk. From 9:30 a.m. until 4:00 p.m., she stared into a Bloomberg terminal, made bets, hedged bets, made side bets, reversed bets, doubled down on bets. The bank gave her some money to play with every morning - not much, only $10 million. The trick was to have more days that ended with $11 million than days that ended with $9 million. On a day when the market was rising, that wasn't too hard: buy an index fund and spend the rest of the day studying for any of the half dozen professional exams she had to take, breaking occasionally to IM with her BFF Brigitte at Georgetown Law.

This wasn't a good day though. Every character on every Bloomberg screen had turned red. Worse, it was a day when the trading department's managing director was having his annual walk around the floor. There'd be no riding the indexes today, or no eking out a small gain on the short side of a mildly downbeat session. This was one of those Armageddons that hit Wall Street a couple times every decade, and the money had fled the market like a school of trout from the sound of an outboard motor. The best a young associate on the equities desk could hope for was to not lose a year's worth of gains before the closing bell's merciful release. To do that with her boss's boss's boss present would be disastrous to her career.

She pictured herself giving up on business, marrying some guy acceptable to her parents and their society friends, probably someone with half her brains but twice her reflexes who was actually able to hack it as a trader. She'd end up spending the rest of her life organizing charity events from the confines of her spacious, tastefully decorated prison in Greenwich, Connecticut. Maybe she'd occasionally be able to make it into the city once every few months to take her kids – the horror! – to some Disney musical or other.

No more Phish tours.

This was not going to happen.

She wasn't aware what transpired next until it was all over. Gazing deeply at the screen, she moved her fingers across the keyboard like Martha Argerich gliding through a Chopin etude. A stock would hit rock bottom just as she pressed the key to buy it. The block of shares would take a ten-cent bounce and she'd sell it just before it reversed direction again and hit an even deeper low. And, as if she knew that was exactly what was going to happen, she'd establish a short position in that stock and make money as it declined. This happened simultaneously with dozens of stocks in every industry. She couldn't know the fundamentals of all these companies, and no recent anthropology grad ever had the math chops to work these miracles through market analysis. The most skilled and insightful traders in the world were being creamed, yet she was holding her own. Whatever she was doing wasn't perfect – she did lose money on some of her bets – but overall, as the trading session wore on, green pixels on her screen gradually crowded out much of the red. The four o'clock clanging startled her, as the time had flown by in a meaningless, undifferentiated haze.

Shaken from her trance, she noticed that she had drawn a crowd. The Dow had dropped over 400 points. The Nasdaq completely collapsed – it was the official end of the dot-com bubble. The U.S. economy was trillions of dollars poorer than it was at 9:30 that morning. Some pension plans would go bankrupt; some fund managers would go to jail. People who considered "master of the universe" their job title would spend the next five years making back the money they had lost that day.

But this one rookie associate had half a screen of red, half a screen of black, and one blue line across the bottom that spelled out: NAV $10,000,000.00 Δ 00.00%.

On the most adverse trading day in years, she had managed to break even.

A wall of slack-jawed but well-coifed heads stared at her silently. One brick in that wall was her managing director. An eighties relic who insisted on continuing to wear solid-collared striped shirts, matching ties and suspenders, and entirely too much mousse in his thinning hair, he peered over his red-rimmed glasses.

"What's your name?" he inquired.

She began to answer, but paused.

"Equity," she said for the first time. I've manifested, she thought. Just like Brigitte. I can't wait to tell her!

The wait would tie her up in knots, but it would be

weeks before she got the opportunity.

BOOM!

"We'll go around the room," Colonel America announced as everyone floated into their seats in the work-in-progress gravity of the Pinnacle of Righteousness. "Let's start with you. You with the flask."

"My name's Bobby Botler," the speedster said, wiping Old No. 8 from his already shaggy chin. "I guess you'll be calling me 'The Blur.'"

"Bobby Botler?" asked Time Tempest, her gray eyes squinting from behind her domino mask, a short crop of red hair poking out behind it. "That sounds familiar. Do I know you from somewhere?"

"The Chadwick Home, about ten years ago. I wasn't there long."

"Yeah, I remember now," said Time Tempest, once a little girl named Tara who was afraid of doctors. She blinked out of existence for a fraction of a second before reappearing exactly where she had been. Her left leg had been crossed over her right, but suddenly that had reversed. And there was a printed sheet of bright-white paper in her hand. "I just checked Roger's records. You were heading into middle school the year they began genetic testing for superpowers as part of the physical. Your markers indicated you as 'high-potential' so your school superintendent sent you to us in a panic. But you never manifested."

"Until now. I caught super-speed."

"It's not a disease. You don't 'catch' it," Pantagruel corrected, rising to his feet and nearly banging his head on the exposed-metal ceiling. "Powers like ours are a privilege, a calling. Most people would give anything to be lucky enough to be seated here in this room. Don't ever be so dismissive of such a gift!"

He was shouting by the end. Midge, who was just

267

floating past the door to get to the support staff briefing, took a moment to glower disapproval. She was accompanied by Shel Shapiro who, in contrast, blew a kiss to his fiancée, the infinitely supple Lisa Lorenzo, now known to evildoers as Anniella. ("Snakewoman" lasted about a month before she cracked open a book on snakes and found the name of a subspecies that had a ring of class to it.)

"Moving right along," Colonel America said, "right next to the Blur I see a young man who's both a Chadwick Home alumnus and part of The Crusaders family."

There was a pause as Orville failed to take the hint that he was to introduce himself next.

"Go ahead, son," The Carbon Avenger said, his voice sounding like it issued from the bottom of a quarry.

"I am Orville Ortley, Mucus-Man. My mother was Olivia Ortley, Looker."

He said all this without any strain in his voice, like he was presenting a status report in a business meeting.

"I was left a helpless, orphaned infant," he continued evenhandedly. "Ta Mok was already in custody and could not have had any connection to the attack that targeted me and killed seven other people who lived in the building. For safety's sake, I was given the surnames Rivera and, later, Chadwick.

"But I no longer seek safety."

{ POW! }

"I'm a full-fledged member of The Crusaders," Midge said in response to a question from one of the dozen of support staff candidates.

"Then why are you in here with us techies instead of with the heroes in the next room?" was the follow-up.

She paused to let out a breath before she said, "Pencils down."

The group closed their notebooks as one.

268

"I made one, huge career mistake, and maybe you can all learn from it," she intoned. Everyone leaned forward in their seats. "Don't become a sidekick."

"How do you do that?" came a question from another quarter.

"You mean, how do you *avoid* that?" Midge smiled, giving the crowd permission to laugh along with her at her misfortune. "Several ways. Number One: don't fall in love with a fellow hero, even if it's someone who is still bucking for hero. That leads us to Number Two: don't get involved in another hero's origin story. You'll spend the rest of your working life in his shadow. You may as well change your first name to 'And.'"

The twenty-somethings in the room didn't know the first or last names of these masked champions, but it was common knowledge that Pantagruel and Midge had recently gotten married.

"But don't you have a power of your own?" asked another candidate.

"Yes, flight, for what that's worth," Midge responded. "Pantagruel is the transcendent genius in the family. He's the one who figured out how to convert dark matter into living-tissue mass. I'm just a technologist who's very good at nanotech. I helped him shrink his gear into something that'll fit into his cowl, and he helped me discover that the four tiny growths on my lower back were actually wings. The trick, which took him about ten minutes to figure out, was how to keep their size constant while shrinking the rest of me down so I could use them."

"Uh, Midge, maybe we could move back into the agenda?" Shel Shapiro prompted, glancing at his over-sized, stainless-steel, NASA-issue Marathon watch.

"The Major's right," Midge replied. "How many people bring mechanical, plumbing, or electrical skills?"

A number of hands shot up. More hands shot up when

she asked about information technology expertise. At this point, the entire assemblage had their hands raised.

"OK. If you have any aspirations of being a hero, put your hand down and don't raise it again. Never, ever display competence in anything besides heroics if you ever want to be a Crusader. There's a whole generation of women with graduate degrees who are executive secretaries rather than executives just because they learned how to type."

Everyone kept their hands up. This was not an ambitious crowd. Midge continued with her dry, prepared presentation, but the questions quickly took her off-track. And the questions grew increasingly personal.

"If I were at normal size," she said in answer to the last question, "like I am now, he'd have to bulk up to about ten feet tall for it to be anywhere near ..." Midge paused, brushing away a lock of hair that had blown into her eye. She put a finger to her lips to hush the crowd. It sounded like a teapot coming to a boil. "Does anyone else hear that?"

BAM!

Doctor Rudy Goldman had recently commissioned a study on the demography of, as the new euphemism went, *persons of ability.* The results revealed that roughly three-quarters were ordinary mortals with a genetic predisposition to gaining powers. This counted all those whose unique talents manifested themselves naturally, as well as those who were exposed to some environmental hazard – radiation, toxic chemicals and so on – that would otherwise have killed them without that genetic trait. It didn't count the billion or so who had the genetic markers but who never manifested an ability.

The remaining quarter were split fairly evenly between two groups. Those who, through sheer force of intellect and will, could invent a device that would enable them to contend with those with innate powers comprised one such constituency. The other was supernatural beings: spirits, angels, demons, elves, even gods. Even so, there was one more sliver – small, but not infinitesimal: extra-terrestrials. They were almost certainly undercounted. Few in the galaxy lived on Earth unless they had no other choice or simply didn't know any better. Some did, but they generally had reason to keep a low profile.

One pretty but not poised young woman of trans-spacial descent was in Bobby's group.

"I am the Princess Xng*nk. But since you can't pro-nounce that, call me Flare Star. I fly and shoot power beams out of my palms," she began. There was nothing regal about the way she spoke or comported herself. Eyes darting, fidgeting in her skimpy, cyan-and-yellow fighting togs, she could have been mistaken for an auto show model. "My planet was a strange, wonderful, entirely alien place, except that everyone was humanoid in every respect, and we had one world government, and we spoke a language that is remarkably similar to English, and we were all Caucasian."

"Verily," began Lugh, "I conjure 'twas as wondrous as the taut, quivering fundament of the moon maid Rigantona, astride her dark steed, its coarse hair poking and scraping at her glittering, shaven—"

"Yes, it was nice," the princess conceded, "what little I remember of it. I was very young when the world ex-ploded."

"How did you survive?" the shale that was once Dirk Henderson asked.

"My parents put me in a small space ship right before the blast."

"Was it a nuclear explosion? A meteor strike?" the Carbon Avenger followed up.

"No, just a spontaneous detonation of the entire planet."

"I have a hard time believing," the Avenger continued, "that any world replete with enough life-granting carbon would ever be so cruel as to destroy that life as well as itself. I have no idea what would drive serene, peace-loving rocks to do that."

"You sound like the people of my planet," Flare Star continued. "They wouldn't listen to my parents. Mother and Father were from the most important family in the world, considered leaders of affairs of state, sciences, arts and letters, but nobody believed them when they said the world was going to blow up. Go figure. Anyway, in a final act of desperation, they put me in a rocket, aimed me at Earth, and lit the fuse. I landed in the American Midwest where a nice family adopted me as a toddler and I've been here ever since."

"The only part of this story I'm having trouble with is that ..." Pantagruel said, then was suddenly distracted. He addressed his distraction, which was flitting around the Saban room. "How many times do I have to tell you not to interrupt me? I have a very subtle, multiple-layered train of thought which—"

"No time for this, hon!" Midge squealed as she buzzed through the room, miniaturized to Tinkerbell size, flapping her wings as fast as she could until she landed in the safety of Pantagruel's palm. They felt a breeze. A breeze on a space station! And it kept getting stronger.

Then the alarm sounded.

What makes heroes heroes, is that they run *toward* trouble. As most of the young recruits climbed over each other to find the Steed they came in on, a select few joined with The Crusaders and ran into the room where Midge and Shel were briefing the support staff.

The question on the minds of many was, where was Major Rhode Island?

272

He fluttered in the support staff briefing room, the source of the breeze, hanging onto a bulkhead by strained, frostbitten fingertips. Bobby was naturally first to arrive on the scene, just in time to witness an information technologist being sucked out of a shattered observation window. A mechanical engineer quickly followed, mouthing a scream that would never be heard. Another was sucked into the vacuum despite his desperate clawing for handholds. And another and another, until there was only one person left alive in the room.

Shel's grip gave way and he plummeted toward the hole. Bobby, braced in the doorway, wasn't sure what to do. Although action had to be taken with all speed, speed itself was not the tool for the job. Bobby began to shut the door on Shel Shapiro to save the integrity of the rest of the statite, and the lives of the rest of its occupants.

But an elastic arm smacked him away. The elastic torso to which it was attached swung around Bobby as three elongated limbs and a neck tried in vain to grab Shel as he tumbled into eternal night.

Shel didn't panic. He was certain, though, that every other soul floating in the statite's orbital trail was likely to meet death in the most horrifying frame of mind imaginable. But a Marine aviator – no less Colonel America's heir apparent – wasn't given to surrendering to terror.

He knew that, despite what he'd seen in movies, bodies don't explode just because they're exposed to a vacuum. He also had the presence of mind to carom off a length of exposed rebar as he fell into the void, deflecting himself to the sun side. Space wasn't cold. It was, in Shel's experience at least, searing hot.

He had two lungs full of air, which would keep him alive for three minutes or more, and he could struggle to remain conscious for most of that time.

Not that consciousness was at all desirable. Knowing

that he wasn't going to explode didn't mean that five pints of AB-negative blood weren't pounding pain through every depressurized vessel. Shel felt his fingertips blistering; he was dressed in a flame-retardant jumpsuit, but with the sleeves rolled up. The best protection he had was the thick, Vibram soles of his flight boots. Shel maneuvered himself so that his feet pointed toward the photosphere and he was staring out into empty space, his bare hands and forearms in front of him in imitation of diving off the highest board ever.

The Pinnacle of Righteousness was a stew of human emotion and superhuman impotence. Pantagruel managed to pry Anniella away before Bobby closed the hatch, sealing off the vacuum-exposed room. Her elastic limbs wrapped around the giant-like tomato vines around a garden lattice. Relaxing her grip, she collapsed onto the deck – slowly in the low gravity – in a writhing mass.

At that moment, she was no longer a Crusader, just Lisa Lorenzo, a woman whose love of ten years was dying less than a dozen yards away, yet she was powerless to do anything to save him. She knew she had little control over her power in space – the lack of resistance could cause her to overshoot any rescue attempt, and the extremes of temperature might render her too brittle.

She imagined her love reaching out to grab her hand, only to have it shatter at the touch of his, then the longing on his face as he tumbled into infinity.

Midge expanded to full size to give whatever comfort she could to her friend – was it six years already since Lisa stood as her maid of honor?

"Time Tempest!" Colonel America, the clearest tactical mind on board, called. "Go back and—"

"Sorry, Elias," Tara replied sheepishly. "I just used my power a few minutes ago, so I—"

"Flare Star!" he called next. "We need you to—"

"Hell, no!" the princess called back. "I'm from a planet just like yours. I can't survive any longer than—"

"Mucus-Man, we need another hole in the wall," the Colonel continued. Orville reached for his pepper shaker. "Wait for my signal. Carbon Avenger, you'll give us a radiation shield."

The Avenger, who had formed an approximation of a head, neck and shoulders, nodded.

"Lugh, we have no choice but—"

"Nay, waste not precious breath!"

"Anniella, give us a barrier!" the Colonel ordered the weeping, amorphous mass on the floor. Without drawing a second breath, he softened his tone ever so slightly. "Look at me. We all care about Clam. We're going to rescue him. But you've got to hold it together for just another minute if we have any chance of surviving the rescue attempt ourselves."

Lisa looked up and locked eyes with Elias O'Neill. She didn't wipe away the tears, but there was no mistaking the grim determination behind her moist eyes.

"Panty, Midge, get yourselves and everyone else off this deck! We'll meet you in the Keep as soon as we're done." As they complied, Colonel America led Mucus-Man, Lugh, the Carbon Avenger and Anniella down the passageway to an observation deck that had a frighteningly clear view of the field of the dead and dying trailing behind the satellite.

Shel was still enough to be dead, Elias considered, but probably wasn't. He was in a survival posture, facing away from the sun. Even so, sparks were quickly forming and just as quickly dying around the soles of his boots. The Colonel was less optimistic about the other bodies floating out there.

"Mucus-Man! Now!"

A section of triple-paned, transparent wall shattered out

as Colonel America broke a cabinet open to collect an oxygen mask for himself. He tossed another to Mucus-Man and a third to Anniella.

The Carbon Avenger, who had morphed into a bipedal approximation of human form for the short trek down the corridor, now took the form of a stack of thick, jet-black tiles that dealt themselves like a deck of cards out into the void. The pieces joined together as a shield between the bodies and the sun.

Lugh left it at, "Ach, fuck-all," before tree-trunk legs launched him into space. Holding his enchanted adze in front of him, the god beelined toward Shel. The major's crew-cut hair was singed, his arms erupting in blisters. His lungs struggled against the reflex to gasp.

Even so, the expression on Shel's face couldn't be mis-read. Moving only his eyes, he waved Lugh off.

Rescue the others first.

Lugh had come to enjoy the company of this fellow warrior, this future comrade. The others hovering nearby, immobile, were of secondary importance to Lugh. Re-specting Shel's gallantry, though, Lugh flew a circuit to see if any of them were left alive.

None were.

So Lugh scooped up Shel in his massive left arm and flew him toward the statite. As Shel succumbed to the inevitable blackout, Lugh saw that the hole in the obser-vation deck was plugged with some malleable material.

Lisa Lorenzo. Except for her face, which hid behind an oxygen mask, her entire body was flattened and molded with the consistency of used chewing gum, adhering to the irregular hole Orville had blasted in the Pinnacle's exterior. She rolled up like a window shade to allow them to enter, then flattened against the breach once more. Facing inward, she saw two things happen simulta-neously. Lugh, known to hate space travel, not because of the exposure or the lack of oxygen but just because freefall played havoc with his digestion, retched violently between vulgar epithets. Far more importantly, Shel, now that he was in an oxygen-rich environment again, burst into flames. Not all of him - just the back of his head and his lower arms.

Lisa threw her rubbery body on top of him, smothering the fire-engulfed tissue while keeping his airways clear to breathe. Behind her, she could hear tiles - the Carbon Avenger - clicking into place to seal the hole she could no longer plug. Once the breach was secured and the room began to fill with oxygen again, Colonel America opened the door out to the corridor as Mucus-Man ushered Lugh, Anniella and Shel Shapiro out of harm's way.

BOOM!

The repairs - and recovery operation - continued in geosynchronous orbit under the Carbon Avenger's direction. Meanwhile, Colonel America piloted the still-glitchy Steed One down to the airfield at Redstone Arsenal, with Midge along to slap the capricious guidance system into compliance.

In the back of the craft, Anniella never left her man's side, nor his front or back, until he was on Dr. Rudy Goldman's table.

Hours went by in the hell known as a surgical waiting room.

"He'll live," Doc Rudy pronounced. "The burns to his scalp are, well, I wouldn't call them superficial, but the only lasting effect will be a nasty scar."

Lisa Lorenzo nodded along impassively. There was another shoe to drop, and she knew it.

"His arms ... I'm sorry, Lisa. I did everything I ... had to amputate. Both of them, above the elbows. It would have been far worse if you hadn't acted so quickly."

She collapsed on Rudy, sobbing on his shoulder. He put his arms around her and gave a sympathetic embrace; her torso gave way like a tube of toothpaste squeezed in the middle. After a minute, Lisa regained her composure and disentangled her arms from his neck, back, waist, and a second loop around his neck.

He stared into her eyes. They were bloodshot from tears and at least twenty-four hours without sleep.

"There is something we can do for him," Doc Rudy continued.

BODY COUNT

◆ t happened so quickly.

Maman Brigitte had snuck up behind Shel Shapiro as Equity snuck up behind The Blur. Simultaneously, they touched their chosen opponent on the hand. Instantaneously, Bobby Botler lost half his speeding ability as it transferred to Equity. They whizzed off in a wide arc, chasing each other around, measuring one another's reactions. Trying to watch them was like trying to watch the first round of a DVRed boxing match on fast-forward.

Maman Brigitte, for her part, came up empty. She found something out about Shel in that moment: as natural as his hands looked, they were mechanical, not flesh-and-blood. She couldn't kill him with just a touch. Simultaneously, Shel realized what she was trying to do and why her effort failed, and he wasn't going to give her another chance. With his other bionic arm, he swung around and grabbed Maman Brigitte by the throat, picking her up so her black, high-heeled boots were at least another heel-length off the short, browning lawn.

He expected her to gag, and she did. He didn't expect her to follow that reflex with a smile.

Sensors informed him that he was touching flesh, 400 pores per square centimeter - very tiny pores. The smooth gleam to her face, the kind that funeral parlors hire cosmeticians to paint on faces of the dead, was Maman Brigitte's natural tone. Her skin was 36 Celsius, not quite normal - a degree closer to death.

That smile, though, was sudden, unanticipated, and eerily beautiful.

He let go of her. He didn't mean to, but his arm no longer responded to his commands. He believed they were responding to hers, but they weren't. Maman Brigitte had given them the gift of life. Carbon-steel cables became writhing creatures like worms or snakes that crawled up Shel's partial humerus, ravenously devouring bone and sinew. Far below the threshold of vision, electronic signals took physical form as a bacterium that entered the brachial vein and spread in seconds to every organ in Shel's body, infecting, corroding, causing collapse.

Shel's life did flash before his eyes, and he regretted little. He was grateful for the opportunity to serve his country as a Marine, and honored to have been considered a potential Colonel America and had long since made peace with being denied that prize. And as tedious, unchallenging and ultimately futile as his TSA career was, it allowed him to be a husband to Lisa and a father to Jael and Matt, and they were the true meaning of his life. His only regret was leaving them.

As he collapsed on a bald patch of dirt, no longer breathing, urine and feces flowing unobstructed, red blotches in his skin erupting in blood, he cast a final glance at his colleagues. Doc Rudy was struggling to run to him, but Colonel America - the successor it should have been his honor to train - restrained him for his own safety. Shel's forearms and hands were writhing masses of living metal but he was able to lift an elbow to a spot near his forehead, a final salute to them. He also gave a nod to Lou Noble, with whom he never really got along. Lou did, after all, waltz into a management job that Shel had teed up, but what did it matter now? He conveyed with the nod that all was forgiven.

Lugh, his best friend. A god, yet powerless to save him. Eye contact was all it took to say goodbye. Floating in midair next to Lugh, Shel could see Eva Peron for the first time. She was figuratively as well as literally a vision, and he gave her a wink to say, take care of the big dope.

He didn't see Bobby, but heard him buzzing around, trying to outrace a similar fate. Shel locked eyes with Kevin and hoped he would understand the more elaborate message he had to convey, you were never much of a hero or much of a man. But I'm dying now, so you're more of either than I am anymore. It's not too late for you. Dig in. Dig in.

But against Maman Brigitte, Equity and – somewhere out there – the Badger, the team would need more than a hero. They would need ...

With his last breath, he whispered, "Mindy."

POW!

"So where is Bobby?" Myron Masters asked as he paced around the Blur Cave. Seth Hill had settled down to play the Colonel America-inspired shooter on Xbox. "Did you know I met him ten years before he even joined The Crusaders? It would be great to see him again."

"I don't know," Seth said, his concentration broken, red pixels splashed around the screen, annoyance creeping into his voice. "I was expecting him back by now."

A few minutes earlier, Porter Peale had announced he was going back on rounds and was, at that moment, heading back to Savini & Nicotero to see if he could make a little more time with that eye-catching funeral director.

BLAM!

To answer Myron's question, though, Bobby was in an exhausting, high-speed duel with Equity. At least, that's what everyone else saw. From their own point of view, as they zigged and zagged around Plainville, it had the feel of an awkward first date.

"So, the semi-famous Blur," Equity offered. "I must say, I'm envious of your power. This speed is invigorating."

"Tell you what, suit: I'll trade you even-up for all your money."

She laughed. Bobby thought she had a pretty laugh – honest, an open, full-throated laugh of someone who knew what it was like to enjoy life. Apparently, she wasn't born in a tailor shop. She actually seemed to have a pronounced fun-loving, down-to-earth side. As he ducked the brick she hurled at him at Mach 6, though, he remembered she was there to kill him.

"You could've had that too, Bobby, if you'd have just done what I did and work for it. Can I call you Bobby? Our dossier on you tells us that's your real name."

"Bobby's fine," he said as he maneuvered behind her and got in a sucker punch, but not a good enough one to rupture her kidney. He just caused her a stabbing pain.

"Oww! Good shot!" Equity said. "I like that: Bobby. Not Robert, not even Bob. You must've had cool parents."

"Until they found out I was a freak, yeah, they were okay." He stood still momentarily and let her charge him, then moved out of the way and, before she had time to stop, momentum took her into the exterior wall of a 150-year-old house. She bounced off it, face scratched and bloodied, but her outstretched arm clotheslined him onto the hood of an old Plymouth.

"That must've been rough," Equity commiserated. "I guess I'm lucky that my powers didn't manifest until I was out of the house."

"Well, me too. But they got all crazed when they found out I had the markers – tried to give me away in sixth grade, if you can believe that."

"But at least you got this amazing gift. So I guess it all ended up for the best."

"Well, like the man said, 'You gave it to me but I really don't want it ...'"

Equity's eyes widened.

"You're into Phish?"

Bobby, although far more skilled and practiced at using bursts of speed, was getting winded. Equity saw to it that they were equally matched for speed, but she definitely had the edge in conditioning.

"Yeah," he said, as he stayed two steps ahead of her for a few laps around a backyard vegetable garden. He'd have to put an end to this quickly or his heart was going to jump out of his chest. "I followed ... them for about a year right before I manifested, and got the Incompletes on my ... college transcript to prove it."

He ran full-tilt toward an old, wooden grain silo, looking over his shoulder at Equity, making her wonder if he knew the silo was there.

"Was that about ten years ago?" Equity asked. She eased off the pace, not wanting to run into the structure that Bobby looked like he was about to plaster himself into.

"Yeah."

Momentum carried him up the side of the tower, a trick Equity had yet to learn. He was trapped up on the domed roof for now, but at least he could catch his breath and think of something else. There was only room for one person to stand there, so it would be easy enough to protect himself if Equity should attempt the same maneuver.

"Did you go to any of the shows at Madison Square Garden?" Equity shouted from below.

"You kidding? I drove up from Austin! I went to *all* their shows at the Garden!"

She improvised a trick of her own, running round and round the silo until she created an artificial tornado.

"Ohmigod! Me too!"

It wasn't the wind that knocked the tower down. It being late October, the structure was filled beyond nameplate capacity, and the low pressure of a cyclone's eye caused it to explode at the seams. Bobby survived the 50-foot plunge just to be buried and crushed amid 70 tons of durum wheat. Most of that was packed below him, but ten times his body weight still stood between him and the cooling air.

Equity saw one of Bobby's deep-treaded boots kick through the wheat. She felt his speeding ability fade from her body, an unwelcome sensation in so many ways. Under other circumstances, she could definitely see herself hooking up with this guy.

As a farewell, she concluded Tom Marshall's lyric from the Phish song, "Julius," the one Bobby had begun less than a second before:

"... I came out on top by the luck of the draw."

BOOM!

There was another consequence to Bobby's death, aside from Equity's deceleration. It also meant that the last Malificium card passed from his possession back to Seth's. And half of all the cards that Seth owned could be possessed by Equity.

Seth held, at that moment, only two cards that he hadn't owned when his shop was invaded: the Malificium that Bobby had been holding onto for safekeeping, and the Domesticus trap that Myron had smuggled away from the Institute.

The two cards seemed to do a little dance on the table where they were placed. You stay, I'll go, one seemed to say to the other. Oh no, the other seemed to respond, I wouldn't hear of it. You stay put.

Eventually, the cards came to some agreement and it was the Malificium that took flight.

It flitted around the hideout trying to find a slot or a crack to wriggle through when Myron spotted it from his perch near the beer fridge.

"Seth!"

Seth didn't waste a second grousing about the new interruption. He dropped his controller and let the shooter-POV screen wash red.

The Malificium card sensed that it could escape to the parking lot and open sky by diving under the rollup gate. Myron grabbed it and was rewarded by being swung by the card over and over into that gate, hard enough to make dents, hard enough to sustain some life-threatening internal injuries.

But he bought Seth the time to play the Domesticus trap. The card was sealed in with them.

Then again, the whole mall was sealed in. An invisible force barrier wrapped like cellophane around the entire two-floor structure, including the part of the roof that was still open to the sky following the action two days earlier.

Seth ran into the first-floor concourse outside the Gaylen Ross screaming for a doctor for Myron. Nobody heard him, though. The crowd was screaming to be allowed to leave. They weren't panicked.

Yet.

And it took the presence of a 40-foot Pantagruel – none too pleased to have an amicable chat with Forrest disrupted – to maintain calm.

{POW!}

Georgiana was closest and went for the fast knockout. Maman Brigitte was faster, though, and stepped into the realm of the dead, emerging a moment later half a block away. Georgiana took flight, closed the distance, and delivered another punch to thin air.

Maman Brigitte reappeared where she had been a moment earlier. Areadbhar, Lugh's singing spear, zeroed in on her with a shrieking war cry – and lodged harmlessly in a tree as Lugh went to retrieve it.

Colonel America was preoccupied with protecting Doc Rudy, so Lou Noble was the only good guy who noticed two other things that were going on. First, Equity was twitching, as if an unseen chain were pulling her. Second, there was a displacement of the rubble that had been the detached garage. Orville lived!

A glove caked in brick and mortar shot out of the pile, dragging a panting face and heaving chest after it.

Lou lunged at Equity, figuring that as the least powerful part of the crew, it would be best if he stuck her with half his power. If she were his equal, he reckoned, she'd be no match in a brawl for any of the rest of the superpowered team.

Preoccupied as Equity was with the tugging impulse, she didn't notice Lou before he grabbed her, held her in a full nelson and threw her to the ground. She tried to roll out of his way but he threw himself down on top of her. All that remained was to induce flesh-to-flesh contact. He planted an impassioned but strictly close-mouthed kiss on her.

The color drained from her – well, not all of it. As Lou pulled away, he saw the ruby-red lips fade to rust-orange. Her exotically hued skin turned sepia. Her eyes darkened to jet.

"Outta sight! You sure know how to get it on with a chick," Equity said to Lou, just before her knee found his crotch.

He got off her in a hurry. In the awkward tumble, his tan trench coat fluttered above him. *Tan!* Maybe it would have been a deeper ochre if Equity had absorbed all of what made him unique but, still, *tan!* Through the pain, he also wondered what his tie looked like in color. But it wasn't there, having been replaced somehow by love beads. And he wondered how his pants had turned purple and flared at the cuffs.

"This is a bust, turkey!" he stated as he regained his footing.

"That would be a stone gas to you and the rest of the fuzz," she said. It was hard for anyone not to notice, let alone America's Greatest Dick, that Equity was clothed in a plaited miniskirt, low-scoop T-shirt and definitely, definitely no bra.

"Dig it," he said.

"Right on, but I can't let that kind of bummer happen," she replied as she backed toward the brick pile.

It occurred to Lou that Equity had not just split the difference with him on period slang and clothing, and not just absorbed half his grayscale. She was also every bit as observant as he was and had already spotted Orville. In mock imitation of Lou, she planted a kiss on Orville, winked at the once-more monochrome anti-hero and picked up a handful of scattered lawn clippings. As the heroes who had given up chasing Maman Brigitte closed in on her, she rubbed the dying grass in her face and sneezed, resulting in a mucous blast with a velocity of explosion of 625 meters per second at 15 degrees Celsius at sea level. A hail of bricks slowed the heroes down and fully uncovered a bloodied but conscious Mucus-Man.

As they tended to him, Equity returned to the field where the Institute's plane was waiting and met up with Maman Brigitte already aboard. They taxied and took off. Lugh gave chase for a while, but he had his limits with speed and maneuverability. The Institute's pilot eluded him easily.

"Brigitte, we have to go back to St. Louis!" Equity gasped, out of breath from her sprint, the engine noise almost drowning her out. Her eyes were wild with excitement.

"Why? What's so important?"

"The card! It's there – and it's calling for me to come get it!"

There was something different about Orville, Georgiana noticed, as she carried him as a groom carries a bride. What it was, she couldn't tell. Maybe it was just a look in his eye –

as if he understood something he didn't understand before.

And he was smiling, something Mindy hadn't seen him do before. She didn't have time to reflect much more on this curious expression. Colonel America threw them both to the ground and the three of them nested there for a moment in darkness under her bulletproof cape.

Lou Noble's muffled shout of "Badger!" echoed off the building fronts of Plainville.

INTERLUDE: 2001–PRESENT

So? What's the big news?" Brigitte asked her cleaned-up-so-nice lunch companion, a couple days later. They dined *al fresco* at a white-tablecloth restaurant in Washington's Adams-Morgan district that served Indonesian-Cajun fusion. A mockingbird perched on a fencepost an arm's length away, entertaining the carb-counters who routinely left their dinner rolls untouched. It performed a medley of robin song, crow caw and car alarm while Brigitte asked, "Promoted? Engaged? Going to law school?"

She worked her mouth soundlessly: powers.

"You manifested?" Brigitte responded, reflexively reaching out to take Equity's hand. "Ohmigawd! What can you do?"

"Anything you can," was the deadpan reply. And with that, Equity reached out at the songster atop the fence-post and the mockingbird keeled over in mid-note, straight onto her plate.

"Waiter! There's a bird in my hamhock satay."

"That's astonishing," Brigitte said. "You actually or-dered meat."

"Lots of changes, girlfriend."

"How did you do that?"

"I focused my attention on the bird, called on Baron Samedi to send Ghede Nibo to—"

"I know how *I* do it," Brigitte interrupted, "but since when do you have the skills of a Voudoun mambo?"

"That's the really cool part," Equity replied. "I have the ability to match the power of anyone I encounter. I just have to touch you – or, in this case, let you touch me – and I'm your equal!"

"That is awesome!" Brigitte exclaimed. "Now give it back."

"Sorry, I'm stuck with half your powers until one of three things happens."

A pause reminded Brigitte that, at some level, this was still her slightly loopy ex-roommate sitting there.

"Like?"

"Oh, like if I touch somebody else, or if you die, or if I have to use my core power, the one that this transference ability is only part of."

Another pause.

"And that is?"

"I can't lose. If I'm in any kind of contest and I'm doing okay on my own, I win. If I'm losing, I just tap into this unconscious sense that I have, and I end up tying or, if tying isn't an option, standing a fifty-fifty chance of success."

"Um, not to spoil your fun, but I'd really like the rest of my powers back as soon as you're done with them," Brigitte said. "Could you maybe grope a hot-looking Mundie or something?"

"Of course! As soon as I get back to the office."

"Office? You moved down here and didn't tell me?"

"Oh, no. I'm still a New York girl – like in *Sex & The City*, but not all wrinkly and dye-jobby and pushy-uppy.

290

But I'm working out of a client's office this week. And that's the other reason I wanted to have lunch with you today, Brigitte," Equity said, her face suddenly contorting from vapid career rookie to calculating villainess. "Clear your calendar. Come back to the office with me."

BAM!

"Brigitte La Vallette," Ta Mok read the name off a dossier, as the woman herself stood right in front of his desk. He had worked hard to affect a standard American accent, but his southeast Asian singsong still managed to poke through. "Graduated Harvard this past May, *summa*, with a major in neurobiology. You speak fluent English, Haitian Creole, Metropolitan French, the Ewe and Fante dialects native to Ghana and I'm sure I'm missing one or two. You were active in Vestis Council, played two years of women's lacrosse ... I didn't even know Harvard had ballroom dancing as a varsity sport but there, again, you are. You sat down for the LSATs cold, no coaching, scored a 179 and got into Georgetown Law, where, after your first round of midterms, you have the highest grades in your class."

Brigitte said nothing. She was sniffling a little, repressing a distaste for, and possibly a mild allergy to, the smell of new, industrial-shag carpet. Equity, meanwhile, beamed with pride.

"In short, I don't see anything that sets you apart." He turned his supercilious gaze from Brigitte to Equity, whose mouth gaped with disbelief. "This isn't the old-boys' network, Equity. Why are you wasting my time with a candidate who's borderline at best?"

"Ta Mok, there's a great deal in Brigitte's background that just doesn't translate well onto a *vitae*."

"That's my point," Ta Mok said, swiveling around to stare at the window, giving the women his back. "I know perfectly well about her ability. It's perhaps the most profound power one could acquire: mistress of life and death, nothing short of that. She touches a live thing and she can kill it. She touches a dead thing and can bring it back to life."

He paused for breath and effect.

"But that's not all, is it, Miss La Vallette?" he asked her spectral reflection in the window, faint, all but gone in the midday southern exposure.

"No, sir," Brigitte replied. Ta Mok didn't say another word, which she took as a command to expound. "I summon the spirits of the dead, human or animal. They answer my questions, reveal their secrets to me. I can put them back in their bodies to serve me, or command them to tear themselves to shreds if I have other uses for their flesh and bones."

"Anything else?"

Brigitte was silent.

"Yes," Equity announced as Brigitte's eyebrows shot up and upper lip curled in reaction to the betrayed confidence. "She can pass through the Realm of the Dead."

"Is this true?" Ta Mok asked, pivoting around to stare straight into Brigitte's wide eyes.

"Not far," Brigitte said. "Cambridge gets cold and snowy. We didn't have that in Haiti, or at the boarding school I went to in North Carolina. Sometimes I walked through the Realm to get to class. If I were to stay there for more than a few minutes, I'd never be able to find my way back."

"And this is how you use your gift," Ta Mok said with scorn, "to keep your feet dry. To get your term papers written and your test answers checked. To get into law school."

He spit out that last charge like gristle from an allegedly lean cut of steak. "I'm detecting a certain lack of ambition. You're like a child who doesn't want to grow up, Miss La Vallette. You just want to keep having slumber parties with your playmate here."

Equity bristled with the backhanded insult but kept silent.

"Your friend got a straight job, so you decided to start a career that would give you an excuse to stay in touch. If she'd kept following that hippie rock 'n' roll band, you'd be living out of the back of a van today."

"Ta Mok! That's hardly fair. Brigitte carried me through college, not the other way around."

"Oh, I'm well aware of your academic mediocrity, *Equality*. If I ever need a primitive-looking basket and The Bombay Company is closed, I'll call you. You were on the verge of washing out of your bank's training loop before you became aware of your own powers, no? So what would have happened to both of you if fortune hadn't chosen that moment? You two would be spending the next couple decades selling apple cobblers at bake sales for the Stepford PTA."

Brigitte and Equity looked at each other with equal parts empathy and shame.

"Equity has charted a new course, though," Ta Mok continued, he now stood behind the chair he was sitting in. "So I can only assume that you, Brigitte, will follow it as well. Only one question remains, and it's an important one. It's important because we need to pass the torch. The days of the likes of me or Schadenfreude or Zaibatsu will soon come to an end. Our leader has presented us with a highly ambitious master plan, one we're too far past our prime to execute. We can help, we can guide, but we can't be the standard bearers anymore."

He directed the rest of his comments directly to Brigitte. The spirits assured her that he was just being as persuasive as he could naturally be; he was not attempting to use his powers on her.

"We need someone to not just take up the fight, but to take up the mantle. Equity will keep the money flowing but if all you want is to continue having lunch every day with your old roommate, there's no place for you here. What passes for excellence in mundane circles won't do at the Institute. If that's all you've got, go back to law school," Ta Mok summed up. He patted the back of the big chair behind the big desk, pulled it out invitingly. "Time to choose a side."

BOOM!

Shel Shapiro made a full recovery. His body accepted the bionic arms as readily as they would have accepted Colonel America's organelles. From a sitting position, leaning against an exterior wall at Doc Rudy's lab, elbow resting on a concrete-reinforced counter, he could curl more than seven tons through ninety degrees.

But that's not what indicated full recovery to Shel. It had more to do with dexterity than strength. When he was able to slip a gold band on the third finger of Lisa Lorenzo's left hand, he considered himself made whole.

Everyone who was anyone in the heroic services industry stood witness. It was an emotional scene.

And it was an irresistible target.

POW!

Maman Brigitte chose, and world events cascaded as a result.

Those who say "time is money" are wrong. Europe spent a thousand years plodding through the Middle Ages and barely broke even. In truth, *risk* is money. Maman Brigitte was in the unique position of having a best friend who took the risk out of anything. Evil had always paid well, but not steadily, relying as it did on the big score. When society demanded a tough stance against property crime, Equity was able to engineer theft on an unimaginable scale through Wall Street's darkest machinations. When the focus shifted to enforcing consumer regulations, Equity was able to calculate the take from every mugging, carjacking and sex-for-food stamps operation, aggregate them, factor them, collateralize them and resell them as derivatives that looked like condo mortgages to everybody else.

It also looked to everybody else as though the money disappeared down a drainpipe but, in fact, it filled the coffers of the American Malevolence Institute. The Institute, in turn, provided a revolving rogues' gallery of villains who split their time between lobbying, Congress, Cabinet positions, the top ranks of private industry and maximum-security prison with cash, perks, influence and full medical coverage. It suddenly became *the* place to put in your resume if you were truly, deeply, irredeemably psychopathic. And Maman Brigitte became known in the circles that mattered as the one who eclipsed all previous masters of evil.

Through the early days of the new millennium, much of what the Institute did under Maman Brigitte was a diversion. Nobody would believe that the most nefarious league of supervillains would spend the better part of a decade intent on little more than collecting trading cards, but Maman Brigitte couldn't afford for anyone to even guess that. So the Institute's operations continued: banks were robbed, armored cars held up, drugs dealt, Disney films pirated and, what's worse, produced in the first place. As it became clear that senior staff members were being recruited just so that they could be captured by heroes and the grand masquerade could continue, it became harder and harder to recruit decent villains. In the end, Maman Brigitte had little to work with except retreads like Ta Mok and idiots like Singh.

But that's getting ahead.

For pure spectacle, though, none of Maman Brigitte's later exploits as the Institute's executive director ever matched her first major attack on the forces of good.

BAM!

Atop one of the two tallest buildings in the largest city in America, a private reception kept eighteen waiters swapping empty trays for full. The bride wore a sheer, diaphanous veil rather than a mask. The newspapers' bridal pages identified her as Lisa Lorenzo of Hartford, Connecticut, not the Crusader known as Anniella. She had no need to hide her face.

Her groom was Major Sheldon Shapiro, USMC, looking every inch the valiant warrior in his evening dress uniform. Lisa had known this man for a decade, always found him attractive, quickly grew to love him, and considered him her best friend as well as her intended. While some loves ranged from formality to epic romance, theirs was playful, familiar, and often a little combative. But as he stood at attention in his midnight-blue coat, the left side of his chest festooned with medals, sash and sabre dangling from his slender hip, red and gold piping embroidering his sleeves and trousers, emanating the comforting scent of fresh wool, she saw him as if through different eyes. He was hers. She knew that. He was a hero. She knew that too. But suddenly he was *her hero.*

Although many superheroes attended, they were as inconspicuous as they could manage to be. Colonel Elias O'Neill stood as an usher, in his army evening dress uniform rather than his cape and cowl. Among the groomsmen - a motley selection of Shel's relatives, Lisa's relatives and Crusaders, only Lugh, the best man, stood out because of a massive frame that no tuxedo could conceal. Porter Peale kept his height to some-where under six feet, thanks to constant glares from matron of honor Millicent May Peale.

The civil ceremony lasted less than fifteen minutes, presided over by the executive director of the Port Authority of New York and New Jersey. He had the same standing to officiate at weddings around the port that a ship's captain had at sea; he was also a friendly acquaintance of Dirk Henderson, who somehow knew this nugget of otherwise useless lore and suggested the man to Shel and Lisa. In fact, Windows on the World was Dirk's idea as well, and he insisted on paying every dime. (He saved a ton by scheduling the affair for a Monday evening, but still.)

The Carbon Avenger himself did his best to stay in-conspicuous. Not wanting the appearance of a quasi-humanoid lump of coal to draw attention that this might be a Crusader's wedding, he bonded his carbon atoms to the metallic overflow bar; what had been about as sturdy as a bridge table was now stronger than a bank vault. Dirk didn't get too lonely; he was fully stocked and Bobby Botler hung out with him for quite a while.

After the exchange of rings, Shel and Lisa were de-clared husband and wife, sealed by a passionate kiss. With no need for a separate room for the reception, the champagne bottles popped right there and then. Crystal flutes made a hasty circuit, and the best man proposed the toast.

"Soft, ye braying herd o' pack-asses! Turn thine ear to me afore I squeeze a wet shit in it!"

Elias's eyes rolled. He was getting the justification he was looking for to make the case that Shel should have chosen him, rather than Lugh, for this honor, that it wasn't just a matter of bruised ego.

Which it was.

"As one who has shared close quarters with Master and Mistress Shapiro, there's much I could tell ye about these two and their congresses – their frequency, their duration, their immoderate din," Lugh began, returned Elias's icy stare, and then winked a steely eye. "But nay, I shall leave that to your own fiendish imaginings. I have braved many a battle with this noble woman at my side and have rarely known so steadfast an ally. She and I share a bond of camaraderie that was cruelly denied to her man but I tell you this: no mortal soul today is more courageous, more willing to sacrifice all for his fellows and for the prevalence of justice and right. So rise, one and all, and join me in a toast. May they e'er know love and ne'er know loss. I say to thee: Lisa and Sheldon!"

They kissed among the clinking of crystal.

BOOM!

Maman Brigitte, who had put in workaholic hours at the Institute's K Street headquarters all summer long, was astonished at the information she was able to access about the superhero teams, particularly The Crusaders.

Olivia Ortley was not the target of the brownstone bombing, according to the Institute's dossier on the woman more widely known as Looker. Her death in battle with Ta Mok was nothing other than what it appeared: a lucky shot by a rookie villain. Her infant son Orville was the bombing's true target. Although his body was never recovered, he was presumed dead by the NYPD, The Crusaders and, for that matter, the Institute. The recent revelation that Roger Chadwick's stepson Marcos was indeed Orville Ortley, and that this young fellow was now the Crusader called Mucus-Man, surprised everyone. The NYPD never solved the case of the explosion that leveled the building where the Ortleys lived; even so, the police assumed – correctly, according to Maman Brigitte's dossier – that little Orville was the intended target.

After two decades, though, the motive for killing the baby was still obscure and no amount of leafing through legalpad-sized files was able to tell Maman Brigitte if the assailant continued to hold whatever sick grudge instigated the attack.

As for more recent events, two hunches she had about the attack on the Pinnacle of Righteousness were borne out by the files. First, although the Institute itself had nothing to do with it, the forces of evil more broadly conceived and implemented the tear in the exterior that caused the deaths of so many of the heroes' enablers. Just a pinprick-sized hole in a seam between window and wall in one compartment showed the world that The Crusaders were vulnerable, and that anyone seeking to help them risked horrid death by exposure to vacuum and solar wind. As for the second hunch, yes, it was an inside job. The Institute had an ally on board the statite.

It was probably this insider who, that very morning, tipped the Institute through a spoofed, intricately-routed email that the Lorenzo-Shapiro wedding in downtown Manhattan was a Crusader function. Maman Brigitte had spent the whole day improvising a response to that.

{POW!}

After the toast came their first dance. Lisa and Shel had very different tastes in music and never did decide on the proper ballad to open up the dance floor. So they let the DJ pick it and, with little wasted thought, she chose one that had begun receiving airplay the week before and went on sale only that morning: The Calling's "Wherever You Will Go." It was a hasty choice. Although the title suggested it would be an ideal wedding song, the lyrics describe a love affair that ends badly, much to the singer's regret. In the case of the new Mr.

and Mrs. Shapiro, though, it would prove prophetic.

BAM!

Ta Mok's Spanish was rusty, but it was still good enough to enthrall the World Trade Center cleaning staff into placing those explosives in the corners of all the sky lobbies.

BOOM!

The crowd danced. They drank.

Orville watched the proceedings with outward dispassion but inward turmoil. If it were a matter of simply lacking emotions that others felt, he believed, he wouldn't have a problem with that. But he did have those feelings, or at least some suppressed vestiges of them. As he stood next to the DJ booth, watching the musical fodder flicker and spin, he was aware that some emotion was rising in him, but he was ill-equipped to identify it.

He surmised it was jealousy, but he couldn't figure out why. He wasn't attracted to Lisa. He wasn't attracted to Shel. He couldn't recall ever being attracted to anyone in particular. So what was there to be jealous about?

A lot, really. Just because he couldn't understand what he was feeling didn't make it any less real. Uncomprehendingly, he envied these two people who understood their own needs and those of their partner. Nor could he fathom that these two, on some instinctual level, recognized that something in each of them fulfilled the other. He had been around them a lot over the past few months and, outside of an occasional "love-you" – not even the complete subject-verb-object sentence "I love you." – they never really spoke about their feelings for each other. And yet they understood those feelings perfectly. Orville couldn't understand how something so profound could be known without being made explicit.

And so he watched the soundboard's lights and dials.

Lisa had strictly forbidden the bouquet and garter toss.

She was poised with a cake knife, prepared to apply the circle-and-spoke method one tier above the dummy layer when Ta Mok's potent, hooved foot stomped hard on the pavement in the plaza a thousand feet below. The shock waves tripped a triggering device that set off the plastique.

The resulting explosion ripped through the 44th and 72nd floors of 1 World Trade Center; in a heartbeat the 45th floor came to rest on the 43rd and the 73rd on the 71st then the rest of the structure immediately pancaked to the ground, the resulting wall of force knocking over the other tower and causing the collapse of every other building in the complex.

The good news was that, moments before it all came crashing down, Time Tempest shimmered out of and back into existence, a dire expression stretching her face, just in time to shout warnings to her comrades to evacuate the reception hall. Lugh's adze sliced a hole in a Window on the World, grabbed a protesting Shel under one arm and a waitress under the other, flew them down to the ground and swooped up for another two handfuls.

Lisa - Anniella now - turned herself into a rope ladder, tying her arms in knots around the antennas on the roof and allowing the guests and staff to climb down her as long as the structure held out.

Pantagruel expanded to his full sixty-foot capability and shimmied down the outside of the building like a tuxedoed King Kong, half a dozen members of the kitchen staff clutching him; at that height, he became slightly translucent and his body took on a squishy, semifluid consistency to which those cooks and dishwashers struggled to cling.

Colonel America radio-called two six-passenger, first-generation Steeds that had been circling on autopilot; he and Midge were able to fly two sorties each from the reception to ground level before everything caved in. The DJ's heart missed a beat when Mucus-Man – without any word of explanation or facial expression that suggested anything the least bit out of the ordinary was happening – grabbed him under one arm and Time Tempest under the other and dove out the window. As they passed the 60th floor and the 50th and the 40th, wind sheered their faces and shredded their clothes. At Mucus-Man's monotone request, Time Tempest held his crystal pepper shaker up to his nose; he looked straight down and sneezed. The recoil slowed their descent and they all survived with windburn scars and broken leg bones to bear testament.

The Blur, gulping for breath after his own efforts to carry two other guests down the C staircase, was already on Vesey Street and toted an unconscious, concussed Time Tempest over to Doc Rudy, who had been on one of the Steeds and was already setting up a triage station. Fortunately, Time Tempest would regain consciousness in another twenty-three hours and fifty-five minutes.

The Carbon Avenger landed with a thud like another building coming down.

The Crusaders couldn't rescue everyone. In addition to the staff and guests who didn't make it out, there were cleaning crews, some but not all of whom were under Ta Mok's control. There were also people working overnight at the financial services firms, making trades in Asian markets or staring down a deadline or just plain workaholics. Dozens died that day. Scores. But not hundreds. Not thousands. Not the tens of thousands that would surely have been lost if such an attack had happened in the middle of the work day.

It was shortly before nine in the evening, September 10th, 2001.

POW!

In a motel room in Portland, Maine, a young man with a broad face, penetrating eyes and short, curly hair watched the replay on the TV news. He grasped his Egyptian passport and two crumpled American Airlines tickets in his hand: a commuter flight from Portland to Boston, and a first-class connection from Boston to Los Angeles.

Arabic was his first language, German his second, his command of English tentative at best. Still, he knew as well as Lugh that English is the mother tongue of frustration. Mohammed Atta, then, aptly selected English for his response:

"Fuuuuuuuuuuck!"

BAM!

The body count was not all it could have been. And, with the economy teetering on the brink of recession, it could be argued that the Institute had done New York a favor by demolishing two million square feet of surplus office space. Still, The Crusaders were on notice: we know who you are and where you are.

With all that done, Maman Brigitte could begin the work that would take her the better part of a decade to complete: collecting the full deck of Malificium cards.

The years went by.

Maman Brigitte gathered her cards and continued to harass The Crusaders, supported by a series of villainous cohorts. She and Equity continued to have lunch at least once a week. And lobbying did take up far more time than she'd anticipated.

Shel retired from the Marines and it would be a decade before he got a chance to meet Major Rhode Island's eventual replacement, Lieutenant Nebraska. He and Lisa promised each other they'd find safer, less stressful ways to make a living. They were no longer in the business of protecting America, freedom, the earth or the universe - just each other and, God willing someday soon, their children. They swore.

Lisa had an elementary education degree to fall back on, but Marine aviation and the Colonel America program were all Shel knew.

Unwittingly, Maman Brigitte and her evil enterprise helped him out in this regard. It was Professor Schadenfreude who wrote the Americans with Abilities Act, which dissolved most groups of superheroes, pressing them into government service to protect America against whatever forces knocked down the Twin Towers - that is, unknown to the government or the public at large, the lobbyists themselves. The strongest, the fleetest, the most gifted heroes in the nation were mandated to become airport screeners. When it became clear that there were far more heroes than the newly formed Transportation Security Administration could possibly deploy at airports, the bill was amended to federalize the private security industry. To prevent rogue operations, the law established felony conspiracy and sedition charges to be applied to anyone who set up a superhero team outside the government structure.

The sole exception was The Crusaders. It was an odd choice considering that it was the one team that was obviously infiltrated by sinister forces. Even so, it was the one team that had borne the brunt of the attack, it had implicit government sanction through Colonel America's participation, and then there was Dirk Henderson's Carbodyne money. And then there was more of Dirk Henderson's Carbodyne money.

After an ill-suited six-month stint in the well-paying but

ethically challenged ranks of Carbodyne middle management, Shel settled into a life as a mall hero supervisor. Lisa wound down her career with The Crusaders with one last mission: to defend the world against invasion from a male-dominated Counter-Earth. All heroes risk being held captive by evil enemies, but Lisa found it particularly demeaning considering that she was a female in a stereotypically female situation and that her adversaries reveled in calling themselves The Chauvinauts. Her own team was in disarray because of a series of communication breakdowns and, if it weren't for Mucus-Man charging to the rescue, she would have been taken back to their home world and enslaved.

Reports of the victory against the Chauvinauts correctly focused on Mucus-Man's daring, single-handed attack on their control center. A doe-eyed seventh grader in Cheltenham, Pennsylvania – Mindy Maguire by name – decorated a wall in her room with press clippings of the silent, sinewy mystery man.

That September, Lisa Shapiro began teaching second grade in suburban St. Louis's Parkway School District. Less than a month later, Bobby Botler burned out on heroics, quit The Crusaders, joined the TSA and crashed on the Shapiros' couch until he could afford his own place.

A year later, Time Tempest went back to school for a doctorate in an obscure philosophical discipline called formal axiology, then went to work for UPS.

Orville left The Crusaders shortly thereafter and tried to make a living as a solo hero. His inability to deal with people worked against him, though, and he soon found himself in St. Louis, looking up his once and future teammates. Shel and Lisa got the sense that, although Orville wasn't about to open up about it, there was some friction between him and one or more of the other

Crusaders.

An inability to deal with people ended Lugh's Crusader career as well. Five more years had passed and Colonel America was injured, battling the Institute over the suspended-animated body of Lou Noble, badly enough that he couldn't address the usual post-action press conference. Lugh took his place with disastrous results. The Colonel was enraged by the way Lugh used obscene, scatological, blasphemous, degrading, and grotesque metaphors to describe the battle and its combatants. When the Colonel recommended Lugh's suspension, The Carbon Avenger went one better and asked Lugh to leave The Crusaders permanently. Nobody else on the team raised a voice in protest.

On that day, Lugh resolved never again to speak publicly. For months he kept up that resolve, until he encountered Pantagruel and Midge in the very public parking lot of the Chesterfield Mall.

And now you're up to date.

SURVIVAL MODE

The Badger screamed. The shriek - a shrill wailing with all the vocal expression of a human being and all the pain, fear and panic of an ignorant beast - drained the blood from Mindy's face.

It was followed a bare moment later by a shredding sound, like construction paper in a guillotine trimmer, which was in turn followed by a string of obscenities from Lugh.

Clawed paws scampered away across pavement and up a tree limb. The sound of rustling leaves grew more distant.

"Draw the curtain. Show's over," Lou Noble said, and Colonel America stood up, letting Georgiana and Mucus-Man gain their feet.

"Atta fella," he continued as the god returned to the ground. He noticed the four, parallel cuts running diagonally down Lugh's cheek. Red rivers flowed in a zig-zag pattern down his face as his enchanted spear, drawn in battle and aroused by the pungent smell, hummed with bloodlust. "You scared the Big Ugly off for now, but there's no telling how long she'll stay scared. We need to find shelter while we work out—"

"Nay," Lugh said, sheathing his spear.

"'Nay'?" Lou repeated. "When someone asks me, 'what part of *no* don't you understand,' I say, 'the part when the guy who means *no* says *nay*. You got something more important to do?"

Without a word, Lugh went over to Shel Shapiro's body and lifted it tenderly, like a bride's.

"You're cutting and running?" Lou asked. "I never thought I'd see Lugh turn yellow."

"I fear not the bitch. I have the power to slay the beast with or e'en without thine help."

"Maybe I can't," Georgiana offered. "Maybe I need a teammate with the power of the gods to back me up."

That gave Lugh pause.

"We need you, Lugh," she concluded.

"Nay, thou needst me not. Thou hast all the power needed," Lugh replied after a breath. "If ye doubt, then withdraw from the field."

And with that, he flew off to take home a warrior named Major Sheldon Shapiro, USMC, Retired.

Under a ton of wheat lay the body of another warrior - one that was more powerful if less accomplished. In the end, though, Bobby Botler had proved himself just as brave. There was just nobody around who was close enough to him to know where to take his remains.

Georgiana glanced at the pile of wheat spilling out across an acre of open land and highway, at how still it was.

That pile would soon quiver with activity, but she wouldn't be there to see it.

Instead, just as she was about to ask, "Where's Kevin?" Orville asked, "Where's Marisol?"

"Who?" Georgiana asked.

"My sister. She's the new Colonel America, the one who just saved us," Orville replied, looking straight into her eyes.

Georgiana couldn't help but notice a relaxed flow to his speech, rather than the usual automatic-sounding recitation. She played it back in her head: a sentence fragment, then a whole sentence with a subordinate clause. She realized at that moment that he'd only ever spoken to her in declarative, subject-verb-object sentences before. And she definitely heard emotion in that voice, a genuine concern.

"She's right over there, Orv," Lou said, gravely, indicating a spot across the street, under a spreading elm where she cradled the body of Doctor Rudy Goldman, the back of his white lab coat a swirl of red and black.

BOOM!

The scene at the Chesterfield Mall was settling down.

Cooler heads among the crowd had figured out that nothing could leave, not cell phone signals, not even light. They were isolated. Jackson or Johnson or Johnston explained via the overhead PA that they were running on a generator that had five days' supply of fuel and a climate control system that could keep the air breathable for at least two of those days. Rescue, he was certain, was on its way.

POW!

On the outside, a few oblivious patrons wandered into the apparently blackened glass doors of the mall never to return; that's all it took to prompt others to call the authorities.

The authorities called TSA, which called Redstone Arsenal, which called the Pinnacle of Righteousness. The military brass was astonished that The Carbon Avenger himself answered on the first ring.

They barely got the question out when Dirk Henderson's rocklike form intoned, "It's a singularity."

"What's that?" General Giancoia at Redstone Arsenal inquired.

Twenty minutes later, she had Dirk's full explanation. Twenty minutes after that, she had Dirk's explanation of his explanation.

The general called back again, asked for Midge, who explained, "It's a point past which you can't see, and nothing can ever come back," thanked her and hung up.

{BAM!}

On the other side of that singularity, Seth Hill and Myron Masters huddled in the Blur Cave.

"Bobby's dead," Seth concluded. "That's why the card transferred back into my possession, and that's why it was pulled toward Equity. I'm glad you came through with that trap card when you did."

Myron nodded, acknowledging the compliment, but would have none of it. "If nothing could enter or exit this mall until The Crusaders or somebody figured out a way to get us all out, that would be good news," Myron figured. "But we've seen people come in even after you played the card. It's a one-way trap, so ...

"... so if the card can't get to Equity, it's calling Equity here."

"She's going to have backup from the Institute - Maman Brigitte at least, maybe Schadenfreude, Zaibatsu - could be even Ta Mok or Singh, who've been known to escape from prison before. Any henchmen we can handle, but there could also be some villains we've never met before - and they can be bad news. I was right there when ..."

Myron didn't finish the statement. Seth knew what he was talking about.

"I got what's left of my card collection."

"I got what's left of my super-strength and damage re-sistance."

"Not going to be enough," Seth summed up. "Even with Pantagruel standing with us."

"Where is he, by the way?" Myron asked.

"Let me check. He gave me his cell number."

BOOM!

Porter Peale was on a break. The cell phone vibrated silently in the pocket of a shirt that had fallen to the floor.

There's no sense judging Pantagruel too harshly. What happened next could hardly have unfolded differently even if he weren't in a funeral parlor, getting laid in a red velvet-finished, satin-lined, mahogany coffin.

POW!

"Well?" Georgiana asked Lou Noble, her shoulders shrugging, one palm pointing up, the other supporting Orville. Her foot tapped expectantly.

"Well what, sweetheart?"

"Well, what do we do now?"

"I'm beginning to think Lugh had the right idea," he replied and turned on his heel toward his SUV. "I don't know about you, doll, but I'm fixing to scram."

She chased after him shouting, "What kind of hero are you?"

"Anti," he said without breaking stride. "I look after myself, sugarplum, and sometimes good things happen. If the Institute had found me before The Crusaders, I might have been on the other side in that fight."

"You have a responsibility, damn it!"

"To who? You? I fired you. And Count Kumquat. And Shel and Bobby, the poor saps. I don't owe any of the rest of you anything. Except Orville," Lou said as he glanced over his shoulder. "You coming, kid?"

"No," Orville managed.

311

"Suit yourself, Schnozzola."

"That's just one less way we have to split the money," Orville said.

Lou froze. So did Georgiana, for entirely different reasons.

"Did you say, 'money'?" Lou asked, and then he froze in place momentarily.

"Did you just comprehend somebody else's motivation?" Georgiana asked.

In response, Orville froze in place momentarily himself. "There are survivors somewhere around here, or at least there were a couple hours or so ago," he said to the back of Lou's neck, marveling at his own lack of precision.

Lou turned around, and their eyes locked. Orville marveled a little at that as well, eye contact being something he instinctually avoided.

"If you see this job through with us and save the townspeople, you get an equal share of the reward."

"What do you want me to do?" Lou asked.

"Um, I don't know!" Orville said, with some excitement. His thoughts weren't racing down one familiar path. So many different ways to proceed passed through his mind, cluttering it up, sometimes disappearing into a chaotic fog before he could grasp it. This experience scared him, but exhilarated him as well.

"Shel was the man with the plan," Georgiana explained. "But he's gone. We've got to figure something out fast."

That was the end of her thought, but Orville and Lou - and, unseen by the others, Eva - kept staring at her.

"I guess we should find whatever cover we can for now," she continued, thinking on the fly. "Looks like this town ends a block north from here. Let's get to the last house, collect ourselves for a moment, figure out how we're going to capture or kill this badger-woman, then sweep the town for her from north to south, where our vans are parked."

Orville and Lou exchanged a glance and a shrug. Eva beamed with pride.

"If that works for everybody," Georgiana concluded meekly.

It did.

"Great," she said, "Why don't you guys go ahead and find us a hiding place? I'll be along in a minute."

"No," Orville contradicted, stopping her as she paced over toward Colonel America. "You and Lou go. I'll follow."

Without a word, Georgiana and Lou trotted up the street as Orville knelt beside his adoptive sister.

Doc Rudy, who had cared for them for as long as either could remember, lay dead, his head cradled on the Colonel's lap, her face now as blank as that of a casino pit boss.

Orville might have been the only one in the world who knew her well enough to recognize that expression. Growing up, their parents were distressed enough that he *couldn't* express emotions because of his medical condition, but even more that she *wouldn't* out of sheer stubbornness.

"Marisol, we have to get out of here," Orville said. "You stay out here on the street, you'll be this thing's next victim."

"Doesn't matter," she said, her tone as inscrutable as her expression. "I've failed in my mission. No Colonel America ever failed in a mission before. I just wasted ten years of my life, taxpayers' money and Crusaders training. I may as well do the honorable thing and—"

"What would Dad say?"

She took the question like a haymaker to the jaw.

"God, I can't even think about that. It's just too shameful."

313

"As I recall, you got into your share of trouble as a kid. I know. I followed you into it. Did Dad – or Mom – ever make either of us feel ashamed? No. Not when we were at our worst. Certainly not when we were trying our best."

He was staring her straight in the eye. She had to break the connection to glance around for the enemy.

"You're looking for the Badger, aren't you?"

She nodded.

"That's because you're trying to save your own life. It's an instinct you have for a reason. Or maybe you're trying to save my life. Either way, Dad would be proud."

Colonel America stared off at a fixed point in the middle distance.

"Marisol, give him the chance to see you in the uniform he used to—"

She grabbed the pepper shaker he wore on a lanyard around his neck, then sprinkled some on her hand which she cupped over his cowl. With a sudden, violent toss, she directed Orville's face and shoulders 180 degrees around and 45 degrees up. She released her hand as he sneezed and braced herself to receive the recoil. Mucus-Man, even at half strength, was still potent enough to knock a pouncing badger across the street.

The Badger was slow to get up.

Leaving Doc Rudy's body behind, Mucus-Man and Colonel America took advantage of the moment to dive on the stunned creature.

"Orville, get out of here! Find your friends!"

Mucus-Man hesitated.

"Now!" the Colonel commanded and, shuffling backward, he scurried northward.

What ensued between Colonel America and the Badger was something approximating a fair fight. They were both lean, strong, born warriors. The Colonel had the advantage in training and conditioning, and the organelles coursing through her AB-negative blood amped them up with the muscle memory of all her predecessors. But the Badger had the sheer ferocity of a bloodthirsty predator; she was frenzied in her attack.

While words such as "subdue" and "incapacitate" crossed the hero's unwelcoming mind, her opponent had no such intrusions; she did not, as such, have a mind to intrude on her instinct. There was only the smell of fresh blood and the promise of the taste of new flesh.

They rolled around in the dusty road for no longer than a minute, but it was long enough for a crimson-spewing gash to open along the entire length of the Badger's snout, and for Colonel America's shoulder to be dislocated, her left arm draped behind her like a lump in the lining of her cape.

In the heat of battle, Colonel America didn't register the pain in her shoulder – until, very suddenly, she did. The pain covered an area as small as a pinprick, but as deep as Hell's dungeon.

The agony coincided with a whistling noise. The whistle dopplered higher as a projectile approached, then suddenly tuned lower as it sped away.

A ricochet! A round had struck her bulletproof cape – right on the shoulder, didn't it have to? – and bounded off.

A second later, another shot, no ricochet. This one grazed the Badger's jaw, just below the gash. Blood, saliva and bone chips splattered across an exposed gully of cross-hatched, mandible-connected muscle. It looked as if half her face had been thrown against a belt-driven lathe.

A third shot punctured a tire in a nearby car, harming no one. The Badger threw Colonel America off her and headed for the camouflaged safety of the canopy of autumn oak. As she leapt from one tree limb to another, the Badger made eye contact with Colonel America before disappearing into the foliage. The Colonel realized she might be projecting too much on that fleeting glance, but she felt a kinship – two worthy adversaries sharing a moment of mutual respect.

The click was barely audible over the rustle of dry leaves and the deflating tire's hiss, but Colonel America surmised that, whoever her unseen helper was, he or she was out of ammo. Not to mention, not such a great shot to begin with.

Still, she was grateful.

Colonel America looked around for her adversary. Instead, she found the body of the man she was sworn to protect.

Suddenly, she wasn't grateful anymore.

Marisol Rivera assumed that there was still at least one resident alive in Plainville and, as she knew from growing up in Iowa, the Midwest was gun country. Likely enough, every house in town had at least one firearm on hand. Whoever it was, she'd offer a commendation later. Right now, she had to drive down guilt and humiliation and focus on bringing low the Badger and rescuing whomever else might still be drawing breath in Plainville, including her brother and his compatriots.

So Colonel America ascribed her rescue to a random middle American stepping up to take his turn at heroics. And, from her point of view, he was. After all, she'd never actually met Kevin Kiley.

BAM!

"Damn. Shit. Fuck!"

Count Karma was no Indomitable Lugh when it came to vocabulary.

Kevin glared out the gabled window of the room of some seven-ish girl with blonde pigtails draped over blue-denim overalls, her glitter-specked socks peeking out above saddle shoes overdue for a polish.

Her appearance wasn't just a mental image based on the pink-and-purple color scheme or the hundred or so plush toys – mostly ponies – that lay neatly on the bed or scattered across the floor. Her corpse was right there, open eyes expressing nothing, black gore soaking into blue fabric, one leg sheared off and gnawed down to the bone. Kevin had taken the revolver out of her hand.

He had fled when the Badger got Schadenfreude, cursing himself with each footfall. The house he occupied now was just the first, in his haste, that he barreled into. Initially, Kevin had almost tripped over what he now decided was the little girl's mother as he galloped across the threshold. There wasn't much left of the mother besides a shredded green-and-gold checkered dress and a splatter of blood, skin, hair and fat on the foyer's sponge-painted walls. That, and the gun that hung loosely from her right index finger. Kevin knew nothing about firearms but guessed that it was a shotgun. He thought the barrel had been sawed off, but then he took two more steps, his foot landed on something cylindrical, and he landed hard on his back. The object he slipped on turned out to be the rest of the shotgun's barrel. It wasn't sawed off. It was bitten off.

Another sibling – brother? sister? older? younger? impossible to tell – had died on the stairs, an automatic in its hand and about a dozen expended rounds alongside it. Kevin had grabbed that pistol as he ran to higher ground, burst into the little girl's room, saw the corpse in its innocent hideousness, and settled into a crouch at the window. He spotted the Badger scurrying across a tree limb as Orville and Marisol had their moment. He pointed the short, silvery barrel at the beast's head and pulled the trigger. Out of ammo, apparently. The kid had gotten off every last shot.

Steeling himself, Kevin had scrambled across the room

317

to relieve the precious little girl-corpse of her revolver, momentarily mesmerized into a staring contest that he could never win. By the time he returned to the window, the Badger had attacked and the two adversaries were rolling around in the street. Not knowing the first thing about what he was doing, never having discharged a weapon before, he had shot Colonel America. Only her bulletproof cape had prevented her from being drilled through the vitals. The next bullet found its intended target, but only a glancing contact. The third round went completely wide. There was no fourth. Apparently, the little girl had gotten off three shots herself.

He needed to reload. But he hesitated, overcome with a gnawing lack of confidence. He didn't know where to find more ammunition, and wouldn't have known the right cartridges from the wrong ones.

{BOOM!}

When Georgiana and Lou Noble sprinted north, they had a destination in mind: a split ranch house that marked the end of town. Not another building was visible along Highway 96 and, in fact, there was hardly a sign of habitation in sight.

But that's not where they ended up. A few steps short of it, someone had gotten their attention with a sharp, two-fingered whistle and waved them over. So they crossed the street and backtracked a block.

While all this was going on, Orville Ortley focused entirely on comforting his adoptive sister.

So they were alone in the last house on the left.

{POW!}

The dials, the dials.

Speed, altitude, fuel consumption. Well into the digital age, pilots still favored analog readings. Not only were they easier to interpret at a glance than LED displays, they were elegant, a bridge to more pioneering times.

And, to Equity, they were unaccountably beautiful. As she sat unbidden in the otherwise empty right-hand seat on the flight deck, she could hear them sing to her, the music of the spheres.

"Equity!" Maman Brigitte yelled, snapping her trance and momentarily startling the pilot, which wasn't easy to do.

"You don't have to shout, Bridge."

"Yes, I did, after calling you three times," Maman Brigitte replied, leaning on the back of Equity's seat, staring - as most people would - at the Great Plains rolling along in multicolored squares ten thousand feet below. "Where were you just now?"

"Fixated on the instrument panel?" Equity responded with an awkward upward inflection.

"Mucus-Man was the last one you touched, right?"

"Right."

"Guess you didn't read the briefing materials on him."

"Didn't have time. I'll read them now," Equity offered eagerly. "All of them."

Maman Brigitte ignored the offer.

"His power is a manifestation of a series of neurological disorders," she began. "He's been diagnosed with Asperger's and OCD, and his mother might have had some of that as well. Anyway, that's the way my sources see it."

"Thanks, I was wondering where this deep focus was coming from. This head trip is definitely different from anything I've ever had before," Equity said, then changed topics. "One of these days you're going to have to tell me where you get your information."

And, just then, a soft beeping came from a bag back in the main cabin.

"This might be that day."

Equity followed Maman Brigitte back as the Voudoun priestess shuffled furtively through a carry-on bag for her tablet computer. As quick as she could, Maman Brigitte pressed a button to take the device off stand-by, filling the screen with a shadowy figure.

"*Gran Houngan!*" Maman Brigitte effused with a tremor of fear in her voice. "What a delightful surprise!"

"Have you identified the entity in Plainville?"

"Yes, *Gran Houngan*. It is some kind of feral, human-animal hybrid. It's capable of incredible carnage, nearly deity-level, but I think it's chaotic rather than evil."

"Have you captured it?"

"Apologies, *Gran Houngan*. We missed the chance. Heroes showed up and—"

"What heroes?" the evil master demanded. "The Crusaders weren't there, I know for a fact. The nearest hero of any renown is Lou Noble, and you're more than a match for him and any of the airport screeners he'd take along."

"He was there, and so was the new Colonel America."

"Marisol Rivera? Why wasn't I informed?"

"I'm informing you now, *Gran Houngan.*"

"Oh. Right."

"And it is my sad duty to report that we lost Professor Schadenfreude and Gay Ray."

"A heavy price," the master said, but with no real inflection.

"Ooh! Ooh! Tell him about Bobby!" Equity insisted.

"I was just getting to that," Maman Brigitte seethed. "The creature killed a couple of Noble's flunkies as well as Doctor Goldman, who was there with Colonel America. I took out Sheldon Shapiro, for whatever that's worth. And Equity here killed the Blur."

"Shapiro? Botler? So it's those same pests who stymied your efforts at collecting that last Malificium card. I will not tolerate your record of failure much—"

"Begging your pardon, *Gran Houngan,* but we are on our way to retrieve that as we speak."

"It's drawn to me," Equity explained. "But it's trapped. It wants me to come and get it. It's at—"

"The Chesterfield Mall," the master completed the thought.

It fit. He already knew about the singularity.

BAM!

They were where it all started, at least, where it started in Plainville: Nick and Rhonda Bayard's house.

It was Nick's cousin Lee Ann who had whistled for them, and so Lou Noble, Georgiana and her familiar spirit found themselves surrounded by a dozen survivors, hunkered down in a basement designed to withstand tornadoes, hoping that it would also protect them from this new force of nature. They huddled at the bottom of a staircase that looked more like a ladder, beneath a multi-bolted door of steel and concrete that looked like it could serve as defense against bank robbers.

"You're with The Crusaders, right?" Lee Ann asked. The surviving Plainville townsfolk were overcome with shock and grief; Lee Ann was marginally more functional and settled in as interlocutor. She propped herself up on the pair of crutches she'd found since responding to the Craig's List ad.

"Civil Service," Lou said.

"Private citizen," Georgiana added.

"They were going to make me vice presid—"

"But The Crusaders are coming, right?" Lee Ann asked, unaware she was interrupting the unseen, unheard ghost of Eva Peron.

"Uh, well, one of them was right outside," Georgiana said, forcing a chipper tone. "Last I saw."

"Yeah, and another mug who used to be with that out-fit," Lou offered.

"Would that be Lugh?" Lee Ann said, brimming with

321

hope, sighing hard enough to send bangs flying past one eye. "I bet he could mash that she-beast into flapjacks without a sweat."

"He was here earlier," Georgiana said, maintaining an upbeat façade.

Lee Ann wasn't biting, though. Her hope faded. Looking around at the faces of her late cousin's neighbors, she realized how naive she must have looked to them to have ever entertained any hope in the first place.

"So he's not here now. Who is?" Lee Ann asked, and Georgiana got as far as opening her mouth. "Don't tell me. I really don't want to know."

Georgiana understood. Out there - maybe, if the Badger hadn't already done her worst - was an untested Colonel America off on her first mission, and Mucus-Man, who never caught on with The Crusaders despite early promise, and was now operating at half power, thanks to Equity's touch. That was quite a handicap, Georgiana had to admit, whatever her feelings for him might be.

And what are those feelings, she wondered.

Focus!

"The fact is, we're on our own," Lee Ann summed up, and all the heroes could do was nod.

"What's wrong with that?" Lou asked. "We got numbers, we got beauty and, not to toot my own sousaphone, we got brains. We got the element of surprise, too. We will get out of this, ladies and gents."

"Did you not see what's out there?" Lee Ann asked Lou. "That thing killed and ate something like ninety percent of this town. And I saw bodies on the street that didn't dress like they're from around here, so I'm guessing they're yours."

"Ours or the bad guys'," Lou corrected gently.

"It never stops hunting. It never stops killing. It never stops feeding. How exactly are we getting out of this, *gent*?"

There was silence in the basement until Georgiana spoke up.

"OK, I'll pass that along," she said to Eva before addressing the others. "The Badger is not natural. Otherwise it would be satisfied at some point. There has to be some kind of otherworldly force behind it."

She paused to listen to Eva again.

"The goddesses think they know who's behind this," she continued. "There's a minor, latter-day deity named Tamora, who revels in giving vermin godlike powers. Apparently she does this out of sheer whimsy."

Another pause.

"But Tamora prefers to work within nature's laws when building these beasts. So ..."

"... So if this Badger dame could be made according to physical Hoyle, she can be unmade," Lou reasoned. "What do we know about this customer?"

"Nothing for certain, but I have a lead," Lee Ann said. "I think she's—"

"Hold your Clydesdales, sister," Lou interrupted. "You know who I am."

"You're Lou Noble, America's Greatest Dick."

"So you know what it means when you spill the beans to me."

"Yes," Lee Ann replied with gravity.

"What am I missing here?" Georgiana asked.

"It's a quirk of anti-heroes," Lou explained. "Giving one of us the last piece of information he needs to solve a mystery is a death sentence. The clock runs out on you some way or another just because you've served your dramatic purpose. Ninety-nine times out of a hundred, you take a dirt nap."

"But this has got to end now," Lee Ann said. Savoring the dank, basement air as if it could be her last breath, she inhaled deeply. "When I got into town yesterday, it seemed

I'd picked up a hitchhiker – a stowaway, really. This woman named Bella Brock rode in all the way from Wisconsin in the back of my dairy truck. She seemed dazed when we let her out, as if she'd blacked out and lost a stretch of hours or days and was trying to piece them together."

"So this Bella Brock is the Badger," Lou summed up. "But she was all woman when you found her, and she was probably all fur and fangs when she got on board. When did she change back into rodent?"

"Late last night, more like the small hours of the morning."

"So what's happening in a stamp-sized burg like this at that time of night?"

"Nothing. Streets would be quiet except for a few second-shift workers coming home. Like Rhonda."

"Rhonda?" Lou asked.

"Nick's wife. She was a tech in the radiology department at–"

"So that's the trigger – radiation exposure," Lou theorized. "That's what turns Bella into the Badger. But what turns the Badger back into–"

And then it struck him: a reminiscence from long ago. It was the mid-1930s and he was still years away from earning the appellation of America's Greatest Dick. But his mentor, Chicago private investigator Hyden Zeke, told him about the three operatives he sent out west to bring in the swindler Double Deal Decker. One of them turned feral any time he saw a mouse and could only return to himself by eating ...

"Cheese."

BOOM!

Someone else died that day, whose passing merits mention.

He wasn't a superhero, or really any kind of hero. He was just an old man, a notch past ninety years. He lived and died in a well-to-do suburb of Cincinnati and his name was James.

The retired auto parts factory owner and retail magnate had five children by three wives. Pushing sixty and ready to retire, he had fathered a newborn baby girl who became the entire focus of his life.

As he sat slumped in the easy chair in his solarium, staring out at the Ohio River for the last time, the aroma of his final cigar wafting toward the vent, midday sun doing not nearly enough to warm him, James's last thoughts were about her. As darkness ensued, he wished he could linger long enough to say goodbye to his little Millicent.

She was so bright. Not only was she a savant with the kind of new technology that his own smokestack experience left him unable to comprehend, it was she who inspired him to get into the trading card game.

"If Mundies have to compete with persons-with-abilities," she explained to him while she was still in high school, "they'll probably pay anything to have an edge."

And that's when he took controlling interest in The Plaquet Box – via a byzantine set of dummy corporations that kept the May family name out of it – and started selling franchises. That was the real reason he was dying richer than he was born.

She said "Mundies," what superfolk, whether heroes or villains, were widely known to call people without abilities when out of earshot. Millicent never displayed any such abilities, but she had her goals even back then.

She had, in some measure, realized those goals. And her father would die beaming with pride in her.

Millicent served as his proxy on the Plaquet Box board as often as her own busy career and faltering marriage allowed. Her smartest move, James recalled, was quietly bringing that Hill fellow in as a fixer, someone who could pose as an ordinary franchisee, avoiding paper trails and official scrutiny, a sleeper unknown even to The Crusaders or The Institute, who could combine his tactical genius with his anonymity whenever the security situation required it.

And it was Millicent who ... who ...

James's consciousness faded fast. Specifics eluded him as emotion overwhelmed him: a swirling puree of love and faith. His religious pieties were more a matter of aspiration than actual belief, but he died with the hope that, even though denied the chance of saying goodbye to his daughter in this life, he would be able to say hello to her in the next.

If so, he'd find out within the next five minutes.

POW!

Follow the signal, she told herself.

Myron Masters, whom Millicent May wistfully remembered was a great lay once upon a time, had managed to plant a tracking device on Maman Brigitte's tablet computer while he was serving as Seth Hill's mole at the Institute.

And Seth was *her* mole. She had no idea what kind of lay Seth would be, although she got the vibe that her dad would have approved of her finding out. He always liked the guy, and hated all the pain and disappointment that Porter had caused her over the years.

Maybe when all this was over ...

Follow the signal. Maman Brigitte may be the tactical leader of the Institute but, Midge was certain, there was somebody above her, anonymously pulling the strings.

As she sat strapped into the low gravity of the Keep, the control deck of the Pinnacle of Righteousness, she reflected on why she was so sure.

When Millicent first got started in heroic services, villains were villains. They wanted to rule the world, and they had to be stopped. But that was more than twenty years ago. Lately, the case could be made that they had achieved many of their aims and were after something different now. And she couldn't figure out what it was. All she knew was that it took more imagination than she was willing to give Brigitte La Vallette credit for.

Midge traced the tracking device as it inched down the Mississippi Valley represented on a GPS screen. Finding the other end of that communication – and, she assumed, Maman Brigitte's boss – was going to be the tricky part. She knew it wasn't going to be a direct link, so she'd just have to sit at that workstation and laboriously trudge through the network path, repeater by repeater. She was surprised that the first one she came across was in Guatemala City. Why there? She'd been to Guate once, backpacking through Central America like every other *gringo* trust fund teen looking for adventure. The guidebooks bragged about its historical importance going back to Mayan times, but she found the place ugly, fetid, impoverished and soaked in sideways-blowing rain. What could the significance possibly be?

She filed that question away and tracked the signal to see where it would lead next.

Meanwhile, she reflected on how the hero business had changed along with the villain business. The regional groups were all gone now, subsumed into the TSA, where their former members suited up in white shirts and black ties like computer repairmen, then got tasked to guard malls or pat down airline travelers for twenty years until retirement ...

Panama City. That at least made sense, Midge thought, at least if you're starting in Guate. It was an international trade hub, the man-made confluence of the world's two largest oceans.

The Crusaders were the only functioning team left. And that was a matter of money. Some people thought it was due to Dirk Henderson's money, but she knew that was only seed ...

Manaus, Brazil. She'd never heard of it. According to the GPS, it was way up in the Amazon River valley ...

The real money behind The Crusaders came from the American taxpayer. Dirk spent just enough to grease the right palms so that the appropriations for the Colonel America program kept flowing. As long as that happened, the costs to build and maintain the Pinnacle of Righteousness, the Steeds and all the other evil-fighting toys – not to mention the generous Crusader stipends – all had a budget line as long as ...

The width of the Atlantic Ocean. Zooming out, Midge could see the Amazon River as an arrow pointed straight at Cape Verde, the island chain off the West African coast. Sure enough, that's where the next repeater was. She saw a pattern emerging, but she couldn't put it together yet. It did seem to favor straight lines and paths of least resistance. Resistance, as in magnetic resistance, she intuited. Guate is directly south – along magnetic polar lines – from the Mississippi. Follow the current to Panama, follow the headwaters to Manaus, then the Amazon to the sea, then the sea currents to Cape Verde. If the evil overlord were in Europe, maybe he'd use a repeater a little farther north in the Canary Islands. No, he's somewhere in Africa or the Middle East.

Algiers? No, that was just another repeater.

Millicent May hadn't had reason to give a second thought to Algiers since eighth grade, when her French teacher assigned her to read Camus's *L'Etranger*. And all she remembered about that novel was that one man killed another man not only without remorse, but utterly without motive.

But no, Algiers was just another repeater.

Next stop, a speck of land called Sao Tome. And that's

where the signal ended. Well, not exactly. It quite clearly repeated, but it didn't go anywhere from there. It just sort of faded to the west a bit and dead-ended in the middle of the ocean. Maybe whoever was the power behind the Institute was on a submarine in the Gulf of Guinea. After all, the GPS wouldn't be able to indicate if the signal's next stop was down, rather than across.

Nor could it tell if the next stop was up.

A penchant for magnetic lines and water currents. A growing indifference to the good/evil dichotomy. These thoughts had occupied different lobes of her brain a moment earlier, but they came together in that second. A look of disbelief crossed her face, and then a look of determination. She had to get off the Pinnacle and warn the world.

Midge unstrapped herself and spun around in her chair. She planted her feet on the floor to push off and get to the Steed bay in one low-g leap.

She didn't expect the wall of gray, striated rocks behind her.

She may have been at her full five-foot stature at that moment, but the Carbon Avenger squashed her like a bug.

BAM!

"The plan's simple," Lou explained to Georgiana as they ascended the stairs. "Lee Ann and I high-tail it out of here, find her truck, act as bait, and stuff the Badger's face full of *le fromage* until she turns back into a dame. Crystal?"

"One question," Georgiana replied. "What am I supposed to do?"

"Open the door for us and close it behind us quick as you can."

"That it?"

"That, and keep looking the way you do, honeydrop."

Georgiana's face didn't betray the feelings her words

329

indicated. "I resent the way you talk to me, Lou," she began. "Getting past how I look – and I've been doing all I can to be less obvious about it – I have super-strength and I can fly. Why are you keeping me out of the fight?"

"Can you drive a truck?"

"No," she said, staring down at her shoes.

"Neither can I. So Lee Ann has to be out there."

"And I can do a better job than you at protecting her."

"I got her into this and I'll get her out. Meantime, if we fail, these people will need you to lead them to safety. Then you form up with your buddy and his sister and take this she-devil out once and for all. Now, *ciao, bella.* That's Italian for 'open the door.'"

She obliged, but she left too and shut it behind her.

Not that Lou and Lee Ann noticed, as focused as they were on figuring out how fast a woman can move on crutches.

BOOM!

Lisa Shapiro heard a whistle of wind and a thud on her front lawn. Peeking out of the living room window, she confirmed her suspicion. It was the unique sound of Lugh coming in for a landing.

She ran to the front door to greet her old teammate, her husband's best friend.

Bearing her husband.

"No," she said.

That was Shel, cradled in Lugh's massive arms.

"No."

Last time Lugh brought him back to her like this, he was alive, barely, but enough to will himself to a full recovery, marry her, raise children with her, and give up the life of adventure with her. Until today.

The god spoke. "Lisa ..."

"*No!*"

Her elastic arms pounded on Lugh's chest and shoulders while she was on the front stoop and he was ten paces away on the edge of the lawn. With every step closer he got, the punches became more forceful, to the point where they actually stung the ancient warrior. Finally, when he was just a step away, she flung herself on him, an amorphous puddle of grief, seeking solace.

Jael and Matt, the Shapiro children, came to the window.

POW!

"Damn well about time, dearie," Eva told her protégée.

The ghost floated alongside Georgiana as she swaggered through the center of town. Georgiana was clearly trying to attract attention – the other heroes' and the Badger's, preferably in that order.

"Sorry, but guys like Lou Noble just make me—"

"Dearie, all guys are like Lou Noble."

"I won't argue the point," Georgiana said, then began shouting. "I hate this power, Evita! Hate it! Did I mention I hate it?"

"Yes, you did. And it's 'Mrs. Peron.'"

"I mean, I thought I hated it when I first got it. But today! It's not just Lou's attitude. He's from another time. No offense."

"None taken."

"First I'm taking orders from Shel. Then from Lou. Meantime, every guy wants to protect me from dangers that I could probably handle better on my own."

"You still don't get it, do you?"

The question stopped Georgiana in her tracks.

"Get what?"

"Beauty," Eva explained, "isn't your power."

"Then whatever it is must be really lackluster, because all anyone notices is my looks."

331

"You're wrong about that, dearie. It's not a matter of what they notice that matters, it's what they respond to. That's your power."

"Talk straight for once, will you?"

"Your power," Eva summed up, "is to inspire."

In the pause, the light of comprehension brightened Georgiana's eye. Eva felt a sense of relief that she soaked in the message, got comfortable with it, owned it. Georgiana pursed her lips to speak.

"That sucks even worse," Georgiana proclaimed. "So I'm a muse. My lot in life is to sit passively by, giving little nods of encouragement to the real heroes. Just kill me now."

"Don't think I wouldn't if I could, you spoiled little bitch," Eva replied sharply. "Is it possible for your humorless, oh-so-literal mind to contemplate anything besides the obvious? Yes, people are inspired by beauty - by *your* beauty. But you know what else inspires people?"

Georgiana drew a blank and Eva filled the silence.

"Courage. Vision. Action. Leadership," Eva listed, then added a note of irony. "Yeah, that Mahatma Gandhi - what a stud."

"And?"

"And you have all of these. Shapiro knew it. You didn't think it was strange that he died with your name on his lips? He was a happily married man - a lifelong love affair cut short halfway through - and he thought of you, not her? Does that make sense? That had nothing to do with your looks. He was giving his last command. He was naming his successor."

Georgiana stood there slack-jawed.

"He wanted you to find a way to complete the mission, then lead us out safely."

Georgiana would've liked a minute to absorb that, but the sound of a diesel engine starting up interrupted the moment.

A quick dash around the corner presented her with the sight of the Badger on the roof of the truck's cab. With the thrill of the hunt etched on her elongated face, furry snout caked in blood like clown makeup, she raised one taloned paw to claw through the metal. Lee Ann Bayard cowered behind the steering wheel. A racket came from the back of the truck – it had to be Lou on the inside, banging on the walls to ring the dairy dinner bell for the former Bella Brock. But the Badger had no interest in taking cold, still proteins when warm, live, pulsating sustenance was four feet away.

A claw punctured the cab's roof but, instead of slashing clean through and skewering a profusely sweating Lee Ann, it was dragged sideways, cutting a scar through the roof clear to the passenger side. The metallic rip sounded like the world's largest creaking door hinge.

What sent the Badger sideways was Georgiana flying to the rescue. The Badger landed on the sidewalk, with Georgiana right on top of her. A super-strong but amateurishly thrown haymaker caught the beast by surprise. Stunned just for a moment, the Badger responded with a smack to Georgiana's cheek that would leave a permanent mark, if she survived.

She would. At just that moment, a bloodied but unbowed Colonel America, one arm hanging limp, jumped the Badger from behind and threw her off Georgiana.

"Sorry, fuzzy, but the Orkin Man is busy," Colonel America wisecracked. "He's catching flies now, because of you."

"Huh?" was all Georgiana could muster.

"Repartee," the Colonel replied as she pinced the Badger's neck between her legs and repeatedly pummeled her with her good arm. "It's literally in the blood. Can't help it. By the way, Supermodel, that's going to turn into a really sexy scar."

"Georgiana, and thanks." She blushed a little as she regained her feet.

The Badger slipped out of the Colonel's grip. The two heroes circled her slowly as she growled low.

"We have to get her in the back of the truck," Georgiana explained. "Lou Noble is in there, ready to shove some cheese down her throat. He thinks – hell, he's betting his life – that the cheese will return the Badger to human form."

"He's probably right. This goes back to when Lou Noble and the first-generation Colonel America were about the ages we are now. There was this detective named Jerome Howard–"

"Can we skip the history lesson, Colonel?" Georgiana asked as the Badger emitted a threatening hiss. Considering the body count that had already been tallied that day, Georgiana had no illusions that two-against-one was a good enough advantage. It was at best a standoff.

"OK, let's talk about current events," the Colonel replied, "like how are we going to get Cousin Ugly here into the back of that truck?"

BLAM!

Kevin didn't know how to load a pistol, so he was completely thrown by the pump-action shotgun. All he knew was that it was lying on someone's lawn, it was loaded, and he'd get off one good shot.

A shot at redemption.

He stuck to the shadows, crouching behind a shrub pruned into a perfect cube no more than a day or two before Plainville's last, hellish night. He'd wait out-of-sight until his moment materialized. It wouldn't take long. From what he could see, the forces of good and the forces of chaotic nature were evenly balanced. His would be the hand that tipped the scales.

This wasn't about winning Mindy Maguire's sexual attention anymore. Chaotic nature had already quashed that. But he did want to prove his worth to her. He didn't need a reason. He just wanted her – and all the rest, even Shel and Bobby, wherever their souls persisted – to see him as being worth something. Or maybe he most wanted to prove his value to nobody more than himself.

BOOM!

Lee Ann watched the delicate dance with fascination, first through the passenger window, then through the side-view mirror.

Georgiana would take a step backward. the Badger would lunge, Georgiana would duck, and Colonel America would circle around, then Colonel America would take a step backward and the *pas de trois* would go on like that.

With subtle ingenuity, they maneuvered the Badger near the truck's tailgate. Georgiana was beginning to feel sanguine about their chances of getting to end-of-job with no more loss of life.

"We can get her in with just one more leap if we–"

BANG!

A spray of tiny metal projectiles stung the back of Georgiana's neck. They caught Colonel America full in the face. Anything not protected by the cowl was a bloody mess. The cowl itself, not bulletproof like the cape, was shredded and stained red.

Some pellets caught the inside of the truck, forcing the strongest language of which Lou Noble was capable:

"What the–? Who's the no-good, dirty–? Why, I oughtta–"

The Badger sensed her chance to escape and find easier prey. She crouched low, then pounced ...

Straight into a sudden cyclone-strength wind, courtesy

335

of Mucus-Man.

His sneeze propelled the Badger into the back of the truck, planting her face into a plateful of mozzarella balls held in place by medium-gray hands sticking out from light-gray trench coat sleeves.

But one of her claws found its way through Lou Noble's rib cage and into a vital.

Immediately, the Badger began her painful return to humankind. As spectacular as that was, nobody paid her any mind.

Georgiana, Colonel America and Mucus-Man climbed into the truck – Lee Ann, too, just a couple paces behind.

"Lou, hang in there!" Georgiana shouted.

"Not this time, kiddo," he gasped. "But it's okay. My time's long gone, and this is how I always wanted to get 86-ed."

"You're not going anywhere," the Colonel commanded.

"Can't ask for a better exit," a wheezing Lou Noble said. "End of the tale, bad guy taken down, internal injuries so nobody sees any blood. This is how I was meant to take my bow. Lee Ann?"

"I'm here, Lou," she said, pushing her way past the heroes.

"Remember what I said before about 'ninety-nine times out of a hundred'?"

"Of course."

"This is what happens the hundredth time."

And, with his final effort, he closed his eyes.

Bella Brock interrupted the solemn moment first, stammering out questions about where she was and who were these people.

Then it was interrupted by Kevin Kiley, looking ridiculous in his Count Karma costume, and carrying a shotgun with a smoking barrel.

"You idiot!" Colonel America said, climbing down to

the street, the better to shout at Kevin. "I don't know what you thought you were doing, but you don't fire into a crowd with a shotgun!"

Adding emphasis, some of the blood that was pooling on her chin splattered on Kevin's chest.

"If you had a rifle and knew how to use it, maybe you'd get a clean—"

"He's not worth it, Colonel," Georgiana said, but that didn't stop her from turning to Kevin and adding, "Lou's dead, thanks to you."

"Mindy," Kevin began, but didn't know what to say.

"Just stay the hell away from us."

"We need to go," Orville said. "I heard Equity and Maman Brigitte talk about returning to the mall. I think they found the card. Kevin, can we offer you a lift?"

But Kevin just turned around, walked away, and was out-of-mind even before he was out-of-sight.

"Let's get to our van," Georgiana said.

"Or we could take my chopper," replied the Colonel.

The offer required no response and the Colonel, Georgiana and Mucus-Man set off toward the ball field where she had landed the Sikorsky hours earlier, taking turns supporting the dazed and exhausted Bella. Eva, as always, floated above Georgiana.

They traveled south and east through the swirl of autumn leaves and stepped over the occasional corpse until they were within sight of the helicopter.

It didn't occur to any of them that they might never reach it.

POW!

The Institute's plane landed in the abandoned parking lot of a bankrupted big-box store across the ring road from the Chesterfield Mall. The pilot was given permission to take off. They wouldn't need him further.

Maman Brigitte knew what a singularity was; Equity, not so much. But people - including cops - stepped aside as they confidently strode into the mall from which nobody had strode out for well over an hour.

They oozed evil, or something beyond it. A crowd of hundreds milled around, desperate for any information from the outside - but everyone left the two villains alone as they paced briskly forward.

"You know where we're going?" Maman Brigitte asked.

"It calls to me," Equity said. "We'll be there in thirty-nine seconds."

And that's exactly how long it took to get to the Blur Cave.

Equity sneezed down the door and the Malificium card flew into her hand.

Seth Hill and Myron Masters would have offered what resistance they could, but the Institute already had its prize.

"Do you," Seth asked Equity, "have any idea what kind of havoc that card can wreak?"

"No," Equity admitted, then indicated her longtime friend with a sideways glance. "But she does."

With whatever mojo was left over from his days as Black Man, Myron pounced on Maman Brigitte. His punch dislocated her jaw, but she was fine with that. She'd never have to eat again in her life and really didn't have anything left to say to anybody.

Meanwhile Myron's life was sucked out of his body the moment his flesh touched hers.

"Maman Brigitte," Equity said with uncharacteristic formality, "the day of days we have worked toward for ten years is now at hand. I present to you, for your collection, the final Malificium card. Your deck is complete. You are now mistress of all evil. Work your will."

And with that, Equity handed the card to Maman Brigitte, who accepted it with an elegant gesture. And, with an equally elegant gesture, she applied her death grip to Equity and watched her fall in a heap to the ground.

Work my will, Maman Brigitte thought, as she added the card to the pocket in her cloak which contained the rest of the Malificium deck. Yes, I'll work my will.

Her will, though, was different from villains of earlier days. She didn't want money or power or conquest or revenge. She was above all that.

She just wanted death.

She wanted death on a massive scale, death feeding on death, an extinction event to turn the entire world into a charnel pit.

But Seth had one last card to play.

"Face-up defense!" he called out as he pulled an ultra-rare out of a sock. "You can't attack me."

That was a half-truth. He was still vulnerable from any traps she might spring or monsters she might turn loose. But he was betting that nobody who spent so much time poring over dossiers on persons-with-abilities would bother much with trading cards. The future of the world rested on a bluff.

Maman Brigitte giggled. Had her jaw not begun to swell, she might have laughed more heartily.

Myron Masters stood up alongside Seth.

"Myron, thank God you're okay. I need you to head back to the Plaquet—"

And then Myron opened his mouth wider than Seth would have thought possible, and bit clean through Seth's tricep. Another bite took off a chunk of Seth's face and a third exposed his intestines to the air.

This undead incarnation of Myron staggered out of the Blur Cave. He would feast well that day, maintaining the element of surprise for some time.

There wasn't much left of Seth, not enough to reawaken anyway. He was not going to be a walking corpse, only their fodder. Maman Brigitte ignored the defense card he had in his outstretched hand and pulled the trap card out of his shirt pocket. As she shredded it, the singularity ended. People could now leave the mall. So could the flesh-eating dead. So could the spell that created the flesh-eating dead.

Then Equity stood up and immediately began gnawing on Maman Brigitte, who did nothing to discourage her.

Enraptured in pain, fading eyesight bearing witness to the unbirth of a new age, Maman Brigitte ignored her jaw's painful protest and died issuing a hearty laugh.

BAM!

Lourdes May knew that someday she would be a widow. You sign up for that when you marry a much older man. And, over the past few weeks of his ill health, she knew that someday would be very soon.

So it was with sadness but not surprise that she discovered James's body, slumped in his favorite chair in the solarium.

She kissed his forehead, then waved her hand gently across his face to close his eyes.

And then the eyes opened again.

PART THREE

EVERY NEW BEGINNING

ALTERNATE ENDING

You hear that?" Porter Peale asked, after spitting Forrest's rose-patterned panties out of his mouth.

It was the first time Pantagruel ever had sex in a funeral parlor. It was the first time Forrest ever had the closed-coffin experience.

"Sounds like a commotion out on the concourse," his new conjugal partner surmised.

"Damn."

"It's okay. You go out there and do what you have to do. I'll keep the mood ..."

"No need. I'm finished."

"Oh. Damn."

"Well, not forever. Let's try again after the mall closes," Porter suggested as he opened the lid and climbed out.

"Yeah, whatever."

Pantagruel tossed on his disheveled TSA uniform and headed for the door. He thought it was odd that there were people wandering around in a funeral parlor which was not yet formally open to the public. He figured they worked there. Out of sheer embarrassment he didn't engage any of them in conversation, and that preserved his life if only for a few moments.

He could see the sun through the atrium skylight, so the singularity – he knew right away that's what it was – had reversed itself. He was left to ponder, then, why was everybody running? Why the screams, the renewed sense of panic? He looked around for someone who appeared calm so he could ask him.

He spotted a black man whom he was ninety-nine percent sure was Myron Masters limping toward him. Considering the circumstances, he risked it.

"Hey, Myron! What's going on? Are you okay? Looks like your legs have stiffened up."

The revenant lurched for his meat organs, and Pantagruel's defense reflex was to shoot up in height. Moments after Myron's teeth sunk into his abdomen, he became the world's largest corpse, and that would be the tipping point. Everyone else in the mall was doomed. In a second, Myron's teeth were buried in Porter's abdomen. The walking corpse was going for the meat organs, but Pantagruel instinctively shot up in height. Moments later, he would be the world's largest corpse, and that would be the tipping point. Everyone else in the mall was doomed.

Simultaneously, the guests of honor at the Jones viewing, scheduled for two days hence, and the Russo viewing, set for the day after that, shared the kill of the woman whom their families had hired to bury them. Forrest was almost sexually frustrated enough to welcome death.

BOOM!

Late in the day, the sun warmed the winds which had slowed since daybreak from breeziness to occasional gusts to total calm. Plainville, Illinois, hot as it was going to get in late October, had started to stink.

More than a hundred unburied corpses littered the tiny village. Most of them were indoors but, even so, Kevin Kiley was left alone to view a gruesome panorama. As he sat on the stoop in front of some random house in the north part of town, he could see bodies lying in the middle of the road, half in and half out of a car, draped over a window ledge across the street. The closest one sat tucked in the nook of a tree limb, practically overhead.

A sour smell, like milk and raw eggs left in a mixing bowl and forgotten, wafted across the porch in waves. Kevin paid the dead little attention as their cells began the work of digesting themselves.

Steeped in self-pity, the only ambient detail that caught his attention was the sound of sirens. At first he thought some all-clear had been sounded and the authorities were at last advancing on the town from their checkpoints on the perimeter.

From such clues as the lowering pitch and decreasing volume, he soon realized the sirens were careening away from Plainville. He didn't stop to think why.

He just sat there and brooded for a while. Kevin had proved he was no use as a hero, nor was he useful for much of anything else. Broke, stranded, and friendless, he was so tired of his lot that he envied the dead.

It was then that a sedan pulled up. Staring down at the dusty ground, Kevin identified the new arrival as a pair of blue jeans over boots – not hero boots but nondescript, brown-suede roper boots like almost every guy in the Midwest owned.

The boots walked up to Kevin, who looked no higher than the kneecaps.

"Do you know who I am?" their owner asked.

That's when Kevin looked up.

"Yeah," he responded without enthusiasm. "You're Anderson Cooper."

"Call me Elias," the stranger said. "I used to be Colonel America. Have we met?"

"Not actually. You were in the fight against Ta Mok a couple days ago," Kevin recounted. "I never made it."

"You must be that Count Karma we'd been keeping an eye on up in Crusaders HQ," Elias said.

"You mean that Count Karma you never actually invited for a tryout. Just call me Kiley."

Elias sat down alongside Kevin on the stoop.

"Well, Kiley, mind telling me what happened here?"

"Bunch of heroes went on a mission to capture this wild badger-woman that moved into town. Met up against villains. Carnage ensued."

"And?"

"Mission accomplished. Some villains died. Some villains escaped. Some heroes died. Some heroes went chasing after the villains."

"And you?"

"And I watched it all from under cover. Totally useless. Maybe I'd have better luck as a villain. How do you think 'Count' would look spelled with a K?"

Elias asked some more questions and a traumatized Kevin, speaking in a hushed monotone, answered them. Kevin had no comfort to extend when he told Elias of the deaths of Shel and Bobby. Nor did he ask for any comfort when describing his own lack of contribution to the Pyrrhic victory.

"So if it wasn't for the harm I'd done, I'd have had no impact at all," Kevin summed up.

Elias looked far off for a second. He did that sometimes when he was concentrating, and stopped when he was sure the fading sunlight was playing tricks on him.

He could've sworn he saw the body on the tree limb squirm.

"Let's think this through. There was Lugh who, despite all his power, was kicked out of The Crusaders. And Mucus-Man and the Blur, who didn't last out the first year in the group. And Shel, who was supposed to have my old job but being a hero cost him the chance to be a superhero. Then there was Georgiana, who never wanted to use her powers in the first place. And you," Elias recounted. "Who's idea was it to come together as a team? Who talked all these people – who had any number of reasons to not want any part of this life anymore – into risking their lives if they failed and risking jail time if they succeeded?"

Kevin just shrugged.

"And here's another thought. You knew you had no real-world abilities, and yet you rode along into grave danger with those who did. That shows some guts."

Elias heard a rumbling in the leaves of a nearby oak. Kevin heard it too.

"And one last thing I'll leave you with before I see if I can find my, uh, friend," Elias said. "You have no firearms training whatsoever. Unless I miss my guess, you've never been to a range in your life. And yet you hit your target one shot out of three – with a pistol you'd never picked up before – from an elevated position, through foliage and a sustained wind, an action which gave Nebr ... Marisol an advantage. And you never sat through the gun safety lecture nor did you know bird-shot from birdshit, but you hit your target again with a shotgun, and no real harm done."

"But Mindy said that Lou would still be alive if ..."

"From what you told me, I don't see what your actions had to do with how Lou died. People just say things like that out of frustration," Elias explained. "I bet

347

if you called Georgiana up and asked her right now if she really meant that, she'd walk it right back."

"Yeah, maybe," Kevin allowed, then brightened a little. "So you think I handled myself okay? With the guns?"

"Kid," Elias said, draping an arm over his shoulder, "Maybe you've got skills you don't know about."

"I never really had the chance to—"

That body which in the nearby oak fell out to the ground.

Which didn't seem strange until it stood up, its body cavity exposed to open air, half its guts already removed by the Badger. Two-thirds of its face was that of a middle-aged man with a close crop of brown hair, while the other third resembled an open blister. It gave voice to a sound halfway between acid reflux and a cry for morphine.

Other bodies picked themselves up off the ground or rained down from other perches. Kevin could see the little girl from whom he took the pistol staring at him from her gabled window.

"I'm very new at this," Kevin said as they both rose to their feet as the resurrected bodies swarmed and advanced on them, "but does this happen a lot?"

"No," Elias said. "This is totally unprecedented."

They checked the door to the house. It was unlocked and they retreated to the relative safety inside. From the front foyer, they could hear bodies slam against the door.

For the second time in an hour, Kevin tripped over a corpse as he crossed a threshold. Like the last one, this body lay quite still.

A window shattered in the double-hung frame in the next room. Elias ran toward the sound. After kicking the intruder in the face, he reached outside to grab the storm shutters and seal them. Kevin took the cue to do the same on the other ground-floor windows before the swarm could break through.

"You think they'll turn into Badgers?" Kevin asked while dashing from window to window.

"Maybe, but I'm more concerned with what they've turned into already," Elias responded as he also dashed around shuttering possible points of entry.

"Which is?"

"Dead, to start with. Some are missing limbs, hobbling around on stumps without any display of pain. Others have trauma to vital organs, or are obviously missing vital organs."

"What do you think they're after?" Kevin asked, shouting over the TV in the den.

Before Elias could answer, one of the house's previous residents – the husk of a teenage girl who might have recently been pretty enough to be a homecoming queen – came charging at Kevin from behind the den's sofa.

Slow and clumsy as it was, it caught Kevin caught off-guard and pinned him to the ground. When he stiff-armed it under the snapping jaw it was trying to apply to his throat, he felt the sticky warmth of its spilling guts through the fabric of his Count Karma costume.

Elias still had his pistol. He pulled it out of his waist-band and aimed it at the reanimate. He stopped before pulling the trigger.

"What are you waiting for?" Kevin demanded.

"Hold on. Just had a thought."

With that, Elias ran back to the foyer to check out the body Kevin had tripped over moments before. Rolling it face-up, he could see it wasn't killed by the Badger. This was a case of friendly fire. The young man's forehead was not just shattered but obliterated by – he surmised based on personal experience - a .30-caliber hollow-point round. Maybe that's what the ghoul in the next room was packing. Maybe he was standing between her and the Badger and she panicked. Maybe they were brother and sister.

Not that it mattered anymore.

"Elias!"

The former Colonel America took one more second to check for any obvious wounds to the body and found none. So he raced back to the fight and pumped two bullets into the back of the attacker's skull. Eyeballs and brains splattered on Kevin's face, so it took him a moment before he got around to saying, "Thanks."

"Sorry about the disappearing act, but we don't have ammo to waste," Elias explained. "Obviously, these things can survive with half their organs removed, and I wanted to see what was keeping that guy by the front door down."

"No prob," Kevin said with a tinge of irony as he stood up. "But maybe we should find better cover. We're right in tornado alley here, so everybody's got a storm cellar."

"Right idea, wrong direction," Elias corrected. "In a situation like this we want the high ground, and to set up barriers behind us."

He handed Kevin his automatic and successfully hunted down the .30-caliber the teenaged girl dropped in the den.

"But you're right in that the cellar should be well provisioned," Elias continued. "Cover me from up here while I grab some supplies."

With that, Elias opened the cellar door and kept a wary eye out for unwelcome company. On the main floor, the thudding against doors and shutters and the moaning, which grew louder as the chorus grew larger, unnerved Kevin.

Elias emerged unscathed, and the two men formed an assembly line taking three loads of water, food, tools and ammunition up to the bedrooms which were, fortunately, unoccupied.

Elias then took a mallet and chisel to a kids' room door, taking it off its hinges. He threw the door down the stairs, effectively turning the bottom eight steps into a sliding board. He had just finished taking an axe to the ninth and tenth steps when the front door gave way under the weight of the mass of bodies.

The two men were very quiet for a while, huddled in the master bedroom suite at the end of the hall, the door shut and blockaded by box-springs.

Finally, Kevin spoke in a low whisper.

"Got an escape plan?"

"Yes," Elias replied, also in a whisper. "The plan is to be rescued."

"You're kidding."

"No. Let's get real. Kevin, you and I have one thing in common. We both lost our powers over the past couple days. We're just two normal guys now. Barring the kind of luck it's unwise to plan on, we don't have the mojo to get out of this on our own. Our best chance is to defend in place until help arrives."

"What makes you think there's any help left alive?"

Elias paused a moment.

"When I was driving into town, the National Guard and local law enforcement were plowing down the road in the opposite direction, sirens blaring. That tells me two things. First, whatever's happening here is also happening elsewhere. The world is mobilizing against this event, outbreak, whatever you want to call it."

"And second?"

"There was - at least as of an hour ago - still a National Guard and local law enforcement. The system is still in place. Society hasn't broken down. Sooner or later, troops are going to come through, or a copter or plane is going to fly overhead. We just have to stay alive until that happens. We got food, water, ammo, electric, a place to sleep, a place to shit, and we know how to kill these things. Let's just wait this out."

"What do you think caused it?"

"This has Maman Brigitte's fingerprints all over it, but I never gave her credit for this kind of ambition. She might be able to execute this kind of grand-scale carnage by herself, but somebody else cooked up the plan."

"You think she's got that trading card she was after?"

"I know she does. It was on the news."

"The news? You knew about these walking corpses before you got here?"

"No, but I was listening to the radio on my drive up, and there was something about a singularity engulfing the Chesterfield Mall. Grant Mazzy was saying that two women - fitting the descriptions of Maman Brigitte and Equity - walked straight into it. Last thing I heard before I pulled up here was that the singularity had been broken and people who were trapped in there were streaming out."

"What's a singularity?" Kevin asked.

Twenty minutes later, Kevin interrupted Elias by positing, "I wonder if there's anyone else in town left alive."

POW!

No, there wasn't.

Scattered through storm cellars and hiding under beds and in closets throughout Plainville, two dozen residents survived the Badger's onslaught.

Shortly after the team led by Georgiana limped away,

most of these survivors gathered in one living room for a communal meal of flapjacks, sausage and sympathy. Among them was Lee Ann Bayard, not technically a resident, but so stunned by the events she was in no shape to drive back to Wisconsin.

"... so then he says, 'This is what happens the hundredth time.' And then he just passed on," she said, choked up. An arm extended a box of tissues to her. "Some people say Lou Noble was just out for himself, but in the end ..."

And then another arm bumped Lee Ann on the shoulder. She looked up and her heart jumped. There he was, walking through the open kitchen door, looking gray and expressionless.

Like he always did.

BLAM!

Meanwhile, where once stood a grain silo there was now just a big pile of freshly harvested wheat. It had lain still in the crisp, autumn air.

All of a sudden a few grains swirled in an eddy. The eddy grew and grew until, a minute later, something bearing the face of Bobby Botler breached into the sunlight.

He ambled toward Georgiana, Mucus-Man, Colonel America and Bella Brock at a relaxed pace. He neither zipped toward them at superhuman speed, nor wandered around in a looping, drunken path.

They missed that sign of trouble and welcomed him.

Bella, in her weakened condition, was the first to be turned, then Mucus-Man as he succeeded in shielding Georgiana from Bobby, but not from the three other flesh-eaters that shambled up from behind – one of which sported a bushy, white moustache and wore a shredded and blood-splattered lab coat.

353

Colonel America made a break for it, but didn't get far - only about three blocks. She was within eyeshot of the house where Elias and Kevin were holed up. As Marisol Rivera went down like a wounded gazelle amid a pack of hyenas, all the two men could do was watch in horror from a distance.

"Wait!" a startled Lisa Shapiro exclaimed, pushing back from Lugh and his solemn burden. "He's alive!"

"Nay," Lugh replied, shaking his red-maned head. "Maman Brigitte herself did lay hands on ..."

"I'm telling you, I just saw him move!"

Lugh looked down at Shel's body, still cradled in his arms.

The children came running outside as Lugh set their father down. Shel was uneasy on his feet but, sure enough, he could stand on his own.

He then waddled up Lisa and stuffed her in his mouth like she was chewing gum.

Lugh at first thought there might be something playful about this, but that idea was quashed. When the deity pulled Shel off Lisa, he was rewarded with an oval of deep teeth marks in his own right ear.

It shouldn't have been a mortal wound, not for a man and certainly not for a god. But the pain from that bite was beyond anything he had experienced in his existence as either mortal or immortal. And beyond the pain were the waves of heat and chills. Seconds after receiving the bite Lugh was, for the first time in millennia, running a fever. His legs collapsed from under him and he slumped to the ground, weak as a slug.

He didn't understand what had happened to Shel, but he guessed it was happening to himself now. Aware that life as he knew it was ebbing, Lugh pondered how that could be. He was a god. Death could not claim him. Then again, whatever claimed Shel wasn't exactly death.

Lugh was still trying to figure this out with his last sentient thoughts while he helplessly watched Shel devour his children, as had the elder gods of so many pantheons.

The electricity stayed on for a week in Plainville although, for almost all of that time, Elias O'Neill and Kevin Kiley were the only two to benefit from it.

Not that they benefited much. Landline phone service had been overwhelmed and crashed under the weight of its antique infrastructure.

Elias suggested that if the power were still on, there was probably a working cell tower around. And there was. They could see it through a window. But Elias had been on the run and living off the grid the past couple days, and Kevin was just too broke and didn't even own a working phone. A furtive search of the space they were confined to on the second floor turned up nothing. They knew there were any number of phones downstairs – the undead were most impolite in declining to set theirs to silent mode – but the risk was too outsized.

Kevin found a set of ear buds and with that they listened to TV news without drawing attention to their presence. At first, they heard reports of rioting in cities. Then came dispatches of mayhem in smaller towns. It took a day for the news media to be unanimous in their assessment that the attackers were reanimated corpses and another to report that their brains were their only vulnerable spot. It took the government another day to organize a concerted plan to rescue survivors and establish safe havens. Another day went by before the plan was implemented.

Those items comprised all of the useful information, most of which Elias and Kevin parsed out for themselves on Day One. The rest of the airtime was taken up with religious ranting and partisan blame.

The next day, the undead of Plainville climbed over each other to breach the door-slide barrier. The following day they forded the gap in the staircase. When nothing stood between the ghouls and their prey except a couple of box springs and a flimsy interior door, Kevin and Elias said their goodbyes.

"Do you want me to do it for you?" Elias asked Kevin with all the kindness left in the world.

"No. I'll take care of it."

With that, Elias put the barrel of the .30-cal under his own chin, cocked the hammer and pulled the trigger. As the back of his head exploded, splattering the wall behind him with what looked to Kevin like Manhattan clam chowder, Elias's face remained as handsome as ever. He needed a shave was all.

The undead howled at the sound of the pistol, or maybe it was the rippling stench of fresh gore. In any case, their determination to get into the master suite redoubled.

Kevin pried the weapon out of Elias's still warm and pliant hand, felt the heat of the long barrel scorch the soft flesh behind his jaw, and pulled the trigger.

Nothing happened.

He pulled it again. Again nothing.

Then he remembered what Elias had taught him earlier in the week: that a revolver needs to be cocked to rotate the cylinder and move the cartridge into position. So he did that, and this time it would have worked.

But he was too late.

The door had come down. Rattled by the sound, Kevin involuntarily jerked while he was firing and inflicted only a flesh wound to his neck.

The reanimates took care of the rest. Intense pain and burning punctured Kevin's calves, thighs, genitalia and guts. He and Elias had made a pact that, if they had to die in that place, they were going to stay at rest. That would have been victory enough.

As he succumbed to the bites, Kevin realized that just as in life, he had failed in death.

BAM!

Eventually, even the most remote outposts of human civilization fell to the undead. When resurrected corpses overran the last Argentine National Gendarmerie outpost along the Pilcomayo River, the name *Eva Peron* dimmed from human recollection. Ghosts, as Professor Schadenfreude observed, aren't immortal. They survive only as long as collective human memory of them does. In consonance, a frustrated spirit's vain shouts of protestation faded to silence.

BOOM!

The Carbon Avenger had done what he set out to do: avenge carbon. Earth was now devoid of consciousness and all-encompassing technology. Six-proton atoms could now exist peacefully, naturally, among those other elements with which they could commune through covalent bonds. No more would his brethren, whether they be diamond crystals or anthracite lumps or petroleum flows or methane clouds, be forced into unnatural alloys with synthetic chemicals.

From his high platform above the Equator, the Avenger decided to return to his planet of origin. But, as a tribute to the world's previous extinction event, the Avenger smashed through the earthside hull of the Pinnacle of Righteousness and propelled himself toward the beckoning seas. Not having nerves, he didn't feel the friction or the heat as he turned from rock to fireball. All he felt was the comfort of his sense of self evaporating in the thickening air. The atmosphere that protected this carbon-rich world wore away intellect, memory and personality, until there was nothing left of Dirk Henderson. There was only a swirl of oxide and alkane gases, and a pebble-sized meteorite that splashed down unnoticed in the vast, salty ocean.

THAT LIVES CAN CHANGE, THAT YOU'RE NOT IN VAIN

r ...

POW!

"What's a singularity?" Kevin asked.

Twenty minutes later, Kevin interrupted Elias by positing, "I wonder if there's anyone else in town left alive."

As if to respond, a booming crack sounded somewhere downstairs, followed by the muffled sound of bodies hitting the floor.

"Shotgun ... eight-gauge and sawed-off," Elias said, and Kevin could tell the qualitative difference between that thunderclap and the spray of birdshot he had sent his colleagues' way earlier.

Amid a surge of undead wailing, a woman's voice issued huffs of exertion.

Elias and Kevin peered down from the blind they'd

set up at the top of the stairs. The undead were abandoning the landing for the mud room in back. That apparently was where the action was.

The two men risked a trip over their barriers back down the stairs. Pistols drawn, they approached the welcome stranger. From a distance and in the dusk, all they could tell was that she had a short crop of red hair and wasn't especially tall. Brown-sleeved arms proved as skilled with pointed weapons as they were with a shotgun. Something sprayed blood in all directions. Elias and Kevin moved forward, firing pistols into the backs of heads to relieve their rescuer's burden.

Elias had six rounds in his revolver, fired six shots, dropped six ghouls and reloaded with such expertise he kept his eyes out for immediate threats, not even looking at what his hands were doing.

Kevin had more trouble. He had Elias's old service automatic, no spare magazine, no loose ammunition that would fit the magazine he had, and no experience in any of this. With the eight rounds at his disposal he thinned out three more walking corpses, and that was nowhere near enough.

Elias, reloaded, was back at his proficient best. And now Kevin was close enough to see what the woman was jabbing with as she grunted her primal war cry.

It was a pair of ski poles.

She was drilling them through the revenantts' eyes two at a time, and they were going down just as fast. It was even faster than shooting them.

Inspired, Kevin dashed the half-dozen steps into the kitchen, pulled a meat cleaver out of the wood block, and brought it back into the fray with a mind to decapitate a few flesh-eaters.

One peeled off from the pack and followed Kevin into the kitchen to oblige him. It had been a big man, six feet of hair, flannel, denim, leather and tattoos covering a borderline obese build.

Kevin's first swing at the twenty-inch neck did little more than trim the man's beard. The next cut the carotid artery, causing a gush of black blood but the face expressed no pain, nor any objection. It just kept coming at him.

And Kevin kept swinging. He maneuvered around the ghoul and took whacks from every angle. On the eighth swing, the spinal cord finally snapped and the head hung at an unnatural angle behind the right shoulder. Another swing and the body went down. Another, and the head came off and the body twitched its last.

He looked up. The battle was over. In the time it took him to bring down one corpse, Elias and their newfound ally had brought down scores.

His Count Karma costume now irreparably soaked in blood and worse, Kevin rose from his kill.

"Kevin Kiley, I'd like you to meet an old friend of mine," Elias announced as he presented the redhead in the UPS uniform. "Time Tempest."

"Call me Tara," she said as, rather than offer a hand to shake, she stuck her ski poles in an archer's quiver she had strapped to her back, right next to the shotgun holster. "We got to get out of here."

"True that," Elias agreed. "We're in a bad situation."

"You think it's bad now," Tara corrected, "just wait a couple days."

And with that she grabbed both men by their forearms and, in a blink, they were somewhere and somewhen else.

BAMF!

When was three days earlier. *Where* was a place of expansive skies, rolling hills and the laughter of children:

the Chadwick home in Iowa.

BOOM!

"... so that's the situation, Roger," Elias summed up as the two former Colonels America sat in the study, accompanied by Kevin and Tara.

"Well, it's hard to get my head around a lot of this," Roger Chadwick mused as he sipped from a mug of coffee. He gave Tara a withering stare. "First of all, somebody's been sandbagging. I thought you could only toggle between your temporal point of origin and a point up to twenty-four hours in the past."

"That's what I wanted you to think," Tara replied with a little bit more defiance than the situation required before dialing it down. "Not you in particular. Everybody. But I've been stretching my power out. I can go back more than four days now, rest up a while and go back just as far. I can even take a passenger or two back with me for a shorter trip."

"But why the subterfuge?" Roger asked.

"Tactical advantage, just like you taught us," Tara replied. "Imagine how much trouble Equity could've caused if she knew she could go back more than twelve hours when she took half my power."

Roger beamed like a father of the bride before turning his attention to Elias.

"And right before things went from bad to worse, as you say, you retired as Colonel America and promoted Marisol. It was full well about time, but I knew she'd wear that cape someday."

Roger's face glowed even brighter, eliciting an eye roll from Tara.

Elias's expression, however, grew furrowed and grim as he recalled Marisol's gruesome end.

"Roger—"

"I can only imagine how proud you are!" Kevin interrupted, cheery and bright. "It's all a testament to the example you set."

Kevin's steely, sideways glance at Elias kept him quiet.

"I need to lie down for a while," Tara said, and with that the meeting broke up.

"Your old bedroom isn't occupied at the moment," Roger suggested as he moved his seat back behind his desk and perched back down. "I'll get started on a strategy. You guys can relax in the living room for now."

"Thanks again for everything, Mister Chadwick," Kevin said as he and his two companions left the study.

"You're welcome, of course. And, Mister Kiley, you're right."

"About what?"

"How proud I am of Marisol. But you may be wrong about something else," he added. Kevin noticed his face was awash with sadness. "I'm not stupid."

POW!

"This is a plan?" Kevin inquired, back in the study the next morning, looking over his copy of the overstuffed three-ring binder Roger had passed around. "I dropped college classes for less required reading."

"And that's part of the problem," Roger replied. "You never really applied yourself, have you, Kiley?"

No answer was the only answer.

"Not all your fault, I suppose," Roger said. "Nobody really challenged you, encouraged you to move beyond your safe zone. I wish it were otherwise, but the fate of the world is in your hands."

Kevin looked around at three pairs of probing eyes.

"No," he said as he got up and walked toward the door. "Between the three of you, there's got to be a better option. Mister Chadwick, you're—"

"Over the hill. No way. My real talent was always in developing others' talents. You're going to be a project, but it's on you."

"Elias?" Kevin pleaded. "Even without your powers, you have the experience to—"

"… back you up if I can, open up a second front if I can't," Elias cut in. "It's just good strategy to keep strength in reserve. I have my role."

"What about all the kids running around this place?" Kevin asked. "You're running a school for superheroes, Roger. There's got to be some go-getter who's dying for a chance like this."

"I have five students enrolled at present," Roger stated. "Two haven't manifested yet. Of the other three, the oldest is twelve."

Without hesitation, Kevin switched gears. "Tara, how about you? You actually have a power."

"Yeah, to get you where and when you need to be," she said. "I'll be too tapped out to be much help beyond that."

"I don't understand why anyone has to go anywhere," Kevin pointed out. "Shel, Lugh, Orville and Bobby barely know me as of today, but they do know you. If you show up and tell them what's going to happen in another couple days, they'll believe you."

"And then what?" Tara reposted. "What am I supposed to say to them? 'Do everything you can to prevent the Institute from getting the last Malificium card'? They're already doing that. The best thing is to get some unanticipated actor - that's you - on the scene dead-bang before the inflection point, just a split-second before Maman Brigitte takes possession. Otherwise we risk having no effect at all."

Kevin stopped his drift toward the door. "There's got

to be someone better for this," he said, and that was the closest he came to volunteering.

"Someone who knows the heroes, the villains and the lay of the Chesterfield Mall? No," Roger pronounced. "But this is going to take some time."

"Time, we got," Tara replied.

BAM!

The physical conditioning was the easiest part. Kevin lacked Roger's broad-shouldered heft or Elias's trim, sculpted physique. But he was wiry, nimble, fit. His sleek body type suggested a middle-distance runner or a point guard. Kevin was both, although only for fun. Nothing he ever worked hard at, until Roger put him through his paces.

Kevin lived in a series of track suits and cross-trainers over those few days. He didn't know what happened to his ripped and soiled Count Karma costume and didn't much care.

Going over the playbook turned out to be not so much a chore as Kevin feared. Roger's solution boiled down to, *Punch out Maman Brigitte's lights before she gets a hold of the card.* There were a couple sheets of paper describing the necessity of wearing gloves when punching someone who can take your life by any physical contact, and how important it is to keep the element of surprise on your side considering her magical powers. A paragraph on dealing with Equity, essentially advised Kevin to allow her to touch him and take half his – nonexistent – powers; since she could only possess one hero's abilities at a time, that tactic would return Mucus-Man to full strength.

The bulk of what his new mentors had to teach him had to do with Plan B – and Plans C, D, E and so on: What if Kevin couldn't get in position in time? What if the situation on the ground was not as Elias described from a secondhand report? What if? What if?

Kevin was also relieved to find out that, although there were a lot of pages in that loose-leaf binder, there were a lot of pictures. What he had to learn couldn't come out of a book.

Problem was, learning out of a book was what the Master of Arts was good at. Now he had to absorb knowledge through the skin, nerves and muscles as well as the eyes.

He'd had the best tutors he could hope for. Patient through Kevin's slow start, they'd taught him an array of useful skills. None of it was part of the Colonel America program. That was all gone, washed out of their systems. But, long before either man donned the red, white and blue uniform, Roger had been an Airborne officer and Elias had been a mechanical engineer. And it was these sorts of skills that would win the day.

Or, more accurately, two days from now.

For her part, Tara tried to stay as rested and relaxed as she could. Over and over, she turned the calendar back two days for herself and four passengers – exhausting work. She tended to spend most of her downtime on the overstuffed couch in the middle of the spacious, sky-lit living room, wrapped in a Snuggie and watching the junk channels that came with basic cable.

She wanted to play with the children who wandered freely and rambunctiously in and out of the room while their guardian was busy on this special project – it amused her how, from their perspective, they were always meeting her for the first time.

But she was too fatigued. Nobody could see how her chest was heaving under the cover, but the gradual hollowing out of her cheeks, bagging under her eye sockets, spots of blood in the whites of her eyes and –

toward the end – little bald spots where clumps of hair had fallen out – these were all on display.

Roger noticed, and it pained him. He empathized with his former student and, well, that churned up a lot of emotions he didn't have the bandwidth to deal with at that time. The important thing was the mission, and he sensed that the mission was in jeopardy. Every hour of training he and Elias could provide Kevin was crucial, but it would all be for nothing if Tara couldn't relay him to the right hour and location. She didn't look like she had another long trip left in her.

Time had become the scarce resource it was to everyone else. Whatever Kevin could absorb over the next day would have to suffice.

Soon came time to make that last jump.

Cable news reported that rioting had broken out in urban centers. Tara would now have to find the strength to take just one passenger back in time only an hour.

Tara, dressed in heavy layers and still shivering, was already in the study when Kevin walked in. He had on his cross-trainers, someone's well-worn denim jeans and a red Western shirt with white and violet piping.

"Don't you want to put your Karma costume on?" Tara asked.

"Count Karma doesn't exist anymore," Kevin said. "If I got to go down fighting, it's going to be as just a regular guy."

"Fancy shirt, though.'

"Regular guy can have a splash of style."

"Kevin, that was Marisol's shirt. She's been looking for it for years."

"I'll give it back to her," he replied. "Not bringing your shotgun or machete? Not even your ski poles?"

"The whole trick is to get there before they're needed," she said and swallowed a gasp of air. "If we show up as scheduled before the flashpoint and I'm packing those weapons, it's likely to cause an altercation with the cops. So no."

The retired Colonels America strode into the room to give their charges a proper send-off. Kevin thought it was kind of awkward. Over the past few days, he had developed a rapport with all involved, but he increasingly picked up an odd vibe from Elias. It was nothing improper, just a little off: eye contact that lasted a fraction too long, standing just a hair too close, a hand resting on a shoulder a tad too heavily.

And, from the way Tara spoke in monosyllabics, Kevin judged there was some unresolved drama between her and Roger.

Concentrating on the spatial location was more difficult. She knew where St. Louis sat on the map, but hadn't ever heard of the Chesterfield Mall before the outbreak. Without that context, Time Tempest's next task proved more taxing than she thought.

"You're going to have to help me," Tara said to Kevin. "Think about your friends. Think about when and where you were all together, before all this business got out of hand. Guide me with those images."

And that's why, rather than finding themselves inside the mall, or out in the parking lot staring into the singularity, Kevin and Tara materialized in the barroom where the team was put together.

BOOM!

As the two younger heroes shimmered out of existence, Roger and Elias shared the moment of envy unique to old soldiers, as the next generation moves forward, leaving them in the rear. Roger was accustomed to it, Elias not so much.

"Guess I should get going," Elias said, staring at the

space Kevin and Tara no longer occupied. "Get the supplies together, get started on building the bunker."

"Here's hoping we don't need it. I'll get the kids' stuff together," Roger replied. He stared out the window at a strange man in tattered clothes staggering slowly up the driveway.

"Lots of changes, Roger."

"And none could be foreseen."

"The Crusaders proving to be so useless in a crisis like this," Elias fumed.

"The fate of the world resting in the hands of such an underachiever as Kevin Kiley," said Roger, "And the only chance of a cavalry charge coming from a motley crew that couldn't even keep their jobs at a shopping mall."

"My turning gay."

"Um. Yes. That more than anything. Never saw that coming. Nope. No way. Uh-uh."

POW!

"Where are we?" Tara asked amid a sudden coughing fit.

She'd have collapsed to the floor if Kevin hadn't guided her down to a seat.

"It's a bar called Hawk's. About two miles from the mall."

He looked around. It looked to be a normal happy hour: no signs of panic, no reanimated corpses; on the jukebox Gerard Way warbled lyrics about demons and non-believers. Kevin asked some random guy for the time.

"Bad news, Tara – it's ten after seven," Kevin conveyed. "We're not just two miles off, we're fifteen minutes late. We have to bounce, now!"

"Go on without me – I'll only slow you down," Tara

squeaked out, her head resting on a table.

Kevin scooped her up anyway. With his arm around her waist for support, he hurried her out the door. A silver Audi was parked - illegally - directly in front of Hawk's. A man wearing shades in the fading light just after sundown, speaking words like "synergy" and "win-win" into a Bluetooth device - that is to say, an obvious douchebag - had one of his honey-colored Gianni Barbato buckle shoes resting on the rear bumper. Kevin let Tara lean against the wall for a moment as he went over to the man, brimming with confidence in his ability to steal a car - by hot-wiring it if necessary.

"Excuse me," Kevin inquired. "Is this your car?"

"Hold on a sec, yes it is, now as I was saying, the optics of the synergy are such that—"

Kevin laid him out flat with a single hammerfist to the temple, reached into the man's jacket pocket for his Blackberry, and started the car with an app.

His mentors had also taught him a little about mixed martial arts.

Kevin practically threw Tara into the passenger seat and screeched the Audi's tires to a jackrabbit start. Pain from the punch's recoil stabbed, then tingled, in his hand and wrist. And he found himself liking it.

He figured he could get to the mall in less than three minutes if he didn't stop for red lights or any other inconveniences. Roger had packed a certain amount of contingency time into the plan, but Tara's fatigued efforts had cost every second of that. He had to make up some time, but not all was lost, at least not yet.

"Why did you take me along?" Tara sniffled, curled up in a ball, leaning against the passenger-side door, clutching the seat belt in her hands. "I won't be any good in a fight in this condition, and I was safer there than I'd be at the battlefront."

Kevin risked a split-second sideways glance as he raced eighty miles an hour down the major thoroughfare, blessedly uncrowded in the post rush-hour lull.

Blood pooled up in the whites of her eyes. Tears of red dribbled down the side of her nose.

"If things go wrong, I might need a quick escape into the past," Kevin said.

"Even if it kills me."

"Well ..."

"Don't say it. I knew the risk," Tara allowed. "Gotta give The Crusaders credit, though. They never used anyone up like this. What kind of hero are you?"

He thought about the people he'd faced death with – over a week ago by his experience, but just that day to almost everyone else. How they all died, and how they might all die again unless he set things right.

He remembered in particular one death that he felt most keenly guilty about.

"The world doesn't need a hero today," Kevin said, and then pressed the pedal all the way to the floorboard.

A zig around one car, a zag around another, an unapologetic sidelong scrape along a third and fourth, rewarded Kevin with open street all the way to the mall's ring road. Pressing his elbow to the horn every inch of the way, the opposing traffic doughnutted rather than collide with him. Over medians, curbs and other barriers, scattering abandoned shopping carts and rent-a-strollers in all directions, the Audi plowed forward until enough of its undercarriage had been stripped away that it just belly-flopped to a skidding stop twenty feet outside the Galen Ross store entrance. The crowd around the mall extended nineteen feet.

As luck or Audi over-engineering would have it, the airbags never deployed. That spared Tara's life.

On the other side of the crowd, the mall looked like it

was shrink-wrapped in black plastic. But as thin as the veneer appeared, the people on the outside could neither see nor hear any signs of habitation on the inside.

"I'm going to leave you here," Kevin told Tara. "Rest up."

"I'll make sure of it," said a woman who peeled away from the crowd. Like Tara, she was a woman in her early thirties, but she was dressed much older - strand of pearls, tailored pants suit, flat shoes, as if she had to toggle quickly between elegance and practicality. She peered into the passenger window. "You okay, Time Tempest?"

"Fine," Tara said defiantly, even though she looked every inch the antithesis of fine.

"Who are you?" asked Kevin, caught entirely by surprise.

"You can't pronounce her real name," Tara said. "Just call her Flare Star."

"I have a perfectly pronounceable name," the woman said. "Missus Roger Chadwick."

"Did you know about this?" Kevin asked Tara.

"I know all about *her*, of course. Didn't expect to see her here. Should've known, though, when I didn't see her around Roger's house."

"I was out running errands when you two and Elias arrived at our home," Flare Star explained. "Roger sent me out here to keep tabs on you. I'll look after Tara, Mister Kiley. You go save the world. Now!"

Without a costume, Kevin Kiley had no outward markings of being the one who would come to the rescue. Maybe it was just something in his step but, as he approached the department store's doors, rows of people moved aside. And some of them wore uniforms.

He pressed down on the bar of the door, the glass of

which was darkened to opaque black by the singularity. It was cold to the touch. He pushed the door open into blackness and, without hesitation, stepped into the mall and out of the sight of the rest of Creation.

BAM!

Inside.

That was Step One. The crowd was on edge, lots of shouting from short tempers and growing claustrophobia, but no primal fear. It hadn't happened yet. Good.

Step Two was to find whatever kind of superpowered assistance was available. Pantagruel was known to be there. How hard could it be to find Pantagruel of all people?

Pretty damn difficult as it turned out. Kevin tore past the row of offices to what he remembered as Shel Shapiro's desk. The Crusader's costume hung on a hook there, but Porter Peale, the man himself, was nowhere to be found.

Where else might he find heroes?

The Blur Cave.

He wished as he raced down the concourse that he had Bobby Botler's speed. Instead, though, he merely experienced time in a way that Bobby would have understood. Seconds were interminable.

Kevin cracked open one of the hideaway's double doors to a gruesome scene, as bad as any that was about to play out in Plainville.

Seth Hill - the card shop owner whom Kevin had seen in passing in recent days - was being eaten alive. He recognized the monster, too. Now a flesh-eating, undead ghoul, but Kevin was well-versed in the history of his chosen profession - and that was none other than Black Man.

It would be so easy to give him his rest, Kevin thought - jump up to grab one of the exposed fluorescent tubes out of the drop ceiling, then jab it straight through the eye socket. Or, with a quick burst of speed, he could grab a drumstick from the Rock Band set or a bumper pool cue. A scissors, a letter opener, a pen - anything he could stab an eye or ear with.

Instead, he did the one thing that he knew would absolutely make him sick of himself.

He hid.

BOOM!

"Why didn't Roger say anything?" Tara asked the former Princess Xng*nk.

"What's to say?" Flare Star said. "My powers are long gone and there's nothing I could do to help train that Kiley fellow. Hey, he's kind of a hottie. Are you two—?"

"No. It's been all about the fight."

"That's how it started out with your dad and me, but—"

"First of all, Roger isn't my dad," Tara said, drawing strength from anger. "Second, he is old enough to be my dad and you're two years younger than me, so yuk."

"Roger always thought of you as his child."

"No," Tara said with slow melancholy. "I was just one of his students. Dozens of others came and went - including you and, I say again, yuk. I was just there longer than any of the rest."

"That's not how he speaks about you," Flare Star said with patience, as if she were the only adult in the conversation.

"I'm surprised he speaks about me at all," Tara replied, settling into the petulant child role. "If he ever did consider me his kid, then I must've been the neglected middle child - sandwiched between Little-Miss-Perfect-

374

Daddy's-Little-Girl Marisol and Our-Precious-Special-Needs-Baby Orville. Those were the ones he loved. Those were his real kids."

"Real, how?" Flare Star asked. "Biologically, they're no more his children than I am, and I'm not even from this planet. The fact is, he loved us all. Even Bobby. Remember him?"

Tara couldn't suppress an involuntary chuckle about the trouble-bound pre-teen who only lasted in the home for only one summer. Flare Star joined in.

"You want some cocoa?" Flare Star offered, reaching into her bag for a Thermos. "I brought some hot cocoa."

Tara hesitated, suddenly unsure why she was angry.

"This doesn't mean I'm going to call you 'Mom'."

POW!

The undead incarnation of Myron Masters staggered out of the Blur Cave, straight past Kevin, who had pasted himself against a wall. This was where the carnage would start. Kevin looked around at the crowd – hundreds of people who would soon be killed, and worse. He could have stopped it. Maybe. If age and neglect had sufficiently degraded Myron's Black Man powers, if those powers were further eroded by his current, revenant state, if there were no other animated corpses already walking around, and if Kevin's own luck held out in a one-on-one fight.

Instead, he chose to stop it from spreading. That was the whole gist of Plan B.

As Myron staggered into the concourse and took a chunk out of one man's neck, a dozen nearby people ran in a dozen different directions. One woman running past Kevin wore a snorkel coat – a little early in the season for that. Kevin figured she had gloves stuffed in the pockets. One shovel-hook punch to the liver and a pair of Isotoners hit the floor before she did. Kevin picked them up, put them on and dove through the Blur Cave doors.

A casually dressed puddle of grue on the floor had Seth Hill's face on it and cards in its pockets. Maman Brigitte eyed those cards lasciviously, which suggested to Kevin that she must never, ever get a hold of them. A diving, knife-hand blow to her third vertebra frustrated her attempt to reach her prize.

She regained her feet, though they wobbled. Kevin could see some swelling in her jaw.

"I wouldn't have guessed," Maman Brigitte said with a smile on the still-functional side of her face. "You punched me almost as hard as Myron Masters. And you thought to wear synthetic gloves. Maybe you're not as useless as your file indicates, Mister Kiley."

Kevin said nothing. He scanned the room for attack vectors he could use to surprise his adversary: left, right, over, under. In a second, though, he realized the best action was none at all. Equity was rising behind her, and he recognized the voraciousness in those dilated pupils. A moment later and Maman Brigitte transformed into a soon-to-be-reanimated corpse. And, unless he was mistaken, she was enjoying it to the fullest.

Kevin took the cards off Seth's remains, inspected them, and understood their importance.

Everybody in the Chesterfield Mall - including him - was likely to die that night and wander forever as a soulless, ravenous husk of a human being.

But as long as the singularity remained in place, nobody else would.

BAM!

"... So I guess that's where the bad habits came from," Tara confessed, lying down flat on the Audi's back bench. "I never thought anyone recognized anything I did, so I stopped trying."

"But as my powers faded away to nothing, yours just got stronger," Flare Star observed. "And it's a good thing they did."

"Yeah," Tara conceded. "Maybe when all this is over, I'll give the hero thing another try."

"You already have," Flare Star replied. "But explain this to me: I get why you left The Crusaders, I can figure out why you went back for your Ph.D., but how did you end up working for UPS?"

"That's the easy part," Tara explained. "What else are you going to do with a doctorate in formal axiology?"

"I don't know. What is formal axiology?"

"It's the study of value. What - mathematically - makes something good."

"As opposed to evil?" Flare Star asked.

"You make it sound like those are the only two choices."

"They aren't?"

"Not by a long shot," Tara said with a smirk. "Kevin and Elias got into this predicament while they were off hunting something chaotic, which doesn't rise to the level of either good or evil."

"So there are at least three choices."

"More than that," Tara explained. "You know what's worse than evil?"

"Worse than evil? No. What?"

"Nihilism. The idea that nothing matters and all humanity's efforts are wasted and worthless," Tara summarized. "At least evil has a purpose. And at least chaos can give birth to order and, maybe, to good."

"So given the choice—"

"Between evil and nothingness? Pick evil every time."

BOOM!

377

Marisol Rivera permitted herself a howl of intense pain.

It took a moment for her to regain enough composure to say, "Thanks, *hermanito*."

"How many times does this make?" Orville Ortley, her adoptive kid brother, asked.

"Lost count," she replied, feeling the organelles shudder at the sound of Spanish. "How pathetic is that? I don't even know how many times you had to snap my shoulder back in!"

"All part of growing up heroes," Orville said with a chuckle.

A chuckle. Marisol mused about how possible it might be to lock Equity away so that she never touched another soul, freeing Orville permanently from half the "static" he sometimes spoke about.

And with that, the small band of the forces of good made their way out of Plainville, Illinois, to give chase to Maman Brigitte and Equity.

Unaware that the two villains were now walking corpses and that the Malificium card's dead-raising enchantment was contained by a singularity trap, other thoughts occupied their minds.

None of the passengers on Colonel America's helicopter had ever been in one before. On another, less exhausting, less emotionally draining day, they might have enjoyed it. At that moment, though, it was just an exercise in loud noise, metallic seats, violent shaking, and stomach-wrenching yaw.

Soon Marisol Rivera, her cowl removed and her lower left cheek a cross-stitch of scabbed-up lacerations, attained an altitude where she could comfortably punch it to cruising speed. Comfortable to her, at least. The experience unnerved Georgiana, who could fly under her own power; it didn't seem right to her that anything this fast should be flying so low to the ground.

Colonel America said something.

Georgiana couldn't hear and asked her to repeat it.

"Twizzler?!" the Colonel offered again, opening up a sunglasses-sized compartment between them, stuffed with chewy, cherry-flavored goodness.

Yes, Georgiana nodded. Twizzler. Exactly what she needed. She savored the dainty bite that transformed her back into Mindy Maguire, clad in her rumpled salmon suit, then devoured the rest of the stick in one chomp.

Leaning back in her seat, getting as least uncomfortable as she could, Mindy took stock of her transformation. *What is Mindy? What is Georgiana? What about me is at root?*

Memory didn't break. As Mindy, she remembered everything that happened when she was Georgiana and, thus, knew that Georgiana remembered everything that happened when she was Mindy.

The personality shifted affect, but subtly. Mindy thought up the name to bury the unwelcome "Supermodel" appellation, but Georgiana herself embraced it without a second thought. It was no Jekyll-and-Hyde transformation.

Even so, the Georgiana persona possessed far more self-confidence. When the goddesses imbue you with transcendent beauty, what's not to be confident about? And Mindy approved of what Georgiana was doing with that beauty – expanding its definition, going beyond the Nordic, workout-video, real-and-spectacular pulchritude that any slobbering imbecile could appreciate, experimenting with skin hues and body types and wardrobe. Not letting beauty define her, she was redefining beauty. Mindy wondered what Georgiana – the mulatto, size-ten Georgiana – looked like with the scar that a single birdshot pellet cut in her cheek. Then she wondered if she still, as Mindy, carried that mark. She rubbed her face where the ball had struck and, sure enough, there was a tiny, new fissure there.

Her cheek.

That put it together for Mindy. That's what she had in common with Georgiana in all her manifestations: the same basic facial shape. Mindy had a face with symmetry up and down as well as left and right. All the iterations of Georgiana shared that trait. And the self-confidence gap wasn't quite so big anymore.

There was one other thing that might have changed when Georgiana transformed back into Mindy but, just as she was about to dedicate some serious reflection to it, she heard something in the second row of seats. She glanced back there, where Orville and Bella sat, and where Eva floated bemused above them.

The sound was the most implausible one she could have imagined under the circumstances: laughter.

Bella was laughing. At Orville.

She wore his TSA-issue windbreaker as he mimicked the postures and gestures of famed Crusaders: the stiff, hunched- over waddle of Pantagruel, the ironic eye roll and half-faced smirk of Time Tempest, the lead-with-his-chin motions of Elias O'Neill-era Colonel America.

And Bella Brock, a complete basket case five minutes earlier, giggled like a high-school mean girl who just found out her rival for prom queen was pregnant.

When Mindy glanced back, Orville caught her eye. He had been smiling all along, but he turned up the wattage when they locked glances.

She recalled her teenage crush on Mucus-Man. Mindy had fantasized about a moment like this since she was still counting her periods. And here it was.

She smiled back, knowing she was forcing it. A short, involuntary, nervous giggle erupted from her throat.

Mindy knew she had one more thing in common with

her alter ego.

POW!

Something's wrong, The Carbon Avenger pondered, without reference to the pink-and-red pancake that used to be Millicent May Peale.

The years of planning, of finding such a gem of anomie as Maman Brigitte, of giving her the tools to destroy everything on earth, the evil as well as the good – it should have all come to fruition by now.

The singularity still sealed the Chesterfield Mall. She must have failed to find a way to dissipate it. For all he could gather, she also failed to execute any of her mission. It was impossible to know.

From the outside.

Just like it was impossible to break the singularity from the outside.

"If you want a job done right ..." he mused as he climbed into Steed Two.

BAM!

"You don't sound surprised," Tara said. She felt better now, sitting up in the Audi's passenger seat, staring out at the sea of people surrounding the blacked-out silhouette of the Chesterfield Mall.

"Oh, I've heard all this before," Flare Star replied. Now she was the one lying on the back bench. "On my world, we had a legend exactly like this: the living dead. In the stories, an outbreak of reanimated corpses becomes a plague, and the plague becomes an apocalypse as smaller and smaller pockets of survivors are overrun and all civilization and central authority break down."

"Sounds stupid."

"Yeah, but a lot of people were into it. They even had a word for the undead. They called them 'zombies.'"

"Really?" Tara inquired. "We have that word here,

381

but it refers to enthralled slaves serving a Voudoun practitioner."

"Hmmm," Flame Star mused. "That's really obscure."

BOOM!

Half an hour later, the helicopter from Plainville approached the mall's parking lot.

"Got a plan?!" Marisol shouted at Mindy, whose hearing had finally adapted to the rotor and wind noises.

"We go in, find the evildoers, stop them!"

"And how do we get out?!"

"Who says we do?!" Mindy replied. "We're heroes! Sacrifice! It's what we're here for!"

"You know, any baddies in there are locked in there!" Marisol advised. "No need to dive in after them!"

"Oh, right!" Mindy said, dripping sarcasm. "Villains never escape!"

"Point taken!" Marisol said, donning her Colonel America cowl again. "Hey, shouldn't you be changing back into Supermodel?!"

"Georgiana! Yes, I should! But ritual requires me to throw up first!"

Never say that to a helicopter pilot.

By the time they landed, not only was the Georgiana transformation complete, but Orville was also looking a little green and Bella – Bella, where to start?

Even Eva looked a little disheveled, her pale impression of a custom-tailored designer dress hanging not quite right.

"Interesting ensemble," she said to her protégée.

"Glad you approve," said Georgiana. This time, the apotheosis of beauty stood solidly, muscular, skin as black as bitumen, tightly curled hair buzzed into a flattop. Her wardrobe consisted mainly of leather and flannel – tasteful, sexy, but intimidating.

"You know what you look like, dearie. You look like a dyke."

Georgiana just raised an eyebrow.

"No!" Eva gasped as she flipped through a mental Rolodex of possible explanations. Suddenly her eyes lit up in comprehension. "Back in that dreadful little village. You matched up against that Ray fellow, didn't you? Didn't you!"

"Look, Evita, we don't have time for this right now."

Orville would have been heartbroken had he been listening to this conversation, but he and Colonel America – along with Bella Brock – were fifty feet away getting debriefed by Time Tempest and Flare Star: "There's probably a horde of resurrected flesh-eaters on the inside, no known way out, a serious risk of spreading the undead plague if they found a way out, and only Kevin Kiley – with no superpowers and only the equivalent of a week's training – went in to save the day."

"Well, I guess we'll go in and rescue him," Orville said. "You two look after Bella. Make sure she doesn't come in contact with anything radio—"

"I'm coming with you," Bella whispered low, but firmly. "It's better that I'm sealed away."

"Bella, I'm sure we can find a cure for your condition," Orville said hopefully. "There's no need for you to risk throwing away the rest of—"

"I need to do this!" Bella said, more loudly. "To make up for what I've done I'd pretty much have to save the world, wouldn't I?"

"Okay, you're in," Colonel America said, looking over the depleted woman in the torn remains of Rhonda Bayard's wardrobe, Orville's windbreaker a necessary layer of warmth and modesty. "If, on the inside, we can locate the triggers that turn you into the Badger and turn you back to human form, I could see how adding chaos to a situation could be an advantage for us. But first let's get you some proper clothes. You look like—"

"Uh," Orville interjected, "We're going to the mall?"

And with that, Mucus-Man, Colonel America, Georgiana with her familiar spirit Eva Peron, and the human alter ego of the Badger strode into the blackened Gaylen Ross entrance to the Chesterfield Mall.

THE EXCITING CONCLUSION

Colonel America was the first one through the door and into the world of women's shoes and handbags. She stepped straight into a fight.

The smell hit her first. Marisol's eyes stung as she wondered how the air could turn so foul so fast. Rot on top of feces on top of diseased urine wafted in the staleness. There was just the slightest undertone of bleach and antiseptic, as if someone had tried in vain to prevent Hell from breaking loose by giving the world a good scrubdown. But the panorama of carnage stretched from one end of her peripheral vision to the other, from blood dripping from the ceiling to a tile floor so slick with bodily fluids that each step was a challenge to the treads of Colonel America's boots. Those boots almost skidded into a pair of zombies crouching over their prey.

The remains of a Brookstone employee and of an acne-pocked freeloader who dropped by at least once a week to browse, relax in the vibrating chair and never buy anything were picking over the ample bones of a bearded-jowled pensioner who had dropped by to fill out the paperwork for his seasonal Santa job.

Both zombies, tangled in the wide suspenders that held up the old man's blue jeans, came across the same meaty femur at the same time. A grunting, snarling, slapping disagreement ensued there on the tile floor. They didn't even notice Marisol Rivera, festooned in bright, primary colors like the barbecued ribs display in a supermarket the day before Fourth of July weekend.

Colonel America walked past without attracting their attention. She could see a half-dozen more of the revenants over the tops of the merchandise displays; a legless one in Banana Republic earth-tones clawed itself along the aisle using its fingernails and bared incisors. They wandered, not quite mingled, silently; the only sound she could hear was that of the two Santavores. She figured if she just moved slowly and avoided eye contact she just might ...

A noise behind her split the silence – an hysterical scream that quickly dropped four octaves to a retching eruption. Marisol turned around to see Bella Brock using a stocking from an aisle-cap display to wipe phlegm from her lips and nostrils, an ochre puddle pooling at her feet.

This attracted more attention than just Marisol's. The two frenzied feeders rose from their haunches as the other reanimates pivoted in the direction of the four heroes.

"You and Orville push on!" Georgiana called out, taking charge. "I'll follow behind with Bella!"

Marisol was about to charge off but Orville stopped her with one word of reason.

"Heels."

It took Marisol a second – which was all the time she had – to figure out what he meant. Swiveling her head, she noticed she was standing beside a column of strappy, stiletto sandals. She pulled a pair out of its open box, one in each hand and drove the heels simultaneously into the eye sockets of the two feeders who had lumbered into her arms' reach. They stiffened, then their heads slid six inches off the spikes as their bodies collapsed in splayed heaps.

Orville went one better. He found a pair of knee-length boots with heels that were just as long. Wearing them like evening gloves, he ran forward, gouging eyes and ears of any zombie in his path. As he took the lead, Marisol fell in behind, holding her impenetrable cape down to serve as a rear guard.

It occurred to Marisol as they emerged into the concourse that they were just running, searching for relative safety, but with no obvious plan or destination.

"Any idea where we're going?" she asked.

"Yes," Orville said with panting breath. "There's an old loading dock sixty-three paces forward then twelve to the right."

"Safe?"

"I don't know," Orville admitted. "But it's stocked with provisions and it's where Count Karma might have established a base, if he's still alive. And Georgiana knows where it is."

Marisol noted a rare twinge of emotion in Orville's voice as he strung the names "Count Karma" and "Georgiana" together in subsequent breaths. Was that a note of disapproval? Jealousy? Swelling romance? In thirty-plus years, she had never known him to express anything resembling any of that.

But she didn't have time to ponder. They weren't in the narrow aisles of the Gaylen Ross shoe department anymore. They were in the widest spot at the center of the Chesterfield Mall and the zombies came at them from all directions. Orville was smart, Marisol conceded, to go with the boots that gave a layer of leathery protection from injury. With her strappy pumps, one of which was already permanently mounted in the eye socket of a burly GNC manager, the only thing between her and a fatal bite was her costume. Yes, it was reinforced with body armor in strategic places, but not all over. She wouldn't be able to run and dive and tumble like Colonel America if she wore a bomb disposal suit. She realized just how vulnerable she was well before she heard that rip in her sleeve.

POW!

Georgiana's charms were utterly lost on the zombie horde. To them, she looked neither more nor less delectable than her comrades. But that was plenty delectable.

Knowing full well it wasn't going to help settle Bella's stomach, she scooped the frail shell of a woman in her toned arms and took to the air. As they hovered fifteen feet off the main floor, Bella responded with another retch. Georgiana marveled at how the undead huddled around the puddle of vomit and lapped at it like kittens around a saucer of milk. Spinning around, Georgiana could see the same scene being acted out around the first puddle. Bella responded by giving the ghouls a third.

"Are you done?" Georgiana asked, not unkindly.

"Think so," Bella said with an uncertain quaver. "Sorry. I thought I'd be of some help. But I'm just making things harder for you."

"Don't even," Georgiana responded. "I wouldn't have taken you along if I didn't think your, uh, skills would come in handy at some point."

"You're saying '*I* wouldn't' and '*I* didn't,'" Bella observed. "Are *you* the leader?"

Georgiana looked around at the mayhem surrounding her. She saw the corridor leading to the office where she first met Sheldon Shapiro and the Indomitable Lugh – either one of them would have been better qualified, but Shel was dead and Lugh was nowhere to be found. There was Macy's, where Bobby Botler had rescued her, even if she didn't know that at the time; whatever attitude problems he had, he also possessed far more experience than she. Next to it was the Plaquet Box, whose owner, Seth Hill, had a proven track record as a tactician. And there was the hole in the roof that Christ the Son tore. Even he would have been a more qualified leader, Georgiana thought.

Then she realized that the same could be said for Mucus-Man, and certainly for Colonel America, the two of whom she spotted crouching in an earring kiosk. But when she gave an order, they followed it. They were content to let her call the shots. Somehow, those around Georgiana were drawing strength from her.

Was she the leader?

"I am today."

BAM!

"How far?" Marisol whispered.

In response, Orville pulled one hand out of the boot, raised his pepper mill to his face and blasted a path toward a pair of push-bar doors between a couple of specialty shops. Reanimates and blood-soaked bones scattered in the gale.

Marisol expected a hurricane. Orville's power, halved by his encounter with Equity, had not yet returned. If he had been at full strength, the twenty-yard dash to the double doors would have been completely cleared. As it was, they had to fight for the last few paces - bare-fisted, as they broke into a desperate, heads-down sprint.

Diving through, they blocked the door behind them with Bobby's foosball table and whatever they could pile on top of it.

Only then did it occur to them to look around to see if they had company.

BOOM!

"Should we follow them?" Bella asked, as she and

389

Georgiana hovered in relative safety in the middle of the atrium. Zombies on the first floor stared up at them while those on the second floor stared across at them. Glancing up, Bella could see the pitch black of the singularity through the gap in the ceiling.

"No, I'm sure they're barricading themselves in," Georgiana replied. "Odds are, if Kevin is still with us he'll be in there. We'll scout around and see if there are any other survivors."

And with that, she swooped through the mall at thirty knots, an unwilling Bella cradled in her arms. Bella's involuntary shrieks had a tendency to attract undead attention as Georgiana banked across second-floor walkways to peer vainly into gated storefronts.

"Slow down, damn it!" Bella screamed more than once. But Georgiana's speed was only barely fast enough to keep the slow but tenacious horde from sinking teeth into their flesh.

{POW!}

Eva Peron's experience of all this was quite different. On her plane of existence, one in which the overhead speakers still pumped out upbeat Christina Aguilera tunes, there were no reanimated corpses - just confused spirits, trying to work or shop or eat, but unable to grasp anything. Their hands passed through anything solid. None could raise a cappuccino to their lips or try on a new suit or stuff unpaid-for books under their jackets.

Eva's attention was caught by one young couple at the counter at Zale's. As a mustachioed sales clerk beamed, the man tried to pick up a diamond ring off the glass to slip on his intended's waiting finger. It eluded him.

"Isn't that the weirdest thing?" he asked her.

Then, after another try, "Isn't that the weirdest thing?"

She looked around and saw that her fellow spirits kept

repeating the same patterns, whether they were attempting to try on clothes that were already in a pile on the floor, or get their ears pierced, or throw a coin in the fountain.

"Isn't that the weirdest thing?"

BANG!

About the time Georgiana noticed the usually obtrusive Eva's absence, she also noticed a clutch of zombies in front of the Cracker Barrel. They weren't there for the cheese logs. Somebody, she figured, must be inside.

Leaving Bella to hang by her armpits for a moment from a wire that supported a banner ad for the new Hyundai, she swooped into the middle of the group. Using her prodigious strength, Georgiana twisted one zombie's head off like a bottle cap. It turned out to be Jackson, or was it Johnson, or Johnston? She was ashamed at how good it felt. Next, she put a conveniently misplaced trash spear through the temples of what turned out to be the reanimated corpse of her former boss at Macy's, Eunice Penobscot Snodgrass, and she felt no such shame.

The problem with zombie fights, she discovered, is that zombies don't scatter. The fight itself actually attracts more of them. Fortunately for Georgiana, she didn't have to spend too much time searching for an exit strategy. A rifle shot rang out from inside the Cracker Barrel and a third zombie dropped. Another shot, and a fourth laid down. The vanguard of the approaching horde was still several stiff-legged paces away. Wasting no time, Georgiana swooped upward to retrieve Bella, then slid with her under the gate which had been momentarily rolled up a foot-and-a-half off the floor.

Closing the gate behind them, smoke coming from the gun slung over his shoulder, stood a high school boy in the sky-blue blazer, white shirt and black tuxedo pants of a movie usher. He had a broad, tan face that beamed intensity.

The two women lay embraced on the floor. Bella was nearly naked, her long, wild hair dancing around her long neck and bare, goose-fleshed shoulders.

He stared gape-mouthed at Georgiana.

"Are you Supermodel?" he asked with a slight Mexican accent.

"Whatever," Georgiana said. It wasn't time to get into the discussion. "Are you alone in here?"

"No," he said. "There are six of us."

Sure enough, five other heads poked cautiously out of cabinets and from behind counters.

"Are you all that's left?"

"I don't think so," the usher said. "We don't know how many others are out there, but at least a couple more stores have holdouts. These freaks seem to wander from one to the other."

"Are you in contact with the others?"

"No," he said, handing the rifle off to the next in line to stand watch. Snarls came from outside the gate as the new watchman kicked aside the spent cartridges and loaded fresh ammo.

"Where did you get the gun?"

"The Crazy One." The Mexican accent conveyed a sense of wonder, not disparagement. "We don't know who this guy is or where he sleeps, but many times he comes to drop off supplies. We share some of our food with him, but I don't think he eats it all. I think he gives most of it to others out there."

"'Many times'?" Bella inquired.

"He was here this morning," the usher explained. "Didn't come around yesterday. Twice the day before ..."

"Supermodel," Bella asked her leader, "how long has

392

this singularity been in place?"

"An hour? Maybe two," was the reply. "Time is obviously passing more quickly on this side of the divide, which explains why this place smells so bad. And it's 'Georgiana'."

"Georgiana," the usher responded worshipfully, and caught her full eye contact.

"Kid, this isn't hypothetical: It's entirely possible that, in a short span of time, you might be the last man alive and I might be the last woman. Even under those circumstances, you don't have a chance with me," Georgiana explained with firmness but no ill will. "Given that, would you still answer a question of mine?"

"Anything," he said, his voice dripping with literal meaning.

"Where did this Crazy One get the gun?"

"I don't know for a fact," he said without hesitation, "but there's only one store in the mall that sells them."

BOOM!

As it turned out, Orville and Marisol were alone in the Blur Cave.

Having stumbled across the eviscerated body of Seth Hill, they realized there was nothing of interest to zombies left on the premises. Except them, of course.

As Marisol sat down in the comfy chair, Orville went over to the fridge to get a couple drinks. The ratio was roughly three overturned bottles of beer to every overturned can of soda. He popped open a can of Sprite and got sprayed by the fizz.

"Time moves faster on this side of the singularity," Orville stated as he offered the next can to his sister.

"Huh?" It wasn't just a request for clarification. It was an admission she didn't have a clue what he was talking about.

"The soda's warm, so the fridge must've stopped working days ago. But just last night Bobby invited the rest of the team to meet here and didn't mention this."

"That's slim," Marisol pointed out. "But I guess we'll find out. Hey, is there any Coke or Mountain Dew?"

"Bobby never touched caffeine," Orville said as he sat down on a bridge chair, actually slouching a little.

"Yeah, I suppose not, but I could really use some."

"Tired?"

"Not so much, Orv, but I have a splitting headache."

"Sorry."

"I'll live," Marisol said. She was wrong and knew it. "I'm more concerned about you, *hermanito.*"

"Never better," Orville replied.

"Don't give me that. I saw what happened out on the concourse just now. Your snots had more firepower when you were fifteen. You were the last one Equity touched, right?"

"Yeah, so?"

"So you're only at half strength."

"So's the static," Orville shot back with yet another subtext with which his sister was unfamiliar: defensiveness.

"Static?"

"The obsessions. The compulsions. The barriers between me and everybody else," Orville said, looking at her straight in the eye, another surprise. "All that misfiring in my brain. It's settled down. And it's not like I'm on meds. I don't feel like ..."

There was a scratching, a pawing at the double doors, followed by a long, low moan.

"... like them."

Marisol listened as she fought against the chills and muscle stiffness that went along with her headache. She was beginning to feel very much like them.

Bella, now dressed in a Cracker Barrel uniform both too wide and too short for her, accompanied Georgiana as they rolled under the gate back out onto the concourse. They had waited until the zombies had forgotten their prey and thinned out. Armed with cleavers used to slice industrial-sized lunchmeat loaves into deli sandwiches, they proceeded toward the far end of the mall and the sporting goods superstore, Dick's.

First they dashed across the narrow walkway so Georgiana could leap into the atrium and take flight. But, once airborne, Georgiana found Bella too much of a burden to bear and looked for an emergency landing zone. Fortunately, she quickly spotted an art framing shop next door to a piano and organ store. The dead ignored those places as surely as when they were alive.

Landing with a thud, they aroused interest and the undead slowly pivoted around toward them.

"You okay?" Bella asked as she regained her feet.

"Not so much," Georgiana replied as she stood up slowly.

"You're not turning into one of *those*, are you?"

"I don't think so, but I may be running into the limits of my powers," Georgiana said. "I've been in super-powered form a lot over the past three days – or however long it's been. The most I'd ever done was a couple hours, and months apart, and ..."

And then suddenly, in a shimmer, she was Mindy Maguire again. Surrounded by scores of flesh-eating corpses. Backed up by the only woman on earth who was possibly more demure than she.

And yet first blood belonged to Bella. One blow with her cleaver, and the nearest zombie's elbow and its outstretched arm dropped to the ground. The next whack took off its jaw. It wasn't exactly harmless, but it was suddenly the least of their worries.

"Don't go for their heads first!" Bella shouted. "Limbs and jaws! Take the fight out of them, *then* kill them!"

The advice served Mindy well as she stood back-to-back with Bella. Within a minute, eight zombies were flailing around their feet in pathetic impotence.

A minute later, and it was twenty.

A minute after that, the two blood-splattered women were exhausted to the point they could barely raise their cleavers above their shoulders.

A minute after that, though, they were rescued.

The Crazy One, the usher called him.

Crazy or not, he was a good pistol shot. The report from his handgun was their first introduction to him. Their second was the way broad exit wounds exploded like monstrous, pus-filled pimples on the faces of their attackers. When finally he came into view, "Crazy One" seemed an apt description. They couldn't see his face because he wore a football helmet with an anti-glare visor. He was tallish, but it was impossible to get a read on his build; brown, insulated coveralls were stuffed with some kind of extra-thick layer of insulation – something green poked out between cuffs and gloves.

"Follow me!" he shouted as he drew a machete out of his web belt and took the legs out from under an attacker.

Mindy recognized the voice. Kevin's.

They followed as he blazed the trail to Dick's Sporting Goods.

BAM!

"They've moved on," Orville said. "We've rested up enough. Time to see if we can meet up with the others."

"No," Marisol said with a wheeze.

There was a tug of war going on in her brother's mind. Mucus-Man, heroic but socially dysfunctional, would have coolly assessed whether or not Colonel America could be saved and, concluding that she couldn't, would leave her to rejoin the group. It would be regrettable to lose such an able ally, but more regrettable for the team to lose them both.

But he wasn't Mucus-Man at that moment. He was Orville. And his sister Marisol was dying. He realized he felt the way he was expected to feel when Marisol's mother – the only mother he could remember – was meeting her end.

"I'm not leaving you."

"You have to. We both know that."

"Like you said, my power is halved. I won't make it ten yards without you, Marisol."

She thought about that.

"You're right, Orv. Help me up."

He did.

"You know what would go down really fine right now?" she asked rhetorically. "A nice, warm beer."

Orville obliged.

The two of them worked together to dismantle, as quietly as possible, the ramparts they constructed to bar the double doors.

Orville reached tentatively for the push-bar but was interrupted by Marisol's fervent embrace.

"I wish you happiness, *hermanito*," she said, kissed him on both cheeks, turned around and kicked open the doors herself.

She ran out, picked up the first zombie she saw before it was even aware of her presence, and broke its spine over her knee. Summoning strength from somewhere, she darted toward the food court, screaming at the top of her lungs something about "free samples!"

The horde followed her.

From across the emptied concourse, Orville spotted Kevin, Mindy and Bella, and quickly fell in step with them.

It felt right. Perfect. As Marisol walked the wide concourses of the Chesterfield Mall, it didn't occur to her how odd it was that her body armor didn't chafe or cause sweat to collect, nor how odd it was that her Colonel America uniform was completely untorn. For that matter, memory didn't suggest that she herself should be untorn. Seeing her reflection in a shop window, the lack of birdshot marks on her face or horde-shredded flesh to her limbs and torso didn't strike her as remarkable at all.

She just wandered the mall window-shopping as a Jennifer Lopez tune – tightly equalized to filter out any jarring highs and lows – wafted overhead.

"*¡Señorita Rivera!*" an unequalized soprano called out. "*¡Marisol!*"

She looked around, wondering whom she might know.

"Colonel America!" screamed the soprano. This shocked Marisol not exactly back into reality, but at least into surreality.

Marisol spun around, moving swiftly but with practiced, unconscious grace, to see a woman in classic haute couture, her bleached hair in a tight bun.

"Do I know you?"

"Only from a movie, I suppose."

Eva Peron introduced herself and explained her mentoring relationship with Mindy Maguire.

"Who?"

"Georgiana."

Marisol's face didn't alter its puzzled, cocked-headed expression.

"Supermodel."

Marisol shrugged, palms up.

Eva looked around at blissful, oblivious faces.

"You don't remember how you got here, do you?" Eva asked.

Marisol replied with a stream of consciousness: "Tranfusion ... new costume ... Doc Rudy ... mission ...?"

"Yes, a mission. Consider yourself still on that mission. You were supposed to find a chaotic entity loose in the Midwest."

"Right," Marisol said.

Eva saw her slump, as if the buoyancy of heaven had left her patriotically clad body, replaced by the lead weight of responsibility.

"You followed her to this mall and died in the pursuit," Eva lied without the slightest tell. "What you see around you are spirits of people who passed away here ..."

"There are an awful lot!"

"I'll get to that later. Meantime, we have no contact with the living. But I think there's an exception. I noticed that, if I concentrate hard enough, I can track Mindy. I can even catch a glimpse of someone she's with if they're speaking or touching."

"Have you tried communicating with this Mindy of yours?"

"I was just about to when I happened upon you," Eva said. "They ran into that sporting goods store at the end of the concourse."

POW!

More like "dove into."

Two strides before running full-tilt into the iron gate at the Dick's entrance, Kevin shouted, "Four alive!" then dropped and rolled; simultaneously, the solid-steel gate rose about a foot off the ground, just enough to shimmy under. Mindy and Bella did likewise, as did Orville coming up the rear a few paces behind. A gray claw in a Pottery Barn-issue sleeve grabbed hold of his ankle but was immediately shot off by a high-caliber round. Before he wiggled under the gate, Orville saw smoke rising from a rifle barrel resting in a slit carved near the top of the gate.

He stood up and heard the clang of the gate slamming. Then Orville saw a sixty-ish man with faded tattoos and no legs below the knees strapped with bungee cords to the top of the ladder. The man clicked the safety on, brushed a spent shell off his perch, and pointed to the floor at Orville's feet.

Orville hadn't noticed that the claw still gripped his ankle.

No one had ever heard Orville scream like that before. The shriek startled the sentry on the ladder and the couple that was working the gates. If Orville weren't as out of breath from running as the rest of them, they'd have heard worse.

"Don't get so worked up," Kevin said between deep inhalations as he emerged from his coveralls and helmet, unwrapping the layer of artificial turf he kept underneath. "That should be the worst thing ... that happens to you today."

"Mucus-Man doesn't like to be touched," Mindy explained, doubled over from exertion.

Orville collected himself enough to ask her how she knew that.

"When you were with The Crusaders," she explained, squatting in a restful crouch, lungs burning for oxygen, "I collected ... every picture I could find of you. It was always Colonel America or Pantagruel shaking hands with whatever ... police chief or politician ... congratulating the team after a battle. I noticed that, of the hundred photos I had of you, I never saw you touch anyone."

"Working on it," Orville said, staring into Mindy's gaze as deeply as he could before he felt some barrier between them.

"I don't think any of us want to be touched by something like that," Bella said, wiping sweat away from her tear ducts.

BAM!

And the late Colonel America heard her.

Saw her, too, although Marisol found it disconcerting how people who looked just as real to her kept walking through this woman whom Eva identified as Bella Brock.

Marisol also wondered about the stop-drop-and-roll she did before entering the Dick's. In the ethereal version of the Chesterfield Mall, she and Eva simply strode in past the snowmobile display.

"That skinny chick in the Cracker Barrel uniform?" Marisol inquired. "She killed me?"

"No, it took more than that, but she did fight you to a standstill in her altered form as the Badger," Eva explained. "Can you see the woman with short hair and sensible shoes next to her?"

Marisol squinted. "Yeah."

"That's Mindy. Anyone else?"

Marisol brightened.

"That's my brother! Hey, Orville!"

"He can't hear you," Eva counseled. "I see one other fellow whom you should also be able to spot. Concentrate."

"I see him. Amazing."

"What's amazing?"

"I used to have a shirt just like that."

BOOM!

As they caught their breath they regarded each other.

401

Kevin, who had been covered head-to-toe with coveralls and helmet, was immaculate except for sweat stains on Marisol's old top. The white shirt of Orville's TSA-approved Mucus-Man costume was streaked in red, like a waiter who had spilled merlot on himself, but was otherwise unmarked by the battle. Bella had done a fair job of keeping the ghouls at a distance but, even so, red dominated the muted brown-and-gold color scheme of the Cracker Barrel uniform.

But Mindy was caked in it. She was splattered in every hue of the human vascular system, from the rust-orange tincture of a mild abrasion to the tar black of deep arterial blood, it stuck to her like acrylic paint to a canvas, saying everything about her encounter with the horde without offering a single, literal detail. Her polyester pants, though, no longer salmon, ran in scarlet streaks.

"I could use a change," Mindy understated. "Is there a working bathroom in here?"

"Water pressure isn't what it should be, but yeah," Kevin replied.

"I'll go with," Bella volunteered and the two women went off in search of the facilities.

As they did, Kevin headed off an awkward moment of silence by offering, "Sorry about your sister, Orville. Roger told me how close you two were."

"Thanks," Orville said, "but we have more urgent problems."

Kevin wasn't sure if that was Orville's emotional cross wiring talking or if it was simply heroic grace under fire, but either way he was glad to take it.

"We definitely do," Kevin agreed. "Believe it or not, the walking corpses are almost the least of our worries."

"I believe it. We have a finite amount of oxygen in here and they don't breathe."

"It's crossed my mind that the only reason I've been

able to survive as long as I have in here is that almost everybody else is dead."

"Which raises the question," Orville pondered, "How many are still alive?"

"Twenty in this store," Kevin began.

But the sentry atop the ladder corrected him. "Nineteen."

"Okay," Kevin continued. "There were twenty when I left to get you guys. Now there's nineteen plus you and ..."

"No," the sentry corrected. "Nineteen *including* the four you brought back."

"Understood, Phil," Kevin said, and saw confirmation of the grim news on the faces of other survivors nearby.

Kevin walked Orville away from prying ears.

"So you see how fast we're dropping. Anyone dies for any reason, he's not likely to go alone," Kevin explained. "Even so, between the hypoxia and the stress, we'll soon be too weak to mount a defense. I figure we've got another day and a half, maybe two, of fight left in us.

"Anyone else left in the mall?"

"There's a handful of people in the Cracker Barrel. Judging by The Badger's wardrobe, they've already met."

"And that's it?"

"Keep your voice down," Kevin said with excessive calm.

"I wasn't aware I was shouting."

"You weren't, but there's a reason I didn't want to be overheard," Kevin continued, his voice remaining light-hearted and conversational despite the dire news. "As far as the mundanes know, there are pockets of survivors in a dozen other shops around the mall. We still outnumber the horde and I'm just the Dick's representative to a council that's ironing out a plan to save us all."

"But that's all bullshit and there's only a couple dozen

403

of us left against maybe a thousand ghouls," Orville said, with a grin of forced bonhomie on his face.

Kevin guessed that he was the first one ever to hear Orville Ortley use an obscenity and felt oddly honored.

"One more thing, Count Karma," Orville stated. "My power was halved when Equity touched me. It should've returned when she died, but I guess what happened to her wasn't precisely dying. Even so, it's going to take me longer to re-energize from my most recent blast. And you yourself never ..."

"Are you getting at something?"

"Mundanes," Orville said. "We're all mundanes now."

{ POW! }

Sheldon Shapiro would be laid to rest according to the traditions of his people, unpreserved, wrapped in a plain shroud inside a nondescript pine coffin, before the sun set twice on the body.

Lugh had tried to make arrangements for Shel's remains to be placed on a wooden raft set to drift down the Mississippi, drenched in pitch, until an archer shot a flaming arrow to set it ablaze.

"If it were up to me ..." Lisa Lorenzo Shapiro muttered, trailed off, and ended with, "... but his parents still live around here."

So, having carried his friend's body to the funeral home of Shel's parents' choosing, Lugh had fulfilled his duty to the dead. Now came his duty to his mates, and to his lady.

With one last nod to Lisa and the two children who were now hers alone, Lugh stepped outside and planted his feet on the cobblestone sidewalk. His massive legs coiled against the masonry which would bear his bootprint as he propelled himself skyward. Leveling off, he bolted in the direction of the Chesterfield Mall.

Lugh did half-expect to see the Steed parked in the lot. He greeted Time Tempest and Flame Star brusquely. They had something they felt was very important to tell him, but the battle blood pounded in his ears, beating a march time that drowned out anything they had to say. Heedlessly, Lugh strode forward into the blackness. He'd see for himself which active-duty Crusaders had joined the battle.

BAM!

"I'm surprised, Kevin," Mindy confessed as they sat with Orville and Bella around the precious, low fire he'd made in the unlit dimness of the store's camping department. Cedar logs intended for children's swing sets boiled a pot of unfiltered coffee. Rested and in fresh clothes, she had no need for warmth or caffeine, but the cedar and Arabica provided welcome relief from the stench of rot hanging in the stagnant air. "I didn't know Dick's sold guns and ammo."

"Honestly, I didn't either," Kevin confessed. "I came here at first looking for tent pegs."

"Tent pegs?" Orville inquired.

"Just the thing for impaling an attacker through the skull," Kevin explained as he blew out the fire to save oxygen. "To quote the Old Testament Book of Judges, 'Then Jael Heber's wife took a nail of the tent, and took an hammer in her hand, and went softly unto him, and smote the nail into his temples, and fastened it into the ground: for he was fast asleep and weary. So he died.'"

"Neither of your friends mentioned you were so devout," said Bella.

"I'm not."

"Then how is it you're able to quote such an obscure verse of the Bible?" Bella asked.

"I'm a Master of Arts," Kevin replied, then turned his

405

attention to Mindy. "What surprises me though is that you're here as *you*, not as Georgiana."

"It surprised me as well. I thought I had a couple more days."

"Days until what?" Kevin asked.

"Part of the blessing-slash-curse of my power," Mindy replied. "The glamour is withheld from me for three days at the end of every month."

"So what's that got to do with it?" Kevin asked. "It was October fifteenth, if memory serves, when we came in here. I'd be surprised if more than a few hours have gone by out there. We're well aware that time moves more quickly on this side of the singularity but it's still been less than a week. So at the most, it's the twenty-second, there's still another ... nine days ... before ..."

At first, he was aware that Mindy was looking at him with an expression suggesting that he was not only stupid, but so profoundly stupid as to merit pity rather than rage. Bella soon joined in with that universal female expression of condescension: eyes wide, mouth closed, chin tilted just a few degrees to the side. When Orville, whom he regarded as the king of cluelessness, joined in the staring contest, Kevin realized what he was saying.

"Oh, right," he muttered but, instead of shutting up, went on to say, "That would explain why you've been so—"

"—much time getting here. Taking," Bella filled in quickly then changed the subject. "I assume you have some kind of plan."

"Yes. First, we get the air re-oxygenated. I've been working on that for days and the pieces are all in place. Bella, I'll need a lookout so you're coming with me," he gave the Badger's human persona a glance, which she rewarded with a grim nod. "Meanwhile, Mindy and Orville, you're going to relieve the siege at the Cracker

406

Barrel. Arm everybody in here, because we're breaking out. You'll lead the charge against the horde. Wipe out every single zombie as you sweep through the mall."

"The charge?" Mindy protested. "We're here to protect these people, not lead them headlong into danger. If there's a battle to be—"

"They're already in danger," Kevin corrected. "You'll be leading them headlong out of it. None of them know about Orville's diminished condition, but they recognize Mucus-Man and that'll be reassuring to them. And I saw in Plainville how people follow your lead."

Mindy's brow seemed weighted down by skepticism.

"I don't know how I'm going to get – including Orville and me – seventeen people more than a quarter mile from one end of the mall to the other."

"You won't," Orville said. "Not all seventeen."

Silence hung in the air like the smell of rotted flesh.

"Any questions?" Kevin asked after a tense moment.

"Yes," Mindy said, rising, then pacing. "What's the point? If we do nothing, we die of asphyxiation in a couple days. If we take up arms, we become ghoul food or worse in a matter of minutes. And even if this battle affords you the distraction you need to get the air breathable again – and don't think I didn't figure that part out in a second – there's no soil or sunlight in here. We'll run out of food after maybe a month, out of fluids maybe even before that. Please tell me you've got a plan to take away that singularity."

"The plan is for a miracle to occur," Kevin said without any trace of apology in his voice, "and for as many of us as possible to stay alive until it does."

"That's some plan, Kevin. Absolutely, positively brilliant," Mindy said, pacing turning to stomping. "The president just called. He's wondering if you've got time to work on the budget deficit. The single most important part of the plan and you're leaving it up to some act of intervention from beyond this plane of existence!"

Kevin said something, but Mindy didn't hear it, captivated instead by a familiar voice that hovered over her shoulder like a cartoon angel or devil.

"I think we have that covered, dearie."

Bella puzzled over whom Mindy was addressing when she said, "I was wondering where you wandered off to."

As Kevin brought Bella up to speed, Eva spoke unheard by anyone but Mindy, "I'm on the mall's spirit plane. At first I couldn't see any of you – only the ghosts of those who passed on since the singularity formed. They're stuck in here as much as you are."

"Why didn't you contact me until now?"

"Sorry, but I wasn't able to."

Eva went on to explain to Mindy how it took concentration, but she was finally able to peer through the veil to find her, find her friends and now, finally, to speak. She also spoke about how Marisol found the ability to focus on her mission and had Bella in her sights.

"The others here are experiencing a cyclical moment, oblivious to anything going on in the mortal world. The only reason I have any sense of time moving forward, I suppose, is that I came in here as a ghost," Eva summed up, then softened her tone ever so slightly. "And not to get too gushy, but I missed you, dearie."

Mindy sniffled back a tear.

"Oh, Evita, I missed you, too!" Knowing it was impossible and not caring how awkward it would look to her mortal teammates, she moved to embrace the spirit. "I was so terribly concerned that ..."

Eva flitted away. "I said I didn't want to get too gushy."

"Not to interrupt," Kevin interrupted, "Well, yeah, to interrupt ... Is there any practical point to this tender moment? I mean, does the Dragon Lady have any thoughts about preventing the spread of the Apocalypse? I can tear down this singularity any time, but that's not happening until I know the problem is contained."

"I heard that," Eva told Mindy. "And yes. I have a thought. Leave it to me."

BOOM!

Fluorescent lights flickered as Mindy provisioned her army. By the time she was done about an hour later, the lights were out for good and the surviving souls in the Dick's store were left to rely on LED lamps fastened around their heads with nylon straps.

By the flashing, darting beams, sixteen civilians donned the uniform that Mindy had picked out for them. It was mainly winter gear. The thick, down-stuffed ski jackets weren't too uncomfortable because the mall was actually a little chilly without sunlight streaming in from the entranceways and atrium, and with so few bodies still giving off heat. Ski helmets and goggles completed the body armor. From their waists down, the group wore all manner of comfortable trousers and athletic shoes; moving fast would be the best protection, Mindy reckoned, and more weight and padding below the waist - where they were least likely to sustain injury - would just slow them down.

Mindy wondered at first what to do about their hands. They needed protection, but not in a way that would interfere with dexterity.

But then, looking around the combat sports department, she had an epiphany. It hadn't occurred to her that what are generally known as boxing gloves are actually boxing mittens. The gloves used by mixed martial artists, though, have articulated fingers and contoured knuckles underneath all that padding. And they'd all need their fingers unencumbered.

Mindy had appropriated a cache of .22-caliber, bolt-action Remington 788s from behind the hunting counter, and distributed them to the half of the group who knew how to shoot them. Automatic rifles would've been nice, but Dick's catered to sport-shooters going out to hunt deer or geese, not platoon-strength militias in a desperate fight for survival.

Those that didn't have firearms experience got trekking poles. She grabbed a fueled-up, gas-powered ice-fishing auger for herself. Everyone got a parang – the kind of knife you should bring if the other guy has a machete.

Everyone, including Orville, had recharged after a few hours' rest and a bite to eat. He sat waiting at the gate while Mindy moved her troop into position. Under her direction, they formed a four-by-four phalanx – two rifles in the center of each rank, flanked by those carrying trekking poles like spears.

She walked around the column, auger resting on her shoulder, inspecting her troops, ensuring safeties were off the rifles and that the jabbing weapons were honed to surgical sharpness. Words of encouragement tumbled from her lips along with words of confidence, and hardly a word of truth.

Finally Mindy came down to Orville, whom she'd tasked as the rear guard. She gave him a tentative half-smile which he returned with a full-faced grin. He had a nice smile, she thought.

"When all this is over," Orville began, absentmindedly twirling his parang, "maybe we could go out. Would you like to go to an art museum? Or if you don't like art museums ..."

"I love art museums," she lied.

"Oh, um, great. You know, Mindy," he stammered his way through his first invitation to a date. "I remember when you first showed up here at the mall. Two years ago.

410

I'd wanted to ask you out ever since then. And now I don't even understand what took me so long. I guess I've been through some changes today."

Don't get me started on that, she declined to say and instead nodded encouragement for Orville to keep talking.

"So it's a date," Orville continued. "I can't tell you what a relief it is to know you might be feeling the same way about me."

"Yes, Orville, I feel exactly the same way about you," she lied again.

She marveled at how it didn't bother her to be dishonest. The odds of both of them surviving a running battle against a thousand ghouls made it unlikely her assertion would ever be put to the test.

But it was put to the test, immediately, as Orville leaned in for a kiss.

Orville's eyes closed in blissful anticipation as his head tilted and lips puckered. A good six inches taller than Mindy, Orville bowed at the waist until their mouths were at the same level.

And Mindy shuddered with revulsion. As much as she truly did admire this heroic individual and would have welcomed a friendly embrace and a chaste buss on the cheek, that was not the choice hovering a finger's breadth away. This was a man in the full throes of ardor, looking to initiate a physical relationship that would go far beyond a kiss.

Her imagination projected a most unflattering picture of him naked. As trim and wiry as Orville was, Mindy's dark fantasy painted him with rolls of fat drooping below thick clumps of body hair swimming in sweat. She imagined what that sweat would smell like and she was suddenly aware of the odor of rot that permeated every cubic inch of the mall. That was enough to make her nauseous, but then her mind took her another place she didn't want to go: Orville's bed. Well aware that people with OCD are notorious neat freaks, Mindy imagined Orville taking her on an old, torn, bare mattress stained with God-knows-what lying on a flea-infested carpet in a room lit by a bare light bulb, and nothing covering the cracked window but graffiti and an eviction notice. She convulsed in disgust at the thought of his member penetrating her, his face a wild and vicious mask of self-absorbed power madness. She imagined the agony of the violence he would cause her, painful tearing as her body refused to ease his entry and his lust refused to care.

Above them, Eva would shake her head, sad-faced but unable to intercede, adding humiliation to pain and repulsion. Then, worst of all, she imagined Orville pulling out and bringing his cock, her blood dripping from its warts and rashes, to her face. She pictured that disgusting length of engorged flesh hovering for a brief moment right in front of her lips.

The lips that the real-life Orville was offering to kiss tenderly. She steeled herself.

Fortunately for Mindy, Kevin picked that exact moment to interrupt. "Mindy's Marauders are looking sharp!" he shouted, even though he was within whispering distance.

"They're the best we got," Mindy said with a touch of sarcasm then added with more conviction, "We'll get through."

"I don't doubt it for a second," Kevin replied, and Mindy found herself on the receiving side of what she knew to be an encouraging lie.

"How are things looking at your end?" Mindy asked, speaking into her walkie-talkie as a test. The question fed back in heavy static on Kevin's unit.

"All the groundwork is done," Kevin said into his walkie-talkie while maintaining eye contact with Mindy, standing right in front of him. He tucked the two-way into his utility belt and addressed Mindy directly. "It's a matter of picking up and delivering one last load of diesel, pouring it in and flicking the switch. With Bella as a lookout and you guys keeping the main force of the horde busy, this should go off without a hitch."

Bella, leaning against the customer service counter, zipped up her overalls and adjusted the artificial turf that stuffed it.

"Look," Kevin said, "I don't have any St. Crispin's Day speech sketched out or—"

"That's okay," Mindy replied. "I did."

And Kevin could see it in the faces of the platoon about to charge once more into the breach.

"They're ready to go," Mindy told Kevin.

"Be safe," Kevin managed after a pause.

"She will," said Orville, injecting himself into the conversation. "I promise – I'll keep her safe."

Twelve years ago, twelve hours ago, Mindy would have melted into Orville's arms at that.

Mindy steeled herself to say, "You be safe too, Kevin. And keep Bella safe as well. And most of all ..."

"Yes?" Kevin prompted.

"Get the job done," Mindy spat out. "Nothing my team does means anything if you fail."

"Mindy," Kevin said after a slow exhale, "I'm going to say to you right now the three hardest words to say."

"Please, Kevin, this isn't—"

"Believe. In. Me."

POW!

Meanwhile, on a surreal level of existence, a smiling Seth Hill stood behind the counter of a miraculously restored Plaquet Box, showing his wares to two giddy, twentyish young women. The slender, ebony-skinned one in the black sheath stared longingly at a Clefable Pokemon, while the caramel-toned one in the tie-dyed, hand-woven summer dress stood mesmerized by a Spellfire booster pack's metallic wrapping. It didn't occur to either of them to ask the storekeeper to pick them up and hand them to them for closer inspection.

"So is there anything else I can show you, ladies?" Seth beamed.

"No, we're just window shopping," the thin black woman replied, then turned to her companion. "What do you want to go look at next, Equality?"

"I don't know. We've never been to this mall before," Equality replied, absent of any hint that she had no idea how they'd arrived or how long they'd been there. "But I'm always game to look at jewelry stores."

"Well, we don't have anything especially high-end here," Seth said, pointing toward the far end of the concourse, "but there's a Kay five stores down."

"How does that sound, Brigitte?" Equality asked.

"Sure. Why not? Like they say, 'Every kiss begins with Kay.'"

"I know," Equality replied. "My ex-boyfriend got all my jewelry from BJs."

"Girls," a supercilious voice cooed from behind, "There are only a dozen stores in the entire world worth getting gems from. And none of them are within a thousand miles of here."

Brigitte and Equality turned around to see a woman in a bright, tropical print dress with padded shoulders, the kind that suggested a night out on the town in 1940s Buenos Aires.

"Incidentally," the supercilious voice continued, "do you know where 'here' is?"

The two friends looked at each other, hoping the other knew.

"It seems we have some catching up to do. You may

call me Mrs. Peron. Perhaps you're acquainted with my colleague here."

Standing right behind Eva Peron was Marisol Rivera in her star-spangled uniform. Seth Hill had always considered himself a good reader of people, but he couldn't parse the expression behind Colonel America's cowl. Was that loathing in her eyes for the two browsing customers? It didn't seem to match the sly half-smile that suggested she had a use for them. He didn't dwell on it; he had other customers.

"Oh my God!" Equality exclaimed. In this idealized world, the body armor accentuated rather than diminished Marisol's supple figure. "Colonel America's a tranny!"

"No," Marisol corrected. "As the lady said, some catching up. Are either of you hungry?"

"No," Brigitte surprised herself by saying. She wasn't hungry. But she'd *always* been hungry.

BAM!

Kevin and Bella raised the gate and the phalanx raced out, Mindy exhorting them to keep their formation tight. They encountered the horde immediately. As trekking poles kept the zombies at length, rifle scopes zeroed in on head shots. Kevin estimated the group was shooting better than he expected. Imperfectly, he counted the number of shots fired and the number of attackers dropped. From his perspective, he reckoned that every three shots yielded two kills – roughly twice what he'd dared hope for. At this rate, he pondered, some of the platoon might actually survive.

Rifle fire and the clink of spent cartridges were constant, meaning that the shooting was disciplined. The Remingtons had the capacity of firing three rounds before they had to be reloaded; at any one time, two weapons on the right were being discharged, two on the left were being discharged, and the other four were being reloaded.

Kevin considered all this a testament to Mindy's leadership. While her troops followed orders she had hastily crammed into them before they left the store's relative safety, she used the whirring, gas-powered auger in her hands to drill through the skulls of any ghouls unlucky enough to be three feet in front of her.

Orville, following close behind, judiciously conserved his Mucus-Man powers and relied on his parang to dispatch two zombies in rapid succession. But mostly, he stuck to his primary mission. It didn't take thirty seconds for the first spear-carrier to fall, then it didn't take another five for the rifleman she was defending to be dragged away by the horde. Orville's main job was to pick up that rifle, and the one dropped a few moments later, and then the next one. Assuming there were any survivors at the Cracker Barrel, the guns would soon have new owners.

Kevin watched as the phalanx made it to the stairs, a place where the living had an advantage over the clumsy dead. He knew there were fewer corpses walking around the second floor, so Mindy's crew - now down to about ten plus her and Orville - had a real shot of making it all the way.

With a grateful nod to the paraplegic sharpshooter on the ladder above the Dick's gate - the man who would now cover their escape by firing on the thinned herd of zombies in front - Kevin tapped Bella on the shoulder and the two of them ran at full sprint toward the Blur Cave.

BOOM!

The four spectral women sat around a table in the food court. None of them hungry, they delighted in the aroma of what Cinnabon might smell like in Heaven.

416

"So we're villains?" Brigitte asked.

"For the past decade, you two have had a hand in just about everything that went wrong in the world," Marisol explained. "When you died in the process of executing your final plot, your spirits reverted to a state when you were both still innocent, still capable of being forces for good."

"It's hard to believe that we're dead," Equality said, long, raven hair swishing as she shook her head.

"Oh, being dead isn't so bad," Eva assured her. "There are worse things – spending eternity in a shopping mall in St. Louis, for instance."

"How did we get stuck in here?" Brigitte asked.

"Just before you acquired the power to raise the dead to exterminate the living, the mall was somehow sealed with a singularity," Marisol explained. "Nothing can escape. Not the spell that reanimated the dead, not the survivors who continue to fight the ghouls, and not the spirits of those of us who've lost our fight."

Brigitte reeled as if she were struck by a punch when Marisol emphasized "you."

"I've always run to the dark side," Brigitte confessed. "But I'm not that person who did this. I can't imagine how I became such a monster, or how I could've dragged Equality into this."

"How do you know I didn't drag you?" Equality said, then turned to face Marisol and Eva. "But, yeah, we'll do whatever we can to help you now. I just have one question ... What's a singularity?"

Twenty minutes later, Marisol felt a little raw in her throat.

"OK," Equality said. "Got it. Thanks."

"And I have a question for you," Eva announced. "What's a tranny?"

"What is this place?" Bella asked, looking around the Blur Cave.

"A monument to wasting time," Kevin answered. "But the real question is, where does it lead?"

"OK. Consider yourself prompted."

Kevin rushed past the bumper pool table, past the comfy chair, past the overturned cable spool that served as a table, and used all his strength to pull the refrigerator away from the wall. In counterpoint to Kevin's grunts, Bella heard bottles and cans rattling around in the fridge. By the time she joined him in his struggle with the two-hundred-pound burden, he had moved it almost entirely off its original floor space. Behind it was a door with the most useless sign ever conceived for any door: no admittance.

"What's back there?" Bella asked breathily, the thinning oxygen proving insufficient to recharge her after her exertion.

"The thing that's going to make everything all right," Kevin said, and waved her through the door first with a gallant sweep of his hand.

They clattered down three landings of metal stairs, Bella's jaw open in astonishment. In the dim backup-battery lights, rows and rows of turbines and compressors stood idle, metal rising from floor to twelve-foot ceiling. It looked like the engine room of some alien spacecraft.

"That's the air conditioner," Kevin explained.

BAM!

Mindy banged on the Cracker Barrel's gate – the old shave-and-a-haircut cadence twice in a row, so those on the inside knew it was living people coming to the rescue.

The phalanx's eight survivors achieved their first objective: drawing the horde's attention away from Kevin and Bella. They achieved their second objective as well:

inflicting maximum carnage on the undead mob. With macabre fascination, Mindy counted forty-two zombies whom she'd personally skewered with her auger. That must've taken at least ten minutes. She couldn't keep count of the rifle shots fired – the noise behind her sounded like a sustained fireworks finale – but the math was easy enough. Eight rifles times three shots a minute times ten minutes – that's two hundred-forty shots. Round that down to two hundred to allow for attrition of the shooters. If half of them were clean head shots, that's one hundred fewer zombies. Plus however many succumbed to the trekking-pole spears or parangs. Who knows? But overall, there had to be at least a couple hundred down-for-the-count ghouls resulting from their blitz.

That was on top of how many Kevin and the civilians might have dispatched before they even got there, Mindy reckoned, and how many she, Bella, Colonel America and Orville slew on their way in. Nobody ever took a zombie census, of course, but Mindy's experience as a retail assistant manager trainee informed her that, at the high side, there were no more than a thousand people in the mall at the time it was sealed by the singularity.

Did Orville take any more out with a nasal blast? Mindy didn't think so. That sort of detonation she would certainly have heard, even if he were at half strength. So she turned around to ask.

"Hey!" she called out to the other survivors, a taut expression of dread falling over her face. "Does anyone know where Mucus-Man went?"

BOOM!

Orville was not, in fact, at half strength. He had fully recovered.

He had kept up with the phalanx as it snaked its way up the stairs but, just as it turned the corner into the hall that led to the Cracker Barrel, the riflewoman standing directly in front of him was grabbed by a gray, arthritic claw in a powder-blue French-cuff sleeve. A quick tug wrenched her off her feet and she tumbled into the thick of the massed attackers. As she lay dying, she mustered the courage to resist the self-preservation instinct and instead tossed her weapon to within Orville's reach. It skittered across the slicked tile floor and Orville chased after it. He no sooner picked it up than he had to discharge it. A zombie was only a step away, but so far off to his side that it was only a flicker in his peripheral vision, more a shadowy presence than a tangible target.

Orville wheeled around, stuck the barrel straight in the female's face and pulled the trigger. His optimism that there might still be a round in the chamber was rewarded as the back of its head exploded, a red, white and gray splatter on the black wall behind it.

And the static returned.

Orville felt his ability to ignore his compulsions, to communicate with others, to be comfortable in his own skin dissipate all in that instant. He fixated on the zombie he'd just slain. Above the neck, nothing was left but the jaw, but a neck bejeweled by a strand of opalescent pearls: twelve of them, each perfectly symmetrical and all exactly the same size. A black, impeccably tailored business suit ended in a skirt hemmed at its knees.

It was once known as Equity and it was now, by any definition, dead and, thus, no longer served as a vessel to contain half of Mucus-Man's powers. Orville was whole again. He wondered what emotion he should be feeling about that.

But not for long. The black wall with Equity's brains splattered on it began to move toward him.

On the spirit plane, Equality rose suddenly from her seat, shuddering, gasping, squealing, eyes bulging.

"Equality! Are you all right?" Brigitte asked, rising as well.

Her friend staggered backward, but Brigitte intuited that her reaction was one of rapture rather than distress. Even so, Equality managed to knock over a garbage can with her flailing, spilling plastic trays onto the floor.

"I'm fine," Equality finally managed. "I feel like a part of me was missing. I wasn't even aware of it. But now I feel ... whole."

"I suppose that means her corpse been re-killed," Marisol said to Eva.

Eva had come to the same conclusion and, everywhere she looked, was confirmation. The newly engaged couple she saw at Zale's was beaming over their new ring. People were carrying around shopping bags. A coin splashed in the fountain. Mothers were picking their babies up out of their strollers and handing them to the clerks at Piercing Pagoda.

"That's great news," Eva said, but her voice was less than convincing. "It means the tide of the battle is turning."

Eva then walked over to Brigitte.

"Of course, it could turn a whole lot faster," Eva said, staring straight into Brigitte's eyes, "if the one who created this plague were to just withdraw the force of will supporting it."

Brigitte said nothing, her face an impassive cipher.

"Most the work's already done," Kevin said as he picked a wrench up off a counter and began wandering down the rows of machinery. "I'd taken the AC off the main power grid to save energy - and to preserve oxygen. It made things awfully stuffy in here, but at least we weren't constantly burning diesel. Of course, the real reason was to give me a chance to make the modifications."

"Modifications?" Bella asked.

"We don't need air conditioning, we need air recycling," Kevin said with only a fraction of his attention, concentrating on tightening a bolt that had worked loose. "I removed the filters, gave them a good scrubbing, then packed them with a concentrated caustic soda solution and ..."

"Where did you get that?"

"Industrial cleaners. If there's one thing a mall's got plenty of, it's caustic soda," Kevin said, removing a panel to show her his handiwork. "You combine that with slaked lime to give you soda lime, which scrubs carbon dioxide from the air. It's pretty much the way they do it on spacecraft or submarines."

"And where did you get this - what did you call it - slaked lime?"

"Some of it came from hair relaxers in the drug store," Kevin said as he wheeled a squat but heavy-looking metal box in front of the first turbine. "The rest of it, you don't really want to know."

"And you did this all yourself?"

"No," Kevin said with as much regret as fits in one syllable.

Bella, who had been giving an occasional glance around to confirm that they were alone, was suddenly a beacon of vigilance.

"My task for the day, until you guys showed up, was to scrape together enough diesel to fill up the tank in this generator," Kevin said, giving the box a pat.

Stripping out of his coveralls, Kevin revealed four canteens hooked to a web belt. He unscrewed the tank's cap

422

and began pouring in the contents of the first canteen.

"This is the last gallon I was able to distill," he continued. "All we have to do is pour this in, flick the switch, the gears start cranking, and the air should start getting fresher pretty fast."

"How much time does this buy us?" Bella asked as Kevin added the second canteen's fuel.

"The generator'll only be able to run for about three hours, but that should be enough to recharge the air for at least another couple days."

"And then?"

"And then we have another couple days to figure out some other way of powering these re-breathers," Kevin said, working on the third canteen.

"You're leaving a lot up to luck," Bella said.

"Yeah but, considering the run of bad luck we've had, we're due for some good," Kevin replied.

The voice of dissent was provided by a low, guttural, unnatural moan two paces behind him.

{BOOM!}

It was the third and final objective that eluded Mindy and what was left of her group: rescuing the survivors in the Cracker Barrel.

The gates didn't open in response to her knocks, nor was there any kind of countersign tapping out. Instead, Mindy listened only to the kind of pregnant silence that inclined her ear toward the gate. She removed her helmet and leaned in to press her ear against the cold stainless steel that formed a solid retractable wall, straining to hear the slightest reply.

The sudden, rattling din of full-body slams against the other side of the gate almost deafened her. At first, it was only one body charging into the gate from the inside but within half a minute it was clear that at least three or four zombies lined up opposite them.

"Too late," she announced to her troops.

One heavy-set man with a trekking pole noted that there might still be survivors inside.

"Maybe, but I wouldn't bet on it," Mindy responded. "We're going in anyway. The gate's still secure, so that means that someone on the inside woke up dead and took everyone else out. There were only six to start with, so we outnumber them. We clear them out, then settle in here."

After a couple shots to the gears atop the gate, Mindy bent down to roll it up. Revving the auger she plunged into the store, skewering the movie usher from ear to ear as an opening move.

"Break ranks!" she shouted and the meticulously formed and impressively maintained phalanx scattered, each individual heading in a different direction as they ducked under the gate. Mindy scored another kill then turned around to reclose the gate before the greater horde outside could charge in. By the time she was done, everyone who had managed to hold out for so long in that store now lay dead twice over on the floor. Mindy fought down despair at how close they came to rescue. With a sniff, she noticed she could detect the smell of cheese and dried meat, exactly as she smelled when she had been there earlier in the day. The scattered organs and lengths of intestines on the ground gave off a putrid odor but didn't completely overwhelm the more whole-some aromas. Not yet, at least.

It might have been just a matter of minutes.

POW!

As the wall slid self-propelled across the blood-slicked floor toward Orville, he didn't back away.

It shuddered, shimmered and changed shape while he

held his ground.

As it stood, bipedal, a foot in front of him, he merely greeted it.

"Carbon Avenger."

In a split second, a black jagged appendage analogous to an arm jutted out from the Avenger toward Orville, grabbing the Remington out of the unblinking hero's hand, crumbling the weapon like a wheat cracker.

"Mucus-Man."

Another anthracite pseudopod erupted in Orville's direction as he stoically accepted his fate. He considered it miraculous he'd lasted this long, isolated and most the time at half strength.

But the column of black rock sailed past his ear and flattened a lone zombie that had shambled onto the scene.

"Your team missed a few," The Avenger grumbled. "But I don't know if The Crusaders could've done better, at least not since your mother was with us."

"Are you here to help us?" Orville asked.

"'Us'? No. You? Yes."

It took three whacks, but Orville's parang separated the head from the neck of what had been a Victoria's Secret sales clerk that was now trying to inflict a bite on the Avenger's humanoid-but-inhuman form.

"I've been watching you, young man, with great interest," The Avenger said with nodding recognition of Orville's prowess with the blade. "At least for the past dozen years, ever since you resurfaced, announcing yourself as 'Orville Ortley'."

"You say you want to help," Orville said. "You could kill every single remaining ghoul as easily as squashing bugs."

"And I would, but there's one problem – I created them."

The Avenger squashed another as it came within range.

"They were created by Maman Brigitte," Orville corrected.

"Yes, but I created Maman Brigitte," The Avenger said with a chuckle. "You know about me and Olivia?"

"No."

"I loved her, although she never felt the same way about me," the Avenger recounted. "When you came along, the object of all her affection, I was crazed with jealousy - even hired some flunkies to kill you when you were still a baby."

That answered a question which had plagued Orville his entire life. His face remained impassive.

"After your mother died, I became increasingly disenchanted with the notions of good and evil," the Avenger continued, slapping down another reanimate. "The final straw was the accident that left me like this. At that point I figured it was best if these two forces cancelled each other out and left this beautiful, carbon-rich world alone. Let the amino acids start the cycle all over and see if such concepts even evolve again. That's when I - secretly - began funding The Institute as generously as I had been funding The Crusaders. Excuse me."

A flock of four zombies had been closing in on Orville, and The Avenger reduced them all to tile stains in less than a second.

"Where was I? Right. Funding. I couldn't be a mainstay of The Crusaders and commissar of The Institute."

"'Commissar'?"

"That's what Ta Mok insisted on calling the shadowy figure I projected. He never knew it was me. But he followed my orders to the letter, bless his naiveté, never questioning my decisions to forego hiring more powerful villains. There were plenty available you know, but it was increasingly hard to find good heroes and it wouldn't do

426

to have them outclassed by the bad guys."

"As long as both forces maintained parity, the struggle between good and evil became a war of attrition," Orville observed.

"Exactly - until Maman Brigitte came along. She had awesome power but, more to the point, she was beyond evil. Her death trip perfectly matched my objectives. But she'd have applied that nihilism to nothing more than lobbying for the chemical industry if I hadn't manipulated events behind the scenes to augment her hippie room-mate with a power, inclined them both toward serving my purposes, and put them on the trail of the Malificium deck."

"So why are you here now?"

"To open up that singularity and let the plague loose," The Avenger said, then sighed, lamenting at wasting yet another zombie about to attack Orville. "I haven't been able to figure out a scientific means of breaking through, so it's probably some mystical energy at work. I'm guessing it's some kind of trap card. Am I right?"

"Why should I help you?"

"I'm not asking for your help," The Avenger clarified, extending an arm toward Orville, but resting it gently on his shoulder. "I'll find that card sooner or later. I just want to offer you the chance to experience the serenity of the end of human existence along with me."

"As a human," Orville began, shuddering with distaste of being touched and already missing the relief from Asperger's that Equity had briefly provided, "I doubt that I'll find it serene."

"Come back with me to the Pinnacle of Righteous-ness," The Avenger offered. "I have a whole lab set up there. I can make you like me."

Orville didn't hesitate to respond: "First, no. Second, why are you extending me such an offer?"

Shale shifted in what passed for The Avenger's face until a very human visage appeared, with soulful, gray eyes that stared straight into Mucus-Man's soulful, gray eyes.

"I'm your father, Orville."

There was silence. The erstwhile Dirk Henderson rocked back to give his son space to process this. Swatting away another random zombie, he braced himself for some groundswell of emotion that would erupt in a banshee cry.

"Oh," Orville said.

"That's it? 'Oh'?"

"It never occurred to me before, but it makes sense."

"So you'll join me?"

Mucus-Man answered with a sneeze: a full-strength, howitzer-power, plaster-shaking, shop window-shattering, zombies-flying-in-the-wind honk. The Carbon Avenger splintered into tens of thousands of fragments scattered across the second floor of the mall and raining down on the first floor. Shards flew with enough force that Orville could see at least a dozen zombies drop as pieces of The Avenger pierced through their skulls. At least as many had arms or legs taken off.

All was quiet for a moment, until the dispersed pieces of The Carbon Avenger began to quiver. Soon they were tumbling over each other to join together again.

Orville continued to stand his ground.

BAM!

"Well, I guess Orville's okay," Mindy said as soon as the echoes died down. It was a louder blast than she expected. She surmised he had regained his full strength.

Her crew had secured the Cracker Barrel with relative ease and now relaxed as best they could, given the hypervigilance they had all become acclimated to. But she knew herself to still be out of breath even though minutes had passed since their last major exertion. They were all still huffing as their lungs strained to take in oxygen from the rapidly thinning air. Mindy wondered how many others were enduring the splitting headache which hypoxia inflicted on her.

One clearly didn't. A sixtyish woman who turned out to have been the best rifle shot of the group had collapsed from exhaustion. Mindy took the gun out of her hands as she lay splayed across a store aisle then kneeled over her. The woman's eyes popped open, and Mindy fed her a .22-caliber kindness.

There was nothing else to be done with this brave woman, yet Mindy felt deeply depressed. She realized that her sudden sadness had little to do with ending that woman's unnatural second life. Mindy had no regrets about that at all. It took her a few moments, but she came to understand that she was coming down from a kind of high: responsibility. She had succumbed to the addiction of leadership and now, her duties discharged, she had no more orders to give.

It was all up to Kevin and Bella now. She took out her walkie-talkie.

BOOM!

Kevin and Bella were at the farthest distance in the mall; in the deepest, subterranean recess, surrounded on all sides by stainless steel and cast iron. But even if radio waves could penetrate, they would have been too busy to respond.

With a flying tackle, Bella had pinned the zombie until Kevin could swing his wrench around. It took a half dozen blows to the face to take the fight out of it, and even that didn't end its existence. Kevin jammed the wrench in its mouth so that it would have something beside his arm to chew on while he jumped up, grabbed the generator and, in an adrenaline rush, picked it up off its wheels and dropped it on the zombie's head. The clang could be heard echoing throughout the enormous utility room. As the echoes became more distant, the groans of the undead inched closer.

"What now?" Bella asked.

Kevin uprighted the generator and flicked the switch. He damned it to hell when it didn't work.

"What kind of weapons do we have?"

"None," Kevin said, working the switch futilely. "Mindy's got them all."

"You have a sidearm."

"What I don't have is a lot of bullets," Kevin said, his focus entirely on grabbing a screwdriver out of his utility belt and removing the generator's front plate. "Just two left."

She nodded that she understood the significance, not that Kevin noticed. He had one thing on his mind, and his own survival wasn't it. It was getting the generator working, something he had absolutely no idea how to do.

Bella picked up the wrench, the only thing within her grasp that could possibly be used as a weapon.

"What are you going to do with that?" Kevin asked, sparing a split-second glance. "Take out one? Maybe two?"

"Well, what else do you recommend?" she screamed.

"A little something I found behind the counter at the CVS," Kevin said as he reached into a pocket, grabbed a heart syringe and plunged it, through her clothes, into Bella's heart.

"Thallium-201," he explained as she began to quiver. "Used in stress tests. Packs about seventy-thousand electonvolts of gamma radiation."

"No!" Bella screamed uselessly, the change already

upon her. She could feel her consciousness peeling away as her snout elongated and her claws, fur and needle-like teeth formed.

In less time than it takes to tell, the Badger's transformation was complete. Kevin played dead for a moment as she tracked the nearest moving thing – a zombie of course. She lurched at it and tore it to shreds. Then another.

Kevin got back up and returned to work on the generator problem. He knew he'd be unmolested by the Badger, who would always gravitate toward the slowest-moving prey. And as long as she was around, he had nothing to fear from the zombies.

POW!

"I'm sorry," Brigitte said. "I just can't."

Eva's jaw dropped.

"Of course you can. A simple act of will," Eva instructed. "Just make up your mind that you foreswear the plague and the hell that's breaking loose on the physical side can all be over!"

"It's not coming," said the spirit that, even as a girl in pigtails, took delight in torturing and killing birds.

"Don't you get it?" Eva said. "As the resurrected ones die, the spirits here manifest and become substantial enough to move things. We stop being happy just living in the moment. We start experiencing time again, which means claustrophobia setting in. And our metaphysical selves will start craving metaphysical food and drink and, as long as that singularity is in place, that stuff is just as finite on this plane as it is on the other."

Brigitte was unmoved. Eva went to slap her face, but her hand passed straight through.

Time to improvise, Eva concluded. Tell her anything and hope nobody ever finds out if it's true.

"We'll all die here, a spiritual death," Eva continued, her voice losing the tone of rebuke and settling into a plea. "We'll run out of meta-food, meta-water, meta-air. We won't go on to any reward. We won't be peaceably at rest. We'll just cease to exist."

"But," Brigitte argued, "that's what I want."

"Maybe for yourself," Eva countered. "But you're also dooming your friend."

Equality stared doe-eyed and innocent back at Brigitte.

"Is it what *she* wants? I don't think so," Eva said. "It's not what I want. It's not what Colonel America wants."

Eva looked around for Marisol to back her up, but the late Protector of Patriots was elsewhere. Eva saw her cape whipping behind her as she tore down the concourse.

BLUR!

Marisol didn't know where she was going, or what she would do when she got there – only that she had been summoned.

Her mission.

She had no idea what was behind those double doors, no way of knowing that her brother's friends referred to the abandoned loading dock as the Blur Cave and no reason at all to tear down the metal stairs at the far end.

But when she got there, the spirit world was overwritten in her sight by the physical world, and the Badger came into focus.

Bella Brock's alter ego stood on all fours, snarling and snapping. It took a moment's concentration for Marisol to broaden her view of the physical world, but she soon saw that the Badger had two zombies pinned to the ground with her forepaws as she eviscerated a third with her teeth. After all its meat organs had been consumed and its spinal fluid had stopped pooling, the third zombie's jaw continued to snap even though it would never again get up. Its two companions were similarly disposed of in a matter of seconds.

Wasting no time, the Badger ravaged another small clutch of ghouls.

Another moment of concentration and Marisol saw, dimly at first, like a distant mountain in fog, Kevin pulling wires out of a generator with its front plate removed. She wasn't sure what he was doing, but it looked important.

"What do you know?" she asked herself. "He actually has a useful purp-"

A zombie stepped forward - from Marisol's perspective, as if out of ether - and stood three shuffling steps away from Kevin, who was too engrossed in his task to notice. Before the reanimated Jamba Juice team member could drag its feet any closer, Marisol instinctively leaped at - but unfortunately through - it.

Jamba Juice guy fell on Kevin, managing to get a mouth full of insulated coverall which it spat out immediately. It had Kevin pinned, its saliva or some other bodily fluid dripping on his ear.

"Bella!" she called out, realizing only after she spoke how futile it was for a ghost to address a living person, and how doubly futile it was if that person were every bit as stripped of her higher-brain functions as the zombies.

The Badger, still in her Cracker Barrel uniform, stopped, reared up and sniffed the air.

"Bella! Over here, girl!" Marisol called out, and the Badger wheeled around.

"That one! You like oranges, girl? I bet he tastes like oranges! Mmmm!"

By the time Marisol was done making the yummy sound, the Badger had leapt over the length of Kevin's body and had made short work of removing the flesh from under the Jamba Juice uniform.

433

The Badger then stared at Kevin with a glint.

"No!" Marisol scolded. "Bad! Bad Badger!"

The Badger whimpered.

Marisol was shocked to learn that she could communicate in this manner, but went with it gamely.

"Good human! No kill human!"

The Badger tilted her head like a puppy being given a command for the first time. Kevin's expression in response to the Badger's odd behavior wasn't much different.

"Make nice!"

The Badger's long, thin, strongly prehensile tongue lashed out and gave Kevin a slurp on the cheek. Kevin recoiled.

"Why did you do that? Don't lick me again! I've seen where that tongue's been!" he shouted at the Badger. Then he remembered how Bella Brock looked in human form. He knew he'd caught her on her worst day but, even so, he liked how she wore her long hair down, how she seemed to have a genuine, healthy, unpretentious attractiveness to her - a wholesome, farmer's daughter look once she cleaned herself up. "We can pick this up later."

Marisol pressed her luck.

"Kiley? Can you hear me?" she asked slowly, then shouted "Kiley!"

No response from Kevin, but the Badger shimmied twelve feet up a support column like a cat hiding in a tree.

"Good Badger! Mommy sorry. Come on down."

Kevin went back to work on the generator but had to stop momentarily to take his wrench to a zombie's temple.

"Who's a good girl? Bella's a good girl! C'mon down, pretty ... Badger."

As the feral woman-beast inched back down, Marisol asked, "Is li'l Bella hungry? Wants some chow? Yum-yums?"

The Badger panted expectantly as Kevin dug in on his task.

"Go get a corpsie! Sic 'em!"

The Badger pounced on the first one available, and kept the carnage up as Kevin puzzled over how to get the generator to kick in without a working switch.

BOOM!

"Care to try that again?" The Carbon Avenger asked the boy he fathered by Olivia Ortley. "I bet you can muster up another blast *almost* as strong right now. Then, after I've reassembled, maybe you'll manage one more degraded shot."

Orville didn't respond.

"But even if you could keep this up all day, I can keep it up all day, all night, all millennium, and until the very moment this world is consumed by its sun and we all become hydrogen together."

Mucus-Man inhaled sharply and braced himself for another discharge. He'd go down fighting.

An ancient Gaelic song of blood lust pierced the air. Areadbhar, The Indomitable Lugh's singing spear, found its mark in the Avenger's belly.

Orville hadn't known if his father had organs or could experience pain, but apparently the answer was yes to both, at least after a fashion.

"Ach, ye grimy pile o' slag, black as a Scythian cumbucket's heart!" bellowed a familiar voice. "Thou wouldst seem like Carrauntoohil's own load o' turd if thou hadst any steam to thee, and if thy smell were a jot more pleasant!"

"And hello to you, Lugh," the Carbon Avenger replied

as he pulled the spear out of his gut. Sweet crude flowed from the wound. He threw the spear down ...

... and, with a will of its own and a song vibrating through its shaft, it jumped back up and drilled through The Avenger's abdomen. The thing which was once Dirk Henderson doubled over in pain and pulled the spear out once more. The enchanted Areadbhar returned with a less lethal but equally painful arc through the Avenger's elbow, entering the convex side and exiting the concave.

"How long didst thou say thou couldst do battle?" Lugh asked, arms parked smugly on his hips. "An immortal prithee answer, shitbeetle."

Areadbhar sang of blood and slaughter as it punctured The Avenger's lungs, kidneys, intestines and testicles – everything but the heart. In its ancient Celtic idiom, it told a tale of an ancient villain for whom the gods designed the slowest, most painful death.

The spear was more merciful, though. Orville watched with stoic intensity as The Carbon Avenger's life ebbed in a tide of petroleum. The immortal weapon's enchantment carried out the task that no mortal agent could – slaying a being made of the most primordial of earthly elements.

"A thousand pardons, young Orville," Lugh said as he put his spear back in its quiver.

"I've seen worse."

"Nay, but I overheard that thou art seed of that knavish, fishwife-ugly, canker-prick'd ass hair," Lugh offered. "Pray ye take no offense."

"None taken," Orville said evenly. "But it was my fight."

"Enemy thine be enemy mine." Lugh went to drape an avuncular arm over Orville's shoulder but remembered in time how much the young man bristled at being touched.

"Not this time. This was my father. It's in the arc of every hero that he has to overcome all the issues he ever had with his father – abandonment, humiliation, lack of affectionate display and so on. In a situation like this, the hero must call upon every ounce of strength and character to best his father in single combat."

"Don the motley, ignoble Lugh!" the god said to himself. "Thou playest the fool."

"Except I was raised perfectly well by Esperanza and Roger Chadwick. Despite my developmental issues, I had as loving, secure, happy and stimulating a childhood as one could ask for," Orville explained. "It was bad form just now. That's all I'm saying."

"Ach, speak of bad form, thou hast not uttered a word of thanks."

Orville blew a small sneeze at him. Lugh stood against the gale, but the two zombies coming up behind him were thrown into a weight-bearing wall hard enough to shatter their skulls.

"Let's just call it even," Orville said.

POW!

The savagery of the Badger's attacks proved so much background noise to Kevin, and Marisol's coaxing completely beyond his ability to perceive. He thought it odd that the Badger would be so protective of him, but was content to wonder about that later. Providing there was a later.

How do you fix a switch?

It didn't come up. Elias O'Neill's mechanical crash course couldn't cover everything. He'd learned how to run the generator, how to run the acre of machinery supporting the air conditioning system, as well as the basics of plumbing, masonry and carpentry. But Elias had stopped short of going into any kind of detail of electrical systems. There was too much to learn and Elias judged that the risks of teaching such a danger-fraught skill set outweighed the likelihood of gaining any benefit from it.

So the zombies were getting slaughtered but, unless he could get the air recycled, they'd still outlast the heroes and the innocents. Kevin still had the trap card which would allow him to remove the singularity at any time, but he'd die of asphyxiation or worse before he'd make that play.

Still, one breath of fresh air would clear his head, he reasoned. If he were to just drop the card on the table and turn it face-down, the singularity would vanish. Pine-scented, oxygen-rich air would flood in. He'd be able to take a deep breath, and another and another, then approach the problem fresh, come up with the solution. Maybe a few reanimates would escape, but not a lot, and he could just flip the card back face-up and the singularity would reappear. Surely the world outside could deal with just a handful of zombies before they spread. Maybe just a couple? Who's to say that any would escape in the time it took to take a few breaths of fresh air?

Kevin chased those fantasies from his head.

Think.

Maybe there was a store here that sold the kind of switch that attached to this generator. He couldn't imagine which one. He didn't remember seeing any. The generator he was using was the mall management's backup power supply, but Kevin did remember that Sears sold something like it. That meant running over to Sears, down a concourse which hadn't been swept for zombies into a store that hadn't been swept for zombies, gasping for breath every inch, then wheeling the heavy-duty appliance back to the Blur Cave and down a thirty-foot staircase, then siphoning the fuel from the old generator to the new one.

Think.

Better to stick with the unit at hand. Even so, it

seemed hopeless. All he knew about generators was how to fill them up and how to turn them on. But how was he supposed to fix the part that actually did the turning on? The only experience he had with electrical systems was how to hotwire a car.

By bypassing the ignition.

The ignition *switch*.

The problem redefined, Kevin allowed himself an embarrassed chuckle before pushing on to the matter of selecting the right wires to bypass the interlock and send battery power to the diesel engine. The process involved trial and error – so many wires! – but in short order Kevin had found the spark. Soon seven thousand watts of electricity were flowing to the subset of air conditioning chillers he had packed with carbon dioxide scrubbers. There wasn't enough power or enough filtration to get the whole roomful of equipment working, but he was confident that this would be enough.

BAM!

Mindy felt like a light on a dimmer switch, her consciousness dialing down. At first it felt like a blessing. When Kevin didn't respond to her walkie-talkie hail, she despaired for the worst. Her auger was out of fuel and the rifle she had taken off her dead comrade had only two rounds left, with no more ammunition to be found. She assumed it was possible to blow one's own brains out with a long-barreled gun and, with her fading consciousness, she tried to imagine how to go about doing it.

But then a shockwave blast, and another, that could have only come from Orville, gave her some hope. And now, suddenly, she could hear and feel the vibration of machinery. Kevin and Bella – Kevin *or* Bella? – had won through. The air was being scrubbed. Almost immediately, the cells in Mindy's body sent thank-you notes to her

439

brain. She looked around the store and saw people who were lying down start to sit up, those who were sitting began to stand. Mindy herself stood up and trained her rifle on the nearest person, not taking the chance that something beside the oxygen revived him. But then he smiled.

They all smiled.

They were all safe, for now.

『BOOM!』

Lugh was a force of nature against the zombie horde. His own, tireless physical strength allowed him to squeeze their neurocrania like toothpaste tubes, and his ability to fly protected him from all attack. The enchanted spear Areadbhar sang of glory and triumph as it pierced more temples than on any day in its storied history.

In less than two hours, Lugh and his war weapon had cleared all the main concourses and every store that had any visible or audible concentrations of ghouls. The battle was won.

Mindy enthusiastically opened up the Cracker Barrel's gate when, accompanied by a raucous pounding, Lugh's thunderous voice called out, "Open! Open, say I! Open like the axle-greased arse of a congress-craving Bogomil!"

Orville stood alongside him. Quite ignoring Lugh, Mindy wrapped her arms around Orville and gave a constricting squeeze.

No passion welled up, no urge to give herself to him even though she had just thrown herself his direction. She collected herself, knowing that she still had feelings for the individual, but no lust for the man.

Orville stood there, at first shuddering at the unaccustomed human touch. He was about to reciprocate the embrace when Mindy broke it off.

The staticky walkie-talkie in Mindy's pocket buzzed.

"Mindy? Copy? Over!"

"Kevin!" she exclaimed. "You got the air on!"

"Still smells like crap in here, but at least we can breathe. Any other survivors, over?"

"I'm here with Orville, Lugh and nine others. Where are you?"

"Blur Cave. With Bella. Sort of. Meet us down here. Bring cheese. Out."

POW!

They trooped down from the Cracker Barrel to find Kevin playing bumper pool against himself. The Badger was curled up in a semi-fetal position on the couch, calmly giving herself a tongue bath as the others walked in. She greeted them at first with a ferocious snarl but quickly calmed down.

"Why isn't she trying to kill us?" Mindy asked.

"I don't know, but I'm not complaining," Kevin replied, giving up his game.

"Perhaps I can shed some light on that, dearie," said a disembodied voice that he couldn't hear.

Lugh could hear her though, as well as her indecent squeal of delight when they reunited in an ardent clasp knowable only to gods and spirits.

The team relaxed in the adequate stash of snack food, beer and, of course, oxygen as The Badger nibbled on a stick of Cracker Barrel sharp cheddar and transformed back into Bella Brock.

"Brigitte La Vallette won't remove the curse," Mindy said, translating for Eva. "So we can't unseal the mall until we can work her over a bit. She's ... wait ... Eva's now telling me that Brigitte's spirit has blinked out of existence."

"Meaning?" Bella asked.

Mindy paused before saying, "Eva thinks it means she

used her Voudoun power to move through some cosmic trap door into another level of existence. Or maybe she ceased to exist."

"I know a little about this stuff," Kevin interjected. "It suggests to me that whatever reality she moved on to, she took her will with her. It no longer applies."

"Evita agrees," Mindy replied.

"So let's focus on the mop-up," Kevin directed. "We can be confident that removing the singularity won't carry the curse into the wider world, but let's not end the singularity until we have some reasonable assurance that no ghouls are left standing. For the fourteen of us to cover every inch of this mall, it'll take the better part of three days. We have the better part of two days' worth of air. We have to find more fuel for the generator, and more material for the carbon dioxide scrubbers."

"What do we need?" Orville asked.

"Something we can distill into diesel. The process is simple enough - it's not a lot different from cooking up bathtub gin," Kevin explained. "But we need some kind of oil - even vegetable oil, but something closer to crude would be a lot better. Also, if we could find anything like activated charcoal for the scrubbers, that would be a huge help."

"I can supply both," Orville said.

BAM!

Putting Dirk Henderson's sharp remains to good use, the group took their time and cleared the remaining mindless ghouls from the premises without any further loss of life.

They bivouacked again at the Blur Cave. Given the assurance that all was secure, Kevin dropped Seth Hill's trap card on the foosball table. Then, without ceremony, he flipped it over.

A crack of sunlight glinted from under the loading bay

gate.

Excitedly, they all rushed out into the atrium to see a marvelous, bright sun beat down. And then they saw something few mortals ever would.

The souls of the people whose bodies had been turned into the objects of Maman Brigitte's plot were suddenly visible to Kevin, Mindy, Orville and Bella. This was the world in which Eva resided and one into which – on occasion, this being one of them – Lugh could peer. The souls took their last steps in their surreal, self-contained world, then rocketed up into an unknown level of being.

The goddesses descended: Aphrodite, Lakshmi, Ishtar and even Tamora.

The heroes beheld them, astonishing in their indescribable beauty.

Then they looked around and noticed that the nine survivors who just happened to pick the wrong day to go to the mall were oblivious to all this.

"This is not for them," called out Eva, and was heard and seen for the first time by Kevin, Orville and Bella.

Mindy dismissed her charges, who ran joyously to the exits and into the welcoming embrace of the day.

"Mindy Maguire, you have proven yourself worthy," Aphrodite intoned.

"Still, we acted hastily in granting you our power, knowing full well what a burden it can be," Lakshmi added.

"We offer to take it back if you prefer, or, if you are willing to use it in the cause of justice, it shall be returned to you at the end of your cycle," Ishtar concluded.

"I can't believe I'm saying this," Mindy said, "but I'd like to keep it."

"So it shall be," the goddesses thundered as a chorus.

"And as for your guide," Aphrodite said, looking at Eva, "You have fulfilled your task, Maria Eva Duarte de

Peron. You may come with us to the throne room of all existence."

"Tempting," Eva said. "But could I ask for something else instead?"

"What could possibly be preferable to what we have to offer you?" Lakshmi inquired. The mortals as well as the goddesses present were just as confused by this.

"To walk this world again – as a goddess," Eva replied, then as she took Lugh's hand, added, "There's a precedent."

"Your desire is granted," Ishtar allowed.

Eva tingled as physical hair bristled on physical skin. Blood flowed through her veins driven by the clockwork beat of a physical heart. And a power, untested and undefined, welled up inside her. She drew a breath.

Eva tugged on Lugh's arm until he bent his ear down to the level of her smiling lips, whereupon she informed him in an excited whisper, "It really smells like shit in here!"

The other three goddesses then glared at Tamora, whose eyes were darting around as if she would rather be anywhere else. Tamora was not a beauty goddess like the others; she resembled a furry woodland creature. Duty-bound or fearing retribution from her peers, she looked at Bella Brock, whom she'd caused so much distress.

"I'm sorry, okay?"

The other goddesses continued to press impatient eyes on Tamora.

"And I will not do that to anyone again. Ever."

The staring from Aphrodite, Lakshmi and Ishtar continued.

"Although, Bella Brock, you are permanently granted the Badger power."

Aphrodite gave her an elbow to the ribs.

"Henceforth, you will be able to control your trans-

444

formation into The Badger and you will be granted a spirit guide to keep you from using your abilities indiscriminately."

Marisol's ghost stepped forth from behind Tamora. Even though she no longer wore the uniform of Colonel America – Marisol was now in the T-shirt and jeans of a Midwestern tomboy on a Saturday morning – Bella recognized her immediately.

"Maria Soledad Rivera, you are steadfast, brave and noble of spirit. In short, you are temperamentally ill-suited to being a goddess," Tamora pronounced, no longer hiding her disdain at speaking to mortals, "but I grant you a return to the flesh if you can turn this anxious, undistinguished woman into a heroine."

The two one-time adversaries, Marisol and Bella, locked eyes and smiled.

"I'll take it on," Marisol agreed. "And I don't think it's going to be anywhere near as hard as you say."

"We have one more reward for you, heroes all," Aphrodite spoke.

"We will return to life one of these two spirits," Lakshmi continued, as the souls of Shel Shapiro and Bobby Botler appeared.

"You choose," commanded Ishtar.

The heroes glanced nervously at each other and avoided looking at the ghosts of their fallen comrades.

"I'll make this easy," Bobby said after a moment. "Shel's got a family who needs him. If there has to be a sacrifice, it might as well be me."

Shel looked at Bobby with renewed respect and a syllable of protest.

"No, Shel," Bobby continued. "After a life as misspent as mine, it's enough to die a meaningful death."

The ethereal world dimmed into cold reality and that was the last they heard from Bobby Botler.

But it wasn't the last thing Bobby said before Oblivion enveloped his soul. That was, "Wait! Wait! Fuck that! I wanna—"

Before the surreal scene completely faded, though, Orville caught a glimpse of a woman on high, wearing a tunic and jodhpurs, her face obscured by opaque, green goggles. She smiled.

WHAT QUINN MARTIN
USED TO CALL AN "EPILOGUE"

Survival mandated a drink. After freshening up, exiting the mall, debriefing the police, and collecting up Time Tempest and Flare Star, the heroes assembled at Hawk's. Lisa Lorenzo Shapiro was two minutes behind them, or roughly the time it took for the news of Shel's resurrection to reach her.

"I'm reconstituting The Crusaders," Orville said, before the first round was even served. "Who's in?"

"Not Shel," Lisa said. "I won't let him."

"What about you, Anniella?" Orville asked Lisa.

"I won't let her," Shel answered as proxy.

And with that the pair threw in ten bucks for the beers and left before either of them had three sips.

"I'll lend a hand, at least until you get things up and running," Time Tempest offered, then turned to her sort-of stepmother. "Coming with, Flare Star?"

"Thank you, no," the otherworldly princess replied. "My powers faded long ago, and I can do much more good back in Iowa working with Roger."

"Do count me in," Eva said.

Orville gave voice to skepticism.

"What powers do you bring?"

"I haven't the foggiest notion," Eva confessed.

"Maybe it's my turn to be your guide, Evita," Mindy offered.

"Presume not, lass," Lugh said, giving Eva a squeeze about the waist. "The task is mine alone."

"Mindy, Lugh, does this mean you'll both serve?" Orville asked.

"Nay, thou hast godhead enow with milady Eva," Lugh said. "This be the day The Indomitable Lugh steps back to serve one greater than he."

"You'll make the most unlikely sidekick ever, Lugh," Mindy said with a chuckle.

"So you'll join?" Orville pressed Mindy.

"We'll talk later," was all she'd say.

Orville gave no indication that he was uncomfortable with that non-reply.

"Bella?"

"Wow? Me? A Crusader!" Bella gushed before being jabbed in the ribs by an unseen elbow. "OK, I'm in. Marisol says she's in too."

"Then count me out!" Time Tempest exclaimed, rising to her feet. "Bella, I understand the Badger was a tremendous help today, but last night it killed a hundred innocent people. There's got to be a price."

Bella's enthusiasm evaporated. Remorse drained her face of all affect.

"I thought about that," she said after a pause. "But maybe, if you'll have me on your team, I could have a shot of redemption and—"

"That's what I'm afraid of," Time Tempest interrupted. "There's actual math behind this kind of moral calculation and I've studied it. Yes, you could redeem yourself, but it's going to entail self-sacrifice. Or you could choose not to redeem yourself, in which case the Universe will exact its revenge in some other way. In either case, you're a bomb waiting to go off, Bella, and I do not intend to be standing next to you when you do."

And with that she threw a five on the table and walked away, still hunched over from her recent exertions.

Bella's eyes welled up and reddened. Nobody had said anything aloud before about the enormity of her crime.

"Cry," Marisol's spirit advised, heard only by Bella, "but later."

Everyone else heard Orville inquire, "Kevin?" as he coolly went down his mental checklist.

"It's all I ever wanted to be," Kevin replied. "But no."

"Why not?" Orville pressed.

"First, I don't have a real power, not anymore at least," Kevin answered. "Second, I don't think I was ever cut out to be a hero."

"You did more to defeat this latest threat than anyone, with or without powers," Orville corrected. "And if that wasn't being a hero, what is?"

"I don't know. Maybe I'll join up when I figure that out," he said, then turned to the Badger's alter ego. "And Bella, I'm here to tell you: There's no such thing as 'karma'."

Kevin then stood and turned to look at Hawk's signature bit of flair pinned to the wall.

The double-holstered gun belt.

Nobody stopped him as he jumped up on the jukebox, grabbed the cracked and weather-beaten leather, and yanked it off the wall with one tug, unanchored wood screws falling out of the masonry with the barest resistance.

He strapped the two-gun sheath around his hips, buckled it and strode out of Hawk's and into the west, illumined by the rising harvest moon.

"We'll need money," Orville said, getting back to business. "Proving that I'm Dirk Henderson's heir will take time, and sure to be contested in court."

"Don't worry about money," Eva announced with a chuckle. "I have you covered."

"Evita, you're as broke as any of us," Mindy chimed in. "As wealthy as you were back in the day, that fortune has been passed through to your relatives if it hasn't been expropriated by the Argent—"

"Dearie, remember that movie you showed me – the opera about my life?"

"Yes."

"And remember that scene where I'm packing up to go on the Rainbow Tour and those porters are lifting all that luggage onto the steamship?"

"Of course."

"And remember that scene where I travel to Zurich?"

Mindy tilted her head.

"No."

"Oh, that must be because it didn't make it into the movie, but it happened in real life," Eva explained. "One more question ... If you were to travel to places like Paris and Milan, how much clothing would you pack?"

"Next to nothing," Mindy pondered. "I'd buy everything there."

"And that would require a great deal of money. So if you had the kind of cash you could only move around if you had diplomatic immunity, and Switzerland was on your itinerary ..." Eva began, then made her point more succinctly. "What do you think was in all those hatboxes? Hats?"

BOOM!

The heroes left in ones and twos, until only Orville and Mindy remained.

"We need you, Mindy," Orville said. "I can step into my

biological father's role and run Crusaders operations, but we need a battlefield leader. There are no more Colonels America."

"And I'm inclined to help out in any way I can," Mindy said. "But there's going to be a tension between you and me. We need to get that out in the open, and I'm not sure how much of this you're going to be able to process."

"I don't understand."

"I know you don't," Mindy said. "These kinds of relationships are new to you."

"I love you, Mindy," Orville said flatly, as he said everything.

"Orville—" she began, expecting to have to say something kind but firm.

"No, listen," Orville continued, uncharacteristically stammering at points. He had never put his feelings on display this way before in his life. "It's difficult for me to express emotion, and impossible for me to guess what emotions others are experiencing. But that doesn't mean I don't have feelings of my own. And those feelings are for you. These crystalized when Equity cut my mental static in half as she cut my power in half. The power and the static came flooding back there in the mall, but I can still remember what it was like to appreciate your touch, to be comfortable around you. I can build on that, I can get back on my meds and—"

"That's not going to help," Mindy interrupted. "Equity's influence ended when you put her down permanently. Gay Ray is another story."

Orville then became the last one to realize what had happened to her back in Plainville.

"It's not forever, Orville," Mindy said. "But I can't ask you to wait. I'd understand if you moved on."

"I can't imagine being without you," Orville replied. "Is there any way to know how long we have to be apart?"

"Three years, eight months," Mindy stated.

"How do you know that so precisely?"

"I went to Smith."

{POW!}

As local police cordoned off the Chesterfield Mall, a containment-suited contingent from the U.S. Army's command at Redstone Arsenal entered the disaster site and combed through the blood-splattered debris. They surveyed the site, got the utilities back on and collected the bodies – including the occasional animated ones.

One of the first they recovered was that of Marisol Rivera, the gutted remains of the last and briefest Colonel America, her brains tugged out through her ears.

None of the soldiers there knew her particularly well, but she was familiar – a face in the chow line, an officer who crisply returned salutes. So they treated her remains with a special measure of respect.

Another presence there treated her with equal respect: an ebony-skinned ghoul with a female frame thin to the point of emaciation. The reanimate, keeping still in a shadow-cloaked corner, had devoured a good portion of the brains that spilled out of the red, white and blue cowl. It had also feasted on organs and muscle. To the zombie, it was as if the muscle contained memories. The more meat it ate, the more it remembered skills developed by a pilot named Marisol Rivera, an engineer named Elias O'Neill, a paratrooper named Roger Chadwick ...

But the best part of that corpse, the ghoul concluded, was the blood. There was something about it that awakened her to a level of consciousness to which other zombies could never aspire. She remembered random things about herself as she was in life: that she had been named Brigitte La Vallette, that she was from some place called Port au Prince, that she was a Voudoun priestess, that her blood type was AB-negative...

Acknowledgements

Foremost, I must pay the satirist's due to those who take the subject matter seriously. This work was inspired by what has come to be known alternately as "the Bronze Age of comics" or "Bill's very lonely adolescence". The works of Denny O'Neill, Marv Wolfman, Chris Claremont, Steve Gerber, Gerry Conway, Steve Engelhart, Jim Shooter, and Roy Thomas provided the blueprints for this world, particularly in terms of the superpowers and the imperfect people who wield them. (The characters and situations owe less to Marvel or DC and more to Mad magazine's "Scenes We'd Like to See" features. Playful nods to pop culture auteurs George Lucas and George A. Romero are blatantly obvious. Other winks go to Harve Bennett and Kenneth Johnson, Frank Lupo and Stephen J. Cannell, Tim Rice and Andrew Lloyd Webber, Phish, and The Three Stooges.)

Let's not forget, though, that the Bronze Age scribes themselves owed much to their Silver Age predecessors (frequently their bosses as well). These include Julius Schwartz, Carmine Infantino, Archie Goodwin, Jim Steranko, Gardner Fox and, of course, Stan Lee. These giants in turn inherited their archetypes from the creators of comics' Golden Age. I admire these storytellers as much as I do their spiritual ancestors who wove tales of gods and heroes which have been handed down to us from antiquity.

Absent in these acknowledgements so far is any mention of the pencil artists who are at least as responsible as the writers for the success of comics before, during, and since the days that I read and collected them. As someone who works entirely in linear forms, I'm not qualified to selectively name them. I'd like to make one exception, though. My choice of a cover artist began with an instant message chat that started with my asking, "Hey, has anyone ever told you that you draw like George Perez?"

If you just glanced back at the cover to check the comparison, I trust that J.A. Fludd's work has impressed you as much as it has me. I am grateful to Joe for taking on this challenge, as well as to the designers at Caryatid for the impressive work they did on the interior, perfectly capturing the *Mighty Mighty* spirit. I would also like to thank editorial director Jayne Southern and the team at Rebel ePublishers for bringing this book from manuscript to market, and my friend and collaborator Ben Parris for his editorial pass. Critique partners Ken Altabef, Kat Hankinson, Miranda Suri, Jake Packard, Amy Lau, and Eric Bresin also provided invaluable advice, as has my lawyer and dear friend Anna A. Volkova, Esq.

My wife, Eileen, and our three boys Eddie, James, and John Liberty deserve great credit as well. It's not easy having a writer in the family. We're a quirky clan to begin with, and my own little obsession adds an order of magnitude to our home's ambient weirdness. I thank them all for putting up with me.

I must also make brief mention of the physical locations. A creature of the northeast United States, I have first-hand knowledge of the settings in greater New York, Washington, and Boston. I am less familiar with other such real-world places as Plainville, Illinois; Redstone Arsenal; and the Chesterfield Mall. Any variance between the map and the territory is on me. Likewise, any errors in fact are mine alone.

Ultimately, I thank you, reader, for coming along with me on this theme-park ride. Hope you enjoyed all the sharp turns.

Warmest regards,
William Freedman
West Hempstead, N.Y.
February, 2014

ABOUT THE AUTHOR

William Freedman is a New York-based satirist who uses science fiction and fantasy tropes. He is author of Mighty Mighty and Land That I Love, co-author with Ben Parris of Supernaturalz, contributor to the 2005 Spirit House chapbook to raise money for tsunami survivors, and a frequent program participant at genre conventions throughout the northeast U.S.

Most recently, he served as editor for the Age of Certainty: What if God Existed? anthology. His non-fiction bylines – covering everything from hot stocks for Investor's Business Daily to the rise of distilled spirits for History magazine to Bram Stoker Awards weekend for Long Island's Newsday – go back more than 20 years.

9780615985060